Practice with Highly Vulnerable Clients

Practice with Highly Vulnerable Clients

CASE MANAGEMENT AND COMMUNITY-BASED SERVICE

JACK ROTHMAN
University of California at Los Angeles

With an introductory chapter by
CAREL B. GERMAIN

 Prentice Hall, Englewood Cliffs, New Jersey 07632

Library of Congress Cataloging-in-Publication Data

Rothman, Jack.
    Practice with highly vulnerable clients : case management and
community-based service / Jack Rothman ; with an introductory
chapter by Carel B. Germain.
       p.   cm.
    Includes bibliographical references and indexes.
    ISBN 0–13–119058–X
    1. Social case work—United States—Management. 2. Social work
with the socially handicapped—United States. I. Title.
HV43.R68 1994
361.32—dc20   93–29021
                                        CIP

Acquisitions editor: Nancy Roberts
Editorial assistant: Pat Naturale
Editorial/production supervision and
   interior design: Bridget Mooney
Cover design: Doug DeLuca
Production coordinator: Kelly Behr

Printed in the United States of America
10 9 8 7 6 5 4 3 2 1

ISBN 0-13-119058-X

Prentice-Hall International (UK) Limited, *London*
Prentice-Hall of Australia Pty. Limited, *Sydney*
Prentice-Hall Canada Inc., *Toronto*
Prentice-Hall Hispanoamericana, S.A., *Mexico*
Prentice-Hall of India Private Limited, *New Delhi*
Prentice-Hall of Japan, Inc., *Tokyo*
Simon & Schuster Asia Pte. Ltd., *Singapore*
Editora Prentice-Hall do Brasil, Ltda., *Rio de Janeiro*

Contents

Preface *xv*

PART I   CONTEXT AND MEANS *1*

Chapter 1   The Severely Vulnerable: An Emergent Clientele and Practice Mode *3*

A NEWLY CONSTITUTED CLIENTELE   3

  Societal Forces Create a New Clientele   3

    The Elderly   4

    The Physically Disabled   4

    The Very Young   4

    The Mentally Ill   4

    Changing Professional Paradigms   5

  Clients and Circumstances   5

  The Nature of Disabilities   5

    Severity   5

    Duration   6

    Scope of Needs   6

  Deficits and Strengths   7

    Skill Deficiencies and Coping Difficulties   7

    Lack of Information   7

    Low Self-Esteem   7

    Strengths   8

  The Social Support Environment   8

INTERVENTION REQUISITES FOR HIGHLY VULNERABLE CLIENTS   9

  Components of Intervention   9

    Community Living Objectives   10

Enhancement Objectives   10

Longitudinal Service   11

Cross-sectional Service   11

Community-Based Service   12

A Supportive Skill Development Emphasis in Direct Practice   12

Environmental Intervention   13

Micro and Macro Practice Perspective   14

Intensity of Practice Relationship   14

A New Practice Paradigm   15

Comprehensive Psychosocial Enhancement   16

Traditional Practice Versus the New Paradigm   16

Common Features of Traditional Practice and the New Paradigm   17

Contextual Factors   18

Community and Organizational Factors   18

Political Factors   18

Community Versus Policy Emphasis   19

Professional Factors   19

Chapter 2   Comprehensive Enhancement Practice: An Implementation Model   23

A MODEL OF COMPREHENSIVE PSYCHOSOCIAL ENHANCEMENT PRACTICE   23

Development of the Model   23

An Empirically Grounded Model of Practice: Fifteen Functions   24

1 Access to the Agency   26

2 Intake   26

3 Assessment (Psychological, Social, Medical)   27

4 Setting Goals   27

5 Intervention Planning   28

6 Resource Identification and Indexing   28

7 Formal Linkage—Agencies and Programs   28

8 Informal Linkage—Social Networks   29

9 Monitoring   29

10 Reassessment   30

11 *Client Evaluation (for Termination)* 30

12 *Interagency Coordination* 30

13 *Counseling* 31

14 *Therapy* 31

15 *Advocacy* 32

ELABORATION AND CLARIFICATION 32

Using the Diagram 32

Explanatory Notes on the Model 33

Points of Clarification 35

Areas Not Covered 35

Feasibility 35

Alternative Models 36

Cultural and Ethnic Considerations 36

Chapter 3 Using an Ecological Perspective *39*
CAREL B. GERMAIN

History and Professional Values 39

The Ecological Perspective 41

Holism: People and Environments 42

Transactional Causality 43

Linear Causality 43

Transactional Causality 44

Examples of Transactional Causality 44

Human Relatedness, Competence, Self-Esteem, and Self-Direction 45

Relatedness 46

Competence 46

Self-Esteem 47

Self-Direction 48

The Stress-Coping Paradigm 49

Distinguishing Between Stressors and Challenges 50

Coping 50

Vulnerability and Disempowerment 52

Withholding Power 52

Exploiting Power 52

Professional Sensitivity   53

Advocacy   53

PART II   PRACTICE FUNCTIONS   57

Chapter 4   Intake, Assessment, and Goal Setting   59

Overview   60

INTAKE   60

Understanding Intake   60

Components of Intake   60

Compiling a Data Base   62

Engagement and Interpersonal Relations   62

Timing Factors   63

Practice Guidelines for Intake   64

Early Steps   64

Engagement Techniques   64

Developing Problem Statements   65

Attending to Population Group Differences   66

ASSESSMENT   68

Understanding Assessment   68

Basic Components   68

Agency and Community Factors   70

Relationship with the Client   71

Practice Guidelines for Assessment   71

An Assessment Framework   71

Assessment Tools   78

Integrating Information   80

SETTING GOALS   80

Understanding Goal Setting   80

Key Aspects   80

Client and Professional Inputs   81

Criteria for Workable Goals   82

Practice Guidelines for Goal Setting   83

Attaining Specificity   83

Encouraging Client Input   85

Summary   85

Chapter 5   Resource Identification and Intervention Planning   *89*

Overview   *90*

RESOURCE IDENTIFICATION AND INDEXING   90

Understanding and Using Resources   *90*

  Definition and Context   90

  Resource Aggregation Methods   91

  Problems   93

  Identifying Key Agency Characteristics   94

INTERVENTION PLANNING   97

Understanding Intervention Planning   *97*

  Definition of the Concept   97

  Treatment and Service Aspects   97

  Strategic and Procedural Aspects   98

  Components of the Intervention Plan   99

  Intervention Principles for Plan Design   100

Practice Guidelines for Intervention Planning   *102*

  Criteria for Designing a Strategy   102

  Strategies for Problems of Vulnerable Populations   104

  Selecting Techniques Within a Strategy   107

  Transforming a Design into Implementation Procedures   108

Chapter 6   Counseling and Therapy   *113*

Understanding Counseling and Therapy   *114*

  The Special Place of Counseling and Therapy   114

  Differences Between Counseling and Therapy   114

  Use of Counseling and Therapy   115

  Key Components of Direct Service   116

  Input from the Client and Others   117

  Alternative Theoretical Approaches to Personal Helping   118

Practice Guidelines for Counseling and Therapy   *121*

  Establishing Relationships   122

  Motivating the Client   123

  Fostering Client Participation   124

  Teaching Survival Skills and Providing Practical Information   125

Providing Support   127

Providing Crisis Intervention   128

Chapter 7   Linking Clients to Formal Organizations   *133*

Understanding the Formal Linking Process   *134*

The Concept of Linking   134

Historical Perspective on Linkage   135

The Practitioner's Role   136

Relationship to Other Functions in the Model   137

Influencing Organizations   138

Barriers to Effective Linkage   140

Practice Guidelines for Linking Clients to Formal Organizations   *141*

Clarifying Client Needs   141

Selecting Appropriate Resources   142

Matching the Client with Relevant Services   142

Exercising Practice Roles with Clients   143

Exercising Practice Roles with Agencies   145

Negotiating Relationships with the Agency   147

Examining Successes and Failures   148

Chapter 8   Linking Clients with Informal Support Networks   *151*

Understanding Informal Linkage   *152*

The Place of Informal Support   152

Functions of Informal Support   153

A Typology of Informal Support Functions   154

Types of Informal Support Networks   155

Characteristics of Informal Networks   157

Integration of Concepts   159

Problems in Informal Support Linkage   159

Practice Guidelines for Informal Linkage   *161*

Defining the Network   161

Selecting the Most Appropriate Support Units   163

Making and Maintaining Linkages   167

Enhancing Helper Capabilities 167

Evaluating Linkage Strategies 169

Chapter 9 Monitoring, Reassessment, and Outcome Evaluation *172*

Overview *173*

MONITORING **174**

Understanding Monitoring *174*

Definition and Purpose *174*

The Unique Place of Monitoring *175*

Client Involvement *176*

Dynamics of Monitoring *177*

Variations by Client Populations *178*

Special Problems in Monitoring *179*

Practice Guidelines for Monitoring *180*

Using Formal and Informal Means *180*

Using Different Levels of Monitoring *181*

Problems with Agencies *184*

Forms to Aid Monitoring *184*

Anticipating Critical Events and Projecting Time Lines *187*

Using Management Information Systems *189*

Using Monitoring with Different Client Populations *190*

REASSESSMENT AND OUTCOME EVALUATION **191**

Tasks and Objectives *191*

Instruments *193*

Key Aspects *194*

Obstacles *195*

The Matter of Discharge Evaluation *195*

Chapter 10 Advocacy *199*

Understanding Advocacy *200*

The Concept of Advocacy *200*

Advocacy and Case Management *200*

Purpose of Advocacy *201*

Characteristics of Advocacy *202*

Diverse Applications *202*

Client Involvement   203

Modes and Tactics   204

Constraints on Use of Advocacy   207

Influence Base for Advocacy   208

Practice Guidelines for Advocacy   208

A Framework for Advocacy Planning   208

Determining When to Use Advocacy   210

Selecting Targets   211

Selecting Tactics   212

Using Tactics   213

Applying Psychological Pressure   215

Chapter 11   Interorganizational Coordination and Agency Access   *218*

Overview   *219*

INTERORGANIZATIONAL COORDINATION   219

Understanding Interorganizational Coordination   *219*

The Place of Interagency Coordination   219

Aspects of Coordination   220

Factors Effecting Collaboration   221

The Task Environment   221

Interdependence and Domain Consensus   223

Linking Mechanisms in Coordination   224

Practice Guidelines for Interorganizational Coordination   228

Practitioner Experiences in Coordination   228

Developing a Strategy for Interorganizational Exchange   230

ACCESS   233

Understanding Access   233

Components of Access   233

Identifying Needs and Targeting Clients   235

Client Outreach   237

Channeling   238

Practice Guidelines for Facilitating Access   239

Roles in Providing Access   239

Targeting the Client Population   240

Employing Needs Assessment Techniques   242

Engaging in Outreach and Social Marketing   246

PART III   SYSTEMIC FACTORS   *253*

Chapter 12   Community and Organizational Issues   *255*

Overview   *255*

THE COMMUNITY CONTEXT   *256*

Community Aspects and Problems   *257*

Aspects of Community   *257*

General Community Problems   *260*

Service Gaps in the Community   *261*

Problems with Service Providers   *262*

Recommendations for Improving the Community Context   *263*

THE ORGANIZATIONAL CONTEXT   *265*

Organizational Problems   *266*

Recommended Organizational Improvements   *268*

Summary of Systemic Factors   *270*

EVALUATION OF SERVICES AND SOCIAL SYSTEM ENDORSEMENT   *271*

Positive Outcome Studies   *272*

Negative Service Results   *275*

Cost-Effectiveness   *276*

PANACEA VERSUS COP OUT: A SUMMING UP   *277*

Appendix   *283*

METHODOLOGY OF THE UCLA STUDY   *285*

STUDY QUESTIONNAIRE: UCLA/DEPARTMENT OF MENTAL HEALTH CASE MANAGEMENT STUDY INTERVIEW FORMAT   *291*

Subject Index   *297*

Name Index   *309*

Preface

This book is concerned with newly emerging client populations in America, people with severe and long-term impediments that diminish their capacity to join the mainstream of community living. The group includes the persistently mentally ill, the frail elderly, physically disabled individuals, the developmentally disabled, and dependent children removed from disfunctional and abusive families. In past years, people in these circumstances were assigned to closed-off institutional facilities where they received custodial services around the clock. Today, there is a societal shift toward serving them in natural community settings, and on a continuing basis (although not always well); in this sense, they constitute a novel clientele for the human services.

For these individuals, the usual methods of the helping professions, particularly social work and psychology, do not apply. The prevailing techniques assume the basic existence of an adequately functioning person, who experiences a destabilizing problem, and then seeks a professional helper who acts to restore proper equilibrium within a delimited period of time. For severely vulnerable clients, however, the notion of cure does not fit in this way. They need to be assisted on a long-range basis to survive and make their way in the community, at the highest possible quality of life, in the context of limbs that will never again flex, an emotional state not capable of becoming fully attuned to common definitions of reality, or the absence of a functional and nurturing family.

New service concepts and approaches are needed that provide sustained care free from institutional confines, and which combine direct personal helping and the linking of clients to a range of formal and informal sources of support in the community. This entails micro practice geared to individualized psychological aid, as well as macro practice involving community and organizational intervention. The human services fields have not yet developed a well-constructed conceptualization and methodology to embody these various requisites. The current approaches go by various names: case management, managed care, community-based care, and service integration. A common definition and set of practice procedures is lacking among them. This book arises out of those circumstances and provides firmer boundaries to guide intervention.

The book is based on 5 years of research at UCLA, involving a survey of case managers in the field and a meta-analysis of existing empirical studies in the literature. From the results, an empirically based model of practice was constructed, keyed to the core functions of the role and their dynamic interrelationships. The model, termed *comprehensive psychosocial enhancement*, with its 15 specific professional functions, constitutes the basic structure of the book.

The introductory section consists of three chapters. The first provides background on historical developments and social forces that led to the emergence of the new clientele and contemporary practice paradigm. The second sets forth the particular model of practice undergirding the overall presentation. The third offers an ecological perspective for applying the model and for relating it to more typical and established principles and approaches in human services practice. That chapter was authored by Dr. Carel B. Germain, who is perhaps the preeminent scholar of ecologically oriented practice.

The middle section comprises the body of the book and reviews each of the 15 functions, providing both conceptual and research information about each function, together with more hands-on "how-to-do-it" guidelines for putting the functions into practice. Each chapter draws on the experiences and views of practitioners who participated in the UCLA survey, in order to elaborate and illuminate the discussion through live reflections from the field. Those functions that are closely related are grouped together in chapters for ease of exposition.

A chapter on interorganizational policies and agency access was placed at the end of this section, even though these functions are carried out early in the process. However, the tasks involve largely macro-level organizational and community actions that precede direct engagement with specific clients. Because most of our readers, we believe, would find it a distraction to delay the discussion of client-specific content, we have taken some liberties with the order of discourse, without prejudice to the general treatment of the subject.

The last section of the book examines contextual factors that surround and shape the exercise of practice. This analysis involves the systems within which practice take place—the sponsoring agency and the community setting. Relevant organizational and community issues are discussed in the final chapter.

The treatment of this subject aims for broad coverage and takes an interdisciplinary approach. It embraces the various severely impeded population groups that require comprehensive enhancement service, and draws from the literature of a cross-section of disciplines and professions. Nevertheless, there is a point of reference that influences the author's outlook. The UCLA research project was focused on mentally ill clients and was conducted from a school of social work. These anchoring points may have skewed the balance of coverage, and the reader needs to be alert to that possibility.

ACKNOWLEDGMENTS

Case management and community-based service call for an extensive coterie of supportive helpers. Analogously, the creation of this book on that subject required a very large company of assistants and abettors. The best way to acknowledge them all is through noting their participation in the various sub-studies that went into composing the book.

The meta-analytic synthesis of case management empirical studies. Reviewers and analysts included Michael Cousineau, JoAnn Damron-Rodriguez, James Shenk, Pauline Siewert, and Anita Tumblin.

The field survey of practitioner experiences and views. Anita Tumblin was field coordinator. Interviewers and analysts included: Eve Cominos, Michael Cousineau, Nancy Harada, Liz LaScala, and Margot Slutka. Professor Manuel Miranda contributed as a faculty research associate.

The pilot study of implementation of the practice model. Anita Tumblin was senior field researcher. Data analysts included Edmond Shenassa and Nancy Harada.

The census survey of case management staff in the Los Angeles Department of Mental Health. Michael Cousineau was project coordinator. Other research staff included Pauline Siewert, Patrick Mace, James Shenk, and Judith Richlin-Klonsky.

Early versions of several chapters, using data and materials from the study, were prepared through a year-long master's project by graduate students at the UCLA School of Social Welfare. Those participating included: Molly Day, Alda Fenster, Jan Honiker, Robin Rubin, Tamar Springer, and L. Katherine Taylor.

The author is indebted to Roberto Quiroz, who was executive director of the Los Angeles Department of Mental Health, for his collegial cooperation in clearing the way for access to the agency and its staff as well as providing fiscal resources. Other staff members whose assistance mattered included Areta Crowell, Jessie Tait, and George Wolkin. Of course, participation by more than 50 practitioners, who engaged in extensive field interviews or in demanding implementation trials, was crucial and indispensable for providing core data ingredients undergirding this analysis of intervention.

At the university, Walter Furman, as facilitator for the Center for Child and Family Policy Studies, aided the undertaking in valuable administrative and consultative ways. Competent and painstaking word-processing assistance was provided, with patience and good humor, by Selena Lu-Webster, Margaret Benjimen, Laura Williams Rigby, and Mitchell Moore. Valuable comments and suggestions on a draft version of the manuscript were given by graduate students Herb Shon and Marelina Narvaez.

Most critically, without the unflinching personal commitment and material support of Leonard Schneiderman, at that time Dean of the UCLA School of Social Welfare, the studies that buttress this book might not have come to light. To him go personal thanks and professional accolades for his dedication to the concept of research for practice.

PRINCIPALS IN THE PROJECTS INFORMING THIS BOOK

Principal Investigator

Jack Rothman

Field Coordinator for Survey of Practitioners and Field Test of Practice Model

Anita Tumblin

Coordinator of Census Survey of Department of Mental Health Staff

Michael Cousineau

Analysts and Preparation of Initial Chapter Drafts

Molly Day
Alda Fenster
Jan Honiker
Robin Rubin
Tamar Springer
L. Katherine Taylor

I
Context and Means

1

The Severely Vulnerable: An Emergent Clientele and Practice Mode

A NEWLY CONSTITUTED CLIENTELE

This book is about vulnerable people made dependent by the chances of life—physical or mental handicaps, infirmities of age, or the death or incapacity of one's parents during childhood. George Santayana remarked, with apparent resignation, "Life is not a spectacle or a feast; it is a predicament." The predicament is even deeper for those who serendipity has dealt a dreadful hand. But Santayana was not a full-scale pessimist. "The diseases that destroy man," he notes, "are no less natural than the instincts that preserve him." An old Yiddish proverb said it more briefly, "God gave burdens, also shoulders." Here, we plan to scrutinize the predicaments of the vulnerable, but our larger attention will be focused on the pathways to preservation.

SOCIETAL FORCES CREATE A NEW CLIENTELE

At mid-century a set of societal currents in America profoundly altered the role of the human service professions. New client populations with a special set of problems emerged. These client types existed previously, but their numbers expanded enormously and the pressure to accommodate them produced a novel phenomenon.

These were people with long-term vulnerabilities, whose disabilities and impediments were not amenable to the usual professional approaches aimed at adjustment and curative results. Rather, they required protracted and multifaceted service, often extending over a lifetime.

The Elderly

One such client grouping was the elderly. Advances in medical science resulted in prolonged life expectancy, dramatically increasing the proportion of older adults in the population. Concurrently, the traditional extended family contracted to a nuclear cluster that excluded the older generation, leading to a significant reduction in the basic responsibility assumed by families for members encumbered by the problems of later life (Frankfather, Smith & Caro, 1981). Other arrangements became necessary in the community to meet the needs of this expanding circle of aging citizens.

The Physically Disabled

The physically disabled was another group transformed by developments in the health field. They were afforded greater proficiency and mobility through medical technology, which freed them from institutions (Brightman, 1984). Their exodus was also affected by legislation and court rulings mandating better access to facilities and more convenient public transportation. Nevertheless, substantial limitations remained, and ongoing support was needed for them in the community (DeJong, 1983).

The Very Young

The child welfare field was also transforming as a result of deteriorating family life—divorce, drug addiction, violence, and a crescendo of child abuse. These circumstances created a class of dependent and harmed children, cut adrift from dependable, natural parents (Goldstein, Freud & Solnit, 1973). These many children required alternative sources of nurturing to bring them safely through the formative years of childhood and adolescence.

The Mentally Ill

The mental health field offers a further informative illustration. Here, the advent of psychotropic drugs provided a means to stabilize symptoms of severe mental illness and increased the ability of many patients to function in normal social situations. About the same time, professional and humanistic voices began calling for the deinstitutionalization of state hospital facilities, so that patients could live and be cared for in the least restrictive environment possible. This movement was joined by conservative politicians who saw the closing of state hospitals as a cost-cutting bonanza. Through this convergence of influences, millions of mentally ill clients were shifted from closed institutions to open community settings, where their need for professional help persisted (Schwartz & Goldfinger, 1981). Much of what happened to mentally ill patients applies also to those developmentally disabled.

Changing Professional Paradigms

The forces of change included alterations in family structure and function, shifting professional and political ideologies, breakthroughs in medical knowledge, and severe economic pressures. These factors have materially changed the social landscape and the tasks of human service professions. (For a more extensive historical review refer to Weil & Karls, 1985). In concert these crosscurrents have churned up a massive clientele with distinctive features and needs, and have made it necessary to construct a new mode of professional practice that can respond appropriately.

This practice paradigm has been referred to using terms such as case management, community-based care, managed care, and community support. We will examine the components of the approach shortly, but first it is necessary to identify the characteristics of the client group and its encompassing circumstances.

CLIENTS AND CIRCUMSTANCES

To understand the common characteristics of this emergent group of clients, we cite literature in several pertinent fields, particularly case management with the mentally ill (Rapp, 1985; Rubin, 1985, 1987), case management with the elderly (White, 1987), services to vulnerable populations (Gitterman, 1991), and the field of psychosocial rehabilitation (Cnaan, Blankertz, Messinger & Gardner, 1988). In the following discussion we draw liberally on these core compilations that synthesize the literature from various fields. In essence, these sources indicate that this emerging group has a wide scope of severe, long-term impairments and impediments. Although limited by skill deficits and often, by lack of information, many of these clients retain basic strengths that allow them to function at a level high enough to maintain a reasonable quality of life in community settings. This typically requires providing them with appropriate supports to compensate for their disabilities. Their support environment, however, is often inadequate, highly complex, and difficult to access. In the following discussion, we elaborate briefly on each of these points.

THE NATURE OF DISABILITIES

Severity

The chronically mentally ill, frail elderly, and physically disabled are in circumstances of profound hardship. Their handicaps are beyond those of the more typical client who goes to a social agency to deal with marital discord or to a psychotherapist in private practice to work through a mid-life crisis. These grand scale impairments often have tragic elements, not rectifiable through adjustments in cognition or behavior patterns. They affect the individual in fundamental and pervasive ways and are outside of the person's volition for their cause or solution. Vulnerable clients, according to Gitterman (1991, p. 1), are overwhelmed by "circumstances and events they are powerless to control."

The young child who is removed from destructive, abusing parents has also been separated from a vital source of shelter, food, and financial support and emotional encouragement. The child lacking these life-sustaining elements faces extraordinary obstacles to progress and survival. In this example, the child is experiencing external impediments rather than internal psychological or physical impairments. Whether sources of vulnerability are internal or external, the affected individual is frequently thrust into a position of forced dependency.

Duration

The impediments of these clients are by nature long term and intractable. Children who are separated from their parents at an early age need substitute care until they can manage independent living—typically at age 18 or older. Physically disabled persons have a condition that is permanent and, ordinarily, irreversible. The infirmity of an elderly individual is not only irreversible, but progressive: hearing defects get worse, visual acuity continues to diminish, and the heart gets weaker. In the mental health field, schizophrenia and other psychotic ailments are generally viewed as persistent conditions with a physiological and probable chemical base that is constitutional. These mental ailments are controllable to a degree through a continuing course of medication, but periods of relative remission are interspersed with episodes of crisis and decompensation. The disability is life-long and cyclical in form. Rubin (1985) notes the limited or slow progress made by this genre of clients and the impatience and frustration practitioners often feel in treating them.

Scope of Needs

Additionally, this client group has a wide range of needs, given the severity of their circumstances. A dependent child needs the array of fundamental material and emotional supports that would ordinarily be extended by a loving family. An elderly individual may require financial help, assistance in homemaking and personal care, medical attention, and transportation. There is a similar extent of need for the individual with a severe mental illness or developmental disability living in a community-based setting, whether with the family or in a board and care facility. Clearly, the difficulties that these individuals face are not particular and focused, as with the typical client seeking counseling or temporary financial assistance, but extremely general and diverse.

DEFICITS AND STRENGTHS

In addition to specialized problem conditions, such as limited dexterity in the physically handicapped or emotional instability in the mentally ill, vulnerable client populations have certain difficulties in common. These include deficits in the skills of everyday living, a lack of information, and low self-esteem.

Skill Deficiencies and Coping Difficulties

According to Cnaan, Blankertz, Messinger and Gardner (1989, p. 64), vulnerable populations "have never learned or have unlearned the relevant skills of independent living." These skills deficiencies can be viewed as a secondary loss that follows in the wake of the primary disability. For example, an individual with psychiatric troubles may not have learned how to make friends, and an elderly person with reduced vision may have lost the ability to navigate on public transportation. People in these circumstances may fail in areas that for others are routine and may also experience a greater number of crisis episodes.

Lack of Information

Lack of information is closely related to poor coping abilities. A salient factor impeding all vulnerable populations, according to Gitterman (1991), is that they are missing necessary information or are guided by misinformation. Because they require a great deal of support from community resources, and the support environment is complex, accurate information is both vital and hard to obtain and keep current. It is this combination of a high level of internal impairment together with a low level of access to external resources that, for Gitterman, symbolizes vulnerability.

Low Self-Esteem

The losses and deficiencies of vulnerable people are real and can be devastating. In comparison to others, these individuals are at actual disadvantage in specific areas. The dependent child does not have a natural parent to teach him carpentry skills and an amputee may not be able to move about as quickly as others. Dwelling on the inadequacy or disadvantage by the individual can easily result in despondency and low self-esteem. Being rejected, disdained, or mocked by other people, as is the frequent reality, or being turned away by service providers favoring higher functioning clients can generate a feeling of defeatism and powerlessness. These attitudes, if not checked, add to the sense of encumberment felt by many vulnerable individuals. Some affective patterns resulting from this that have been described by Ballew and Mink (1986) include: pessimism, apathy, fatalism, anxiety, aloofness, and cynicism.

Strengths

Despite these deficits, vulnerable populations can demonstrate remarkable resiliency. They possess an underutilized capacity for growth and change, even within the context of handicapping circumstances (Cnaan et al., 1988). These are the "shoulders" that the earlier proverb noted. Such assets, Gerhart (1990) indicates, may be environmental (an adequate income, caring family, friends, a lovely garden) or personal (good health, a sense of humor, religious beliefs, an ability to learn). We have, appropriately, been advised to

> recognize the elder as a person still capable of joy and giving and productivity, regardless of the deficits that have led to the need for case management. Life-long learning and foster grandparents programs are but two examples of ways in which elders can be more than passive recipients of care. They can continue to develop themselves and help others until the very end of life (Burack-Weiss, 1988, p. 25).

Acknowledging this potential, Rapp and Wintersteen (1989) formulated a "strengths model" of practice for work with severely vulnerable groups.

THE SOCIAL SUPPORT ENVIRONMENT

Internal deficits need to be balanced by strong external supports. But another social trend accompanied those we already identified, and it operated in a countervailing way. A growth spurt in social programs was one of the notable developments in the sixties. The War on Poverty and the Great Society spawned a proliferation of human services, often in disjointed and even contradictory form. The problem presented for the client group of our concern has been depicted cogently by Intagliata (1982, p. 55):

> As a result of this expansion, the overall availability of services increased significantly. Because public funding for these programs was provided primarily through narrow categorical channels, however, the network of services that has resulted is highly complex, fragmented, duplicative, and uncoordinated. Countless individual programs have been developed to provide extremely specialized services or to serve narrowly defined target groups. While these factors interfere with service accessibility for all potential users, the barriers are particularly burdensome for those persons whose complex problems require them to engage in multiple, disconnected programs in order to get the assistance they need.

Stated slightly differently, the task confronting clients was to "maintain an optimal level of independence in the midst of a . . . confusing 'nonsystem' " (White, 1987, p. 96).

These circumstances made for a daunting support environment. Clients who were already materially thwarted in life were forced to seek help in a humongous and indecipherable community service network. Even the professionals in the agencies did not know what was available in other organizations. Clients found themselves in a "revolving door mode" as they scrambled from one organization to another to meet eligibility requirements and connect with the right service niche.

The pattern of services was not only fractured, it was also in perpetual flux as program policies shifted, funding levels oscillated, and political regimes changed hands. Clients were at a loss to know what services still existed and how to access them.

In moving from the expansive sixties and seventies to the retrenching eighties and nineties, services dried up substantially. Fewer support opportunities were available and access became more harsh and forbidding. While the number of services shriveled, the delivery system somehow remained as chaotic.

Long-term vulnerable clients faced one additional obstruction to needed support; they were not among the most desired class of clientele. Their impairments were fixed and, for many professionals, they were not the easiest people to treat. Some presented themselves with bizarre behavior or physical deformities. With them, agency records would not be able to reflect as high a rate of success in program evaluation statistics and annual reports. This could negatively affect funding and public relations.

Professionals preferred to work with higher functioning clients with whom progress was more immediate and clear-cut, and professional satisfaction was more predictable. They favored engaging problem patients in whom psychotherapy was a more dominant aspect of service (Rubin & Johnson, 1984).

The pattern of characteristics and circumstances defining this population has decided implications for the kind of professional intervention they require. As we will see, the appropriate helping role calls for a paradigm of practice that is in many respects different from the traditional approach in human services.

INTERVENTION REQUISITES FOR HIGHLY VULNERABLE CLIENTS

COMPONENTS OF INTERVENTION

We have used the characteristics and needs of the client group as our point of departure, refraining from beginning with the more professionally enticing exploration of the intricacies of practice. Just as form follows function, intervention, responsibly, derives from the requirements of the group being helped. We are focusing on a population with a condition that is grave and incapacitating, one that is deep-rooted and rather immutable, and that in the past has caused people to be sequestered from the mainstream of life. To address this problem in an efficacious and humanistic way, a responsive intervention approach has evolved that includes the following components:

Goals
    Community living objectives
    Enhancement objectives
Intervention Structure
    Longitudinal service
    Cross-sectional service
    Community-based service
Foci of Practice
    Supportive and skill development focus in direct practice
    Environmental intervention
    Micro/macro practice perspective
Practice Style
    Practice intensity

We will elaborate on these components, drawing substantially on the key literature sources previously cited. The longitudinal and cross-sectional phraseology is taken from Test (1979).

Community Living Objectives

A fundamental intervention aim is to situate seriously handicapped individuals in the least restrictive environment possible, one that allows for maximum freedom and natural social intercourse. The services offered to the client, it is asserted, should not "set him or her apart from other citizens in our society" (Lamb & Peele, 1984, p. 799). This approach has been referred to as *normalization* by Cnaan and his associates and is also sometimes called mainstreaming. Aviram and Segal (1973) speak of it as an antidote to the "ghettoization" of people that is reflected in the medical model. Rapp (1985, p. 40) maintains, "The task of the worker is to build the mechanisms that will enable the client to meet the social demands set by 'normal' settings, so that a client's sense of competence can be respected." Among other things, an implication of this orientation is that intervention inherently must include addressing residential needs of clients, whether arranging for an individual apartment, placement in a group facility, or satisfactory location with the family.

Enhancement Objectives

Most helping professionals seek to bring clients to a normal level of functioning by removing stumbling blocks. The blocks may be immediate and situational or can be rooted in the basic personality of the client. With severely vulnerable clients, impediments or "blocks" are frequently permanent, and established modes of treatment generally are not relevant. Normalization with the vulnerable refers to acquiring a normal residential or community living situation, not to attaining full functional parity with people in general.

Rubin (1985, p. 14) admonishes practitioners not to "hold unrealistic expectations about 'healing' these patients." Rather, he observes, practitioners have been able to achieve success with mentally ill clients "not because they cured or alleviated psychopathology, but because they enhanced the living conditions or facilitated [the client's] role performance" (p. 3). Speaking of the elderly, White (1987, p. 93) indicates that the aim, likewise, is to "enhance client self-care." Maintaining the client in the natural community setting at the highest possible quality of life is paramount. The terms *enrichment, dignity,* and *greater opportunity* apply.

It may be useful to think of the objective as *optimization*—recognizing firm limits, but reaching for the full measure of potential within the limits. This is the sense in which the term *enhancement* is used. The strengths possessed by all individuals make this possible.

Longitudinal Service

As impairments are protracted, intervention has to be long-range. This indeterminate practice orientation is referred to by such terms as *continuing care* in the mental health field and *permanency* planning in child welfare. Turner and TenHoor (1978) envisage care-giving in a fluid framework, perhaps for life. The service posture is expressed vividly by Rapp (1985, p. 40): "The professional commitment must be forever; not that it will necessarily last until death, but . . . case closing dates are not part of the case plan."

Cross-sectional Service

The needs of disabled clients are broad and varied. This calls for invoking a wide range of different community resource supports: governmental and private, formal and informal, specialized and general. The practitioner has to bring a "holistic orientation that views all aspects of people, their situation, and environment" (White, 1987, p. 93). Cnaan et al. (1988, p. 68) observe that staff members "are concerned with all aspects of the lives of clients and are interested in them as human beings with many dimensions," in contrast to the more usual involvement with "one limited area of service." The emphasis is on helping in breadth. The practitioner is an orchestrator of diverse services, some of which he or she controls, and others over which the practitioner has no direct authorization.

Cross-sectional activities imply interdisciplinary involvements. Services to clients draw on a multiplicity of competencies and outlooks. Those playing the primary practice role include social workers, psychologists, nurses, teachers, gerontologists, psychiatrists, and physicians. This primary practitioner, regardless of professional discipline, must relate productively to professionals from diverse backgrounds. A cross-sectional orientation applies to the use of time as well as resources. The practitioner, according to Intagliata (1982, p. 658), has to offer availability that is "open-ended . . . and around-the-clock."

Community-Based Service

Obviously clients who are in a normal living setting ought to receive services that are community-based and convenient. Logistical considerations alone speak to this arrangement, but there is also another rationale. When the living situation and the service provider are in proximity, skills can be taught in vivo, which makes for an optimal learning environment (Beardsley, Kessler & Levin, 1984). The service agency may provide not only direct service to link clients to external resources, but can also offer its own organized programs locally, such as day treatment for mentally disabled clients and sheltered workshops for those needing physical rehabilitation.

A Supportive, Skill Development Emphasis in Direct Practice

Typical human service agencies emphasize clinical tasks and therapy to serve clients. For the severely vulnerable client, this is not the preferred course. These clients have limitations that make basic personality restructuring or insight development a difficult or unattainable objective. There is professional consensus, for example, that persistently mentally ill patients are not choice subjects for such treatment (Hogarty, 1981). The infirm elderly have similar barriers and are firmly set in their ways. Given their life-span projection, the investment in staff and funds for personality restructuring is not a practical use of professional resources. In addition, as we noted earlier, deficits in skills, information, and self-esteem are the basic factors inhibiting the social functioning of these individuals. In direct work with clients it is productive to place the emphasis on cultivating social survival skills and providing emotional support to engender positive attitudes toward the self. Direct assistance in practical matters of everyday living is also important. The professional literature offers strong support for these observations (Baker & Weiss, 1984; Perlman, Melnick & Kentera, 1985).

Cnaan et al. (pp. 64, 72) state, "It is the absence of skills, not clinical symptoms, that is the determining factor in the rehabilitation process. . . . The current level of functioning and the here and now are the focus." Intagliata (1982, p. 661) gives greater specificity in stating that practitioners need to *"assist their clients with the management of simple life activities and practical daily problems"* (emphasis in the original). This, according to Rubin (1985, p. 12), translates into methods relying on "components of problem-solving, task-centered and behavioral models of practice." He cites research showing these modes were associated with successful outcomes. Practical help may get clients through points of crisis. In working with vulnerable populations, Gitterman places major emphasis on developing coping skills, using such techniques as role playing, role modeling, coaching, and dramatization. Other practice roles he proposes include providing information, clarifying misinformation, offering advice and interpretation, specifying action tasks, and preparing plans for task completion. Reid (1992) sets out an array of "task strategies" for implementing these kinds of problem-solving roles.

The earlier discussion of client capacity for growth supports employment of these "psychoeducational" approaches. The research cited above gives empirical support for the prospects of client achievement in these areas.

Environmental Intervention

Community-based practice inherently implies environmental intervention. Disabled clients living in natural settings are in dire need of support from these settings. Environmental intervention aimed at insuring this support takes four forms.

1. Connecting clients with community support resources and assuring service

We have spoken of the difficulty experienced by vulnerable clients in knowing about available community resources and obtaining services from them. Rubin (1987, p. 212) proposes that "a core maze of direct service providers . . . assume ultimate responsibility for seeing that the service delivery system is responsive." The trick is to know which available programs match the needs of the client, and then to make sure that the client gains access. That may require advocacy on behalf of an individual who is denied an entitlement. Linkages need to be to both formal agencies and informal helping networks, including families, friends, and neighbors.

2. Helping to develop new needed services

When there are gaps in services needed by clients, the practitioner may want to fill the void. Easton (1984) calls for the creation of missing elements or the enhancement of inadequate elements as a facet of the approach. The latter function clarifies that the practitioner's focus on enhancement relates both to optimizing the client's capacities and also to enhancing the capacity of the environmental setting to provide for the client. The psychosocial perspective that is involved in the practice is highlighted by this dual emphasis.

3. Coordinating mini client-centered support systems

It is not sufficient only to link the client and see that the service is delivered. The need for this practice approach stems in part from a defective level of integration among community services. Practitioners need to impose a degree of coherence within the various mini support systems that they compose for each client. This involves coordinating among and between formal and informal support elements.

4. Promoting system-wide policy changes and community education

Changes in service patterns may require policy action at the level of the overall service system or even at the broader community level. Cnaan et al. talk of "restructuring and reeducating the environment to better absorb and care for people" (p. 70). This is an undertaking that is generally beyond the reach of the typical direct service practitioner and needs to be viewed, rather, as the role of the executive and the agency system. It is an ambitious and formidable intervention function that needs to be acknowledged, but not underestimated.

Micro and Macro Practice Perspective

The service professional works directly with individuals in guiding and counseling roles, and also deals with systems and environmental elements. This is sometimes aptly described as a "boundary-spanning" approach. The professional has to span the territory between the client and community support agencies; to tread between various agency entities, bringing them together on behalf of the client; and to span the sometimes inhospitable borders between clinically oriented direct practice professionals and those with community organization or administrative commitments.

Psychosocial practice is a way of framing the role, but that may trivialize it to some degree. A psychosocial perspective ordinarily defines a clinical worker who takes the broader social context into account in designing a treatment plan for a client. The PIE, or person-in-environment, phraseology is sometimes used to signify this (Karls & Wandrei, 1992). The focus is on how the external world impinges on the client, and how the client needs to adjust independently to those influences. The practice role we have described goes beyond this; it requires that the practitioner have baseline competency to operate proficiently on both sides of the psychosocial fence. The ecological systems perspective, which is presented by Germain in Chapter 3, offers a comprehensive and balanced conceptualization for carrying out that role. Cnaan et al. (1989) in another study closely analyzed 15 different theoretical perspectives for utility in psychosocial rehabilitation. They concluded that the ecosystems perspective is by far the most promising.

Intensity of Practice Relationship

The notion of practice intensity is more difficult to convey than the others. It concerns practice style and the climate of relationship with clients. Because clients are often significantly impeded in many areas of life, frustrated, and discouraged, the form of association with them needs to be closer, more encompassing, and more expressive than in typical service settings. We encapsulate these practice attributes in the term *practice intensity*. The style is described in various ways in the literature.

Rapp uses a three-fold formulation of attributes to portray the concept: unconditional positive regard, empathy, and genuineness. *Unconditional positive regard* involves communicating respect, acceptance, liking, and concern in an open-hearted way. Cnaan et al. (1988, p. 67) describe this as demonstrating "genuine concern with the well-being of clients." *Empathy,* according to Rapp, calls on the practitioner "to perceive and communicate accurately and with sensitivity both the current feelings and the experiences of another person and their meaning and significance" (p. 39). Cnaan et al. similarly enjoin practitioners to be "in close and trustful rather than remote contact with their clients" (p. 69). *Genuineness* for Rapp entails practitioners "being themselves in the moment rather than presenting a professional facade" (p. 39). In the words of Cnaan et al., there should not be "neutrality of staff members toward clients. Staff members respond to what clients say or do, including in instances regarding non-therapeutic issues, in positive or negative ways" (p. 68).

The Cnaan group goes on to add another practice attribute, projecting unswerving conviction and enthusiasm about the possibilities of enhanced functioning by clients. "Even when clients are losing their determination, staff must be expected to persist in the belief that progress is feasible" (p. 69).

This helping posture has a related element: encouraging a high level of participation by clients in the practice process. Their maximum feasible input is actively sought and promoted in every phase of intervention. Clients with low self-confidence and defeating life experiences need to know that their ideas are valued, and that they can contribute to and shape their progress. For this reason, the empowerment of clients is a crucial component of this paradigm's approach. While client participation is by no means a unique consideration, it receives special accent here.

A final aspect of practice style for Cnaan is a broad scope of helping involvements with the client, allowing for easy access as needs arise and crises occur. This harkens back to Intagliata's point about around-the-clock availability. That time availability can refer to the agency system rather than exclusively to the primary practitioner.

Serving vulnerable clients well, Gitterman tells us, requires a touch of "heroism." There are implications here for the size of the case load that will permit this kind of close attention. It also suggests structuring the job for adequate supervision and support, and cycles of release for staff, to avoid burnout.

A NEW PRACTICE PARADIGM

When these components are put together in a service setting, they give rise to a new paradigm of practice. Not that it is altogether distinctive and apart; some components have been used here and there in the human services. For example, the ordinary information and referral function of agencies parallels the linking of clients to community support resources. Typical clinical practice sometimes includes educational aspects geared to skill development in clients. And, certainly, most services are based in community settings rather than in closed institutions.

It is when the components are used fully and in close interplay that the configuration represents something unique. This is not simply community psychology or "old-fashioned social work." It is most akin to the cluster of practices that go by terms such as *case management, care coordination, community support,* and kindred designations. For purposes of convenience, the case management terminology will be used to represent the lot.

A difficulty remains that the general case management approach has so many definitions and different applications in practice that it takes on a multifarious and amorphous coloration. Some frustrated scholars have concluded that the term is somewhat akin to a Rorschach test in that it can be interpreted to mean whatever its user wishes it to mean (Schwartz, Goldman & Churgin, 1982). For example, some view case management primarily as community outreach and linkage, sometimes in a strictly short-range service framework (Roberts-DeGennaro, 1986).

Comprehensive Psychosocial Enhancement

We believe the term *comprehensive psychosocial enhancement* is an emblematic phrase that conveys the practice paradigm, and we failed to discover a briefer adequate expression. The concept seems to aptly contract the spectrum of paradigm components. *Comprehensive* embodies both the longitudinal and cross-sectional aspects of the approach. *Psychosocial,* a micro/macro construct, signifies both individual helping in connection with skill development and emotional support and environmental interventions involving linkage to community supports. *Enhancement* conveys the notion of optimization rather than cure, and allows for the objective of helping to maintain the client in a community setting. A fuller encapsulation would be *comprehensive psychosocial enhancement for community living,* but the author shrinks here from testing the full extent of the reader's linguistic tolerance. In this book the abridged term *comprehensive enhancement* will frequently be used interchangeably with the term *case management,* but represents a distinct conceptualization or subset.

Traditional Practice Versus the New Paradigm

The distinctiveness of the paradigm for practice with severely vulnerable populations can best be highlighted by comparing it with features of the traditional mode based on psychotherapy. The chart below presents features of traditional practice in one column and contrasts these with features of the new paradigm in the parallel column.

Traditional Clinical Practice	The New Paradigm
• Cure: elimination or reduction of original impairment	• Enhancement/optimization: enables clients to maintain themselves satisfactorily in the community with the original impairment
• Delimited, short- to medium-term duration of service	• Continuous, long-term duration of service
• Helping in depth, focused needs	• Helping in breadth, multiple needs
• Practitioner is primarily a direct service provider (micro orientation)	• Practitioner is substantially a linker to community support resources (micro/macro orientation)
• Primary focus on client insight, emotional growth, personality development	• Primary focus on developing client coping skills to function in a community setting
• Single helper	• Multiple helpers; practitioner as coordinator of a helping system
• Agency or institution as locus of help provision	• Community as locus of help provision (community-based service)
• Practitioner authority is clear and sanctioned (fixed boundaries)	• Practitioner authority is unclear and variably sanctioned (fluid boundaries and boundary-spanning role)
• Eventual full self-sufficiency for client; practitioner disengages	• Partial self-sufficiency for client; practitioner maintains connection
• Case termination or discharge	• Ongoing monitoring and reassessment

Common Features of Traditional Practice and the New Paradigm

To clarify distinctions, this analysis has emphasized the differences between the paradigm for working with severely vulnerable populations and the ways of more normative practice. There is, however, a core of fundamental overlaps and similarities between the two, and these must be examined in the interest of accuracy and balance. Basic principles of all professional helping are commonly known and applied. They include, among others:

A service ideal: the needs and interest of the client are primary and inviolate
A commitment to professional integrity, including ethical conduct (confidentiality, truthfulness) and the maintaining of practice competency
Use of a rational and systematic problem-solving methodology that is based on empirical knowledge and practice wisdom
Conscious and disciplined use of the self as an instrument of purposive change
Individualization of client problems and of approaches for dealing with them
Respect for the integrity of the client as a person: cultural values, personal style, and aspirations

There may be other principles, but these suggest the common types of critical elements that define the professional helping role regardless of theoretical orientation or client characteristics.

Contextual Factors

This discussion has emphasized direct service to clients, with the practitioner as the focus of attention. But no practitioner of human services operates in a professional vacuum; there is the context of community influences, the structure of the employing organization, and the climate of professional culture. These community and agency variables both give direction and impose constraints on the particular way practitioners implement services.

Community and Organizational Factors

The community background is an especially salient factor in work with severely vulnerable populations because of their intense need for manifold help-rendering supports. The practice is highly dependent on a substantial community resource base as a fundamental component of the work. The professional role presupposes existence of concrete resources that can be drawn on as needed to sustain the client (or calls for activity to fill in gaps or supplement community supports as required). When these supports are not in place, the practice is compromised or even nullified.

Political Factors

It is important to stress this because the case-management approach often has been distorted by planners and politicians. As discussed earlier, the case-management approach emerged historically in connection with the movement for deinstitutionalization of the mentally ill, the developmentally disabled, and others, and their relocation in natural community settings possessing minimal restrictions. At the time deinstitutionalization was promulgated, there was an understanding that adequate funds would follow the discharged clients in order to ensure the needed sustained care. Research studies and writings show that the funding did not materialize at an adequate or proportionate level (Segal & Aviram, 1978; General Accounting Office, 1977). In addition, sufficient dedicated funds were not allocated for new clients served in the community rather than in an institution. Deinstitutionalization was widely used as a money-saving tool.

This resulted in a structural problem: clients needing community support services often were abandoned and left without a funding policy or delivery system to assure assistance. Into this breach was thrown a cadre of workers, often designated case managers, whose role it was to extract various services for their wanting clients from a human service system constricting under extreme fiscal pressure. The professionals were in a squeeze. A reasonable law of sociology would hold that structural problems are rarely solved by the independent actions of individuals. Practitioners' efforts become diminished or futile when they have to contend personally with a structural pattern of insufficient or detached human services. Professional efforts can result in incremental improvement beyond where clients would be if left alone to engage the community system, but fall far short of what would be possible if structural elements were in place.

From a policy standpoint, it is important to incorporate structural elements of community resource development into the broad conception of the comprehensive enhancement role. Otherwise, the role can be used as a device by politicians to evade their responsibility toward our most vulnerable citizens.

Community Versus Policy Impulses

A distinction between community and policy impulses generating case management approaches is useful. The paradigm presented here starts with a concern for a client population in the community—i.e., the deinstitutionalized mentally ill—and seeks to formulate a service mode that meets their needs in a responsive and effective way. The prevailing question is, How can we best meet the needs of highly vulnerable clients? An alternative conception of this practice comes from managed care and receives its impetus in the fields of medicine and gerontology. Here the community concern is over the rapidly escalating costs of medical services, and the prevailing question is, How can we contain medical costs while still providing a reasonable level of health care? The purposes are different and each has its own validity. Also, the emphases on effectiveness versus efficiency are not mutually exclusive.

Both approaches are referred to under the same rubric and are discussed interchangeably, causing practice confusion and conceptual chaos. A useful step would be to separate them out and let each develop on its own terms. We hope to contribute to that purpose in this book by clearly articulating one of them.

From an organizational standpoint, the practice paradigm calls for assigning a fixed point of responsibility for the coordination of the multiplicity of needs of clients. The professional role grew out of the difficulties clients had in obtaining a viable mix of services on their own, and was made necessary by the segmented methods of both workers and agencies. It is important that the professional assigned to the case hold resolutely to the principle of comprehensive coordination, even when other staff members become involved. Also, some agencies use a team rather than an individual approach to implementation, and in those instances, designating a central point of personal accountability within the team is essential.

PROFESSIONAL FACTORS

There are some aspects of professionalism that also provide context. The approach we are considering is rather new, unorthodox, and not well-established in the human services from a professional standpoint. Case management is often not well understood, in part because of its vague definition. It does not have the status and legitimacy that other areas enjoy: it's clients are not as high functioning, it does not feature the clinical methods that are in vogue, and it is sometimes carried out by paraprofessional staff.

Standards. For some, the approach just does not require the same demanding professional standards of other practices. Three aspects of this merit comment. The first point relates to the proficiency level needed to implement the practice. Comprehensive enhancement is a compound, multi-dimensional intervention mode calling for across-the-board competencies that are contained in clinical, community, organization, and administrative roles. Knowledge of human behavior, organizational interaction, and community processes is essential. White (1987, p. 93) believes that this necessitates a higher order of professional application than other areas: "While casework remains an integral part of case management, the dimensions of managing and monitoring systems, service delivery, interagency agreements, finances and provider efficiency add complexity to more traditional methods." The breadth of sophistication required of the professional, in both knowledge and skills, to conduct this practice effectively may well exceed those in more circumscribed areas. A legitimate question is whether the demands are actually greater than is reasonable to expect. One of the purposes of this book is to articulate and codify the substantive professional undergirdings of the practice, which should help to answer that question.

Knowledge and skills. Another professional issue concerns the place of human behavior knowledge and clinical skills in this practice. Chapter 6 (Counseling and Therapy) will discuss this in detail, but a few preliminary remarks are in order here. As mentioned earlier, an emphasis on psychotherapy is not the best approach for severely vulnerable individuals. Professional help focused on skill development, psychological support, and crisis intervention is what most fully meets the needs of the client group. This empirically based reality has to be firmly acknowledged in order to avoid becoming infatuated with technique at the expense of serving people.

Still, we know that extreme life conditions that drastically impede and frustrate individuals can bring on feelings of helplessness, anxiety, and defeatism. All contacts with such individuals need to be carried forward with enormous psychological sensitivity and knowledge of the dynamics of human behavior. Making a referral to an agency, encouraging completion of a self-care plan, resolving a dispute in the family, or promoting compliance with a medical regimen will draw on a wide range of psychotherapy skills. Transference, managing mechanisms of defense, use of ventilation, and confronting are all concepts that apply. The treatment goals and broad intervention strategies are not the same, but the able practitioner will draw widely and wisely on the full array of techniques and insights of psychotherapy to assist the seriously impeded client.

Criteria for success.   Another professional issue bears on criteria for success. Professionals ordinarily gauge success and derive satisfaction from the trajectory of client improvement. Cure or substantial improvement of clients toward normal functioning receives high marks on the professional scoreboard. Providing continuing care that maintains the client stably at a reasonable but impaired level of living, however, does not. This is a professional task without status or glitter.

It is appropriate, however, to measure success not only by the distance we raise clients up, but also by the distance we prevent them from falling. Severely vulnerable clients if not buttressed can sometimes sink to a dire and grievous level of human existence. Many professionals working with these individuals consider themselves on a rescue mission to prevent this—as reflected in the practice intensity and dedication they manifest in the role. If practitioners come to view enhancement and prevention of precipitous downward movement on par with cure and promotion of strong upward movement, the professional value of case management and a comprehensive enhancement approach will attain an elevated position.

In the next chapter we will move from general and rather abstract concepts to the specific functions of practice. A model for implementation will be presented as a concrete guide to carrying out the paradigm that was put forward.

REFERENCES

Aviram, V. & Segal, S. (1973). Exclusion of the mentally ill: A reflection of an old problem. *Archives of General Psychiatry, 23*(2), 120–131.

Baker, F. & Weiss, R. (1984). The nature of case manager support. *Hospital and Community Psychiatry, 35,* 925–928.

Ballew, J. R. & Mink, G. (1986). *Case management in the human services.* Springfield, IL: Thomas.

Beardsley, C., Kessler, R., & Levin, E. I. (1984). Education for young adult chronic client. *Psychosocial Rehabilitation Journal, 8*(1), 44–52.

Brightman, A. J. (Ed.). (1984). *Ordinary moments: The disabled experience.* Baltimore: University Park Press.

Burack-Weiss, A. (1988, fall). Clinical aspects of case management. *Generations,* pp. 23–29.

Cnaan, R. A., Blankertz, L., Messinger, K., & Gardner, J. R. (1988). Psychosocial rehabilitation: Toward a definition. *Psychosocial Rehabilitation Journal, 11*(4), 61–77.

Cnaan, R. A., Blankertz, L. Messinger, K., & Gardner, J. R. (1989). Psychosocial rehabilitation: Towards a theoretical base. *Psychosocial Rehabilitation Journal, 13*(1), 33–56.

DeJong, G. (1983). Defining and implementing the independent living concept. In N. M. Crewe, I. K. Zola, & associates (Eds.), *Independent living for physically disabled people: Developing, implementing and evaluating self-help rehabilitation programs.* San Francisco: Jossey-Bass.

Easton, K. (1984). Psychoanalytic principles in psychosocial rehabilitation. *Journal of the American Academy of Psychoanalysis, 12*(4), 569–584.

Frankfather, D. L., Smith, M. J., & Caro, F. G. (1981). *Family care of the elderly.* Lexington, MA: Health Lexington.

General Accounting Office. (1977). *Returning the mentally disabled to the community: Government needs to do more* (HRD-76–152). Washington, DC: U.S. Government Printing Office.

Gerhart, U. C. (1990). *Caring for the chronic mentally ill*. Itasca, IL: Peacock.

Gitterman, A. (1991). Social work practice with vulnerable populations. In A. Gitterman (Ed.), *Handbook of Social Work* (pp. 1–32). New York: Columbia University.

Goldstein, J., Freud, A., & Solnit, A. (1973). *Beyond the best interests of the child*. New York: Free Press.

Hogarty, G. E. (1981). Evaluation of drugs and therapeutic procedures: The contribution of non-pharmacological techniques. In G. Tognoni, C. Bellantvono, & M. Lader (Eds.), *Epidemiological impact of psychotropic drugs*. Amsterdam: North-Holland Biomedical Press.

Intagliata, J. (1982). Improving the quality of community care for the chronically mentally disabled: The role of case management. *Schizophrenia Bulletin, 8*(4), 655–674.

Karls, J. & Wandrei, K. (1992). PIE: A new language for social work. *Social Work, 37*(1), 80–85.

Lamb, H. R. & Peele, R. (1984). The need for continuing asylum and sanctuary. *Hospital and Community Psychiatry, 38*(8), 798–802.

Perlman, B., Melnick, G., & Kentera, A. (1985). Assessing the practice effectiveness of a case management program. *Hospital and Community Psychiatry, 36,* 405–407.

Rapp, C. A. (1985). Research on chronically mentally ill: Curriculum implications. In J. Bowker (Ed.), *Education for practice with the chronically mentally ill: What works?* (pp. 32–49). Washington, DC: Council on Social Work Education.

Rapp, C. A. & Wintersteen, R. (1989). The strengths model of case management: Results from twelve demonstrations. *Psychosocial Rehabilitation Journal, 13*(1), 23–32.

Reid, W. J. (1992). *Task strategies: An empirical approach to clinical social work*. New York: Columbia University Press.

Roberts-DeGennaro, M. (1986). The case management model in employee assistance programs. *Employee Assistance Quarterly, 1*(3), 63–74.

Rubin, A. (1985). Effective community-based care of chronic mental illness: Experimental findings. In J. Bowker (Ed.), *Education for practice with the chronically mentally ill: What works?* (pp. 1–17). Washington, DC: Council on Social Work Education.

Rubin, A. (1987). Case Management. In A. Minahan et al. (Eds.), *Encyclopedia of social work* (pp. 212–222). Silver Spring, MD: National Association of Social Workers.

Rubin, A. & Johnson, P. (1984). Direct practice interests of entering M.S.W. students. *Journal of Education for Social Work, 20*(2), 5–16.

Schwartz, S. R. & Goldfinger, S. M. (1981). The new chronic patient: Clinical characteristics of an emerging subgroup. *Hospital and Community Psychiatry, 32*(8), 470–474.

Schwartz, S., Goldman, H., & Churgin, S. (1982). Case management for the chronic mentally ill: Models and dimensions. *Hospital and Community Psychiatry, 33,* 1006–1009.

Segal, S. & Aviram, U. (1978). *The mentally ill in community-based sheltered care: A study of community care and social integration*. New York: John Wiley & Sons.

Test, M. (1979). Continuity of care in community treatment. In L. Stein (Ed.), *Community support systems for the long-term patient*. San Francisco: Jossey-Bass.

Turner, J. & TenHoor, W. (1978). The NIMH community support program: Pilot approach to a needed social reform. *Schizophrenia Bulletin, 4*(3), 313–348.

Weil, M., Karls, J. M., & associates. (1985). *Case management in human service practice*. San Francisco: Jossey-Bass.

White, M. (1987). Case management. In *Encyclopedia of aging* (pp. 93–96). New York: Springer.

2

Comprehensive Enhancement Practice: An Implementation Model

A MODEL OF COMPREHENSIVE PSYCHOSOCIAL ENHANCEMENT PRACTICE

Alfred North Whitehead reminds us that "the aim of science is to seek the simplest explanations of complex facts." In keeping with this insight, this chapter presents a discrete model of the multifaceted paradigm of comprehensive enhancement practice, one that specifies a finite set of core functions of the practice and their approximate sequencing in application.

While advocating the need to unmask a complex process, Whitehead also warns us of the downside. We may err in believing that the original facts are, in reality, simple because our quest was to arrive at a simplified construct. Therefore, he admonishes: "seek simplicity and distrust it."

DEVELOPMENT OF THE MODEL

As we have stated, the major effort to put into operation the comprehensive enhancement paradigm has been through case management practice. To gain a better understanding of how case management was carried out in the field, the author directed a series of collaborative studies between the University of California, Los Angeles Center for Child and Family Policy Studies and the Los Angeles Department of Mental Health. The department conducts a large, geographically varied, and ethnically diverse program that encompasses most of the problems found in urban centers nationally. The department itself identified case management as the priority area to be investigated because of the lack of an agreed on definition and wide variation in practice, both within the department itself and in the country generally. Action and research steps were taken to explore and clarify. The project staff carried out the following activities:

Composed from the literature a preliminary set of 13 case management functions in rough sequential order

Conducted an in-depth field survey of 48 case managers to adjust the preliminary list based on their experiences (eliminated some, added some, rearranged the order) (Rothman, 1987c)

Conducted an extensive retrieval of research literature on case management in numerous fields of service to vulnerable clients; completed a research synthesis of findings of 132 studies (Rothman, 1987a)

Constructed an initial model of practice from the field survey and broad research synthesis

Reviewed and refined the initial model through reactions and suggestions of a select panel of eight experienced practitioners rated as possessing high competency

Constructed a working model of practice (Rothman, 1987b)

Field-tested the working model through structured application by agency-based case managers; assessed the feasibility of the intervention from this trial (Rothman, 1988a)

Carried out a parallel appraisal and critique of the working model through a re-survey of 15 practitioners who were interviewed in the original field survey (Rothman, 1988a)

Constructed an advanced model of practice from the operational field-test and re-survey (Rothman, 1988b)

Detailed information about this process is available in the references cited.

Through these procedures, the original list of functions devised by the researchers was reconstituted in a number of ways. None of the functions was eliminated, but two new ones were added. The terminology for some functions was changed, and the flow of activity was altered and became more dynamic. Some functions became somewhat overlapping in the sequence; others became alternative options at given points. There were several functions that were now viewed as recurringly entering or leaving the process at points along the sequence.

AN EMPIRICALLY GROUNDED MODEL OF PRACTICE: FIFTEEN FUNCTIONS

The current model was derived from the practice experience in one large, complex setting and the findings of existing social research in numerous fields of service to vulnerable populations (see Fig. 2–1). Interviews and informal discussions with professionals from various fields of service suggest that it has wide applicability. It is based on the typical functions performed in case management practice and on the interrelations among functions. The model identifies and proceduralizes the steps ordinarily taken to implement case management practice. Fifteen functions are depicted representing a time-phased process.[1]

The functions are not strictly separate and discrete. Often they flow into one another and overlap. Areas having a high degree of overlap or compression are grouped together in the discussion below. A concise definition for each function assists in providing conceptual concreteness. We begin by describing

[1]This discussion is based in part on Rothman (1991).

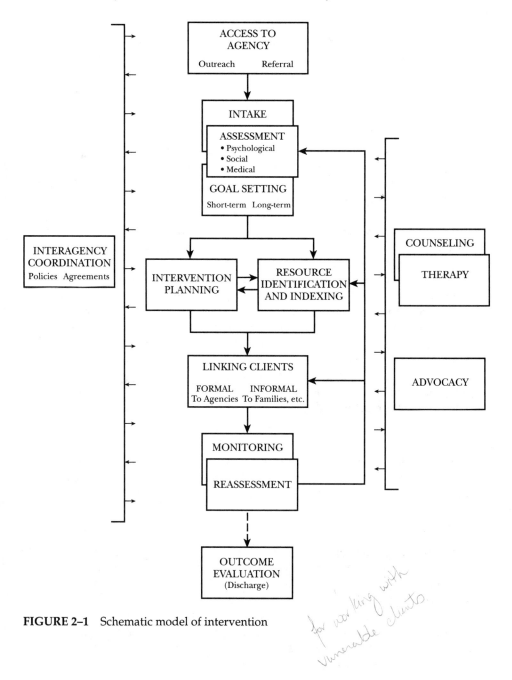

FIGURE 2–1 Schematic model of intervention

the sequential functions from top to bottom in the center of Figure 2-1. We will then move to the left-hand intermittent function, and then the right-hand intermittent set of functions. The definitions grew out of the field interviews with case managers, supplemented by findings from the research synthesis.

Channeling Clients

1. Access to the Agency

The flow of clients into the organization can come through *referrals* of various kinds (agencies, families, community organizations, clergy, police, schools, self-referral, etc.). In that instance, the agency needs to be ready to receive clientele as they approach the system. Many agencies function primarily in this mode. The other access mode is that of *outreach*, in which the agency extends into the community, to both search for and encourage clients to enter its service system. This often involves seeking client groups that are most in need of service and who do not themselves make contact with the agency, such as the homeless and frail elderly. Outreach suggests, in some agency situations, either the absence of a sufficient ongoing natural client flow, or the availability of resources to accommodate a greater number of clients than is currently being served. Generally, the matter of providing access for clients is an agency or system function rather than one falling to the individual practitioner. The practitioner participates in the access function but does not direct it.

For new clients, research suggests it is effective to have a quick turnaround time. An appointment should be set within days, and the worker should make prompt direct contact with the client (Research Synthesis [RS], pp. 17–18).*

Intake, Assessment, and Setting Goals

These three are separate functions, but they also overlap and interact. Often they take place at the same time, allowing the practitioner to move back and forth among them. Sometimes, however, they exist independently.

2. Intake

Intake includes identifying the client's problem and situation. Also, the practitioner will seek to determine if there is an appropriate agency–client match. Eligibility is examined and the financial situation is appraised. The client is given information about agency services, requirements, and limitations. Sometimes this is done on a group basis and referred to as orientation. Some preliminary intervention planning may begin. Intake often is a rather formal process, involving the gathering of designated information, filling out standard administrative forms, and giving routine instructions.

---

*Citations to specific research studies will be found in the research synthesis, which was expanded in Rothman, 1992. The page numbers are for the 1992 publication.

3. Assessment (Psychological, Social, Medical)

Assessment further examines the problem to understand its causes and dynamics. The level of the client's social, psychological, and physical functioning is clarified. For highly vulnerable clients, needs are typically broad and assessment must be inclusive. There is traditional case history development. Outside informants may be relied on, including the family and previous agencies that saw the client.

Because client empowerment is a major goal, clients are encouraged to participate to their maximum potential in assessment and every other phase of the process. Participation is frequently acknowledged by practitioners, but then treated in a off-hand and perfunctory way, serving as a slogan rather than as a protocol of practice. For this reason, we will explore the client input factor throughout this entire book. It is too easy, otherwise, for it to slip away.

Research points to a careful assessment of the family in terms of its potential benefit to the client and its capability to cope with a long-term client. Professionals in the agency, from several disciplines, may need to participate in the assessment. To deal with family and other dynamics, sufficient time needs to be given, and appropriate assessment tools need to be used or developed (RS, pp. 34–37).

4. Setting Goals

Establishing service goals builds on assessment. Most case managers attempt to obtain the client's perception of areas needing improvement and to include the client's personal objectives in their own construction of professional objectives. Typically, short- and long-term goals are formulated—for example, acute stress and immediate housing needs versus enhanced self-esteem and occupational aims.

Respondents in our survey pointed to the importance of a realistic outlook on given limitations of severely vulnerable clients. A maintenance program to allow the client to function stably in the community or to reduce hospital recidivism may be a sufficient goal in many situations. Expectations have to be realistic, in addition, to sustain staff morale and avoid burnout. With a service goal established, there are two alternatives for the next function in the sequence.

Intervention Planning or Resource Identification

A logical progression of steps at this point would be to first engage in planning intervention services aimed at specific goals, then to seek necessary resources to carry out the plan. The problem with this progression is that service resources are frequently in short supply and the system of services changes rapidly. The means are not always there to reach the desired goals. Therefore, some case managers first determine what is available in the resource pool and build their service plan from that reality base.

5. Intervention Planning

The notion of intervention planning encompasses both *treatment planning* in the sense of the direct provision of counseling and therapy, and *service planning* involving the linking of clients to informal and formal external supports for more practical assistance. Intervention service planning usually involves methods of achieving both short- and long-term goals. As suggested earlier, planning is heavily tied to resource identification and linkage, and these work hand-in-hand. In developing a plan, many case managers consider the barriers that may be encountered, both on the client and system level, and begin to consider contingency steps to cope with these. The research indicates that clients should be involved to the greatest extent possible in intervention planning (and earlier stages) as they often are able to accurately identify their own needs, thus contributing to more effective service outcomes (RS, pp. 19–20).

6. Resource Identification and Indexing

This function entails obtaining information on relevant service resources and organizing the data for easy access. A number of means are available for such resource identification: telephone contacts with agencies, attending meetings where agency representatives are present, informal networking, setting up a personal resource file, and using an office resource file or directory. Information may sometimes be obtained from clients as well. Most case managers use multiple means. Be aware of possible inaccurate or out-of-date information due to frequent changes in agency policies and programs.

Services for atypical clients with double or difficult diagnoses (such as AIDS together with drug abuse) are especially difficult to locate. The case manager may also need to develop new resources when certain opportunities for clients are absent or in short supply. Licensed community care facilities are one example of this.

Linking Clients to Community Supports

Linking was identified as a frequent activity among all case managers in the study. Formal and informal supports have to be considered in tandem and as a package. One may precede the other in action steps or they may be dealt with rather concurrently. There was no clear pattern among these possibilities in the survey responses.

7. Formal Linkage—Agencies and Programs

Formal linkage functions include such activities as clarifying the service need, careful matching of clients to agencies, initial telephone contact, orienting the client, preparing papers, and visiting agencies. The research suggests that more effective linkage is active and facilitative, with the practitioner often serving as a "traveling companion" (RS, p. 20). The practitioner needs to give both concrete and emotional support to facilitate a productive connection. Linkage requires the use of organizational skills (who to contact, at what level) and community-oriented skills (knowledge of what new services are developing, what legislative policies are applicable, what funding is available) to optimize service connections. The agency ordinarily needs to pave the way at the administrative and community level if the linkage function is to be accomplished most effectively. Preparing the client for the experience includes such things as providing detailed information, anticipating difficulties, role playing appropriate client behavior, giving emotional support, and accompanying the client on the first visit.

8. Informal Linkage—Social Networks

This entails drawing on a range of natural helping networks. Family members can be important, but must be assessed first to determine whether they have the potential to be helpful, and whether they can sustain the burden. The practitioner has to structure time to provide the necessary orientation, training, and consultation needed for natural helpers to carry out the informal support roles. These linkages also extend to friends, neighbors, and community groups. Ethnic considerations should be examined in determining whether a formal or informal approach should be emphasized, as different groups have available, or favor, different options. Some groups (Hispanics, Asian–Americans) may have large extended families and may prefer to rely on assistance within the family circle (RS, pp. 37–38). We will discuss cultural issues in more detail later in the chapter.

Monitoring and Reassessment

These two functions overlap to a great extent. The purpose of monitoring is to keep current on whether existing arrangements are satisfactory for the client. Monitoring includes a reassessment component to determine whether changes are necessary.

9. Monitoring

Systematic contact with agency service providers and with informal supports is at the heart of monitoring. Its purpose is to appraise the suitability of provisions made to sustain the client in the community. This can be accomplished through telephoning the contacts, visitation, phoning clients, or having the support individuals or client phone the practitioner. The research indicates that this requires a definite and substantive allotment of time (RS, pp. 22–23). The research also indicates that crisis situations will arise, and that the case manager should anticipate dealing with these—necessitating some degree of flexibility in working hours (RS, pp. 22–23).

10. Reassessment

Given a long-term continuing care outlook, recurrent appraisal of the situation is a necessity and may be required at established intervals by agency rules. Each initial client assessment will, in time, require a reassessment. These can be formal or informal, periodic or ongoing, and at various intervals of frequency. Respondents indicate that the client should ordinarily participate in the reassessment.

A number of factors were identified as hindering reassessment: ill-defined goals make assessment difficult; sometimes clients withhold information or their progress is irregular and uncertain; collateral agencies occasionally fail to provide information; work pressures and time restraints may interfere.

Reassessment often leads to looping back in the sequence to a new linkage, different intervention plan, or revised goals.

11. Client Evaluation (for Termination)

Evaluation differs from reassessment in that it carries the sense of termination or discharge. It ordinarily occurs when a client is ready to operate in a fully independent way without further service, based on the professional judgment of the practitioner. Since most long-term vulnerable clients are in a continuing-care mode that requires ongoing professional attention, such final outcome evaluation is rare. For this reason, a broken line has been used in the diagram, signifying that this point is seldom reached. Nevertheless, the function has been included in the diagram of the model because it occasionally applies and should not be discounted. For example, in child welfare, dependent children become capable of independent living, which results in purposive termination of active service. In gerontological work that point may not be reached.

Intermittent Functions

The intermittent functions that follow do not occupy a specific or regular position in the flow of the case management sequence. They may enter and leave the sequence at various points in recurring fashion.

12. Interagency Coordination

Interagency coordination function deals with the establishment of relationships among agencies to facilitate the linkage function, either through formal policies or by informal agreements between organizations. Formal policies are typically arranged at the highest hierarchical levels. Informal agreements are less binding and "legal," and are sometimes brought about at the program level by direct service professionals. These interorganizational understandings relate to service patterns, type and number of clients, and financial payments. As the diagram shows, such interagency understandings can be made before a service program begins, or at any time during the operation of the program.

The research suggests that optimally the primary service organization should clear the way initially at the administrative or policy level. Further, interorganizational relationships are more likely to engender linkage if they are based on an "intrusive influence" involving fiscal remuneration, authority, and the like (RS, pp. 42–45). The research also points to meaningful exchange among agencies as a means of encouraging successful linkage, such as sharing information about clients, making mutual referrals, sharing a common facility, and sharing staff functions (RS, p. 46).

13. Counseling

In field interviews respondents referred to counseling in terms of information and advice giving, for example, cuing clients on how to deal with fellow clients in a residential facility. Supportive encouragement of the client is also emphasized, such as pointing out strengths and reinforcing efforts at self-direction. This is typically not highly intrapsychic (as is traditional therapy) and involves "here and now" problem solving, reality testing, imparting socialization skills, and giving practical help in such areas as housing, finances, parenting, and employment. The research shows that effective counseling approaches included such things as teaching basic living skills, using role playing, and modeling desirable behavior (RS, pp. 20–22). Since counseling is ordinarily short-term, it can be offered recurrently and at various points in the process.

14. Therapy

Respondents distinguished between long-term therapy, which focuses on deep-seated personality problems, and short-term therapy, which is concerned with immediate problems in living, such as a conflict with a roommate or a family crisis. Most of the reported activities were short-term. Respondents thought it important to include family members in order to reinforce or maintain positive behavioral change. The majority view was that even in mental health settings therapy should have a present-time emphasis and assist clients to cope with day-to-day living situations, as the severity of their condition affords them only a limited capacity for basic personality change.

This is in keeping with research findings that intervention concentrating on the management of immediate reality, social adjustment, and the connection of clients with social supports is the most useful form of intervention. Therapy, as defined, can occur at many places in the sequence, and may be provided and withdrawn recurrently as required.

As indicated, with severely vulnerable populations, counseling and therapy overlap functionally, and it is difficult to make sharp distinctions between them. While the term *therapy* was used, the actual intervention tasks generally involved counseling. The choice of terminology may be related primarily to the higher status attributed to therapy. In some fields, such as gerontology or child welfare, clients are typically linked to outside sources for extended therapy when appropriate. Thereby, the function is exercised indirectly, through referral, rather than in a direct way.

15. Advocacy

Advocacy is another intermittent function. It might be needed early in the sequence (exerting pressure on a landlord on an emergency basis to allow a client back into his apartment so that reflective assessment may begin), or may take place later, perhaps at the time of linkage, where an external community agency is refusing to provide a service. Advocacy involves an affirmative and assertive approach to assisting a client to receive services or amenities that are being unfairly withheld. The advocate assists the client to move through bureaucratic blocks in order to obtain benefits. There are a number of intensity levels of advocacy, including discussion, persuasion, prodding, and coercion. Typically in intervention, one increases the level of intensity in stepwise fashion as is necessary. Advocacy requires a sophisticated understanding of how organizations are structured and work, including an appreciation of organizational politics.

The model focuses on the functions of case managers in providing care to individual clients. However, case managers also work in the community and with organizations in order to promote benefits for clients collectively. These broader "macro" tasks were pointed to by participants in the field survey as follows:

> *Education:* Of other professionals within and outside the agency, residential care operators, and citizens' groups
> *Group approaches:* Support and self-help groups for families of clients
> *Community meetings:* Attending interagency planning councils, for example, the United Way
> *Supervising staff:* Mentor for new case managers and advising less-trained staff

ELABORATION AND CLARIFICATION

USING THE DIAGRAM

The diagram can be viewed as a road map to comprehensive enhancement practice. A map tells the traveler how to get from one point to another, often in unfamiliar territory. The diagram does this also, from the point of seeing a client for the first time, to nesting him or her securely in a supportive situation, and allowing for the highest possible quality of life in a natural setting.

Like a road map, the diagram does not detail the sharp curves, the jarring bumps, and cloudbursts along the way. It does not tell the reader in advance when a truck suddenly will pull out into the road or when a drunk driver will go into an unpredictable swerve. Still, a road map is a useful tool of travel management within its limitations, just as the diagram can give direction for case management. Through its flexible features of feedback loops and overlapping functions, the diagram does allow for special and individualized conditions that arise.

The diagram helps to make practice more systematic and consistent because the professional does not need to figure out fundamental steps in the process for each case. Within limitations, the diagram is a working tool to regularize, to some degree, the complexities of helping severely vulnerable clients and achieves the kind of simplification proposed by Alfred North Whitehead.

EXPLANATORY NOTES ON THE MODEL

When practitioners reviewed the schematic diagram developed from the field survey, they agreed with the depiction, but thought it lacked some subtle and particular aspects of practice. Through their comments, notes were developed to accompany the model. These provide nuances that counteract the reductionism produced through model building, which Northhead warned us about. Explanatory items include the following:

Flexibility.   The diagram is meant to be flexible rather than rigid, allowing for individualized use of the feedback loops and the overlapping functions. By having the arrows loop back into the process, service provisions can be tailored to the varying needs and goals of particular clients. Also, functions often overlap in various ways. Thus the sequence is approximate and suggestive rather than a precise and lockstep progression.

Time.   There is an explicit time element involved in the process. First, the entire process with any client can be highly time-consuming, measured in years. Second, when case loads are heavy, time pressures exist and priority decisions must be made in providing care across a practitioner's full client group. Third, each specific function may vary in its time demands. Thus, differing periods of time may be needed in moving from one function to another. Finally, the administrative tasks related to carrying out these functions, including the filling out of forms and attending meetings, require a heavy time allotment and do not show up in the diagram.

Administrative discharge.   The diagram indicates the possibility of an occasional termination discharge as a function, based on a positive evaluation by practitioners. However, administrative discharges that are not professionally based can take place at any time. These are client-initiated acts rather than practitioner-initiated acts. The client may voluntarily withdraw from service, move out of town, change to another agency, or die. The practitioner reacts to these situations rather than carrying out a purposive function.

Cyclical, interrupted process. The diagram represents one sequential experience with a client. However, in those relatively few instances when a long-term patient is evaluated as well enough to receive a therapeutic discharge, the commitment to continuing care does not terminate. New circumstances may require reestablishment of services, with a looping back to the access or intake functions. The same may be true when clients break off service, move, or are ill, and then return after a time lapse. In one sense the process is beginning again, in another sense it is continuing.

Dynamic character. This activity has a great deal of vitality. It is alive with human and organizational relationships, pressures, successes, and disappointments. The diagram does not explicitly depict this quality, but recognizes and acknowledges it. The diagram provides the structure of practice, not its drama. The diagram may appear stiff or routine on the surface, but this is an artifact of all conceptual models. Actually, robust human factors animate all functions.

Some functions are not implemented. The diagram shows a range of functions that are carried out by the preponderance of case managers. However, in certain situations a practitioner may not, nor be expected to, include a particular function, such as outreach, interorganizational relations, therapy, or advocacy.

Internal linkage. Linkage in the diagram ordinarily refers to connecting clients with external services and supports. However, in some large service systems in metropolitan areas, internal linkage (to other units or regions in a county department) may involve complex, informal processes equivalent in character to linking with external agencies. Within a particular service unit, linkage (or referral) may be quite informal. Internal linkage is carried out at any point in the practice sequence, involving referral for intake, collateral diagnosis, and service planning. As an example of internal linking, making arrangements with another unit of the organization for medical diagnosis or dispensing is common.

The model is strongly empirically based in that it reflects a consensus of practitioners in a large and diverse field setting concerning their functions. It also incorporates findings from a broad spectrum of empirical research on the subject. The diagram, accordingly, is descriptive of the practice as it is conducted in real world contexts, but at the same time it provides a more comprehensive and well articulated formulation than is currently in use. While accurately reflecting the varied components of typical practice, it is probably more complete and systematic than the performance of any single practitioner. The model is an ideal-type in the sense of incorporating the widest range of fundamental functions and designating their interaction, thus revealing some steps and actions that might likely be overlooked by any given practitioner in serving a client. The model is prescriptive as well as descriptive, in that it sets forth a set of action steps through which practitioners can guide and evaluate their professional actions.

POINTS OF CLARIFICATION

Areas Not Covered

The angle of vision in this discussion has been from the individual practitioner. But there are also other viewing positions involved in the service: the administrator who is concerned with organizing the overall program; the policymaker who wonders about where funding will originate and how to gain service integration in the community; the politician who is listening for signs of public demand or discontent; and the clients and their families who care intently about how the program will affect their immediate life circumstances.

Each of these perspectives raises different questions and requires a different level of analysis. For example, from the administrative standpoint there are matters of recruiting and training the staff, organizing them into operational units, and determining case loads. Also, the administrator is concerned with obtaining adequate funding, promoting interdisciplinary relationships, assessing community need, and maintaining stability in the program. A book could easily be written from any one of the different viewing positions. At this stage of practice development, there are distinct advantages to focusing on the essential roles and functions of the core professional helper, recognizing, at the same time, that something will be missed. Broader system issues will be discussed in Chapter 12, which deals with organizational and community factors.

Feasibility

Focusing on practice leaves open broader inquiries about feasibility: Will the role be adequately funded? Will it be backed up administratively in agencies? Will it be given political and moral support in the community? Are professionals able and willing to carry out the required functions? All of these are valid and essential probes, but they probably cannot be answered satisfactorily until this still nondescript role is sufficiently clarified and articulated—a prime purpose of this book. Only reasonably defined practice can be mounted in a systematic way across the field and tested for feasibility. Indeed, the very act of crystallizing it conceptually serves to advance its reality as a service mode and to enhance the feasibility of its enactment.

In emphasizing conceptual coherence, associated problems and contradictions have not been discussed here. These significant problematic aspects will be explored in the chapters dealing with implementation of the functions, and in the analysis of organizational and community considerations.

By focusing on the practitioner, we have taken the stance of an individual professional carrying a broad responsibility. The remainder of the book continues that outlook, but the functions that are identified in the model can also be used by a team of professionals who share the responsibility for executing them and coordinate their activities to achieve that end. In some situations that may be a more feasible format. The construct of the model can logically be carried forward in various ways. Many instances of this practice involve team arrangements, although the research conducted on the subject has not as yet shown any strong advantage by one or the other of these forms of professional implementation (Steinberg & Carter, 1983; Goldstrom & Mandersheid, 1983).

Alternative Models

Just as there are variations in staffing patterns, alternative models of case management/comprehensive enhancement practice exist in the field. The author has described some of these elsewhere (Rothman, 1992). They include, among others: the *therapist-case manager* formulation in which therapy is a designated function; the *supportive care* model, which bases the service in a neighborhood and involves natural helpers as the main vehicle of intervention; the *psychosocial rehabilitation* center approach using a residential facility with saturated services that include vocational training; the *paraprofessional* format emphasizing community referral activities; and the *family as case manager* service concept. Because the service mode generally is emergent, experimentation with different forms is natural and useful. As yet, none of the variations has won predominant professional acceptance or has been found empirically to be superior to others.

Cultural and Ethnic Considerations

In the previous chapter we indicated that the service paradigm calls on the practitioner to respect individual differences (such as age, gender, sexual preference, and personal style) and cultural norms among clients. This suggests cultural variability in the way the model is played out. For example, some ethnic minorities rely less on formal agency services and more on informal social supports, including the extended family (Greene & Monahan, 1984). In work with such groups, the practitioner ought to anticipate the possibility of greater use of natural helping networks.

The style of relationship with clients needs to be geared to the cultural values of different groups. Illustratively, with traditional Latino clients interpersonal contact typically should emphasize courtesy and social amenities. Getting to the point quickly and focusing on specifics operates in opposition to the client's more holistic world view. For this reason, the practitioner may have to allow extra time—including engaging in casual conversation—for problem identification and assessment to take place. Also, for some Latino clients their fear of embarrassment often is greater than their dread of failure. The same for Asian-Americans, who sometimes experience a profound sense of shame for not meeting family expectations. Problem exploration that may imply underlying criticism needs to be carried forward in a particularly understated and nonjudgmental manner, and confrontation techniques would be used judiciously and sparingly. For some ethnic groups, the goal of independent living does not preclude close attachment to the family.

Clients of various backgrounds who use English as a second language can experience vexing communications problems in ordinary discourse. The best solution is to provide a practitioner of the same background, or for the practitioner to learn the language of the clientele. In the absence of that occurring, the practitioner can speak slowly, provide specific information and instructions, explain explicitly why something needs to be done, and rely minimally on formal written communication. Taking time to help clients read written instructions and fill out required forms is also beneficial.

Because there are so many different ethnic and racial groups in American society, and given that there are many differences within each of these groups by geography, generation, dialect, and rate of acculturation, it is impossible in this presentation to embody comprehensively the dynamics of ethnically responsive practice. We will, however, include an ethnic dimension in the chapters that follow. A checklist for examining cultural competence in agency service has been developed by Dana, Behn, and Gonwa (1992), and provides a framework for the application of ethnically sensitive intervention on an across-the-board basis. The main criteria for fostering multicultural practice are reproduced below and provide a guidesheet for applying all the functions of the model to particular practice situations.

Practices (staff/policy/attitudes)

> Bilingual
> Bicultural
> Culture broker
> Flexible hours/appointments/home visits
> Treatment immediate/day/week
> Indigenous intake
> Match client-staff
> Agency environment reflects culture

Services

> Culture-relevant assessment
> Cultural context for problems
> Cultural-specific intervention model

Relationship to Community

> Agency in minority community
> Easy access
> Uses existing minority community facilities
> Agency ties to minority community
> Community advocate for services
> Community as advisor
> Community as evaluator

Training

    In-service training for minority staff
    In-service training for nonminority staff

Evaluation

    Evaluation plan/tool
    Clients as evaluators/planners

This chapter and the previous one establish a foundation for comprehensive enhancement practice to aid severely vulnerable population groups. The following section provides specifics, particularly about techniques and actions, including examples, obstacles, and promising approaches, treating each function systematically and in detail. The UCLA survey of practitioners will be drawn on intermittently throughout to provide illustrations and share observations by those working closely with clients. The qualitative character of the study makes it especially useful for this purpose. A concluding section of the book deals with community and organizational factors and examines what research evaluation has found about this type of intervention.

REFERENCES

Dana, R. H., Behn, J. D., & Gonwa, T. (1992). A checklist for the examination of cultural competence in social service agencies. *Research on Social Work Practice, 2*(2), April, 220–233.

Goldstrom, I. & Mandersheid, R. (1983). A descriptive analysis of community support program case managers serving the chronically mentally ill. *Community Mental Health Journal, 19*(1), 17–26.

Rothman, J. (1987a). *Case management action guidelines: A synthesis of social research.* Los Angeles: University of California, School of Social Welfare, Center for Child and Family Policy Studies.

Rothman, J. (1987b). *A model of case management: Systemizing case management intervention.* Los Angeles: University of California, School of Social Welfare, Center for Child and Family Policy Studies.

Rothman, J. (1987c). *The practice of case management: A study of case managers' experiences and views.* Los Angeles: University of California, School of Social Welfare, Center for Child and Family Policy Studies.

Rothman, J. (1988a). *An empirically-based model of case management: Results of a field study.* Los Angeles: University of California, School of Social Welfare, Center for Child and Family Policy Studies.

Rothman, J. (1988b). *Performing case management functions: A handbook.* Los Angeles: University of California, School of Social Welfare, Center for Child and Family Policy Studies.

Rothman, J. (1991). A Model of Case Management: Toward Empirically Based Practice. *Social Work, 36*(6), 520–528.

Rothman, J. (1992). *Guidelines for case management: Putting research to professional use.* Itasca, IL: F. E. Peacock Publishers, Inc.

Steinberg, R. & Carter, G. (1983). *Case management and the elderly.* Lexington, MA: Lexington Books.

3
Using an Ecological Perspective

Carel B. Germain

All human service fields contribute in their own fashion to the important work of giving support to the most needful among us. The particular view presented in this chapter is derived from the history and value system of the social work profession. It also includes a particular emphasis—an ecological perspective—that fits well with Dr. Jack Rothman's comprehensive psychosocial enhancement model of practice with highly vulnerable client groups.

HISTORY AND PROFESSIONAL VALUES

In 1915 Abraham Flexner, a social scientist, addressed the National Conference of Charities and Corrections (NCCC) and thereby started a notable chain of events in the development of professional social work.* Flexner had introduced improvements into medical education, and his social work audience expected advice on improving professional education for social workers. However, Flexner's address was entitled, "Is Social Work a Profession?" And to the dismay of the audience, his answer to the question was no, because social work lacked transmissible knowledge and skills of its own. Social workers, after identifying a need or problem, had to call on other professions for the solution. The social worker merely invoked the authority of another. However, he said, social work did provide a useful service in connecting people to other sources of help.

---

*The NCCC was the only association of a newly identified occupational group and therefore the only forum available in 1915 for the exchange of ideas. In later years, it was renamed the National Conference of Social Work, and later still, the National Conference of Social Welfare, but it gradually lost status and power as the National Association of Social Workers, other forums, and journals were developed.

This outraged Mary Richmond, a leader in the charity organization movement (the forerunner of social casework). She asserted that ". . . behind his back, apparently, there was developing a skill quite different in method and in aim from the work that he described." She identified this skill as discovering the social relationships that shape a personality, identifying the difficulties in those relationships, and utilizing the action of mind upon mind in their adjustment. "We shall have a skill of our own . . . and shall act as middleman [sic] to the extent that any professional worker who wants to do a good all-round job must so act and no further" (Richmond, 1915, pp. 112–115).

Richmond's apparent disdain for the knowledge and skill in connecting client and resource was apparently as strong as Flexner's own. Her response is understandable given the striving for professional status. Yet the disdain for the liaison or management activities of the social worker is ironic in the light of the prominence given in today's practice to brokerage and advocacy. This is especially characteristic of the rapidly developing specialty of case management. In Dr. Rothman's empirically based model, such activity is part of four major functions: resource identification, linkage of clients to formal and informal support systems, interagency coordination, and advocacy. All require high level skills.

But history has more to tell us. Flexner's speech was a significant factor in casework's determination to establish itself as a profession through the development of transmissible knowledge and methodology and method-centered training (social group work and community social work had not yet appeared). What might have been a unique social purpose was left undeveloped until much later. An emphasis on what came to be called function (method) was increasingly contrasted by Conference speakers, and later writers, to the social reform emphasis of another group within the Conference, the settlement house workers. The great Jane Addams of Hull House and other settlers shunned charity and embraced a philosophy of help based on being good neighbors to the immigrant poor. Their emphasis was on social reform, and they were leaders in the social change efforts of the Progressive Era.

The contrasts grew between settlers and caseworkers as many caseworkers focused on a method for "treating" individuals and families, rather than helping people-in-the-mass through social change. They introduced the method into settings beyond the charity organization societies, such as hospitals, courts, and schools. Some explored new ideas from psychiatry and later from psychoanalysis; others worked on issues of professionalism, and on specialized training and its relationship to the university. Recognition of the psychological and social complexities involved in one person's helping another accompanied these developments, despite an earlier emphasis on moral defect and the so-called disease of pauperism.

By 1929 the tension between those who supported social action and those who favored individual rehabilitation was clear enough to be identified by Porter Lee, in his presidential address to the Conference, as a polarity of cause (social reform) versus function (methodology). Lee's great contribution, perhaps not recognized at the time, lay in his vision of a synthesis that would blend cause and function as comprising social work's purpose in society (Lee, 1929).

Nevertheless, the issue was debated down the decades. For example, Howard (1954) referred to continuing calls in the Conference for social workers to return to a more active participation in broad social affairs and reform activities, out of which the profession had evolved, and to relinquish their primary focus on technical matters. Burns (1958), a social policy analyst, referred to the professional myopia of social workers, suggesting that in order to profess a commitment to social welfare they must become social actionists on behalf of programs responsive to social needs. Towle, a noted casework educator, said to the Conference in 1941:

> The worker, who staunchly maintains that he [sic] can help only the person who can use a certain kind of relationship, frequently is saying that he can relate himself only to that individual who least needs help. . . . While this stand may be reconciled with the function of some agencies, it cannot be reconciled with our profession's purpose as a whole. (Towle, 1941, p. 259)

As late as 1961 she felt constrained to write,

> This is a time for the social work profession to have faith in its cause, to reaffirm its humanistic values, and to work positively for conditions of life that will promote man's humanity to man . . . the union of cause and function. . . . (Towle, 1961, p. 396)

By the late 1950s, acceptance of a person-in-environment focus in social work, proposed by Richmond in her later years and advocated by Hamilton (1951), began to spread. The formulation implied an equal interest in both people and their environments. While a method existed for working for change in people, however, none existed for changing environments, which therefore were largely overlooked in practice. Hearn (1958) introduced into social work the *general systems theory,* which had something to say about environments but was abstract. Gordon (1969), using several systems ideas, reduced the abstraction somewhat by declaring that social work's social purpose was to bring about growth-promoting transactions between people and environments by simultaneously working to improve people's coping patterns and their environment.

THE ECOLOGICAL PERSPECTIVE

These contributions opened the way to the development of an ecological perspective on people and environments that was not abstract and was close to human experience (Germain, 1973). The ecological perspective is not itself a practice model. But used as a metaphor, it provides a conceptual lens through which the complex phenomena faced by social workers may be more fully understood and more effectively handled. For example, in addition to the traditional study of personal factors, it describes and analyzes the nature of historic, political, economic, physical, and social environments and how they influence human development and behavior within varied cultural contexts (Germain, 1991).

As we will see, Rothman's model of case management and the perspective are remarkably congruent. Thus his model lends empirical support to the perspective, which in turn lends additional theoretical support to the model. Ecologically speaking, they enjoy a reciprocal relationship. Both reflect the unity of cause and function, and both activate the person: environment commitment of social work.

The following section describes five concepts that, *in combination*, constitute the ecological perspective:

> "Holism" and person(s): environment transactions (exchanges)
> Transactional causality
> Human relatedness, competence, self-esteem, and self-direction as transactional outcomes
> Life stress and coping as transactional outcomes
> Vulnerability and disempowerment as transactional outcomes

Herein, the fit between practice principles derived from these concepts and the functions identified by Rothman is highlighted. Only general considerations are presented, as space does not permit content specific to the varied conditions that require these particular services, such as advanced age, physical or mental status, abuse and neglect, and so on.

HOLISM: PEOPLE AND ENVIRONMENTS

In the biological sciences, ecology is the study of the relationship between living organisms and their total environment, including other organisms and species and the physical setting. Used as a metaphor, the ecological perspective calls attention to the holistic aspect of people:environment relationships. That is, we can approach full understanding of either person or environment only in the context of their relationship to each other and their continuous exchanges. *(Use of the colon between p:e symbolizes the inextricable connection.)*

The human being's maturation, psychosocial development, and social functioning take place in particular environments over time and across space. Together with the particular culture and subculture in which the person is embedded, these varied settings, in interaction with the individual's genetic potential, shape life's course. Reciprocally, human beings shape their physical and social environments to greater or lesser degrees.

All forms of life strive to reach a favorable fit with the environment so that needs are met and survival is ensured. Additionally, human beings also strive toward a favorable fit so that not only their needs but also their rights, goals, and aspirations are met. Indeed, when the fit is favorable a human being's emotional, cognitive, biological, and social potentials are released and development proceeds. When the fit is less than favorable, a person's growth and continued development may be adversely affected at any point over the life course, and the environment may be damaged for all those who function within it.

Technically, a favorable p:e fit is called adaptive balance. The term is wrongly assumed by some to refer to a person's passive adjustment to the status quo. But in the biological sciences, the term *adaptive balance* refers to an action-oriented p:e fit that releases genetic (innate) potentials of organisms (in this case human beings) and simultaneously benefits or, at least, does not harm the environment.

People strive for adaptive balance (p:e fit) by using an infinite variety of biological, social, emotional, cognitive, behavioral, and cultural adaptations. This list represents the active methods of change that are possible:

> *change oneself* (e.g., as in learning, undertaking a new role, religious conversion, and the like)
>
> *change one's physical environment* (as in moving from a rural community to an urban one) or one's social environment (as in entering a hospital day care program, moving into a group home, and the like)
>
> *change both environment and self* (as in going to school to become a social worker or other human service professional).

Environments are also changed by acts of nature (as in earthquakes, floods, fire, behaviors of other species, and so on) as well as by human actions. In every case, however, human beings, like all organisms, must adapt anew to whatever changes are made in themselves or in the environment, whether by the environment or themselves. Thus adaptation is a continuous active process.

Holism, like the comprehensive enhancement model, requires in assessment and intervention our taking into account continuously, and as simultaneously as possible, both personal and environmental features and their interplay. Complex life issues that people, including clients, face cannot be viewed as solely the result either of personal characteristics, deficits, and pathology or of societal dysfunction (although the latter is likely to be the case in some instances). It follows that traditional, simple linear cause-and-effect relationships to explain complex human phenomena must be relinquished in favor of transactional or circular causality that analyzes p:e exchanges.

TRANSACTIONAL CAUSALITY

Linear Causality

In linear causality, the question asked is, "Why did this predicament, Y, come about?" And the usual answer is "Because it was caused by X." Therefore, it is assumed that if we remove or diminish X, we will eliminate or reduce the predicament. Such a linear or one-directional explanation of cause and effect relationships may serve us well in explaining simple, everyday phenomena: "Because *X* was done, *Y* happened." This simple, linear explanation ignores context and interactional sequences over time, and assumes that one element, *Y*, is changed while *X* remains unchanged. If we apply such simple explanations to the more complicated life transitions and life events faced by case management clients and their families, we are apt to be less effective in helping them manage the condition from which they suffer or the life issues that erupt from time to time.

Transactional Causality

By contrast, transactional causality is concerned with repeated exchanges over time, in which each unit's behavior represents both a response to the other's behavior and a stimulus for the other's next response that affects both units. This is the case whether we are considering individuals, collectivities, cultural factors, or varied environments. The question for the practitioner, then, is not "*Why* did this predicament come about?" but rather "*What* is going on, and *what* must be done to manage the predicament or perhaps resolve it?"

Examples of Transactional Causality

Let us assume a sequence of exchanges between a chronically mentally ill person, George, and a group home operator, Alice, that ends with George's removal from the home. Linear causality might suggest that George's behavior caused Alice to request the removal, thereby solving the problem but leaving George in a predicament and assuming it is largely his fault. George and his situation are changed, while Alice and her situation remain unchanged. Transactional causality might explain the sequence as follows: George's behavior is the cause of anger in Alice (an effect). Her anger becomes a cause that elicits a vindictive response (effect) from George. His response is then a cause that intensifies Alice's anger, which leads to George's slamming the door and leaving the house (effect). Each time this sequence is repeated, George stays away for a longer period, which escalates the problem for himself, the group home operator, and the case manager. Ultimately, it leads to George's removal from the home and another failure for him. This analysis began with George's behavior, but we could just as well begin with Alice's behavior because, in such a feedback loop, who is cause and who is effect is irrelevant. "The fact that a transactional description is inherently circular is not to be deplored but exploited in observation, description [and intervention]" (Coyne & Lazarus, 1980).

Asking why Alice and George behave in this way is less important than asking, "How can these reciprocal but dysfunctional exchanges be interrupted and supplanted by more adaptive ones?" The "why's" may be embedded in genetic make-up, very early life experience, or in a fixed environmental feature, or all three. None of them can be changed. Instead, the practitioner's attention to current exchanges in order to help change them has a better chance of reducing the tensions in the relationship between Alice and George. Note that this approach does not deny the reality of George's mental status, nor does it place blame on either participant. Instead, the focus is on that which can be changed and what each participant can do to reduce the maladaptive transactions. Through George and Alice's accumulative learning of more effective interpersonal communications, the handicapping nature of George's condition may be reduced and Alice's functioning may become more productive for her and her other residents.

Holism and transactional causality with their focus on personal and environmental strengths and resources, while taking account of vulnerable areas of client functioning, are consonant with the assessment, goal-setting, and intervention-planning functions in the comprehensive enhancement model.

HUMAN RELATEDNESS, COMPETENCE, SELF-ESTEEM, AND SELF-DIRECTION

These four sets of human capacities are significant forces in all adaptation. They are major personal strengths to be mobilized and enhanced through this practice. Like other concepts in the ecological perspective, these capacities are transactional outcomes of p:e relationships, past and current. They are not attributable to personal or environmental features alone but have been shown to arise from the nature and quality of p:e transactions from birth to old age (Germain, 1991).

The four appear to be relatively free of cultural bias as in the following example.

(1) All societies value some form of human relatedness, if only through adherence to varied systems of kinship that define authority and decision making, acceptable mates, childrearing responsibilities, and so on.

(2) All societies train their young for competence in performing adult roles valued by the culture. However, what is defined as competence may vary from society to society, and from one cultural group to another in our own society.

(3) In some cultures the self-concept and self-esteem may be linked more strongly to family, clan, or tribe instead of the individual.

(4) Most societies probably value self-regulation in accord with their own cultural norms. But self-direction in the sense of personal autonomy in thought and action—highly valued in American culture—is likely to be lodged in the family, clan, or tribe in other cultures. These particular cultural differences operate in our own multicultural society and often lead to generational conflicts in newcomer families.

Finally, it appears that the four sets of attributes are interdependent in their development and persistence over the life course, that is, each is continually influenced by the other three.

Relatedness

The biologist Dubos (1968) pointed out that human evolution took place in the context of small bands in which the members knew one another personally. Within such bands, there was a strong pull to remain in close proximity for protection against predators. In contemporary life, most of us sustain personal relationships, characterized by intimacy and sentiment, with only a small band or network of others, such as relatives, friends, neighbors, workmates, and religious affiliates. Such networks may serve as resources for dealing with difficult life issues. In networks with a predominance of positive feelings, members provide emotional support, information and advice, and tangible aid to one another. In providing effective support, informal systems also contribute to members' self-esteem and relatedness and may enhance the sense of competence and self-direction.

The practitioner's role. The concept of relatedness refers also to the importance of the practitioner's being realistically supportive, empathic, and respectful of the client. The professional relationship serves as a model for the client's relationships with others. This relationship and an affiliation with informal supports not only strengthen the capacity of relatedness, but also enhance self-esteem, competence, and self-direction.

The ecological emphasis on relatedness is clearly congruent with the function of linkage to informal resources in Rothman's model.

Competence

Competence in one's environment is a concept developed by White (1959), who viewed the person as a source of influence on the environment as well as being shaped by environmental influences. He proposed an "effectance" motivation (an urge to act effectively in one's environment) that is independent of thirst, hunger, and the libidinal and aggressive drives of psychoanalytic theory. White suggests that effectance is satisfied by exploration and action, and leads to learning about the environment. He also proposed the term *efficacy* for experiences of successful action in the environment. Together, satisfaction of the effectance drive and the accumulation of efficacy experiences lead to the sense of competence.

For White, effectance is an innate attribute of human beings, having been built into the genetic structure of the species because of its survival value in the evolutionary environment. However, as with all genetic potentials, opportunities must be furnished by the environment for effectance motivation to be released. Notably, all forms of life have some degree of competence in their environments or they would not survive for long, but competence reaches its highest level in human beings.

Infancy and competence.   Effectance, efficacy, and the sense of competence begin early in life. For example, during the first year the baby who is secure in his or her relationship to the caregiver tests the environment, explores it, finds out what can be done with its varied components, human and otherwise, and takes an active part in learning about the world (Ainsworth & Bell, 1974; Srouf, 1978). But continued experiences of efficacy are necessary over the entire life course if the sense of competence is to be sustained.

Competency and the vulnerable client.   Effectance motivation in highly vulnerable clients may have been dampened by life's circumstances, so that efficacy experiences and a sense of competence have dwindled and may even be entirely absent. White's ideas provide an optimistic position for the practitioner in such instances. Because effectance is biologically based, it can be reawakened for many by providing opportunities to practice efficacy in the environment. For example, simple life tasks in the environment that have meaning to the client can lead to efficacy when worked on jointly with a case manager. Later, tasks can be designed to be performed by the client alone. Failure can be devastating to someone who lacks a sense of competence. Hence the tasks must be planned carefully to ensure reasonable success while stretching capacities. *Encouragement and support are essential.*

Self-Esteem

Self-Esteem is the most important dimension of one's self-concept and reflects one's judgment of one's value, that is, the extent to which an individual feels capable, significant, effective, and worthy (Coopersmith, 1967). Rosenberg (1979) suggests that self-esteem is a major influence in human thinking and behavior. And Sullivan (1953) believed that the prime motive in human striving is to protect and enhance one's self-esteem. High self-esteem reflects self-respect and feelings of self-worth, along with recognition of faults hoped to be overcome. Low self-esteem reflects lack of respect for oneself and feelings that one is unworthy, incompetent, inferior, unloveable, and seriously deficient as a person. Studies consistently show that low self-esteem and depression are often associated.

Infancy and self-esteem.   The self-concept and feelings of self-esteem have their start in infancy, as the behavior of the parents or caregiver toward the baby conveys feelings that the baby is loveable. Rosenberg (1979) believes that throughout the life course, a positive self-concept and feelings of self-esteem are sustained or are diminished, not necessarily consciously, by the following:

Reflected appraisals of significant persons toward oneself in regard to appearance, capacities, race or ethnicity, gender, behavior, goals, and so on. Rosenberg points out, however, that race, socio-economic status, gender, or physical or mental condition do not affect the self-concept directly. But experiences of prejudicial discrimination, segregation, powerlessness, and poverty do affect it, depending on personal interpretation of these experiences.

Social comparisons to others on these dimensions as made by oneself

Self-attributions as bases for explanations or conclusions about one's behaviors and outcomes

Psychological centrality of the components of the self-concept in terms of their relative importance, each to the others

The developing self-concept.

The self-concept continues to develop or to change over the life course, and levels of self-esteem may shift for most of us, given the ups and downs of life. For example, growth in relatedness, competence, and self-direction also enhances self-esteem. But interpersonal rejection, so often experienced by vulnerable clients, can be a life stressor that threatens self-esteem, morale, and the self-concept. Hence, in every contact with the client, the practitioner must support and enhance self-esteem through conveying respect for the person (even while having to call attention to, or correct, dangerous or destructive behaviors) and empathic communication that leads to the person's feeling understood and accepted. Realistic support and commendation for adaptive functioning is also important.

Self-Direction

The sense of having some control over one's life and environment and being the master of one's destiny to some degree is critical to the development of self-direction, as well as to self-esteem and competence. Self-direction includes the ability to take responsibility for one's decisions and actions while respecting the rights and needs of others. This capacity must be supported throughout childhood, youth, and adulthood by community institutions and the family. For example, young children will develop the ability to do things for themselves if opportunities are provided by the caregivers, and if teachers and parents recognize and value the child's self-direction. Opportunities over the life course for taking responsibility for oneself, making decisions, and pursuing purposive action (however modest because of age, physical or mental status, culture, and environmental features) are needed to sustain the capacity for self-direction just as they are for competence.

The practitioner's role.

In trying to help with self-direction, case managers directly confront issues of client vulnerability and powerlessness. When people's life circumstances are such that few options exist in their environment so that personal choices are meaningless—and one has no control over undesirable life events and no financial security—then the sense of self-direction, as well as competence and self-esteem, may be threatened or diminished. A sense of vulnerability and powerlessness is heightened, and some persons may retreat into chronic rage or succumb to feelings of help-lessness and hopelessness. Those who are poor or members of oppressed groups can benefit from learning to recognize when circumstances that inter-fere with self-direction are not personal in origin, but societal. Such recogni-tion can emerge through the use of analogy, pointed, Socratic-like questions, story-telling, presentation of facts, consciousness raising and, where appro-priate, through support groups of those in similar situations. The issues involved are discussed in the final section of this chapter.

The ecological emphases on competence, self-esteem, and self-direction are congruent with the assessment and counseling functions of Rothman's model and its emphasis on growth promotion.

THE STRESS-COPING PARADIGM*

From an ecological perspective, the conditions underlying vulnerability and any subsequent, difficult life issues faced by those in need of services are con-ceived as life stressors. They may be generated by the following:

> *Life transitions* that represent new statuses and roles such as those involved in moving from institutional to community care or family care, entering ado-lescence, beginning a new job, becoming a parent, or growing old cause stress. Some are universal, others are expected for most but may not be expected by some. Any or all transitions may be extremely stressful for some persons.
> *Unanticipated life events* such as serious injury, physical or mental illness or dis-ability, family violence, loss of a family member or friend, and loss of hous-ing or a job are severe stressors. They also tend to impose new but unwanted statuses and roles that are added stressors for many.
> *Particular life conditions* such as poverty, prejudicial discrimination and disem-powerment, social isolation, chronic mental or physical illness, lack of appropriate housing, and prolonged unemployment are chronic stressors. They usually expose those suffering from them to many more acute stressors with fewer resources for managing them than are faced by others in better life circumstances.

Life stressors and life stress reflect a maladaptive p:e relationship in which a critical life issue involving a harm or loss, or threat of harm or loss, evokes emotional and physiological experiences of stress. Neither the stres-

---

*This section draws, in part, on the work of Lazarus and Launier (1978), Coyne and Lazarus (1980), and Germain (1991). It is not about the daily hassles and tensions (often termed *stress*, and calling for stress management) encountered at work, in school, and at home. Behaviorally oriented physicians and others teach people to reduce such strains and tensions through biofeedback mechanisms. Such an approach overlooks the cultural and environmental context in which the tensions arise, so that when the person returns to the same environment, the tensions frequently reappear.

sor nor the stress can be understood in terms of the environment alone or the person alone, or even in simple stimulus–response terms. Rather, they are outcomes of complex transactional processes.

Life stress arises when the person unconsciously or consciously appraises an environmental demand (life stressor) as exceeding environmental and personal resources for coping. A particular combination of personal and environmental variables meld in the appraisal in each instance. This is more complicated than it seems: People differ in what they define as a life stressor or serious life issue, depending on factors of cognition and emotion, age, health, gender, past experience, culture, and the nature of the environment. They may differ in the meaning they ascribe to the particular stressor (for example, it was God's will, punishment for my sins, someone else's negligence, or my own fault) and how they plan to manage it.

Distinguishing Between Stressors and Challenges

It is important to note the distinction between stressor and challenge. A life issue experienced as a stressor is accompanied by negative feelings such as anxiety, guilt, anger, helplessness, depression, despair, and by lowered self-esteem. By contrast, a life issue experienced as a challenge, even though it may be "stressful," is associated with positive feelings of anticipated mastery, cheerfulness, and a favorable level of self-esteem. Some people may define a life issue (such as job loss or a serious illness) as a challenge, while others may define the same life issue as a life stressor, depending again on environmental and personal characteristics, including the meaning attributed to the life issue or event.

Once we recognize a discrepancy between the stressor and our resources, we call up special adaptations to manage the stressor and restore or even improve the prior p:e fit. These efforts are referred to as "coping." Coping is transactional inasmuch as its effectiveness requires both personal and environmental resources. Personal resources include motivation to deal with the life issue; resilience; knowledge about the stressor and how to manage it; and favorable levels of relatedness, competence, self-esteem, and self-direction. Environmental resources include an informal support system; a receptive, caring community that provides adequate housing, finances, health care, and social services; and accessible sources of information about the stressor and how to cope with it. Few if any of us possess all of these, but some of both are needed. Some may be acquired with the help of a wide-gauged practitioner who is familiar with the common coping tasks in managing certain life issues (e.g., Germain, 1990).

Coping

While coping consists of an almost infinite variety of behavioral or cognitive actions, it also has two major functions: problem solving and regulating the negative feelings so they do not interfere with problem solving. There is a paradox in this because negative feelings are not likely to diminish, nor will self-esteem be restored, until there is at least a start in problem solving. Yet it is difficult to begin problem solving until one's anxiety, guilt, anger, depression, or despair begin to subside.

One way people resolve the paradox is through unconscious defenses; *these can be adaptive, but only temporarily*. For example, the person may deny the existence, extent, or the implications of the severe life issue (stressor), rationalize it, or project the blame for it on to something or someone else. This maneuver, because it shuts out awareness of the reality and dulls the negative feelings, may provide an intermission in which one can take a few first steps in problem solving. Having taken them, the person is then able slowly to relax the defense, and accept the reality and some of the associated negative feelings. However, a defense that is too rigid or that continues beyond an optimum time can be severely maladaptive and may block all problem solving and interfere with rehabilitation or a medical regimen.

The practitioner may need to provide emotional support to the client by gently affirming the painful reality and validating the fears and guilt. This can help to relax the defense, which then allows enough tolerance of the reality and of some negative feelings so that problem solving can begin. With some success in beginning to manage the stressor, more of the negative feelings can be tolerated, thus allowing more vigorous problem-solving. Similar social–emotional support from family members, friends, and other staff also helps the person to begin coping with the issue instead of defending against it. Relatives and friends may need guidance from the practitioner on how best to be helpful in this effort (Anderson, Hogarty, & Reiss, 1986; Strauss & Glaser, 1975).

Some persons may err in perceiving a discrepancy between the environmental demand (life stressor) and their resources for managing it. That is, they may overestimate or underestimate the demand or their resources. Or, they may misunderstand the implications of the demand. In these instances professional helpers need to assist the person in developing a more realistic view of the demand, the resources, or both, by providing information, affirming personal and environmental strengths where indicated, raising questions about unwarranted assumptions, hewing to reality, and interpreting elements of the stressful demand. Some coping efforts can themselves be maladaptive. For example, resorting to alcohol or illicit drugs may be an effort to cope by allaying negative feelings. If abused, however, alcohol or illicit drugs add to the existing stress or create new stressors in other areas of life. In such instances, clients usually need to be linked to other kinds of therapeutic or institutional help than what is discussed here.

Clearly, the complex issues of stress and coping fall into all functions specified by Rothman. For example, assessment, goal-setting, intervention planning, and resource identification may be uppermost at one point, linkage, counseling, and advocacy at other points, and monitoring and reassessment at still other points.

VULNERABILITY AND DISEMPOWERMENT

Misuse of power by dominant groups in society, such as corporate and public bureaucracies, is the antithesis of growth-promoting, self-healing life forces. Misuse of power creates vulnerability, exclusion, and oppression of large segments of the population. Two forms of misuse are withholding power and exploiting power.

Withholding Power

Withholding of power from vulnerable groups on the basis of personal or cultural characteristics (such as color, ethnicity, gender, age, sexual preference, religion, social class, and physical or mental condition) results in oppression and powerlessness of those groups. Such disempowerment creates and maintains social pollutions of poverty, institutional racism, repressive gendered roles in family, work, and community life, and homophobia. Other social pollutions include poor schools; chronic unemployment or underemployment of those whom the schools fail to educate; physical and social barriers to community participation of the physically or mentally challenged; homelessness and lack of affordable safe housing; inadequate health care; and differential rates of longevity, infant mortality, and chronic illness among people of color as compared to whites.

Exploiting Power

Exploiting power by dominant groups leads to universal frightening results. Abusive exploitation by corporate and governmental institutions creates technological pollution of the air, food, water, and soil. It tolerates the presence of toxic materials in dwellings, schools, and work places, and of hazardous wastes in communities—especially, but not exclusively, in poor communities. Vested interests in expanding defense systems and increased militarism during the 1980s, together with scandalous greed in financial systems, drained national resources away from desperately needed services and programs. Together with the virtually uncontrolled use of firearms in the population, technological and social pollutions contribute to the erosion of our moral and value systems so that violence and other degradations are increasing at international, national, community, family, and personal levels.

Disempowerment and pollutions are major life stressors that structure the conditions of life, the very context in which the continued development and functioning of vulnerable groups take place. They limit access to opportunities for self-direction, competence, self-esteem, and relatedness, and threaten health, social well-being, and life itself. They express unacceptable p:e relationships in which the social order permits some people to inflict grave injustice and suffering on others (and other forms of life). Disempowered people, including many case management clients, are apt to suffer many more disruptive life stressors with long-term consequences than the rest of the population. At the same time, they have far fewer societal resources for modifying disruptive, stressful life issues or coping with their consequences.

Professional Sensitivity

It follows, then, that an effective practice must be an empowering and ethical one. This requires sensitivity to racial and ethnic differences that exist between the practitioner and the client, especially in the areas of cultural values, behaviors, language, family structures, and family functioning. The last two refer to newly emerging family forms, role assignments and expectations, child-rearing practices, influence of spirituality, and for many, the impact of years of war followed by uprooting, migration, and cultural adaptation. All professional helpers need to learn about these aspects specific to the particular people they serve who are culturally different from themselves. Knowledge may be obtained through consultation with clients and others, experience, or reading (see, for example, Devore & Schlesinger, 1981; Jacobs & Bowles, 1988; Lum, 1986; McGoldrick, Pearce, & Giordano, 1982; Red Horse, 1980). It is also essential in each instance to be aware of how these cultural factors bear on all the functions specified in Rothman's model.

It is equally imperative in an empowering and ethical practice that all human service professionals learn about their clients who are different from themselves on other dimensions that frame their life situations, such as gender (Van den Bergh & Cooper, 1986), sexual preference (Moses & Hawkins, 1982), age (Germain, 1991), and physical or mental conditions (Anderson et al., 1986; Corbin & Strauss, 1988). And, finally, an empowering and ethical practice requires skillful advocacy on behalf of vulnerable clients. Hence this chapter concludes with underscoring the strong congruence between Rothman's comprehensive enhancement model and the ecological perspective in respect to the function of advocacy.

Advocacy

Both the model and the perspective emphasize the absolute necessity of having in place accessible, ethnic-, racial-, gender-sensitive, and empowering formal services. Therefore, professionals must undertake knowledgeable and skilled advocacy on behalf of individual clients vis-à-vis one's own agency and other organizations when they are unresponsive to need or are insensitive to difference. Professionals must also be knowledgeable and skilled in policy and legislative advocacy on behalf of all clients (Brager & Holloway, 1978; Germain & Gitterman, 1980; Mahaffey & Hanks, 1982). Only by meeting these requirements can cause and function be melded in practice—the union of environmental change and methods that release human potential for personal growth.

REFERENCES

Ainsworth, M. D. & Bell, S. M. (1974). Mother-infant interaction and the development of competence. In K. J. Connolly & J. Bruner (Eds.), *The growth of competence* (pp. 97–118). New York: Academic Press.

Anderson, C. M., Hogarty, G. E., & Reiss, D. J. (1986). *Schizophrenia and the family: A practical guide to psychoeducational treatment.* New York: Guilford Press.

Brager, G. & Holloway, S. (1978). *Changing human service organizations: The politics of practice.* New York: Free Press.

Burns, E. (1958). Social welfare is our commitment. *The Social Welfare Forum, 1958: Proceedings of the 85th National Conference on Social Welfare* (pp. 3–19). New York: Columbia University Press.

Coopersmith, S. (1967). *The antecedents of self-esteem.* San Francisco: Freeman.

Corbin, J. M. & Strauss, A. (1988). *Unending work and care.* San Francisco: Jossey-Bass.

Coyne, J. C. & Lazarus, R. S. (1980). Cognitive style, stress, perception, and coping. In I. L. Kutash & L. B. Schlesinger (Eds.), *Handbook on stress and anxiety* (pp. 103–127). San Francisco: Jossey-Bass.

Devore, W. & Schlesinger, E. G. (1981). *Ethnic-sensitive social work practice.* St. Louis: Mosby.

Dubos, R. (1968). *So human an animal.* New York: Scribner's.

Flexner, A. (1915). Is Social Work a Profession? *Proceedings of the 42nd Session (Baltimore, MD) National Conference of Charities and Corrections 1915* (pp. 576–590). Chicago, IL: Hildmann Printing Co.

Germain, C. B. (1973). An ecological perspective on social work. *Social Casework 54(6),* 323–330.

Germain, C. B. (1990). Life forces and the anatomy of practice. *Smith College studies in social work, 60* (2) March, 138–152.

Germain, C. B. (1991). *Human behavior in the social environment: An ecological view.* New York: Columbia University Press.

Germain, C. B. & Gitterman, A. (1980). *The life model of social work practice.* New York: Columbia University Press.

Gordon, W. E. (1969). Basic constructs for an integrative and generative conception of social work. In G. Hearn (Ed.), *The general systems approach: Toward an holistic conception of social work* (pp. 5–12). New York: Council on Social Work Education.

Hamilton, G. (1940). *Theory and practice of social case work.* (2nd ed., 1951). New York: Columbia University Press.

Hearn, G. (1958). *Theory building in social work.* Toronto, Ontario: University of Toronto Press.

Howard, D. S. (1954). Social work and social reform. In C. Kasius (Ed.), *New directions in social work* (pp. 159–175). New York: Harper & Row.

Jacobs, C. & Bowles, D. D. (Eds.), (1988). *Ethnicity and race: Critical concepts in social work.* Silver Spring, MD: National Association of Social Workers.

Lazarus, R. S. & Launier, R. (1978). Stress-related transactions between person and environment. In L. A. Pervin & M. Lewis (Eds.), *Perspectives in interactional psychology* (pp. 287–327). New York: Plenum.

Lee, P. (1929). Presidential address. *Proceedings of the 56th session (San Francisco) National Conference of Social Work* (pp. 3–20). Chicago, IL: University of Chicago Press.

Lum, D. (1986). *Social work practice and people of color.* Monterey, CA: Brooks/Cole.

Mahaffey, M. & Hanks, J. W. (Eds.). (1982). *Practical politics: Social work and political responsibility.* Silver Spring, MD: National Association of Social Workers.

McGoldrick, M. Pearce, J. K., & Giordano, J. (Eds.). *Ethnicity and family therapy.* New York: Guilford Press.

Moses, A. E. & Hawkins, R. O. (1982). *Counseling lesbian women and gay men: A life-issues approach.* St. Louis: Mosby.

Red Horse, J. G. (1980). Family structure and value orientation in American Indians. *Social Casework 61,* (October) 462–467.

Richmond, M. (1915). Response to A. Flexner. *Proceedings, National Conference of Charities and Corrections* (pp. 112–115).

Rosenberg, M. (1979). *Conceiving the self.* New York: Basic Books.

Srouf, L. A. (1978). Attachment and the roots of competence. *Human Nature 1* (October), 50–57.

Strauss, A. L. & Glaser, B. G. (1975.) *Chronic illness and the quality of life.* St. Louis: Mosby.

Sullivan, H. S. (1953). *The interpersonal theory of psychiatry.* New York: Norton.

Towle, C. (1941). Underlying skills of casework today. *Proceedings, National Conference of Social Work* (pp. 254–266).

Towle, C. (1961). Social work: Cause and function, 1961. *Social Casework 42*(October), 385–396.

Van Den Bergh, N. & Cooper, L. B. (Eds.). (1986). *Feminist visions for social work.* Silver Spring, MD: National Association of Social Workers.

White, R. W. (1959). Motivation reconsidered: The concept of competence. *Psychological Review 25* (September) 271–274.

II
Practice Functions

4

Intake, Assessment, and Goal Setting

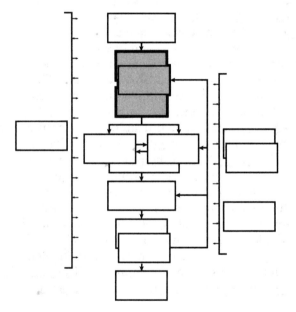

OVERVIEW

"Now vee may perhaps to begin. Yes?" That is the concluding sentence of *Portnoy's Complaint*, and one of the most famous lines in recent American literature. It is spoken by the protagonist's psychiatrist and, by the time we come upon it in the novel, we know there will be a bumpy road ahead. Starting out on something new combines a sense of promise and excitement about a fresh undertaking, and apprehension over what is obscure in the unknown. This duality surely describes a first encounter with a client, whether in psychiatry or case management.

In this chapter, we address the early phase of comprehensive enhancement practice, when a client makes contact with a service agency, presents a troubling problem or difficulty, and a decision is made about what to do. That decision, which we refer to as *goal setting*, needs to be based on accurate information about the situation and its cause. Only then can well-grounded interventive service be devised and implemented.

To serve clients well, an understanding of both the problem situation and intervention aims needs to be clear and rational. The functions involved in this process are *intake, assessment,* and *goal setting*. These three functions are discrete but interactive. The diagram of the comprehensive enhancement model depicts this separate but overlapping pattern (Fig. 2-1). Often the functions take place in close time proximity, allowing the case manager to readily move back and forth among them. In that sense, they may be viewed in common as the early phase of the process; however, they can also exist independently. For example, intake ordinarily requires one session, but assessment may extend over three, four, or five meetings.

In the discussion that follows, intake, assessment, and goal setting functions are presented separately, with the understanding that they are components of a loop process involving intertwining tasks. Because these three overlapping functions are presented in one chapter, the presentation may appear somewhat broken and compressed. The other chapters do not cover as many separate functions and have a smoother flow.

INTAKE

UNDERSTANDING INTAKE

Components of Intake

Intake involves the earliest contact with the client and a process of becoming acquainted. From the practitioner's standpoint it includes *obtaining basic information* about the client, including demographics such as age, sex, residence, and financial circumstances. Often a *case history* is composed at this stage in order to trace previous manifestations of the client's difficulty and past services that were provided. There is effort directed at *clarifying the presenting problem* as viewed by the client and as understood by the practitioner. This will be defined more precisely during assessment, but intake establishes a base from which to start. Finally, intake determines the *eligibility* and appropriateness of the client to receive the services that are offered by the agency. Does the client fit into the service niche claimed by the human service organization?

From the client's viewpoint, intake is a time at which to decide whether this is the best place, or an acceptable one, to receive help. Will the aid be effective? Will it be given in a sympathetic and convenient way? Are the expectations and demands required for service reasonable?

Intake can involve clients in a group, include several intervention functions in a telescoped fashion, and sometimes involve several different staff members.

Facts about the client's financial situation are a high priority for service eligibility in some settings, because economic dependency can be a core criterion. Other programs have different key eligibility criteria, such as whether the client is among the most seriously at-risk population (Weissman, Epstein, & Savage, 1983). In all instances, consideration of the agency's mandates and policy strictures will be necessary to decide if the client has come to the right place. Frequently, standard administrative forms must be filled out and routine instructions given.

In the University of California, Los Angeles, case manager field study the majority of the staff (40 of 48) indicated direct involvement with the intake process. They described intake as a relatively well-structured activity. The major activities that were reported (Table 4–1) included problem identification and psychosocial case history. There was also attention to reviewing previous services and treatments and noting current medication needs.

TABLE 4–1   Intake Activities Reported by Case Managers

ACTIVITY	NO. OF TIMES REPORTED (N=48)
Problem identification	31
Psychosocial/case history	21
Demographic information	5
Determine prior treatment activities	14
Determine medication use	11
Initiate treatment planning	11
Determine mental functioning	8
Orientation to treatment program	7
Determine agency appropriateness	4
Financial capability/determination	5
Supplementary Security Insurance eligibility	4
Determine drug/alcohol abuse level	4
Determine physical/sexual abuse experience	3

As indicated in the table, a number of those interviewed noted that they initiated intervention planning as a part of the intake process. Although intervention planning generally follows assessment, a number of those respondents pointed to the natural inclusion of some intervention-related considerations during the intake sessions. It is worth noting that many of those interviewed, particularly those with considerable practice experience, conceptualized intake as a fluid, holistic process—responding to each client's unique circumstances—rather than as a mechanical, lockstep procedure.

Compiling a Data Base

We may view intake as the task of compiling a data base to guide further activities with the client. This data base, according to Silverstone and Burack-Weiss (1983), contains varied information:

> name
> living arrangements
> referral source
> age
> sex
> marital status
> ethnicity
> religion
> family members and their locations
> education
> work history
> medical history
> financial information
> presenting problem and precipitating event
> previous service provision
> emergencies contacts
> behavior in the interview
> professional contacts and consultations that are arranged

This information needs to be elicited in a way that is sensitive to the client's situation, ethnic background, and emotional state. Obtaining accurate, perceptive information is not a routine activity, but rather one that requires human relations skills and cultural sensitivity.

Engagement and Interpersonal Relations

Ballew and Mink (1986) address the optimal climate for service to vulnerable clients and stress that it begins in the very first interview. The climate needs to engender productive communication and relationships, and it commences with early engagement. During the engagement stage, the practitioner seeks to develop trust by conveying a sense of concern and capability. It is this rapport that helps the practitioner both to understand and accept the client, and transmits the message, "I care." Reflective listening demonstrates an attitude of thoughtful concern. Being organized and focusing actions on purpose and direction show the client that the practitioner is competent. Providing an initial concrete service at this early time, like getting a meal for a homeless person, will signal to the client that the worker is capable and reliable.

Two client attitudes often addressed in the intake interview are negative feelings about taking help and unrealistic expectations. Vulnerable people needing this service typically have multiple, long-standing problems, and may have had aversive experiences in receiving or using help. They often feel powerless, inferior, guilty, and afraid. Our culture places great value on independence, so the recipients of service, especially those from ethnic groups that emphasize informal mutual aid, frequently feel discouraged or embarrassed about their plight and need for formal professional service. Also, practitioners sometimes have ambivalent feelings about severely impaired, dependent, or highly abrasive clients with whom they are obligated to contend.

The other common problem, unrealistic expectations, often centers on who is to do what. Clients can be confused about what is expected of them or their families. They may have amorphous or erroneous ideas about what the practitioner can or cannot provide. The worker must carefully negotiate and delineate roles during the engagement phase. Role clarification at this stage can reduce the number of clients who discontinue service prematurely and can enhance service outcomes. It is key that client and case manager expectations become joined.

There are start up problems and issues unique to different populations. The elderly may be difficult to engage because of physical losses such as hearing impairment and may exhibit depression due to these losses. Mentally ill homeless clients, according to Cohen (1989), have great fear of agency programs because their contacts with professionals frequently have involved confinement in institutions, and their illness and homelessness rob them of control over their lives. Their capacity to trust is eroded. Cultural groups speaking only their own native language may be reluctant to enter into impersonal bureaucratic structures. Overcoming this fearfulness is critical to the engagement process, and a path to overcoming it is through working toward a sense of personal empowerment by conveying respect and encouraging participation.

Timing Factors

Various research studies round out this picture and call attention to timing. Some studies show that effective intake efforts are related to a prompt response. Wolkon (1972) found that keeping short the time lapse between the initial inquiry and the first scheduled appointment increased the percentage of interviews that were kept. Three days is suggested as a maximum delay.

When working with the frail elderly, the importance of rapid follow-up to requests for service was found to be critical. "The frail older person may be ambivalent in the search for aid or too worn out to keep on trying . . . a lack of timely response to his or her effort may well discourage further attempts and a crucial opportunity to help is lost" (Silverstone & Burack-Weiss, 1983, p. 78).

One of the practices that was most strongly associated with overall quality of service in child welfare was found to be a prompt response to incoming reports (Wells, 1985).

A study of the impact of changing life events on long-term mental patients gives insight into the types of intake questions that are relevant to this population (Baker & Burns, 1985). When the types and frequencies of stressful life events the patients experienced were identified, 85.1 percent of problems involved alterations in the life situation, such as shifts in *structured daily activities, residence, health, finances, hospitalization, family relationships, and other close associations*. The findings can help practitioners focus on background information that is useful to obtain during early contacts.

PRACTICE GUIDELINES FOR INTAKE

Early Steps

The preceding professional concepts and research findings point to guidelines for the intake function. Put together with additional information that will be introduced, a set of specific practice procedures for intake emerge.

The first interview should be scheduled as soon as possible after the initial request. The practitioner needs to quickly determine whether the client has come to the correct place for help. Eligibility for service is sometimes predetermined by a referral source. If not, the practitioner should move to review the agency's criteria for service with the client and clarify eligibility. It is important to give the client ample opportunity to bring forward personal wants and concerns in order to learn which (if any) the agency will be able to provide for.

A first order task in intake is to construct a data base as described on page 66, including demographics, living arrangements, family situation, income, and ethnicity. In addition, the Lazarus (1971) *Life History Questionnaire* provides a useful guide to compiling a case history of the client.

Engagement Techniques

As mentioned, the engagement process begins with the first interview and is critical for going forward with service. According to Ballew and Mink (1986), the content of the first interview needs to include introductions and role clarifications.

Clarify the situation.   The client may still be feeling confused and anxious in a new context. In that case, the case manager might take a set of specific actions that are both obvious and necessary:

1. Ask the client to state (or perhaps write) exactly what he expects of the case manager and of himself.
2. Restate the client's communication to verify what it means, and to let the client know that it is understood.
3. State (or write) the general responsibilities of each as discussed.
4. Discuss any differences and come to an agreement on each person's role.

Respond to the client as a unique person.   In the engagement phase, the practitioner has to focus on understanding the client and his or her life situation and should avoid criticism or an abrupt manner. This is especially true for certain minority groups, such as Asians, where shame over inadequacy may be present. This does not preclude taking the initiative when appropriate with clients by talking about sensitive areas in a frank and open manner. This often stimulates the client to participate similarly. The worker can also express some hunches about the client's problems and suggest some possible consequences if problems continue, as a stimulus to collaborative decision-making.

Make a personal connection.   See if there is anything similar in your mutual interests or experiences that you can point to. This often helps the client feel that the practitioner has interests or attributes in common and is able to understand.

Recognize negative feelings.   Let the client know that his or her feelings are acceptable and realistic in the circumstances. Cohen (1989) provides a framework for engaging the homeless mentally ill, specifically:

* Give clients the choice of accepting or rejecting the service.
* Be flexible in your manner.
* Respond to client's personally perceived needs: housing, money, food, and physical safety.
* Be willing to move slowly and carefully at the client's speed. They need time to develop trust.
* Do everything *with* the client, rather than to him or for him.
* Strive to build trust.

Developing Problem Statements

It is recommended by some professionals that the client and the practitioner develop an initial problem statement. Work done at UCLA by Damron-Rodriguez suggests a useful approach to this, focusing on service to the elderly.[1] A common difficulty is a tendency to confuse the underlying causeof the problem with the manifesting problem or symptom.

Example:

> Memory impairment (cause)
> versus
> Forgets to pay bills (problem/symptom)

Another difficulty in developing problem statements is not describing the problem in enough specific detail.

Example:

> Forgets to pay bills
> versus
> "For the past 4 months, Mrs. M. has consistently forgotten to pay her rent bill due to short-term memory impairment of approximately 4 to 6 months duration. This has resulted in an eviction notice dated 5/1/89."

This problem statement may be too inclusive. A middle ground and probably better way to state this problem is as follows:

> "Failure to pay rent due to memory impairment has resulted in an eviction notice dated 5/1/93."

Strategies for developing problem statements include:

Write it out.
Make it sufficiently detailed.
Avoid fuzzy or global statements.
Avoid entwining multiple problems.
Include the cause if it is known. (Remember to separate the problem, the immediate, symptomatic difficulty, from the underlying cause.)

Attending to Population Group Differences

Developing initial problem statements is aided by knowledge of characteristics of a particular population and attention to personal factors, as stated previously. For example, work with the elderly is facilitated by understanding that the client usually has a variety of problems that are caused by depletions and physical losses (Silverstone & Burack-Weiss, 1983).

Bloom et al. (1971) discuss a set of concrete practice behaviors to employ when interviewing the elderly.

---

[1]This discussion is based on shared lecture notes.

To Address Hearing Limitation:

> Directly face the elder in close proximity.
> Speak slowly in a normal voice.
> Use clear, short sentences.
> Write the questions if necessary.

To Address Vision Limitation:

> Speak clearly to announce your presence and credentials.
> Ask the elder about his visual acuity. (Depending on the cause of the vision problem, objects may be seen only in the center or only on the sides of the visual field.)
> Be calm, quiet, and reassuring.

To Address Language Function Limitations:

> Be patient. Time is required for understanding and response.
> Accompany your speech with visual cues and gestures.
> Listen carefully to find out the elder's communication style.
> Nod when you understand.
> Reword what the elder says to check on the meaning.
> Show interest and concern, even when you cannot understand.

To Address Mental Limitations:

> Give the elder time to understand the question, gather his thoughts, and report his decision.
> Stay in the immediate and the concrete as much as possible.

For different population groups it is necessary to take into account different aspects of the client's life situation. The procedures followed in a local mental health clinic studied in the UCLA survey gave a great deal of attention to biological and psychological factors. The intake form detailed psychiatric history, medical history, and medications currently and previously prescribed, including the degree of compliance in taking them. Case managers looked for stress-producing life changes in routines, residence, or relationships. Information was obtained on how the client looks, feels, thinks, and behaves in the interview situation. This can tell a great deal about emotional state and ability to function. A structured psychiatric diagnostic instrument was employed later, at the point where assessment is undertaken. In working with the elderly, medical factors and activities of daily living are prominent. A comment from a practitioner in the UCLA field study succinctly summarizes some of the flavor of intake:

> I determine, in talking with and observing the client, what the present difficulties seem to be. I try to see what the client is asking and what the client needs. I try to learn if there is a history of previous illness and what the family's current situation is. I try to learn about financial circumstances and whether the client goes to work or school. I try to get a his-

tory of past medications and drugs—did the client take medications in the past and which were helpful? I try to gauge mental status. Is he having delusions or debilitating anxieties? Is he dangerous to himself or others? I also try hard to describe our service process in a way that is understandable.

ASSESSMENT

UNDERSTANDING ASSESSMENT

Basic Components

Once a problem has been identified in approximate form during intake, more pinpointed and specific data need to be marshaled to help shape interventive goals. "The purpose of assessment is to gather the information necessary to evaluate what is to be changed, what factors are maintaining or currently controlling the problem, what resources are necessary to bring about changes, what problems might result from bringing about changes, and how change can be evaluated" (Fischer, 1978, pp. 249–250).

A client complains of inability to hold a job as the problem for which she needs help. During intake the practitioner becomes convinced that this has been a recurring pattern that needs to be resolved. Assessment would seek to determine whether the client lacks adequate vocational skills, exhibits sloppy work habits such as frequent tardiness, has a poor self-image that results in passivity on the job, or is experiencing a level of stress that results in inattentiveness or strident interpersonal relations in the workplace. There are markedly different intervention implications and goals for each of these.

Assessment has both a factual and an analytical component, referred to by Northern (1987) as the "collection" and the "appraisal" of data. Appropriate information needs to be obtained, and the information then needs to be treated in a disciplined, interpretative manner. The analytical component entails projecting forward to intervention goals.

Kurtz and Bagarozzi (1984) report on the frequency of assessment type activities performed by the case managers they studied (Table 4–2).

TABLE 4–2 Report on Frequency of Assessment Activities

FREQUENCY OF PERFORMANCE	OFTEN	SELDOM
Telephone contact	31	69
Office contact	50	50
In-home visits	4	96
Emergency screening	34	66
Family interviews	38	62
Information from agencies	43	57

The figures reflect the percentage of respondents who engaged in each assessment activity.

Office contacts are somewhat frequent and home visitation is rare. Other modes are employed to a moderate degree.

The data from the UCLA field study indicate that the most frequent assessment activities consisted of refining the problem, determining the client's current level of functioning, and interpreting the previous history of service. Also, examining potential social support was frequently mentioned. The approach was described by one respondent as follows:

> In psychosocial assessment I want to know what the person's actual level of functioning is. And secondly, I want to try to figure out what could be beneficial for the person. What kind of social support would be most helpful— general relief, board-and-care, SSI?

A considerable number of the respondents made active use of external informants—family members, other staff, and previous agency contacts—as important sources of information in compiling the psychosocial assessment:

> I first gather information from the relatives or family members of the client, piecing together the client's history. I also meet with agency staff persons and gather their comments. I read through records and ask staff to supplement the records and answer any questions I have. Following this I meet further with the client.

Respondents saw psychosocial assessment as implicated early in the intake process, and they found it difficult to conceive of these start-up activities as totally discrete functions. Overall, assessment was one of the functions that respondents claimed took a considerable amount of their time.

The specific amount of time for assessment may vary depending on the client and the circumstances. For example, in a crisis situation assessment has to be rapid, particularly if there is an immediate threat to health or safety (for example, an infant is in danger of serious child abuse). If the child instead faces *potential* neglect because of a contentious divorce, assessment takes place normally and continues with reassessment during monitoring. Assessment is an ongoing activity throughout the interventive process, but receives focused attention during the early start-up phase. Epstein (1988) suggests that the basic assessment is preceded by a "rapid early assessment" to identify a problem to target, and followed by a "working assessment" for purposes of client involvement and contracting.

Assessment involves social and psychological diagnosis and may include medical factors as well. Positive factors, including *client potentialities and strengths,* are also brought out. It is a multifaceted activity and may require multiperson, multidiscipline involvement.

The rationale for a broad needs-based approach is predicated on the highly vulnerable client population—"people who have multiple needs and who may not be able to meet these needs by themselves" (Moxley, 1989, p. 25). Moxley defines needs in terms of deficits in resources to sustain biological, social, and psychological integrity. Stated in another way, needs relate to the potential for independent living (Weil & Karls, 1989). Clients' needs, as related to independent living, fall into such diverse areas as income, housing, health care, mental health, recreation, and education. Viewed from a broad psychosocial perspective, Reid (1978) proposes the following assessment framework: interpersonal conflict, dissatisfaction in social relations, problems with formal organizations, difficulties in role performance, decision problems, reactive emotional distress, inadequate resources, and psychological or behavioral problems not elsewhere classified.

Agency and Community Factors

Looking at assessment from an organizational view rather than a practitioner's view, Austin (1981, p. 91) states that "assessment is part of a larger organizational process by which agencies determine the kinds and quantities of services clients will receive." She views clients "as individuals enmeshed in a system of relationships and exchanges with the individuals and groups that make up their environment" and is therefore concerned with the complex context within which assessment activities occur (Austin, 1981, p. 96). This context includes the agency service system and the client's surrounding social system. An important question is who performs the assessment. Accountability in the organization must be fixed and responsibility for conducting the assessment needs to be assigned clearly and consistently. Otherwise, clients can fall between the cracks of the agency's infrastructure. A variable that affects assessment is the agency's sense of mission and organizational self-interest. This can affect the quality of assessment and its objectivity. "There is ongoing tension between the organization's survival needs and the clients' service needs" (Bertsche & Horejsi, 1980, p. 81). The practitioner ought ordinarily to assume the role of client advocate within the agency, taking account of, but not being immobilized by, organizational realities.

Assessment obviously involves examining the person–environment balance: how the individual deals with the environment, how the environment affects the individual, and the interaction between the two (see Chapter 3). Is the problem located in the client, in the situation, or in the match, and at which points in this configuration should change efforts be targeted? The environmental appraisal includes examination of supportive resources available from the individual's informal helping network.

Relationship with the Client

The working relationship between client and practitioner is a key ingredient in the assessment process. Kanter (1985) speaks of the personal commitment of the worker as an important feature. He views the relationship as including a learning element for the client. Generally with this type of practice, the client's input through optimal participation should be encouraged. The client is an expert informant about his or her own perceived needs, feelings, and wishes. However, one of the difficulties in the relationship is the handling of the authoritative role that the practitioner must assume at times. If the relationship is to be genuine (based on trust), the practitioner must be straightforward about acknowledging legitimate areas of authority. A potential difficulty in the relationship is that the helping process can foster dependence in the client; the client may come to see the worker as a determining parental figure. Client attitudes of this nature impede assessment, as well as intervention generally. The severely vulnerable client can see the situation as hopeless, and therefore refuse to become engaged. These hindering attitudes need to be recognized and dealt with as a part of the assessment and intervention planning.

PRACTICE GUIDELINES FOR ASSESSMENT

An Assessment Framework

Assessment in comprehensive enhancement practice is the process of determining the client's varied needs, weaknesses, and strengths in an environmental context. Sufficient time needs to be allocated for the task and appropriate assessment tools need to be used or developed.

An assessment framework by Moxley (1989) provides a useful format and guides this discussion. The dimensions of assessment fall into four categories: (1) the nature of client needs; (2) the client's capacity to address these; (3) the contribution of informal supports; and (4) the contribution of human service agency supports. The framework is broad—overlapping intake inquiries—and suggests varied areas that can be drawn on differentially as needed in specific client situations.

Screening specific needs.   For the first category, identifying specific needs, the case manager can delve into relevant areas from among the following:

1. *Income.* This should be adequate for the basic necessities of life. Find out if the client has the ability to provide this himself. Investigate the client's eligibility for entitlements, such as public assistance, social

security, or unemployment compensation. Sources of income may exist in the client's social network.

2. *Housing and shelter.* These needs interact with other variables: income, the client's capacity for independent living, accessibility of housing, safety in the neighborhood, and how the client views satisfactory housing. Support the client in the establishment and maintenance of a suitable living arrangement. The client may be eligible for publicly sponsored or subsidized housing or may make an arrangement with family or friends.

3. *Employment.* Understand the client's employment history and skills. Identify vocational guidance, evaluation, placement, and training opportunities. If the client cannot meet this need through personal initiative or a social network, make a connection with the employment program of a public or nonprofit agency.

4. *Health care.* This is a critical area and includes physical, optical, dental, nutritional, and preventive aspects. Get a health history and find out about the client's cultural and personal beliefs about health.

5. *Mental health.* These needs are manifest by the client's behavior, subjective expressions, and how the client copes with daily life. Being free of depression and anxiety, having a positive outlook, and opportunities for self-actualization are aspects of mental health.

6. *Social and personal relationships.* These assist in fulfilling the needs of intimacy, social integration, nurturance, self-worth, and mutual aid. Evaluate the skills and capacities of the client relating to social relationships. Seek to define the client's social network.

7. *Recreation and leisure.* This affects quality of life. Focus on the availability of recreational opportunities. Are they appropriate for and accessible to the client? Ask the client if they are acceptable.

8. *Activities of daily living.* Such activities are assessed to find out if the client can maintain an independent life. One needs to be able to feed, bathe, and dress oneself. Find out if the client is able to shop, clean, and pay bills. *Highly vulnerable clients commonly require careful assessment of this area.* The social network and human service agencies are sources of support.

9. *Transportation.* Can the client get around independently or is help needed? The practitioner may need to assess the eligibility of the client for specialized transportation programs.

10. *Legal assistance.* This is related to criminal charges and issues of competency and protection. You may need to link the client to an attorney or legal aid if necessary.

11. *Education.* These needs are assessed by learning the client's deficits and orientation toward education. Education may be needed for vocational, communication, social, and other basic skills or for intellectual or cultural growth.

Gauging capacity for independent functioning. The second category, client capacity, involves the degree to which the client can function independently.

1. *Assessment of physical functioning status* looks for the presence or absence of illness, disability, physical energy and strength, coordination, medications, disfigurement, sensory capacities, and other characteristics that indicate psychological or health status.

2. *Assessment of cognitive functioning status* examines reality orientation, intellectual capacity, judgment, flexibility, coherence of cognition, values and their consistency with behavior, and self-concept.

3. *Assessment of emotional functioning* is related to the presence or absence of depression, anxiety, or debilitating affect. It also concerns the range of emotions and the style of controlling them. Check to see if affect is situation-appropriate.

4. *Behavioral functioning status* is assessed by evaluating social skills (sensitivity to others, cooperativeness, and assertiveness), personal hygiene, grooming, degree of organization, listening skills, self-expression skills, behavioral reaction to frustration, presence or absence of aggression, level of motivation, and willingness to be responsible.

Appraising informal support. In the third category, mutual care, there is an appraisal of the degree to which the client's informal helping network can fulfill some of the client's needs. Identify the number of people in the social network, obtain their names and locations, gather information on the nature of the relationships, and determine what type of support exists. The case manager is interested in instrumental, material, and socio-emotional supports. The relationship areas to review with the client are household members, kin, co-workers, neighbors, other community contacts, and members of clubs, churches, social groups, schools, and human service organizations. Specific procedures for this type of assessment are discussed in Chapter 8.

Appraising formal agency support. The fourth category concerns professional care, or the contribution of formal human services. This overlaps with the function of resource identification and indexing, which is treated in Chapter 5. While resource considerations become critical in the later stage of intervention planning, they need to be considered here also. It is necessary to match the client's needs with professional care resources to assess whether formal services can fulfill the needs. Professional care is found in broad community and public services, human service agencies, and specialized welfare programs. These services are used to sustain and strengthen the client and the client's helping network in their effort to keep

FIGURE 4–1 Level of functioning assessment

Instructions: Circle the number that best describes this person's *typical* level of functioning on each item listed below. *Be as accurate as you can.* If you are not sure about a certain rating, ask someone who may know or consult the case record. **Mark only one number for each item. Be sure to mark all items.**

Self-Maintenance

A. Physical Functioning	No Problem	Problem But No Effect on General Functioning	Slight Effect on General Functioning	Restricts General Functioning Substantially	Prevents General Functioning
1. Vision	5	4	3	2	1
2. Hearing	5	4	3	2	1
3. Speech impairment	5	4	3	2	1
4. Walking, use of legs	5	4	3	2	1
5. Use of hands and arms	5	4	3	2	1

B. Personal Care Skills	Totally Self-Sufficient	Needs Verbal Advice or Guidance	Needs Some Physical Help or Assistance	Needs Substantial Help	Totally Dependent
6. Toileting (uses toilet properly; keeps self and area clean)	5	4	3	2	1
7. Eating (uses utensils properly; eating habits)	5	4	3	2	1
8. Personal hygiene (body and teeth; general cleanliness)	5	4	3	2	1
9. Dressing self (selects appropriate garments; dresses self)	5	4	3	2	1
10. Grooming (hair, make-up, general appearance)	5	4	3	2	1
11. Care of own possessions	5	4	3	2	1
12. Care of own living space	5	4	3	2	1

Social Functioning

	Highly Typical of This Person	Generally Typical of This Person	Somewhat Typical of This Person	Generally Untypical of This Person	Highly Untypical of This Person
C. Interpersonal Relationships					
13. Accepts contact with others (does not withdraw or turn away)	5	4	3	2	1
14. Initiates contact with others	5	4	3	2	1
15. Communicates effectively (speech and gestures are understandable and to the point)	5	4	3	2	1
16. Engages in activities without prompting	5	4	3	2	1
17. Participates in groups					
18. Forms and maintains friendships	5	4	3	2	1
19. Asks for help when needed	5	4	3	2	1

	Never	Rarely	Sometimes	Frequently	Always
D. Social Acceptability					
20. Verbally abuses others	5	4	3	2	1
21. Physically abuses others	5	4	3	2	1
22. Destroys property	5	4	3	2	1
23. Physically abuses self	5	4	3	2	1
24. Is fearful, crying, clinging	5	4	3	2	1
25. Takes property from others without permission	5	4	3	2	1
26. Performs repetitive behaviors (pacing, rocking, making noises)	5	4	3	2	1

(continued)

FIGURE 4-1 (*Continued*)

Social Functioning (*Cont.*)

E. Activities	Totally Self-Sufficient	Needs Some Verbal Advice or Guidance	Needs Physical Help or Assistance	Needs Substantial Help	Totally Dependent
27. Household responsibilities (cleaning, cooking, washing clothes)	5	4	3	2	1
28. Shopping (selection of items, choice of stores, payment at register)	5	4	3	2	1
29. Handling personal finances (budgeting, paying bills)	5	4	3	2	1
30. Use of telephone (getting number, dialing, speaking, listening)	5	4	3	2	1
31. Traveling from residence without getting lost	5	4	3	2	1
32. Use of public transportation (selecting route, using timetable, paying fares, making transfers)	5	4	3	2	1
33. Use of leisure time (reading, visiting friends, listening to music)	5	4	3	2	1
34. Recognizing and avoiding common dangers (traffic safety, fire safety)	5	4	3	2	1
35. Self-medication (understanding purpose, taking as prescribed, recognizing side effects)	5	4	3	2	1
36. Use of medical and other community services (knowing whom to contact, how, and when to use)	5	4	3	2	1
37. Basic reading, writing, and arithmetic (enough for daily needs)	5	4	3	2	1

	Highly Typical of This Person	Generally Typical of This Person	Somewhat Typical of This Person	Generally Untypical of This Person	Highly Untypical of This Person
38. Has employable skills	5	4	3	2	1
39. Works with minimal supervision	5	4	3	2	1
40. Is able to sustain work effort (not easily distracted, can work under stress)	5	4	3	2	1
41. Appears at appointments on time	5	4	3	2	1
42. Follows verbal instructions accurately	5	4	3	2	1
43. Completes assigned tasks	5	4	3	2	1

Other Information

44. From your knowledge of this person, are there other skills or problem areas not covered on this form that are important to this person's ability to function independently? If so, please specify. _____

45. How well do you know the skills and behavior of the person you just rated? (Circle one)

Very Well   Fairly Well   Not Very Well at All
  5   4   3   2   1

46. Have you discussed this assessment with the client? (Circle one)   Yes   No
If *yes*, does the client generally agree with the assessment? (Circle one)   Yes   No

the client living in the community. Formal aids may be used to fill in when natural resources do not exist. Examples are adult day care, meals on wheels, income maintenance and social security, and homemaker services. Community senior citizen centers offer many services for the elderly, such as mental health, ambulatory health care, transportation services, and legal aid.

Assessment Tools

To facilitate assessment, a variety of standard instruments are readily available. These are sometimes referred to as *rapid assessment instruments* (RAIs). A package of such measures has been compiled by Hudson (1982) and a similar sourcebook has been issued by Corcoran and Fischer (1987). An older, comprehensive compendium is by Hersen and Bellack (1976). These compilations offer tools geared to different stages of intervention and types of problems, such as marital difficulty, anxiety, addiction, and children's problems. For gauging psychological and emotional deficits there is the DSM-III-R (*Diagnostic and Statistical Manual of Mental Disorders*), which provides uniform nomenclature, categories, and procedures across mental health professions. Disorders are classified using five axes: clinical syndromes, personality disorders, physical conditions, psychosocial stressors, and changes in stress level.

Such highly clinical measures, we have stated, may not be the assessment tools of choice in comprehensive enhancement. Kanter (1985, p. 66) observes that for serving clients in community-based settings, "traditional psychiatric diagnosis have little bearing on rehabilitative potential." He recommends focusing on skill capacities for functioning in key life situations; thus, assessment tools that examine functional capacity are particularly pertinent for this purpose. The *Specific Level of Functioning Scale* (SLOF) of Schneider and Streuning (1983) is a serviceable instrument along these lines. It uses a five-point rating system to examine a range of skills. Because of the importance of the clients' level of functioning to serving vulnerable clients, the scale is reproduced (Fig. 4-1).

A related scale, Instrumental Activities of Daily Living (IADL) by Lawton and Brody, gauges the ability of the elderly to function independently (Fig. 4-2). It screens eight areas of self-sufficiency.

These assessment tools suggest possibilities that are available. Many agencies have their own forms and scales that staff are expected to use routinely. Additional or specialized options can be found in the sourcebooks referenced. These tools must be used with sensitivity to individual differences and cultural diversity. For example, communicating "to the point," as incorporated in one of the illustrative scales, is not a typical cultural mode for some ethnic groups.

FIGURE 4–2   Instrumental Activities of Daily Living Scale (IADL)

A. Ability to Use Telephone

1. Operates telephone on own initiative—looks up and dials numbers, etc.   1
2. Dials a few well-known numbers.   1
3. Answers telephone but does not dial.   1
4. Does not use telephone at all.   0

B. Shopping

1. Takes care of all shopping needs independently.   1
2. Shops independently for small purchases.   0
3. Needs to be accompanied on any shopping trip.   0
4. Completely unable to shop.   0

C. Food Preparation

1. Plans, prepares, and serves adequate meals independently.   1
2. Prepares adequate meals if supplied with ingredients.   0
3. Heats, serves, and prepares meals, or prepares meals but does not maintain adequate diet.   0
4. Needs to have meals prepared and served.   0

D. Housekeeping

1. Maintains house alone or with occasional assistance (e.g., "heavy work domestic help")   1
2. Performs light daily tasks such as dishwashing, bedmaking.   1
3. Performs light daily tasks but cannot maintain acceptable level of cleanliness.   1
4. Needs help with all home-maintenance tasks.   1
5. Does not participate in any housekeeping tasks.   0

E. Laundry

1. Does personal laundry completely.   1
2. Launders small items—rinses stockings, etc.   1
3. All laundry must be done by others.   0

F. Mode of Transportation

1. Travels independently on public transportation or drives own car.   1
2. Arranges own travel via taxi, but does not otherwise use public transportation.   1
3. Travels on public transportation when accompanied by another.   1
4. Travel limited to taxi or automobile with assistance of another.   0
5. Does not travel at all.   0

G. Responsibility for Own Medications

1. Is responsible for taking medication to correct dosages at correct time.   1
2. Takes responsibility if medication is prepared in advance in separate dosage.   0
3. Is not capable of dispensing own medication.   0

H. Ability to Handle Finances

1. Manages financial matters independently (budgets, writes checks, pays rent, bills, goes to bank); collects and keeps track of income.   1
2. Manages day-to-day purchases, but needs help with banking, major purchases, etc.   1
3. Incapable of handling money.   0

Integrating Information

The basic information gathered during assessment needs to be analyzed in a way that integrates the data, draws conclusions about the interrelated factors contributing to the problem, and sets the stage for decisions about which interventions to implement (Northern, 1977, p. 180). In other words, critical thinking and reasoned professional judgment have to be applied in order to interpret the raw data. Inferences have to be made about causation and about how different aspects of the problem configuration are linked together. The practitioner draws on theoretical perspectives from varying fields—individual behavior, family dynamics, social psychology, small group behavior, and others. Whatever intellectual resources and past experiences the practitioner has acquired provide the basis for this complex task that is partially scientific and partially artistic. It is through this process that goals for intervention are formulated.

SETTING GOALS

UNDERSTANDING GOAL SETTING

Key Aspects

Intervention goals shape the service plan. Goals need to be stated clearly and realistically, incorporating the client's own perceptions of both long- and short-term requirements. This provides the foundation for intervention planning. The rationale is that "case management emphasizes decision making . . . an orientation toward service provision based on the attainment of specific objectives and goals for clients" (Weil & Karls, 1985, p. 367). The function includes determining which of varied needs to work on and for what purposes.

Practitioners in the UCLA survey offer useful perspectives. The most frequent goal-setting activity, according to those interviewed, was explicating client-identified areas of needed improvement. A reality check by the professional involves an appraisal of the client's "true" problems and a determination of whether the necessary resources for change are available. A participant in the study commented:

> Trying to find out what the client wants to accomplish in the program consists of getting the client to break things down to the most basic level . . . I get clients to talk about their goals in many areas of their lives. I probe for their interests. In my work, goal setting sometimes involves a formal contract with the client.

While a variety of activities were mentioned by the respondents as being a part of the goal-setting process, they agree that these activities could be separated into short- versus long-term objectives:

I collect the information needed to establish goals during the intake and psychosocial assessment periods. I then set short-term goals for purposes of alleviating symptoms (such as distress, anxiety, and housing problems). I also consider long-term goals in relation to occupational development and improving self-esteem.

Goals vary by client population. In setting goals with the long-term mentally ill, the balancing of psychosocial treatment and drug treatment has to be weighed. Medication has had beneficial effects, but can be overemphasized. Davidson and Jamison (1983, p. 139) present clinical vignettes that show that the alleviation of symptoms by drug treatment may not always be worth the severe physical, social, and psychological side-effects. They show how "drugs can reinforce a client's self-image as a deviant person, encourage drug overdependence, lead the client to avoid confronting pathogenic environmental conditions that exacerbate his or her psychopathology, and present the problem of potential misuse." Other goals may be salient for different client groups. The goal of re-entry into mainstream educational institutions is important in work with adolescents who are institutionalized (Ferdinande & Colligan, 1980). Students were found to have strong apprehensions about their return to school. This study revealed a primary goal for this particular group and the need for careful planning to attain it.

Client and Professional Inputs

We have emphasized that the client's interests are a key consideration, and client participation should consciously be drawn on at every stage. The client often can articulate what needs stand out in his or her own mind. Even if these are questionable in some way, the case manager should take them seriously and explore them interactively. When the client "owns" practice goals, the likelihood increases that personal effort will be directed toward attaining them. The practitioner, we know, joins in the choice of goals. Professional inferences are made about causes of problems, potential effective solutions, and the feasibility of implementing alternatives.

A number of respondents in the UCLA study stressed the importance of maintaining a *realistic perception* of how much progress a seriously impaired client can make. Being aware of the standing problems that have prevented clients from living normal lives in the past greatly helps practitioners to be hopeful but patient. A respondent comments:

> At this point you have to address what both you and the client see as a practical set of goals. The goals must be attainable. Most of my clients have severe problems going back many years. So goals for them must be within their abilities to achieve, otherwise the whole process can be very negative.

Society's expectations and demands, often incorporated within the service delivery system, also play a part. The client's needs and society's demands can be in tune or discrepant. Child welfare is an example: A child protective service agency asks for prescribed, normative behavior by parents toward their offspring, regardless of the parents' personal views of what is acceptable in rearing and disciplining their children.

The importance of focusing on quality of life in community living as a goal was revealed in research by Baker and Intagliata (1982) when they studied the community support system programs in New York. The findings emphasized several client-based factors:

1. a need for maintenance and comfort rather than cure
2. a need for complex programs for complex problem conditions
3. a need to keep the customer happy
4. a need to use a holistic perspective

Criteria for Workable Goals

There are two important qualities for workable goals: specificity and discreteness (Ballew & Mink, 1986). Different people can have the same understanding of a goal when it is unambiguous. Short-term perspectives have to be considered. Needs that require immediate attention generate such goals (usually high-risk situations, conditions, or events). A child who is subject to serious abuse obviously requires immediate attention, as does an elderly person who can no longer walk to the market for food. Even if a client's goal is not high risk, meeting it promptly can serve to strengthen the professional relationship and give hope to the client. This can be highly motivating to further effort. When the goals are not accomplished within the set time frames, reassessment is required. The goals may be continued or modified. This process helps the practitioner reach an increasingly better understanding of how the client functions and copes. Guidelines for specificity are presented in the following practice section.

Long-term goals emerge from needs that will usually require considerable time, energy, and resources. This type of goal has value because it specifically addresses the continuity of care component and invokes a maintenance program that will keep the client functioning in a stable, ongoing fashion in the community. These long-range objectives are the basic goals comprehensive enhancement aims to achieve. Though they are relatively distant, they also need to be reasonably specific and measurable. "Overgeneralized and open-ended objectives such as 'psychosocial adjustment,' 'environmental fit,' or 'stable adaptation' are desirable but impossible to measure" (Silverstone & Burack-Weiss, 1983, p. 49). An example of a specific long-term goal for an abused child is return to the family under conditions where the father has obtained regular employment, is under reduced stress, and expresses an understanding of acceptable disciplining methods.

Goal statements should be given emphasis in the case record. There has been a prevalent human services practice of recording client problems using a process-oriented, highly descriptive approach. Objective-oriented case recording is important because it focuses on what the client, practitioner, and other persons will seek to do in concrete prescriptive terms.

PRACTICE GUIDELINES FOR GOAL SETTING

An analysis of the practice literature and research conclusions leads us to some specific practice strategies and techniques for this function.

Attaining Specificity

Goals set forth the kinds of changes that should be aimed for, in specific and tangible form. Should certain behavior be increased or decreased? Should its duration be modified? Or its place of enactment be shifted? The case manager can aid the client by laying out alternatives, their probable consequences, and unanticipated outcomes. Steps in the process of setting goals according to Ballew and Mink (1986) include:

- forming goals based on the assessment data in collaboration with the client
- prioritizing the goals

Concrete steps need to be taken to translate assessment information into goals. Ballew and Mink (1986, p. 63) state that this process is easier if "the [goal] statements are expressed in clear, specific and unambiguous language." They add that describing actual behavior makes it even more clear. For example, a goal for Mrs. M. could be, "Mrs. M. will pay her rent by mailing a check on the tenth day of each month, beginning on May 10th."

These two goals developed for Mrs. M. also illustrate other techniques for setting goals. They have been introduced previously but are given an application emphasis here:

- Be behaviorally specific, e.g., mailing a check.
- Make the goal observable, e.g., a check stub can be seen.
- Make the goal measurable, e.g., the number of times in a year the rent is paid by the tenth of the month.
- Establish a time base, e.g., beginning on May 10th.

Ballew and Mink (1986, p. 145) recommend additionally structuring goals through use of special dates like important holidays or the client's birthday: "... you should place a date for completion right in the goal statement itself as an integral part of the goal."

Let us consider two strategies to help the wording of goal statements. One is to *state goals in positive terms* (Modrcin, Rapp, & Chamberlain, 1985). "John will work until 5:30 PM," states what is expected of the client. ("John will not leave work early," is the negative way to word the goal.) The second strategy is to *avoid vague adjectives and adverbs*. To say "Mrs. M. will successfully manage her financial affairs," leaves us wondering what she really needs to do. It is especially difficult to measure "successfully manage." Success may instead be keyed to having expenditures not exceed income for a 6-month period.

Previously, sections have addressed the requirement to partialize by *breaking goals down into smaller workable segments* when useful. The goal about Mrs. M. paying the rent is suggestive. It may be that she can not negotiate the public transportation system, and to pay the rent she needs to get her social security checks to the bank. One segment of the rent-paying goal may be "Mrs. M. will learn to use the service of the transportation program at the community senior citizen center. When this is mastered she will pay the rent as specified. Until then, the case manager will call on her daughter to carry out this task."

Goals need to be in tune with reality. If Mrs. M.'s physical examination reveals cognitive impairment due to a stroke, the goal for her to pay the rent herself should be reconsidered. Perhaps her daughter should do it.

Paying the rent is a short-term goal. As previously stated it is necessary to also keep in mind long-range goals. What capacity or status is desired as the outcome? What maintenance program is required? The practitioner needs to develop this with Mrs. M. and her daughter. It may be, "Mrs. M. will receive these services in order to maintain her regularly in her apartment." Or a basic change may be decided: "The daughter will invite Mrs. M. to live with her permanently." Or they may decide upon a board and care facility.

In setting a goal, it is important to check at least tentatively to see if necessary resources are available. Is there a transportation service at hand? Is Mrs. M. eligible to use it? Also check the adequacy of the components of the goal formulation. The goal of using transportation service to get to the bank may fail if the buses run irregularly, at the wrong time, or if Mrs. M. can't remember how to get to the bus.

Clarifying and selecting goals is a multifold process, involving an understanding of the client's various problems and needs. It is an evolving process that undergoes refinement and reassessment in working with clients over an extended period of time.

Encouraging Client Input

Practitioners sometimes have difficulty in getting their clients to participate in setting goals. Entrenched negative perceptions can keep clients from believing that their needs can be met. They also may have a conflict about making some type of changes, such as moving from a posture of dependency (Kanter, 1985). Effective contending with these conscious and unconscious blocks to involvement in goal setting can include: waiting patiently—assisting strategically when appropriate; taking a lead role in early decision-making to get things moving; partializing—working on one goal, possibly short-term, at a time, moving to the next goal only after initial success (Ballew & Mink, 1986).

Many of the clients do not comprehend how they can move on from a powerless, one-crisis-after-another existence. While total "cure" usually is not possible, the client and practitioner can work toward greater comfort, independence, and capability. This needs to be explained to clients. Individuals can, through the very process of setting goals, begin to take control of their lives and enhance the quality of their existence.

SUMMARY

The model of comprehensive enhancement practice indicates that intake, assessment, and setting goals are an interrelated and overlapping set of functions in the early phase of service. The end product of this phase is a set of aims upon which the practitioner and the client will base an individualized intervention plan. These goals will also serve as a basis for evaluation as the practice process proceeds.

Intake establishes whether there is a client–agency match. It should be initiated in a timely fashion in order not to discourage the client's motivation. Since the practitioner and the client will be working together for a long time, interpersonal engagement is an important feature from the beginning. Information is exchanged so that the client knows what to expect and the practitioner can obtain an initial understanding of the client-in-situation. Working problem statements are developed.

Assessment has to be broad, frequently involving other disciplines, agencies, and family members. Psychological, medical, and social factors are considered in order to adequately determine the client's needs and resources. Assessment includes gathering case history data, establishing current functioning, and clarifying problems. The practitioner, through assessment, aims to define the areas of the client's life that need support.

Setting goals is the bridge to intervention planning. The case manager and the client, in a collaborative process, determine the service objectives that are attainable, specific, and measurable. Time frames, priorities, and preferences come into play. Setting goals involves decision making about enhancing the client's ongoing capacity to function satisfactorily in the community.

REFERENCES

Austin, C. D. (1981). Client assessment in context. In H. Weissman, I. Epstein, & A. Savage (Eds.), *Agency-based social work: Neglected aspects of clinical practice* (83–96). Philadelphia: Temple University Press.

Baker, F. & Burns, T. (1985). The impact of life events on chronic mental patients. *Hospital and Community Psychiatry, 36*(3), 299–301.

Baker, F. & Intagliata, J. (1982). Quality of life in the evaluation of community support systems. *Evaluation and Program Planning, 5,* 69–79.

Ballew, J. R. & Mink, G. (1986). *Case management in the human services.* Springfield, IL: Charles C. Thomas.

Bertsche, A. V. & Horejsi, C. R. (1980). Coordination of client services. In H. Weissman, I. Epstein, & A. Savage (Eds.), *Agency-based social work: Neglected aspects of clinical practice.* Philadelphia: Temple University Press.

Bloom, M., et al. (1971). Interviewing the ill aged. *The Gerontologist, 11* (4, Pt. 1), 292–299.

Burack-Weiss, A. (Fall 1988). Clinical aspects of case management. *Generations,* p. 23–25.

Caires, K. B. & Weil, M. (1985). Developmentally disabled persons and their families. In M. Weil & M. Karls (Eds.), *Case management in human service practice.* San Francisco: Jossey-Bass, Inc.

Cohen, M. B. (November 1989). Social work practice with homeless mentally ill people: Engaging the client. *Social Work Journal,* 505–509.

Corcoran, J. J. & Fischer, J. (1987). *Measures for clinical practice: A sourcebook.* New York: The Free Press.

Davidson, M. & Jamison, P. W. (1983). The clinical social worker and current psychiatric drugs: Some introductory principles. *Clinical Social Work Journal, 11*(2), 139–150.

Diagnostic and statistical manual of mental disorders (1987). Third edition—revised. Washington, D.C. American Psychiatric Association.

Downing, R. (1985). The elderly and their families. In M. Weil & M. Karls (Eds.), *Case management in human service practice.* San Francisco: Jossey-Bass, Inc.

Epstein, L. (1988). Helping people. *The task-centered approach: Vol. 2.* Columbus, OH: Merrill Publishing Co.

Ferdinande, R. J. & Colligan, R. C. (1980). Psychiatric hospitalization: Mainstream reentry planning for adolescent patients. *Exceptional children, 46*(7), 544–547.

Fischer, J. (1978). *Effective casework practice: An eclectic approach.* New York: McGraw-Hill.

Garrison, V. & Podell, J. (1981). Community support systems assessment for use in clinical interviews. *Schizophrenia Bulletin, 7*(1), 101–108.

Gerhart, U. C. (1990). *Caring for the chronic mentally ill.* Itasca, IL: F. E. Peacock.

Germain, C. B. & Gitterman, A. (1980). *The life model of social work practice.* New York: Columbia University Press.

Germain, C. B. & Gitterman, A. (1987). Ecological perspective. In A. Minahan (Ed.), *Encyclopedia of social work* (Vol. 1, p. 495). Silver Spring, MD: National Association of Social Workers.

Gwyther, L. P. (Fall 1988). Assessment: Content, purpose, outcomes. *Generations: Case Management*, pp. 11–15.

Hersen, M. & Bellack, A. S. (Eds). (1976). *Behavioral assessment: A practical handbook.* New York: Pergamon.

Hudson, W. W. (1982). *The clinical measurement package: A field manual.* Homewood, IL: Dorsey.

Identification, case management and treatment of child abuse and/or neglect. Rockville, MD, NIMH, 1977, 159–171 in DHEW Publication No. (ADM) 77–344, Child Abuse and Neglect Programs.

Intagliata, J. (1982). Improving the quality of community care for the chronically mentally disabled: The role of case management. *Schizophrenia Bulletin, 8*(4), 655–674.

Kailes, J. I. & Weil, M. (1985). People with physical disabilities and the independent living model. In Weil M. and Karls J. I. (Eds.), *Case management in human service practice.* San Francisco: Jossey-Bass, Inc.

Kanter, J. S. (Ed.). (1985). *Clinical issues in treating the chronic mentally ill.* San Francisco: Jossey-Bass, Inc.

Kurtz, L. F. & Bagarozzi, D. A. (1984). Case management in mental health. *Health and Social Work (9)3,* 201–211.

Lawton, L. P. & Brody, E. M. (1969). Assessment of older people: Self-maintaining and instrumental activities of daily living. *Gerontologist, 9* (3), 179–186.

Lazarus, A. A. (1971). *Behavior therapy and beyond.* New York: McGraw-Hill.

Los Angeles County Department of Mental Health. (1985). *Human resource development: Issues in case management.*

Los Angeles County Department of Mental Health. (1989). *Case management needs assessment training for departmental trainers.*

Lowy, L. (1985). *Social work with the aging.* New York: Longman.

Meyer, C. H. (1987). Direct practice in social work: Overview. In A. Minahan (Ed.), *Encyclopedia of social work* (Vol. 1, pp. 409–422). Silver Spring, MD: National Association of Social Workers.

Modrcin, M., Rapp, C. A., & Chamberlain, R. (1985). *Case management with psychiatrically disabled individuals: Curriculum & training.* Lawrence, KS: University of Kansas.

Moxley, D. (1989). *The practice of case management.* Newbury Park: Sage Publication.

Northern, H. (1987). Assessment. In A. Minahan (Ed.), *Encyclopedia of social work* (Vol. 1). Silver Spring, MD: National Association of Social Workers.

Platman, S. R., et al. (1982). Case management of the mentally disabled. *Journal of Public Health Policy, 3*(3), 302–314.

Reid, W. J. (1978). *The task-centered system.* New York: Columbia University Press.

Richards, M. & Murphy, P. (Fall 1988). Case management in nursing homes. *Generations: Case management*, pp. 50–53.

Schneider, L. D. & Streuning, E. L. (1983). SLOF: A behavioral rating scale for assessing the mentally ill. *Social Work Research and Abstracts, 19*(2), 9–21.

Silverstone, B. & Burack-Weiss, A. (1983). *Social work practice with the frail elderly and their families.* Springfield, IL: Charles C. Thomas.

Stone, C. & Bernstein, L. (Fall 1980). Case management with borderline children: Theory and practice. *Clinical Social Work Journal, 8*(3), 147–160.

Weil, M. & Karls, M. (1985). *Case management in human service practice.* San Francisco: Jossey-Bass, Inc.

Weissman, H., Epstein, I., & Savage, A. (1983). *Agency-based social work: Neglected aspects of clinical practice.* Philadelphia: Temple University Press.

Wells, S. J. (1985). Children and the child welfare system. In M. Weil and J. M. Karls (Eds.), *Case Management in human service practice* (pp. 119–144). San Francisco: Jossey-Bass, Inc.

Wolkon, G. (1972). Crisis theory: The application for treatment and dependency. *Comprehensive Psychiatry, 13*(5), 459–464.

5

Resource Identification and Intervention Planning

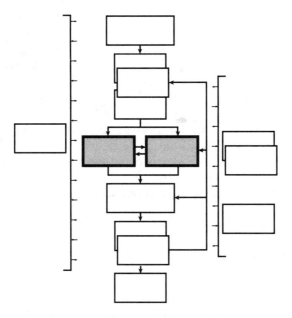

OVERVIEW

Client well-being is advanced by conceiving of beneficial goals and creating the means to bring them about. This chapter emphasizes the issue of means, fortified by Oliver Wendell Holmes' trenchant observation that aims acquire greatness "when greatly pursued." Means involve both a strategic plan and the material elements for its execution: in essence, the functions of intervention planning and resource identification. As the diagram of the comprehensive enhancement model shows, these two functions are in a parallel position in the sequence of practice. This is because once a practice goal is established these functions are alternatives for the next step.

Some practitioners in our field studies proceeded immediately to devise a plan for service, and then sought available resources to implement it. The problem with this is that few communities contain a full array of help-giving components, hence the plan often has to be revised and retrofit accordingly. Recognizing this interplay, other respondents first examined the resource situation and then constructed a feasible plan based on what they knew was accessible to work with. Neither progression commands a consensus of professional opinion or empirical support in the research literature. For this reason, it is useful to think of the step following goal setting as a combination of the two functions, joined together in an order that may vary.

Resource identification is the more straightforward and, in some ways, routine of the two functions. There are prepared indexes, directories, and computer-generated data bases accessible in some agency situations. For this reason, that area is presented briefly and will precede the more complex and demanding function of intervention planning.

RESOURCE IDENTIFICATION AND INDEXING

UNDERSTANDING AND USING RESOURCES

Definition and Context

An intervention plan is obviously enhanced through use of available service resources. Milton Berle was fond of saying that whether you are rich or poor it pays to have money. We can restate that point for our purposes with more propriety: "Because resource identification should be an integral part of service planning, the case manager needs to know what services exist that can help meet a client's needs" (Weil, 1985, p. 33).

Resource identification involves the location of useful services and programs, and indexing includes describing their characteristics and storing the information for easy access. Broadly speaking, this function is an aspect of the information and referral component of the human services, and has been carried out alternatively as part of an individual practitioner's role, as a specialized role in an agency, or by a specialized agency established for this sole purpose. Eighty-eight percent of the practitioners interviewed in the UCLA survey reported engaging in this activity. Those who did not, stated that they wished to but were not given time, or that their own agency provided them with whatever they needed. This function, then, can be carried out by the organizational system rather than the individual case manager.

While compiling resources may be a mechanical task in some circumstances, and an already-completed one in others, the vast proliferation of services in contemporary urban settings can also make the undertaking daunting. Expansion of welfare state features has resulted in a substantial proliferation of services, but not of their coherence. A presidential study group concluded:

> It would be difficult to design, or even imagine, a more confusing, inefficient, costly and less productive enterprise than the existing human services delivery system. For example, there are more than:—140,000 community based organizations, 28,000 local governments, 50 different State governmental configurations. These agencies are funded, guided, guidelined, regulated, visited, assessed, assisted, reviewed, monitored, evaluated, and audited by more than 100 Federal programs in 10 Federal agencies spending $22 billion on human services (Levinson, 1980, p. 15).

An even more vivid image of the tangled maze of service arrangements is contained in Figure 5-1, which shows the number of contacts and interactions that were required for one client in one agency. The visual reflects a set point in time: consider also that policies, programs, funding, eligibility, and staffing are concurrently changing from day to day. Rein (1970) aptly comments that clients are frequently over-serviced but underserved.

Resource Aggregation Methods

Practitioners use a variety of tools to keep abreast of service patterns and to codify the information. Levinson (1981) states that these can range from a battered shoebox file to an ultra high-tech computer system. In the UCLA survey, respondents reported the following as frequent methods:

using an office resource file
making telephone contacts with agencies
gathering information at community and agency meetings
networking and personal exchange with colleagues
making a personal resource book or folder file

Less frequent means included:

receiving information by mail
getting information from a supervisor
using telephone books and directories
using hotline information sources
making a mental note of information that presents itself

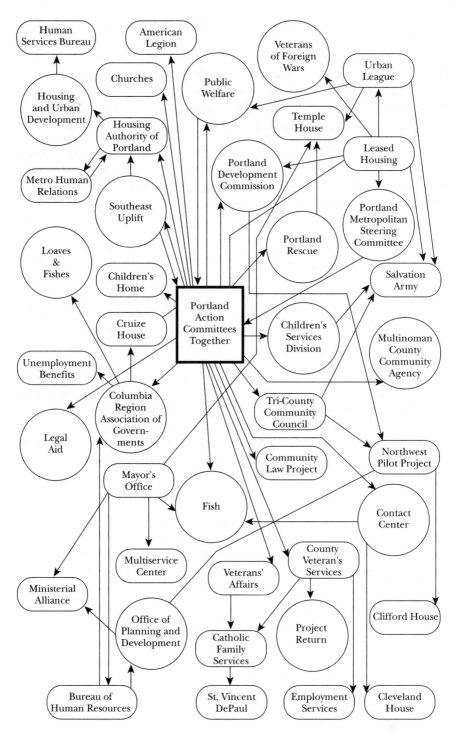

FIGURE 5–1 Frustrations of ping-ponging efforts to obtain services for a client took a caseworker to 41 agencies and required 35 hours. Source: United States General Accounting Office, *Information and Referral for People Needing Human Services* (Washington, D.C.: Comptroller General's Report to Congress, HRD-77-134, March 20, 1978), p. 12.

Further comments by the respondents provide useful elaboration. Usually the practitioners, especially those who were on the job for a longer time, employed several means simultaneously:

> I get resource information in a few different ways: telephone calls, meeting with various agencies, getting information from my supervisor, talking to other social workers, learning about resources through various mailings, and looking in the phone book.

Several respondents noted that this is not necessarily an official part of the job:

> It's something I do wherever I may be going. Anything I read, anyone I talk to, I immediately follow-up or ask a staff person to. It's not like I'm on the phone going through a list. But who knows, I might be out shopping and read something and say, 'Hey, that's something we might be able to use.'

After a time the function may become rather automatic and intuitive, for example:

> It's all in my head. I've been with the department since 1973. I just know the resources. I keep files and folders, but mostly it's all in the computer up here [points to head]. Well, they don't give us any other computers after all.

For the new worker, though, the activity is more difficult and self-conscious. The rookie might start out with a set of typical steps: seeing if there is an office file, networking informally with other workers, checking with the supervisor for leads, creating a personal file, making telephone calls to agencies to verify or clarify information, and later expanding and updating information in the course of community and agency meetings. The objective for many is to get to this kind of situation:

> I have my own, indexed, formalized file of resources (emergency, food, public assistance, housing, alcohol, employment, helplines, etc.)—pretty thorough. I helped put it together as a region-wide thing, and others contributed.

One additional source of information is clients themselves. In speaking with clients about places they turn to for help and what has been useful to them, additional resources surface, some off-the-beaten-track. In some agencies a resource team is established to take responsibility for finding resources for the full staff.

Problems

A number of vexing problems impinge, making this more complicated than initially expected.

Agencies provide inadequate or misleading information:

When you have only a directory book and you can't visit the site, you hope that what they're telling you is what they actually have.

Programs and facilities are in constant flux:

Resources do change so much—some places go out of business, some suddenly require money so that I need more rapport with the free ones—the frustrating thing is that these tend to be less professional.

Atypical clients appear who require supports beyond what is at hand:

I sometimes have to work with a particular client on a particular need. You get to be pretty creative. You go through the telephone book. If this doesn't yield anything (as was the case with a client who was an orthodox Jew and needed special dietary considerations) and I can't find a suitable residence, I call other agencies that may be able to act to bridge the gap. I can spend hours on this.

Most respondents mentioned the importance of this function in their work. They suggested ways to facilitate it, such as having intimate knowledge of the services and facilities through making visits and achieving good communication with a friendly contact person in the facility. At the same time, they pointed out difficulties: the activity takes time, initially and also on an ongoing basis. But time is not always allowed for it.

This kind of activity requires a lot of hours to develop good connections and properly sort out resources. Unfortunately, I receive no credit for the time that I spend developing contacts. I recently met a man who owns several board-and-care facilities. Because he has all kinds of connections I thought it would be very productive to speak with him. However, I had to do it on my own lunch hour in the field. Resource development is not identified with a "case" and, therefore, I receive no time credit for that work. The system's just not set up that way—all of the stats are linked to cases.

Typically when we think of resources we think of formal agencies of various kinds. This has been the emphasis here. But, as we know, community-based resources also include informal networks—families, friends, neighbors, and grassroots organizations. The composition of such networks will vary uniquely for each specific client, and a baseline of such supports cannot be garnered across-the-board and in advance. The informal resource profile, by and large, has to be individually devised at the time. For our purpose here, it is enough to note informal support as another type of helping resource for clients. For more detail see Chapter 8.

Identifying Key Agency Characteristics

There are particular characteristics of resources to keep in mind when making a reconnaissance of the support capability of a community or service area. Some key factors include:

The function of the agency. Is this a single service or multi-service program? What types of service are offered?

There are various ways of categorizing services. Health versus welfare is the broadest. Other service areas include employment, day care, recreation, and mental health. Sometimes services are visualized along the life cycle: children, youth, family, and aging. One of the most comprehensive and widely used classifications is the Service Identification System of the United Way, which is by goals and sub-goals of human service agencies.

Access and eligibility. Who can obtain the services? What are the requirements?

Is it necessary to reside in the service area (county, city)? Does economic status apply (below the poverty line)? Is the character of the client's condition relevant (severity of mental illness)? Is age, religion, ethnicity, gender, or other personal characteristics a consideration? Is it necessary to be a member of the organization (such as with the YWCA)?

Fees. Is there a price tag for this service and is this flexible?

Many social services are given at no cost. With increasing budget constraints and privatization of services, fees are becoming more common. It is necessary to know whether the service is free and if not, whether there is a standardized fixed cost for everyone, or if there are exceptions, "scholarships," and sliding scales based on ability to pay.

Availability. How accessible is the service and with what ease of initiation?

Is there a waiting list before onset of service? How long is the wait and is there any flexibility in this? What are the hours of service, including evenings and weekends? Where is the service located (in a remote area of the community or at a central, convenient geographic point)? Is public transportation available to the location?

Quality and reliability. Is this a high standard service and is it provided in a stable manner?

What kind of reputation does this agency have? Is it well established? What has been your previous experience with clients linked to this program? Are the professionals well trained? Has the funding pattern been consistent or are policies and programs subject to sudden or frequent fluctuations?

Climate and accommodations. Is the ecology of service user-friendly?

Is the service style receptive and congenial to clients? What is the ethnic orientation and composition of staff? Is there a multi-lingual capability on site? Is the physical set-up comfortable, reasonably aesthetic, and respectful of privacy? Is the place hassle-free?

Key people in the system.   *Are there some key people who the practitioner can relate to in a productive way?*

Is there a specific contact person the case manager can rely on for information and help? Should the client make contact directly or should the practitioner call first? Who should the client see for reception, who should be avoided? Which staff members are best for specific clients or needs? Who controls decisions about acceptance for service, service provisions, and assignment of staff?

This type of information can easily be put into a loose-leaf notebook that the worker uses to index resources. A sample form for this is suggested in Figure 5-2. Such a personal notebook can be used as a tailored supplement when the agency or service unit keeps such information centrally. In that case, the unit secretary or a designated staff member is ordinarily responsible for beginning and updating such a resource file. In either case, pages can be indexed by type of service, geographic area, or other categories that optimize the planning of intervention.

FIGURE 5–2   Resource Agency Identification Form

Agency Name _____

Address _____ Telephone ( ) _____

Service Area _____

Hours of Service _____

Transportation/Directions _____

_____

Services _____

_____

_____

Eligibility _____ Fee Requirements _____

Waiting Period _____

Languages Spoken _____

Ethnic/Religious Orientation _____

_____

Agency Climate _____

_____

Key Contacts _____

_____

Comments: Quality of service, special services offered, who is not served well, reliability, etc. _____

_____

_____

_____

INTERVENTION PLANNING

UNDERSTANDING INTERVENTION PLANNING

Definition of the Concept

Someone once defined planning as the act of thinking about what to do about certain human affairs, while life is meanwhile bringing these affairs to a firm conclusion. The aim of professional intervention is to somehow actually shape beneficial outcomes, even if this runs counter to natural proclivities.

Intervention planning is a vital link in the chain of functions in the comprehensive enhancement model, and indeed, has been identified by Schneider (1988) as the core case management function. In this function the practitioner concretely addresses the client's problems by formulating a structured plan for achieving both short- and long-term goals. This is in keeping with professional intervention methods generally, but there are particular emphases unique to work with highly vulnerable clients.

This function adds a sense of motion to the model. Up to this point, the practitioner's attention has been focused on understanding the pain and needs of the client. Intervention planning focuses on means. It provides a route for reaching the highest level of client fulfillment in a natural community setting.

Although the development of a plan of action for meeting client needs is an essential aspect of service provision, this step from assessment to the crafting of a concrete intervention plan may be "the most poorly specified part of the case management process" (Kane, 1985, p. 190). Many writers fail to separate intervention planning from assessment and goal setting, or they dismiss it in a sentence as the clerical task of filling out a form documenting how needs will be met. Figure 5-3 depicts intervention planning and presents a structure for the discussion that follows.

Treatment and Service Aspects

Intervention planning encompasses both *treatment planning,* in the sense of therapy and counseling, and *service planning,* which involves the linking of clients to external agencies and informal networks for more varied and comprehensive assistance (Schneider, 1988). We have shown that this entails a "person-in-environment" helping perspective. The client's personal rights, needs, and goals are considered in their interrelatedness with the external realities of physical space, social supports, family structure, and the community's social and political climate (Germain & Gitterman, 1987, and Chapter 3). The disciplined emphasis in this type of service on situational analysis and linkage is what gives the practice a distinctive character. This two-pronged outlook must inform all aspects of intervention planning.

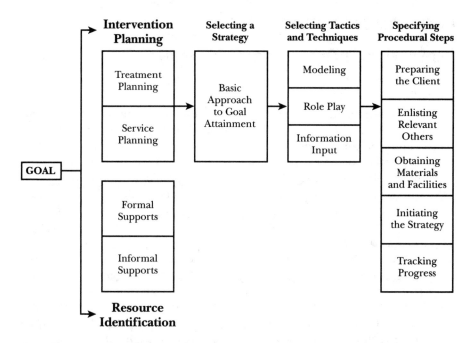

FIGURE 5–3   Diagram of intervention planning and resource identification

To illustrate, hypothetically, is Mrs. Westly, who has been taken to the emergency room with symptoms of hyperventilation. The practitioner discovers that Mrs. Westly is the sole caretaker for her husband, who is in declining health and requires round-the-clock care. She has refused any offers of assistance because she is highly independent and suspicious of all strangers, afraid they will take advantage of her and her husband. The intervention plan for Mrs. Westly is two-pronged. The psychologically oriented treatment plan could recommend a support group for Mrs. Westly as she continues in her role of primary caretaker, as well as counseling to address and lower her suspiciousness (so she can access other forms of service). The situation-oriented service plan would address community agency resources for concrete help in the home to care for her husband and to manage housekeeping tasks.

Strategic and Procedural Aspects

The intervention plan is a design of action that incorporates strategic elements and procedural elements. The case manager must strategize about how best to achieve the goal previously determined. These strategies may range from developing client skills to changing aspects of the environment, and are discussed in more detail in the section on practice guidelines for intervention planning.

Procedural elements specify how the strategy will be enacted. This includes the tasks to be carried out by both practitioner and client—the sequencing of steps, logistics of timing and coordination, the anticipating of obstacles and calculating how to overcome them. As with other aspects of case management, research indicates that the clients should be involved to a substantial extent in intervention planning as they are often able to accurately identify their own needs, thus contributing to more effective service outcomes (Ewalt & Honeyfield, 1981). Also, involving the client in the planning process generates motivation to use the services delineated in the plan (Gerhart, 1990, p. 213). Involvement in the planning process may also be a significant way to build a sense of confidence and competence in the client.

> The specificity of the service plan makes it a useful therapeutic and planning tool for the client, involving him or her deeply in problem solving and decision making. This involvement is the earliest step toward client empowerment in the case management process (Weil, 1985, p. 368).

Components of the Intervention Plan

Intervention planning results in a tangible treatment–service plan, which often takes the form of a written document with several basic features. It can comprise a contract between the client and practitioner. Although the particulars of such plans vary, it is generally agreed that the following aspects are necessary.

Clearly defined goals.   This feature requires the practitioner to determine which needs are most significant, or in what order they most logically flow. It reflects the case management principle of individualization of services, as the client's own particular situation serves as the basis for identifying the goals.

High potential for attainment.   For example, the intervention plan might specify if the family or neighbors are to be used for social support; if economic enhancement would be sought through Supplementary Security Income or self-employment; if insight counseling or behavioral teaching of skills would be emphasized. Resource identification needs to take place as a component of this. The strategy ordinarily entails an interrelated treatment plan and service plan. Strategic considerations are expanded upon in the next section, which reviews relevant research.

Specific actions.   Here, detailed, step-by-step planning allows the practitioner to clearly delineate the tasks assigned to client and practitioner, and the manner in which these tasks will be accomplished. It is also a way to make sure that the objectives are not unreasonable or impossible for the client or the agency to achieve.

Realistic time frames.   Many cases require the provision of services on a long-term, indeterminate basis, but the specificity of the intervention plan (in terms of actions, actors, and agencies) requires time-related planning within a more open-ended context. This fosters accountability and facilitates monitoring.

Potential barriers.   Potential barriers can include eligibility criteria, client attitudes or resistance, and nonexistent services. The intervention plan, in tandem with resource analysis, should identify and anticipate these obstacles and suggest ways to surmount them.

In addition, a calculation of the costs of providing services for a specific period of time with an indication of the sources of payment is required by many agencies. Fiscal elements, including feasibility, need to enter into designing a plan.

Intervention Principles for Plan Design

Intervention planning is guided by basic principles on which practitioners generally agree (Gerhart, 1990; Schneider, 1988). Key points, some of which have been discussed in a more general context, include:

1. Individualizing services
2. Providing comprehensive aid
3. Addressing parsimony
4. Fostering client empowerment
5. Addressing cultural differences
6. Assuring continuity of care

Individualizing services. Individualization of services considers the uniqueness of each person with regard to such factors as differential response to medication, emotional development, and level of socialization. Therefore no two clients are to be treated exactly alike and intervention plans cannot be standardized. Because the intervention plan is unique, it needs to be altered as circumstances in each individual's life change.

For example, a practitioner at a homeless shelter prepares intervention plans for two women who appear similar in terms of age, number of children, racial and cultural background, and who are both married to violent, abusive men. Nevertheless, these two women are not identical, and may differ significantly with regard to their ability to handle cramped living quarters, to care for their children, or to manage appointment calendars. The intervention plans prepared for these two women should reflect their uniqueness. In a sense, discerning individual characteristics is part of the assessment function, but often the picture is not complete until the planning stage when the client has some concrete options to consider.

Providing comprehensive aid.   *Comprehensive service* includes planning for all services that are appropriate for the client, both formal and informal. Because human needs are so diverse, and the tasks of this process so encompassing, the intervention plan has to have a cross-sectional perspective (Schneider, 1988). Planning for an elderly individual might include medical treatment, aid with transportation, homemaker service, and visits from kin.

Addressing parsimony.   The principle of *parsimony* refers both to cost consciousness and the provision of services that are targeted with some precision. In other words, neither too many nor too few services should be planned. Duplication ought to be avoided. Generally, expecting clients to deal with more than two or three service organizations at one time creates an obstacle to service delivery (Gerhart, 1990). Intervention planning needs to take into account the capability of people with severe vulnerabilities to keep track of procedural requirements such as numerous dates and places for appointments, to manage transportation, and to arrange child care. Too many referrals may overwhelm clients and discourage them from making any attempt to contact the service agencies, while insufficient referrals may frustrate clients and in other ways curtail progress.

Fostering client empowerment.   Client empowerment, as we know, is fostered when the client participates to the maximum degree feasible in the selection of approaches and services. This deflects the practitioner from being overprotective. Consideration of client rights overlaps this principle. In the process of intervention planning, clients ought to be informed of their rights to challenge an assessment or refuse a service. They should be entitled to evaluate and provide feedback on the quality of the service (Downing, 1985, p. 163). Enabling clients to be their own case managers, by including them in the intervention planning process, is a vital way to address issues of clients' rights and to maximize long-term client capability for self-direction.

Addressing cultural differences.   Cultural relevance requires that the intervention plan take into account the values, norms, and language patterns of the clients being served. For example, with Mexican Americans the folk medicine *curandero* approach to health service could be drawn on. With Asian Americans the views and needs of elders in the family have to be given special prominence. Certain behavioral patterns, such as low-assertiveness, which are considered dysfunctional in American society, are accepted as appropriate in other ethnic groups. These cultural expressions need to be acknowledged in the plan design.

Assuring continuity of care.   The principle of *continuity of care* applies to providing services on a long-term, indeterminate basis. The assumption behind the principle of continuity of care, or permanency planning, as we have seen previously, is that there is often no ultimate cure for the client's condition, such as is the case with the frail elderly, orphaned children, and the persistently mentally ill. The intervention plan, accordingly, must look toward providing services on an open-ended basis, for as long as the impairment or condition hinders the functioning of the client.

The notion of time-limited planning (Schneider, 1988), in which the practitioner makes plans for a bounded period of time, is consistent with and supplements the principle of continuity of care. Time-limited planning clarifies both for the client and for the professional what is expected and in what time frame, along a sequential course. Having a definite time set for reassessment or completion works against creating dependency in the client. A bounded plan is important for those particular clients who may be able to work toward emancipation or a recovery date, or those who are in the midst of learning new methods of coping.

It is evident that intervention planning draws on information that has already been obtained in the assessment and goal setting functions, and in resource identification. The product of these functions shapes the intervention plan, which in turn enables the case manager to link clients with both formal and informal sources of assistance.

Professional judgment gauges the client's appropriateness and eligibility for services. As the practitioner writes the intervention plan, discernment and discipline assist in the selection of appropriate types of services, and in choosing between goals that may be in conflict, such as autonomy at the expense of security. While intervention plans are created in concert with clients and other colleagues, ultimately they are the responsibility of practitioners. As Kane (1985, p. 190) phrases it, "The road from the assessment tool to the care plan is still paved by clinical judgement." Both client input and professional responsibility are necessary, and there is a potentially creative tension between the two.

PRACTICE GUIDELINES FOR INTERVENTION PLANNING

This section examines how an intervention plan is constructed, including both strategic and procedural elements. The case manager faces two related tasks, each containing a series of decisions: (1) identifying plausible strategies and techniques, and (2) operationalizing strategic approaches into procedures.

Criteria for Designing a Strategy

After completing the functions of assessment and goal setting, the case manager determines the type of change required to reach the stated goal. The practitioner may consider internal change, such as altering the client's cognition or emotional state, or external change, focusing on altering the client's environment.

For example, Jim, a latency-age child in foster placement who demonstrates excessive aggression at school, may benefit from an intervention plan that focuses on internal changes, such as increasing self-control through role playing appropriate behavior, while he remains in the current foster home and in a regular classroom. A different intervention plan would result from a focus on external change, on the assumption that a more powerful environmental impact is necessary. This might involve removal from the home to a more structured setting, or enrollment in a special education class designed for the aggressive child. If the case manager decides that both types of change are necessary, the intervention plan might include a combination of strategies.

Each strategy selected for possible inclusion in the intervention plan needs to be evaluated specifically in terms of its applicability to the individual client's situation, thereby employing the principle of individualization of services.

Suggested criteria, adapted from Gambrill (1983), include the following:

1. Feasibility

Can this strategy be used given the constraints of the situation?

In Jim's case, a plausible external strategy for change involves situational structuring. This entails working with the teacher and foster parents to introduce a program that sets clear and consistent limits for behavior in the classroom and at home and provides immediate caring feedback. The child is already linked to these two sources of aid. The objective is to strengthen the linkages and maximize appropriate helping capabilities. Given the constraints of Jim's hypothetical classroom, with a full complement of students, with limited teacher resources and an already stressed relationship between Jim and teacher, is this strategy feasible? Is the teacher equipped to or willing to cooperate? Can the proposed program mesh with existing classroom routines? Is Jim capable of learning new behaviors in this situation? Clearly, the idea of the approach should be discussed thoroughly with the parents, the teacher, and Jim before deciding to proceed. All individuals should participate actively in assessing the plan as it proceeds.

2. Effectiveness

Will this strategy effectively produce the desired change?
Is it efficient?
What are the positive and negative side effects?
Can the plan be generalized beyond the immediate situation?
Will the effects last?
Will it lead to measurable, reasonably immediate results?

With reference to our example, the strategy for the classroom might reduce Jim's aggressive behavior in that situation, but will it foster new positive behaviors elsewhere? How much time and energy on the part of the school and the child will be involved in producing change? Is this the most efficient option in terms of time and effort by the teacher? Does it involve unfavorable changes in the classroom environment? How will achieving the change through this strategy affect the teacher's overall relationship with the child? Once the program stops or the school year ends, is there any reason to believe that the effects created by this intervention strategy will continue? Can the program be designed so that results in classroom behavior change can be measured and identified immediately, both by the practitioner and Jim? Does the approach need to be supplemented by counseling with the child?

3. Acceptability

Is this strategy culturally appropriate?
Does it match the value system and frame of reference of the participants?
Does it have a positive rather than a punitive focus?

A program that sets clear limits for behavior and provides immediate feedback requires the cooperation of the child and the child's peers, as well as the teacher and the foster parents. Will the foster parents have culturally based objections to singling the child out among classmates for this kind of attention in class? Will this strategy produce change without encroaching on some aspects of the child's assertiveness that are valued by the family? Will the foster parents regard this as a helpful strategy, or will they resist its implementation? It is a less intrusive strategy than removing Jim from the school entirely, but will it further isolate Jim from his peers?

4. Implementability

Can this strategy be made operational?
Are there techniques available for carrying out this strategy?

The strategy can be conceptualized as effecting change in the aggressive child's self-control by altering the classroom and home environment through a special program to include clear limits for behavior and immediate feedback. Is it possible to do this in a realistic, systematic manner, with practical steps that lead toward achievable results? Is the teacher sufficiently knowledgeable and reliable for taking the necessary steps? Is the strategy consistent with the policies, norms, and procedures of the school? Will more information or training for the teacher be needed in order to implement this strategy?

Strategies for Problems of Vulnerable Populations

If intervention planning is perceived as the means by which the client is guided to arrive at intended end states, then planning needs to incorporate strategies that can accomplish these objectives. For long-term vulnerable clients such end states can include greater assertiveness, better social skills, and increased ability to locate employment, each responsive to a problem condition impeding the client. Practitioners faced with choosing a strategy can be aided by examining empirical studies that bear on these issues.

A useful synthesis of research supporting this purpose was compiled by Krumboltz, Becker-Haven, and Burnett (1979). The discussion that follows reflects their analysis and describes specific studies that are relevant to client problems frequently encountered in severely vulnerable populations.

The discussion emphasizes approaches involving internal processes, but planning typically includes a wider range of factors than the single strategy addressed. Treatment planning and service planning are clearly the necessary components of a rounded intervention strategy. For example, modeling may be an approach chosen to increase assertiveness, but at the same time a comprehensive intervention plan would include more diverse elements, such as linking the client with agencies dealing with financial aid or housing, or activating informal supports. A range of family members, agency professionals, or neighbors can be brought into the plan to foster greater assertiveness. Assertiveness can be tied to greater client initiative in pursuing external services. In comprehensive enhancement, the practitioner may be viewed as orchestrating a helping strategy that involves several themes and a small system of collateral helpers. The traditional concept of therapist as sole operator does not apply.

Unemployment. Many vulnerable clients have difficulty in finding employment, owing to a physical disability, advanced age, or cognitive deficits. The case manager may assist these clients in acquiring job interviewing and job searching skills. Several training programs are available for the case manager, including such techniques as simulated job interviews and videotaped feedback (although research does not reveal which specific components of these programs make them effective).

An encouraging study by Azrin, Flores, and Kaplan (1975) describes the development of a job club in which participants emphasized sharing job leads in the framework of a support group, and learned new skills such as resume writing and searching help wanted ads. The modeling and rehearsing of job search skills proved successful in assisting participants in getting jobs, and at a higher starting salary than those in the control group. Direct contact by the practitioner to selected potential employers might appropriately accompany this strategy.

Low Assertiveness. Many vulnerable clients have a low level of assertiveness because of long-standing impairments such as physical or mental disability. Clients who have a low level of assertiveness may benefit from instruction in appropriate interpersonal skills (Twentyman & McFall,

1975). An effective approach is to focus on changing cognitive self-statements from negative to positive (Wolfe & Fodor, 1977). Once clients can conceive of themselves in positive ways, their anxiety is reduced and they are able to use the new interpersonal skills. A spouse, residence manager, or day-care professional can be enlisted as part of the plan to encourage affirmative self-expression.

Social Isolation. Lack of social contact is a problem faced by the elderly, persistently mentally ill, and abandoned children, whose life situations inhibit social interactions. Practitioners may link their clients to an adult day-care situation or after-school program to counteract loneliness. Research suggests that this intervention is most effective when clients are coached in friendship skills.

Research with socially isolated children indicates that instruction, with encouragement, in the development of friendship skills is more effective than using peer-pairing—also referred to as a "buddy system" (Oden & Asher, 1977). Clients may lack the skills needed for cooperative behavior and friendship with peers. Several studies have identified four skill areas as important to peer acceptance: *participation, cooperation, communication,* and *validation* (Hartup, 1970). Oden and Asher (1977) developed a friendship skills training sequence with a set format:

1. Verbal instruction
2. Practice of skills with peer
3. Evaluation and discussion between instructor and client
4. Suggestion to use skills on a daily basis

Excessive Aggression. Uncontrolled aggressive behavior is a symptom of some clients who have endured long-term frustrations growing out of the limitations they experience. The mentally ill sometimes exhibit this behavior, as do neglected or abused children. This aggressive behavior, in addition to affecting general relationships and adjustment, may prohibit the client from effectively linking with referrals or from being accepted at recommended residential or family placements. The reduction of aggressive behavior requires the acquisition of new overt social behaviors by the client. At the same time, contact can be made with the family, an employer, or residential home to urge tolerance and encourage assistance to the client while he or she works at behavior change.

Studies with aggressive school-age boys indicate that impulsive associative processing dominates over verbal mediation (Camp, 1977; Camp, Zimet, Van Doornick & Dahlem, 1977; Goodwin & Mahoney, 1975), suggesting it is useful to plan intervention strategies that teach the client self-instructions to use in the presence of signals that formerly provoked aggressive responses. Novaco (1977) has developed a cognitive behavioral treatment approach that has been applied effectively with adults. His "stress inoculation" program includes assisting the client in creating self-instructions for each of the four stages of a conflict situation:

1. Getting ready for a provocation
2. Impact and confrontation
3. Managing arousal
4. Consequent reflection.

These elements can be readily included in a treatment plan.

Physical Pain. Elderly clients and those with physical disabilities and serious medical conditions may have to cope with chronic pain. Strategies for pain alleviation may include helping clients to control the perception of physical pain. Several studies (Chaves & Barber, 1974; Levendusky & Pankratz, 1975; Spanos, Horton & Chaves, 1975) demonstrate that this can be done by training clients in various coping strategies, such as imagining pleasant activities or developing an insensitivity to pain. Relaxation exercises have been demonstrated to be effective in the alleviation of the clinical pain of migraine headaches (Chesney & Shelton, 1976; Cox, Freundlich & Meyer, 1975; Epstein, Hersen & Hemphill, 1974; Mitchell & White, 1976), dysmenorrhea (Tasto & Chesney, 1974), and phantom limb pain (McKechnie, 1975).

A broad-spectrum pain reduction plan may be most effective, as Holyrod, Andrasik, and Westbrook (1977) suggest. In their study, subjects were taught stress-coping skills that focused on distinguishing the precursors and consequences of tension-generating behavior, reappraising perspectives and beliefs about the stressful circumstances, and learning new self-instructions or ways to use imagery in coping with pain.

This array of techniques provides potent components for an intervention strategy. The intervention plan, as we have suggested, may involve the practitioner serving as a consultant to other helping professionals in outside agencies or family members, rather than providing counseling or other services directly to the client.

Selecting Techniques Within a Strategy

Strategies aimed at developing new behavior may draw on specific techniques such as modeling and behavior rehearsal. These techniques, and other forms of the behavior modification approach, are effective strategies for enhancing client assertiveness, developing social skills, and finding employment.

Model presentation. Model presentation refers to the acquisition of new behavior by observing someone else perform the behavior. For example, to provide self-instruction to Jim in the example, demonstrations of children successfully handling problem situations can be shown on videotape to parents.

Modeling is most successful when the behaviors which it is intended to foster are easily observable and concrete. Components involved in the effective use of modeling include identification of the behaviors to be developed or increased; demonstration of an appropriate model that the observer is able to scrutinize; ability of the observer to imitate the behavior and to retain the behavioral components; and reinforcement for imitating the behavior (Gambrill, 1983). An illustration in our continuing case example might be to pair Jim for team work with children who ordinarily exhibit the desired behavior and to reward the team for its success. Jim might be asked to enact the desired behavior in a trial that serves as rehearsal.

Behavior rehearsal. Behavior rehearsal consists of the simulation of selected interactions and is also known by the term *role playing*. This technique can be effectively used in combination with a model presentation. Behavior rehearsal teaches new skills but can also provide an avenue for participants to understand what it feels like to be in a particular situation. When instructions are clearly defined and constructive feedback is given, behavior rehearsal offers a safe environment in which to practice skills.

Cognitive methods. Cognitive methods of change involve altering the functions of environmental events and feelings so that they result in cues for constructive thoughts, feelings, or actions rather than dysfunctional ones. For example, clients who cope with chronic pain can learn to transform the trigger of a stressful events into a cue for the use of a relaxation exercise. In Jim's example, instances of threat and competition might be a stimulus to trigger aggression. A cooperative approach using collaborative teams might be a stimulus-control procedure established as the usual classroom routine.

Providing information. For some clients, an appropriate strategy involves providing helpful information rather than specifically altering behavior. Clients frequently request facts on how to obtain certain results. For example, elderly tenants on a fixed income who face a sharp increase in rent may request information about their legal rights as tenants or about alternative housing arrangements. Parents who are anxious and preoccupied with their child's behavior might become calmer upon learning that the behavior reflects normal child development. The foster parents in Jim's case could perhaps benefit from this kind of input. An information-giving approach is useful when there are no serious emotional blocks or cognitive limitations that stand in the way of using new knowledge.

Transforming a Design into Implementation Procedures

An intervention plan is in contract form for implementation to the extent that it is an explicit agreement or understanding between client and practitioner about a course of action (Epstein, 1988). Both written and oral contracts are used, depending on the preference of practitioner and client. The intervention plan, in this formalized state, makes evident the target problem and goals, client and practitioner tasks, and logistical elements such as scheduling, location, and duration of the intervention. In this sense, a contract is a shared articulation of the intervention plan, in written or unwritten form.

Identifying operational tasks. Operational tasks in the plan state the specific actions the client or worker is to take. They may be broken down into subtasks and constitute the procedural aspects of the plan. The following example illustrates the correct and incorrect way to subdivide tasks.

Correct	1. Provide information to teacher regarding how to conduct self-instruction, behavior rehearsal, and use of timeouts.
	2. Reach agreement with teacher, Jim, and foster parents on the specifics of the special program.
	3. Provide referral for foster parents to parent education classes at Hill Community Center.
	4. Schedule weekly appointments with Jim for counseling and to monitor progress of program.
Incorrect	1. Set up program.
	2. Counsel Jim.

Remember that the idea of task planning is to clarify and specify procedures for both client and practitioner. Minor details should be handled in a common-sense manner and not be allowed to clutter and overmechanize the process. Logistical considerations such as scheduling, location, and duration of the intervention should reflect the reasonable level of precision and specificity of the formulated intervention plan. The anticipation of any obstacles to service use and delivery, and the proposed solutions to these obstacles, may be stated in a similar manner as follows.

Duration	Arrange conference with teacher within 2 weeks. Set up meeting with foster parents, Jim, and teacher to occur within 1 month.
Location	Meetings will be held in the conference room at Washington Elementary School.
Potential obstacle	Jim may resist the program and demand to go home.
Proposed solution	Include foster parents and teacher in session with Jim to demonstrate that all three are in agreement that Jim will be obliged to cooperate with the program at school.

Activating intervention principles. After focusing on procedural elements, it is valuable to examine how the principles of intervention planning discussed at the beginning of the chapter impinge on the overall plan. A review of any particular plan considers the degree to which it reflects general principles of intervention planning and incorporates aspects of resource identification.

1. Individualization of services. *Does this intervention plan fit the unique aspects of the client's situation?* Will it provide Jim with the structure he needs in school as well as equipping the foster parents to handle his agitation at home?

2. Comprehensiveness of service delivery. *Does this intervention plan cover all supports that are appropriate for the client?* Have those resources been identified and found to be available in the community? Are there untapped informal resources such as friends and neighbors who can give the foster parents a reprieve while maintaining the environment Jim needs?

3. Parsimonious service. *Are the services provided through this plan neither too few nor too many for the client to use?* Will Jim and his family be overwhelmed by all the logistical aspects of this plan, or will they perhaps feel as though nothing much is being done?

4. Fostering empowerment. *Does this intervention plan deflect the practitioner from exerting excessive control?* Is it clear that the foster parents and the teacher agree with the approach and are willing to learn to assist Jim in this way? Can they change or discard the approach? Does Jim understand what is being done and what it can contribute to his development? Will there be provision for reassessment to determine when a less intrusive strategy is appropriate?

5. Continuity of care. *Does this intervention plan allow for the provision of services on a long-term, indeterminate basis, while also making arrangements for a bounded period of time?* As a foster child, Jim may require services for many years, yet this particular issue of excessive aggression at school may be time-limited. The practitioner should be alert to monitoring unproductive aggressive behavior in other settings and over time.

The most exquisitely designed plan is of little use if it is not applied. In comprehensive enhancement practice, this involves linking the client to service agencies in the community, enhancing linkage with informal social supports, or providing counseling. It could also entail advocacy. These are areas that we will turn to next.

REFERENCES

Azrin, N. H., Flores, R., & Kaplan, S. J. (1975). Job-find club: A group-assisted program for obtaining employment. *Behavior Research and Therapy, 13,* 17–27.

Camp, B. W. (1977). Verbal mediation in young aggressive boys. *Journal of Abnormal Psychology, 86,* 145–153.

Camp, B. W., Zimet, S. G., Van Doornick, W. J. & Dahlem, N. W. (1977). Verbal abilities in young aggressive boys. *Journal of Educational Psychology, 69,* 129–135.

Chaves, J. F. & Barber, T. X. (1974). Cognitive strategies, experimenter modeling, and expectation in the attenuation of pain. *Journal of Abnormal Psychology, 83,* 356–363.

Chesney, M. A. & Shelton, J. L. (1976). A comparison of muscle relaxation and electromyogram biofeedback treatments for muscle contraction headache. *Journal of Behavior Therapy and Experimental Psychiatry, 7,* 221–225.

Cox, D. J., Freundlich, A. & Meyer, R. G. (1975). Differential effectiveness of electromyograph feedback, verbal relaxation instructions, and medication placebo with tension headaches. *Journal of Consulting and Clinical Psychology, 43,* 892–898.

Downing, R. (1985). The elderly and their families. In M. Weil & M. Karls (Eds.), *Case management in human service practice* (pp. 145–167). San Francisco: Jossey-Bass.

Epstein, L. (1988). *Helping people: The task-centered approach.* Columbus, OH: Merrill Publishing Company.

Epstein, L. H., Hersen, M., & Hemphill, D. P. (1974). Music feedback in the treatment of tension headache: An experimental case study. *Journal of Behavior Therapy and Experimental Psychiatry, 5,* 59–63.

Ewalt, P. & Honeyfield, R. (1981). Needs of persons in long-term care. *Social Work, 26*(3), 223–231.

Gambrill, E. (1983). *Casework: A competency-based approach.* Englewood Cliffs, NJ: Prentice-Hall.

Gerhart, U. C. (1990). *Caring for the chronic mentally ill.* Itasca, IL: F. E. Peacock Publishers.

Germain, C. B. & Gitterman, A. (1987). Ecological perspective. In *Encyclopedia of social work* (Vol. 1, pp. 488–499). Silver Springs, MD: National Association of Social Workers.

Goodwin, S. E. & Mahoney, M. J. (1975). Modification of aggression through modeling: An experimental probe. *Journal of Behavior Therapy and Experimental Psychiatry, 6,* 200–202.

Hartup, W. W. (1970). Peer interaction and social organization. In P. Mussen (Ed.), *Carmichael's manual of child psychology* (Vol. 2). New York: Wiley.

Holyrod, K. A., Andrasik, F., & Westbrook, T. (1977). Cognitive control of tension headache. *Cognitive Therapy and Research, 1,* 121–133.

Kane, R. A. (1985). Case management in health care settings. In M. Weil & M. Karls (Eds.), *Case management in human service practice* (pp. 170–203). San Francisco: Jossey-Bass.

Krumboltz, J. D., Becker-Haven, J. F. & Burnett, K. F. (1979). Counseling psychology. In M. R. Rosenzweig & L. W. Porter (Eds.), *Annual review of psychology* (pp. 556–602). Palo Alto, CA: Annual Reviews Inc.

Levendusky, P. & Pankratz, L. (1975). Case reports and comments: Self-control techniques as an alternative to pain medication. *Journal of Abnormal Psychology, 84,* 165–168.

Levinson, R. W. (1981). Information and referral services. In N. Gilbert & H. Specht (Eds.), *Handbook of the social services* (pp. 13–34). Englewood Cliffs, NJ: Prentice Hall.

McKechnie, R. J. (1975). Relief from phantom limb pain by relaxation exercises. *Journal of Behavior Therapy and Experimental Psychiatry, 6,* 262–263.

Mitchell, K. R. & White, R. G. (1976). Self-management of tension headaches: A case study. *Journal of Behavior Therapy and Experimental Psychiatry, 7,* 387–389.

Novaco, R. W. (1977). A stress inoculation approach to anger management in the training of law enforcement officers. *American Journal of Community Psychology, 5,* 327–346.

Oden, S. & Asher, S. R. (1977). Coaching children in social skills for friendship making. *Child Development, 48,* 495–506.

Rein, M. (1970). Coordination of social services. In M. Rein (Ed.), *Social policy: Issues of choice and change,* (pp. 103–137). New York: Random House.

Schneider, B. (1988). Care planning: The core of case management. *Generations,* Fall, 16–18.

Spanos, N. P., Horton, C., & Chaves, J. F. (1975). The effects of two cognitive strategies on pain threshold. *Journal of Abnormal Psychology, 84,* 677–681.

Tasto, D. L. & Chesney, M. A. (1974). Muscle relaxation treatment for primary dysmenorrhea. *Behavior Therapy, 5,* 668–672.

Twentyman, C. T. & McFall, R. M. (1975). Behavioral training of social skills in shy males. *Journal of Consulting and Clinical Psychology, 43,* 384–395.

Weil, M. (1985). Key components in providing efficient and effective services. In M. Weil & J. M. Karls (Eds.), *Case management in the human services* (pp. 29–71). San Francisco: Jossey Bass.

Wolfe, J. L. & Fodor, I. G. (1977). Modifying assertive behavior in women: A comparison of three approaches. *Behavior Therapy, 8,* 567–574.

6
Counseling and Therapy

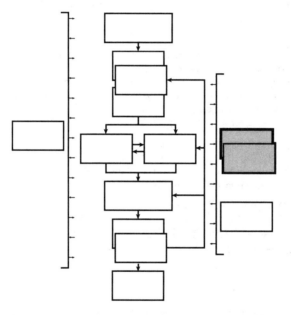

UNDERSTANDING COUNSELING AND THERAPY

The Special Place of Counseling and Therapy

The big advantage of emotions, according to Oscar Wilde, is that they lead us astray. But when someone is already astray, we may be talking here about too much of a good thing. Rather than reveling in further emotional release, counseling or therapy could add up to an advantage.

Counseling and therapy are functions of comprehensive enhancement practice that are provided directly to clients. Unlike linking, which has an environmental focus, these functions deal one-to-one with the cognitive and emotional inner world of the client. This includes aiding the client to use external community supports to greater benefit. The purpose is to strengthen the severely vulnerable client's inner resources and bring about the personal wherewithal to "make it" in the community. This role with vulnerable clients has been described, in part, as follows:

> It is not unusual for frustration, anger, feelings of defeat, and loss of motivation to well up in a client. The response . . . is to sustain the client by imparting hope, by providing praise for his or her efforts, by listening closely to his or her concerns and feelings, and by identifying the small successes and progress the client has made in advancing his or her interests. Thus, empathy, enabling, and sustaining become major strategies. (Moxley, 1989, p. 91)

Counseling and therapy are probably most prominent following intervention planning, as an aspect of plan implementation. Such direct helping, though, is not concentrated at one stage of the process, but rather can come into play at any time. For example, a mentally ill homeless woman may need to be calmed down at intake, reassured, and given information in order to obtain such necessities as food, clothing, or shelter. Only then will the client be freed up to proceed with the other steps in the process.

Differences Between Counseling and Therapy

It would be precarious to draw ironclad boundaries between counseling and therapy. In fact, many practitioners interviewed in the UCLA field study used the terms rather interchangeably with comments such as, "How do you separate one from the other? It is really difficult to sort the two out." Moreover, the literature reveals that the conceptual definitions of counseling and therapy are blurred, especially in the context of case management (Caragonne, 1983; Downing, 1979; Greenberg, Austin, & Doth, 1981; Kurtz, Bagarozzi, & Pollane, 1984; Schwartz, Goldman, & Churgin, 1982). Several factors explain this lack of differentiation: both functions deal with emotional and cognitive processes; they share some of the same theoretical knowledge base; and they use many similar techniques.

Baker and Weiss (1984) try to differentiate by emphasis in method and purpose. *Therapy is more inner-directed* and aims to alter the pathology of an individual's personality through psychodynamic introspection, whereas *counseling is relatively more outer-directed* and endeavors to help clients function adaptively in the community by often giving concrete advice and guidance. Generally, counseling entails help-giving with regard to here-and-now problems of daily living. Therapy involves "talking" methods that focus on fundamental and enduring psychic elements within a client.

Use of Counseling and Therapy

Applying both approaches. Research has shown that personal helping interventions have, indeed, been applied and were found to be effective in positively modifying the behavioral patterns of highly vulnerable clients (Hogarty, 1979, 1981). Kurtz et al. (1984) found that the mental health agency directors they studied generally expected practitioners to assume a degree of responsibility for psychological helping. A preponderance of practitioners interviewed in the UCLA field study reinforced this research, stating that they were involved in providing some form of counseling or therapy to clients.

Rapp (1985) indicates that numerous professionals give preferential attention to the therapeutic interventions at the expense of community-oriented tasks such as advocacy, linking, monitoring, and coordinating services. He summarizes research findings on this by noting that mental health workers with a clinical orientation favor doing psychotherapy and eschew chronically mentally ill clients (Rapp, 1985).

However, other studies found that practitioners who give direct service do not necessarily neglect social support functions (Kurtz et al., 1984). A reading of the professional literature reveals some variance and uncertainty about the use of therapy, but not about counseling. We will offer a perspective on this question that has substantial support in the field.

Emphasis on support for community living. It is important for the practitioner to recognize that "curing a client's symptomatology" is ordinarily not the paramount goal in comprehensive enhancement intervention. Rather, direct service focuses on moving the client toward competency in community living. This stance is upheld by the relevant practice literature, which emphasizes that a productive focus is to assist that client in coping with basic life tasks in a self-directed fashion (Baker & Intagliata, 1982; Baker & Weiss, 1984; Brill & Horowitz, 1983; Downing, 1985; Hogarty, 1979, 1981; Linn, Klett, & Coffey, 1982; Stein & Test, 1980; Weick, Rapp, Sullivan, & Kisthardt, 1989). Bowker suggests that "traditional psychotherapy," especially when working with psychiatric patients, is of "limited value" (Bowker, 1985). Her view is that such clients would benefit to a greater degree from a "specialized kind of psychotherapy" that supports the client in grappling with pragmatic issues, rather than attempting to reshape the client's personality.

Lamb (1982) likewise cautions against a curative orientation that implies intensive psychotherapy. He suggests that the role of the practitioner in continuing care for highly vulnerable patients is to expand the remaining "well part of the person" (Lamb, 1982). This position is particularly salient, he states, with clients such as the elderly and the developmentally disabled, whose impairments are not reversible and in some cases may be progressive.

Most UCLA field study respondents shared the view that actively assisting the client to deal with day-to-day living situations and focusing on communication and socialization skills serve as major helping tools. Typical comments were: "You try to give the client practical ideas on parenting, housing, money." Or, again, "I give guidance, advice, information and material aid."

Imagine a case in point where a patient is about to be discharged from a psychiatric hospital and is anxious and fearful about re-entering mainstream society. There will be questions about where to live, how to bring in an income, engage in recreation, maintain a medication regimen, and keep from becoming isolated. The kind of present-oriented help that was advocated above would appropriately address these matters.

Key Components of Direct Service

The key components of direct service to highly vulnerable clients analytically can be broken out as follows:

- teaching the skills of daily living, including managing interpersonal relationships and performing practical tasks;
- providing emotional support: encouraging, fortifying, and motivating;
- giving cognitive support, including information about how to find help and use community resources;
- extending concrete practical aid: finding a baby sitter, calling a tow-truck, or buying a meal;
- using crisis intervention to bring the client through unexpected episodes of stress.

Many professionals favor a specifically time-limited form of psychological aid (Reid, 1978; Reid & Epstein, 1972; Roberts–DeGannero, 1987). Hollis (1980) has postulated that few professionals employ classic, extended in-depth psychotherapy in actual practice (even when they refer to "therapy"). The concept may embrace a series of short-term, problem-focused interventions over a long time frame. The UCLA respondents perceived short-term targeted interventions as a major factor in reducing recidivism rates in rehospitalization. A respondent stated it this way: "I think that in counseling . . . the main purpose is not to get into deep issues . . . but to be more immediately supportive of the client. We focus on the immediate crisis and situational difficulties. For broader problems, we refer clients to long-term treatment."

Among the interventions that Hogarty (1979, 1981) found to be the most useful for aiding long-term patients were teaching, role playing, and modeling desirable behaviors. His conclusions concur with several other studies that also support social learning theories and behavioral modification techniques as particularly effective with this population (Schutz et al., 1980).

Some authors and practitioners suggest eliminating the clinical functions from this practice altogether and making that the responsibility of therapy specialists. Lamb (1980) rebuts this by asserting that engaging with community resources should not be foreign to any "conscientious clinician." He folds the clinical functions in and renames the professional's position a "therapist case manager." This blend assumes the practitioner's role to encompass *all* functions that will restore the balance of the person–situation fit.

Lamb (1980) further identifies several benefits from synthesizing the clinical and community linkage roles. The practitioner will have access to firsthand "psychological knowledge" that is necessary to thoroughly understand the client and get through with supportive help. The confusion of a separate, compartmentalized bureaucratic layer, which has the potential of depersonalizing the helping situation, is eliminated by the merger of the roles. It also simplifies the process of coordinating referrals for the client. Additionally, in this formulation, there is no loss of valuable time in going from one professional to another to extract essential information about the client. While Lamb retains the word "therapy" in his formulation, the actual tasks he envisions lean in the direction of counseling and comprehensive enhancement.

While therapy in a strict clinical sense is not central, the skills and insights of psychotherapy come into play in all aspects of this work: understanding clients, forming relationships, and motivating behavior. Psychotherapy perspectives can provide the oil to lubricate the helping process.

Input from the Client and Others

The goal of maximum client self-direction and empowerment is nullified if the client is a passive recipient of services. The client who is an active participant in the process is likely to be better prepared to manage his or her own affairs (Roberts-DeGannero, 1987). Adopting a participative role requires that the client be accountable for a share of the intervention process: brainstorming and offering input regarding the problem and the means required to bring about desired ends. Frequently the helping professional and the client jointly establish a verbal or written contract in order to specify agreed upon goals, roles, and actions (Reid, 1978; Reid & Epstein, 1972).

Sanborn (1983) urges emphasizing client self-sufficiency because many clients with severe impairments have been made to feel powerless and are caught in the cycle of a defeatist self-fulfilling prophecy. Practitioners have the task of empowering them with the ability to help themselves (Grosser & Mondros, 1985; Pinderhughes, 1983; Shapiro, 1983). Sanborn notes three advantages of promoting self-direction in this way: self-sufficiency is cultur-ally valued within the society; it can attenuate a client's dependency on oth-ers, including professionals; and it serves to enhance a client's sense of self-worth.

Research confirms that service should consider the active involvement of the client, for the reason that clients have shown themselves to be knowl-edgeable about what is required to satisfy their personal needs (Ewalt & Honeyfield, 1981; Kinard, 1981; Kolisetty, 1983; Levine & Fleming, 1984).

The practitioners in the UCLA study reported that the treatment was "very interactive," with a good deal of encouragement of client input. Some practitioners indicated that they also frequently engaged the client's family members in the treatment process. One view of this was as follows: "Coun-seling often advances when you bring a significant other into the situation such as the family, spouse, children, etc. If the client is not progressing, you may have to counsel other parties involved in the process."

Alternative Theoretical Approaches to Personal Helping

While personal helping in this model of practice does not emphasize psy-chotherapy, many of the insights, concepts, and tools of ego psychology come into play. These are used for such purposes as understanding person-ality and behavior, forming relationships, providing encouragement and support, and disciplining personal intervention by the practitioner. The insights and techniques of ego psychology can inform intervention, even when not applied formally.

Personal helping functions in work with vulnerable clients can draw on a panoply of practice theories to service the needs of clients (Epstein, Savage, & Weissman, 1983; Meyer, 1987). Four of these theories will be covered as grist for the practitioner's mill: ego psychology, behavioral practice, cogni-tive practice, and crisis intervention. This discussion includes a brief and consequently simplified overview of these methods, but it is sufficient for a basic orientation to alternative approaches. We will start with ego psychol-ogy, the approach that is probably most familiar and encompassing, recog-nizing that the other three probably have more direct applicability in working with highly vulnerable clients.

Ego psychology.   Ego psychology's course relies heavily on the impact of early life experiences on the client's personality and functioning (self-image, self-perceptions, and interrelational patterns) (Schamess, 1983). Many practitioners in this mode focus on the client's ego deficits arising from an arrest in one of Erikson's stages of development (trust vs. mistrust, auton-omy vs. self-doubt, initiative vs. guilt, industry vs. inferiority, identity vs. identify diffusion, intimacy vs. isolation, generativity vs. stagnation, and ego integrity vs. ego despair) (Blanck & Blanck, 1974; Craig, 1986; Erikson, 1950).

To survive in the environment, the client is assumed to use maladaptive defense mechanisms such as denial and projection. Ego psychology postulates that these mechanisms externalize the client's feelings of failure, which serves to create patterns of negative interaction with the environment.

The goal of intervention is to encourage ego adaptability and the development of mature defense mechanisms through the exercise of ego supportive techniques (Blanck & Blanck, 1974; Goldstein, 1986). To counteract feelings of anxiety or depression, the clinician encourages what Hollis (1972) refers to as "person-in-situation reflection." This enables the client to explore previously unconscious behaviors, feelings, and perceptions in order to bring maladaptive defense mechanisms to the fore for the purpose of changing them. The practitioner offers support by emphasizing the strengths and accepting, not judging, the client's limitations. This includes taking a nurturing stance and providing the "mirroring" or validation for the client, which had presumedly been absent during the identified period of arrest.

The behavioral approach. The behavioral approach (or behavior modification) focuses on overt behavior, with purposive intent to decrease undesired behaviors or to increase those that are desired. It deals specifically with problems in functioning around actions that are observable and where improvements are measurable. The presenting problem is a key consideration and a valid basis for guiding intervention (Fischer, 1978).

The approach is based on learning theories derived from the work of B. F. Skinner, wherein behavior is seen as learned, rational, and adjustable. Unlike ego psychology, the approach does not dwell on unconscious emotions, nor does it concentrate on early developmental factors in a client's history. Attention is directed at current conditions in the environment that maintain dysfunctional behavior or impede the development of more adaptive behavior.

At the heart of the behavioral approach is contingency analysis and the management of contingencies (Wolpe, 1973). This framework conceives of *antecedents, behavior,* and *consequences.* The practitioner has the task of rearranging antecedent events by means of stimulus control, or rearranging consequences through structuring favorable or unfavorable outcomes of behavior. Reinforcement theory plays an important part in that regard. If rewarding results flow from behavior, the behavior will be increased or strengthened. If unpleasant or aversive reactions follow the behavior, it will be decreased or weakened. The intervention mode is based in large part on increasing or decreasing behavior through applying or withdrawing such consequences.

Behavioral approaches have relied substantially on modeling techniques (Bandura, 1971). The principle applied is "imitative learning," whereby behavior patterns are changed through observation and vicarious experience. The modeled behavior is then internalized through practice or "behavioral rehearsal," more commonly called role playing. In behavior modification, role playing is viewed as a basis for retention of desired behavior because it provides for motoric reproduction of the basic elements of the behavior. Both modeling and role playing have been advanced technically in the behavioral approach because of their potency as tools of social learning.

Behavioral intervention has a number of key characteristics. Client problems are tangible and time frames for service are constrained. Environmental conditions have an important place in the orientation. Outcomes are specified concretely, with clearly defined techniques proposed to attain them. Assessment is rigorous, and the link between assessment and intervention is closely integrated. There is an emphasis on evaluation, and empirical research is relied on heavily to inform intervention (Kazdin, 1978). The application of "self-change" by clients (Watson & Tharp, 1972) is an especially pertinent feature.

The cognitive orientation.   The emphasis in the cognitive approach is on modifying irrational cognitions in order to bring them into alignment with reality (Beck, 1976; Werner, 1986). It is assumed that maladaptive behaviors can be adjusted reciprocally through mental control and behavioral learning techniques. For example, a depressed client can be helped to alter negative self-statements about the way she looks or talks. This approach operates on the premise that dysfunctional behaviors are learned and incorporated through faulty thought processes. They can be unlearned by focusing on reframing distorted cognitions and negative self-perceptions that have engendered the demoralization and derailment of the client (Speigler, 1983).

The practitioner helps the client identify the irrational thoughts and motives that preceded the inappropriate behavioral patterns, and then employs *cognitive restructuring* as an intervention technique. This guides the client in coming to a new understanding of his or her situation and in being able to formulate positive, constructive self-statements. The client can come to realize that her appearance is not unfavorable, or that other personal attributes and resources are of greater moment. The process seeks to enhance both the client's perception of the environment and sense of self-worth. Further, the client is encouraged to learn, integrate, and practice a more constructive behavioral repertoire, concordant with the revised cognitions. From application to one problematic situation, it is assumed that the client will be equipped with the confidence and tools necessary to generalize this remedial strategy to other situations.

Crisis intervention.   Crisis theory postulates that either a major external catastrophic event, or a series of internal disjunctures, precipitate a homeostatic imbalance. This condition is presumed to characterize long-term patients such as the elderly and mentally ill, who are vulnerable to entropy (the tendency for a system to breakdown or become disorganized) and who lack the necessary skills to cope with circumstances of stress (Golan, 1986;

Patti, 1983). Engaging in dysfunctional behavior serves to exacerbate the pre-existing feelings of heightened anxiety, inferiority, and hopelessness.

As with other methodologies, the role of the professional is to instill in the client the belief that this bounded dilemma is remediable and to lay the groundwork for a helping relationship. Once rapport has been established, the practitioner collaborates with the client in assessing the immediate presenting problem and in identifying a means to rectify the predicament. At this juncture, they agree on a set of concrete tasks, a structured plan of execution, and a time-limited action frame that will result in a near term solution (Parad, 1965; Reid, 1978). Crisis intervention will be discussed further later in the chapter.

The person-in-environment ecological perspective undergirding this book encourages the practitioner to be eclectic in selecting and using these and other theoretical orientations. It encourages an understanding of internal and external problem etiology and of sources for progress that come from within the person or from without. A multimodal approach to intervention would seem appropriate (Lazarus, 1981) because of the fluidity of the situations in which practitioners work, and the many variations among clients served. For example, some clients appear with presenting problems that have a crisis dimension, while others do not. However, crisis situations may arise from time to time for all. As we know, some problems require the learning of new coping skills, while others need to be addressed through social support or emotional adjustments. Whatever the issue, most clients will probably need time-limited crisis services at various points in conjunction with what may be viewed otherwise as a long-term helping relationship. The broader the conceptual frame of reference, and the more theoretical resources that are available, the better equipped the practitioner will be to provide competent assistance.

PRACTICE GUIDELINES FOR COUNSELING AND THERAPY

This section examines specific actions and procedures that constitute the practice of counseling and therapy with severely vulnerable populations. Although some aspects have been touched on in the preceding discussion, the most salient will be reintroduced and discussed in greater detail, with specific emphasis on practice implementation. Some fundamental tasks of counseling and therapy include:

1. establishing a relationship
2. motivating the client
3. fostering client participation and empowerment
4. providing survival skills and relevant information
5. providing support
6. providing crisis intervention

These areas are recurrently cited in the literature as critical in work with long-term clients (Burack-Weiss, 1988; Ballew & Mink, 1986; Lamb, 1980; Modrcin, Rapp, & Chamberlain, 1985; Sanborn, 1983). While these tasks will be addressed sequentially, in practice they interrelate and frequently overlap. The emphasis will be on situational problem-solving rather than traditional psychotherapy. As we know, for highly vulnerable clients this is consistent with both the professional literature and empirical research.

Establishing Relationships

The bonding of the helper and the client is a key element in professional intervention (Austin, 1983). There is widespread agreement that establishing a relationship with the client is the preliminary step toward meaningful service (Lamb, 1980; Sanborn, 1983).

Self-validation.   To help establish a relationship, the practitioner must convey a strong sense of respect (Sanborn, 1983). The practitioner can communicate this attitude by validating the client's unique constellation of feelings, thoughts, experiences, and goals. To illustrate, when working with a physically disabled mother who is encountering conflict with an adolescent daughter, the practitioner can assure the client that this concern is widely shared by other people in the same circumstance and is taken as common by the practitioner ("normalizing" the client's feelings).

Empathy.   Conveying this message requires empathy, which Basch (1988, p. 145) describes as finding "one's way into another's experience." Others use the metaphor of "stepping into the shoes of the client" to express the same notion (Berger, 1987; Raines, 1990). The practitioner can reveal attunement to the client's subjective experience with comments such as: "it must have been difficult for you to have been fired from your job" or "at times finding a job must seem like a hopeless proposition" (Raines, 1990; Wolf, 1988).

Such empathic responses will often encourage the client to be at ease and begin to perceive the helper as a nonjudgmental ally with whom it is safe to ventilate feelings. Empathic understanding can be especially effective when serving an elderly individual who is unwilling to ask for help because of denying the aging process and admitting to a physical or mental deficiency (Burack-Weiss, 1988).

For many long-term vulnerable clients sensing such empathy in the practitioner may be a unique experience. They often have been made to feel unimportant and labeled untreatable or "a problem case." Showing genuine positive regard, and simply being there each week for the client, serves to strengthen the client's belief that the practitioner is dependable and has the potential to help (Garvin & Seabury, 1984).

The practitioner needs to be aware of personal feelings toward the client and not overstep the line between empathy and condescension (Berger,

1987; Raines, 1990; Wolf, 1988). The distinction between sympathy and empathy comes into play here. Sympathizing with a client often involves feeling the full depth of another's distress. Empathy is a more constrained vicarious entry into another's feeling state for purpose of perceiving how the individual might be experiencing a problem (Wolf, 1988). Greenson (1960, p. 148) distinguishes between the two by noting that in empathy "one partakes of the quality . . . and not the quantity of another's feelings."

Knowing the client. There are other initiatives that can facilitate the helping alliance as well. For instance, Basch (1980) suggests getting acquainted with clients by finding out something about them and "being yourself." Learning about a client's ethnicity or culture; finding common interests in music, sports, or cooking; providing small comforts by offering the client a cup of tea; and accepting social amenities at the beginning or end of a weekly session allows the client to perceive the practitioner as an unintimidating person. Extending to the client in these ways may appear simplistic or obvious, but can serve as a powerful vehicle to establish mutuality and a comfortable emotional environment.

Examples of relationships in this mode are described in one study:

> One case manager took a client to lunch once a week. From this case manager's perspective the client was being resocialized. From the client's perspective the case manager was providing a pleasant social occasion. The client said, "We go out for a sandwich. Sometimes I pay, sometimes he pays. We change off. It's a nice outing."
>
> For some clients the case manager functioned like an older brother or sister, offering the kind of advice and guidance that might be obtained from a caring nonprofessional. The better-functioning patients viewed the case managers as helpful and knowledgeable people not intrinsically different from themselves. These clients felt that whereas psychiatrists and social workers were distanced from them by their status and authority, case managers established a more peer-like friendliness.
>
> One patient emphasized that she felt respected by her case manager, something she felt was missing from her relationship with other members of the treatment team. (Baker & Weiss, 1984, p. 926)

In traditional clinical practice the professional also gets involved in the details of the client's life, but mainly in the interview room and through the client's eyes. In the comprehensive enhancement paradigm the involvement is more direct, in vivo, and hands-on. The practice style is intensive, as described in Chapter 1.

Motivating the Client

Many of the points pertinent to establishing a relationship apply as well to motivating the client. Inadequate client motivation, according to Ballew and Mink (1986), is typically rooted in the individual's "internal impediments." These serve to maintain the client's feelings of "pessimism, fatalism, and cynicism." Ballew and Mink (1986) identify long-term clients as those most likely to require a high degree of motivational encouragement, as they are especially susceptible to distorted self-imagery. The authors believe that motivation can be elicited if "internal resources" are mobilized to overcome the internal impediments.

To facilitate this effort, these authors suggest using many tactics previously discussed, but with special emphasis on energizing the client. Exhibiting empathy, encouragement, and respect all apply. Taking the role of a "personal cheerleader" is particularly relevant here (Modrcin, Rapp, & Chamberlain, 1985).

Giving a client a sense of mastery and success can be key to motivation. Some steps to follow include:

1. encouraging the client to pinpoint particular problems to target for change;
2. defining "doable" tasks that are within the realm of the client's abilities and interests;
3. practicing those tasks for mastery.

A critical aspect of this partializing approach involves practicing the behavior and achieving recurring *rewarding outcomes*. Small initial experiences of success not only breed further success, but are stimuli for increased interest and desire to pursue additional targets of competency.

Fostering Client Participation

Client participation was previously designated a positive force for effective and empowering intervention (Ewalt & Honeyfield, 1981; Kolisetty, 1983; Levine & Fleming, 1984; Kinard, 1981). Here we discuss more specifically how to bring this about in practice. For the reason that the environment has typically made clients feel powerless, they may lean toward a passive stance in the client role and need to be invited in.

Before the client is guided toward a participative role, however, the practitioner should assess the individual's particular capabilities and limitations for involvement. This will suggest what level of involvement will be promising in the interaction (Burack-Weiss, 1988; Roberts-DeGannero, 1987). Such data could divert the practitioner from a standardized approach that could set the client up for failure (Meyer, 1987; Perlman, 1957; Siporin, 1983).

At the outset, the worker should be aware of the extent of the client's experience and understanding in service settings. It is erroneous to assume that the client is well acquainted with the "rules" of counseling or therapy. In fact, many times severely impaired clients do not know or have forgotten what is expected or required of them in such an environment (Sanborn, 1983). It is advisable often to explain that actively expressing feelings, concerns, and preferences is an acceptable and welcomed aspect of the relationship (and to use an occasional mini quiz to check comprehension). The practitioner can convey the notion of a problem-solving team and move toward actualizing this by drawing the client into concrete decision-making. There may be times, however, to become less active or remain silent, in order to create space for client initiative. If the helper consistently comes to the rescue by offering solutions to problems, the client may become complacent and dependent.

The practitioner may employ structured behavioral techniques, such as modeling, shaping, and role playing, as participative techniques. For example, a developmentally disabled client may need to learn how to identify and use the community's appropriate transportation facilities. After assessing the individual's strengths, the participants may agree that by the next session the client will obtain a bus schedule, read it thoroughly, and attempt to outline a route that would most easily get the client to the agency. In subsequent meetings, the client and practitioner can pinpoint additional steps necessary to facilitate this goal. The practitioner may then involve the client in a role-playing scenario in which the patient learns ways to communicate with the bus driver.

Teaching Survival Skills and Providing Practical Information

Research mentioned earlier identified teaching basic living skills and conveying information on resources as crucial for service to long-term vulnerable clients. The approach has been referred to as *life skills counseling* (Schinke & Gilchrist, 1984). The goal is to enable the client to use and integrate information, and to generalize practical daily life skills learned in the service setting to external situations involving independent living.

One community-based program has set up a structured community living educational program, whereby skills are imparted to clients on a group basis. The program aids clients in the following areas:

1. *Personal Skills*
   grooming
   hygiene
   laundry
2. *Interpersonal Skills*
   socialization
   planning leisure activities
   managing own time
   making decisions
   sharing chores
   settling conflicts
   assertiveness
3. *Community Skills*
   making use of community resources
   knowing about mental health and other emergency services
   developing awareness and communication skills
   knowing about self-help groups and community services
   developing community and political awareness skills
   exploring involvement opportunities

4. *Consumer Skills*

nutrition	meal planning
marketing and shopping	cooking
banking	budgeting
	housekeeping

5. *Housing*
   applying for public housing
   negotiating with management companies

Leavitt (1983) adds safety skills, vocational skills, illness management, and transportation skills. She breaks each of these into small units. Illustratively, vocational skills include:

following orders from production of a product or provisions of a service, on a
   continuum from close supervision to no supervision
learning a job skill from on-the-job observation
learning a job skill from reading and applying the skill
preparing a resume of past work
participating in an employment interview
supervising others in the work place
training others (Leavitt, 1983, p. 34)

A valuable aid to this area of practice is found in the *social and independent living skills modules* (SILS) developed by Liberman, Mueser, and Wallace (1986). These include recreation, grooming, job finding, money management, dating, and others. The models have been carefully developed, systematically tested, and videotaped to facilitate transmission and training.

The literature supports employing behavioral techniques such as role playing, modeling, shaping, and positive reinforcement in working with highly vulnerable clients. To initiate service the practitioner and client might jointly identify one or a few specific tasks to be mastered. After this has been decided, the professional may model the skill in a way that is clear and comprehensible, with the client encouraged to learn the task by practicing. Immediately following completion of the activity, the client should be positively reinforced in an appropriate way: the practitioner could simply say "great" or "good job," or could even use a token system (Speigler, 1983).

Providing information can further skill development or give the client a basis for taking actions or making decisions. An example of implementation involves what has been termed *an information broker role,* described as follows:

Pat Williams is a case manager working at an independent living center located in an inner city neighborhood. The center specializes in supporting the independent living of persons with severe physical disabilities. Pat works with a number of clients who have special needs regarding transportation, housing, and recreation. For the most part, his clients are well-motivated and able to respond to these special needs. However, he has developed a reputation for being quite knowledgeable of housing resources within the community, especially housing which is physically accessible to persons who use wheelchairs. Members of the independent living center who are looking for housing often drop in to see Pat. They discuss their housing needs and review with the case manager the desirable attributes of the housing which they are seeking. Very often Pat is able to identify several housing alternatives that the members can subsequently investigate on their own initiative. It also is not unusual for some members to be unclear about their housing needs. In these cases, Pat explores their needs and then helps them to identify appropriate options that they can investigate on their own. (Moxley, 1989, pp. 88–89)

As a way of imparting information, the client may be reached through verbal or written communication. The practitioner can, in daily conversation with a client, act as an "information specialist" who simply lets the client know how to locate a relative or access social security, medicare benefits, or housing resources. As a backup measure, this same information could be written to assure that the client will remember correctly. The point is that these need to be seen as valid and essential tasks by the practitioner, meriting time and attention.

Providing Support

Support for a client can come in many forms and can be emotional or practical in character. Initially, this discussion explores the psychological aspects of support.

Emphasizing the client's strengths, rather than concentrating on pathology, has a supportive effect (Ballew & Mink, 1986; Lamb, 1980; Weick et al., 1989). For example, the practitioner may laud a client for an ability to arrive on time for an appointment, to be well-groomed, or to select the appropriate bus route. Giving accent to the client's personal strengths will convey a belief that the client has the internal resources necessary to realize positive change.

Support aims at reinforcing the client and promoting a positive self-image. The following hypothetical situation demonstrates this.

Mrs. Hoffman comes to the practitioner's office for assistance in dealing with a reprimand from a workplace supervisor for selling cookies at the wrong price. This criticism on the job has thrown her into a familiar downward cycle of self-deprecating thoughts about self-worth. Several supportive initiatives can help her cope better. The practitioner provides balance by pointing out that all people make mistakes in the process of experiencing growth. Concurrently, the practitioner does some reality testing with her to negate the distorted thoughts that she perceives as valid. Also, highlighting the tasks that were positively implemented helps restore a measure of self-esteem and hope.

The supportive role as perceived from the client's viewpoint is described in the following passage:

One client said that when she felt "down" she would get in touch with her case manager, who would then help her get "up." Asked how the case manager did this, the client suggested that simply being taken seriously and being treated as worthy of attention helped repair her feelings of low self-esteem. Undoubtedly the client was also helped by the reassurance that she could call on the case manager if she needed to. (Baker & Weiss, 1984, p. 926)

A practitioner described the impact of support to the author in the following words:

> It is amazing just how far one compliment can go in lightening up a client's day. For example, one client got out of control in the clinic and was potentially violent. Another client came along and very calmly lifted this 190-pound male up in the air and quietly escorted him to the exit door. Staff and fellow members applauded and loudly commended him, after which he walked around with his head held up high for the next three days. In another instance, a young bipolar woman whose moods had stabilized began wearing make-up again. She then began to get compliments from the staff and fellow clients like, "Gosh, you really look pretty" or "I didn't know you were so nice looking." This lifted this woman's spirits immensely and her attitude became even more euthymic.

Another illustration of psychological support is in a brief excerpt from Ballew and Mink (1986, pp. 216–217), focusing on a client with weak ego strength:

> [Rosemary's] pessimism is so pervasive that she will not become involved. She believes that she has failed at anything important that she has ever attempted. She learned responsibility from her parents and feels responsible for everything that goes wrong. She is afraid to attempt anything new because she thinks that she will spoil it. This conviction about herself immobilizes her. . . . Rosemary and I discussed her attitude today. I told her that I thought she didn't give herself enough credit. She said she had no reason to take credit. I said that she had two beautiful children and that someone had to take credit for that. She said that was God's work, but I could tell she was pleased.

Empathic listening is another means of giving support (Lamb, 1980). Sanborn (1983) describes it as "acting as a sounding board" for the client. This incorporates elements of interest, attention, concentration, and unswerving concern.

As indicated, support can also involve taking actions of a practical nature for those clients who have limited capacity or require concrete help. Helping a client complete application forms, assisting in making arrangements for a trip, and locating emergency child care are other instances where the practitioner extends practical help.

Providing Crisis Intervention

Clients may need personal counseling during periods of crisis that all individuals encounter. Severely vulnerable clients are susceptible to critical occurrences in life because of a high level of impairment or ongoing dependency that saps their resiliency in dealing with unexpected events. Dixon (1979, in Moxley) indicates that these events leave such clients in a weakened state, with intense feelings of depression, anxiety, loneliness or failure. He defines a crisis event as one that overwhelms the individual's ordinary problem-solving mode, resulting in the inability to cope with the situation. Another way to understand the phenomenon is through the concepts of risk and stressors (Leavitt, 1983). Risks may include the possibility of grave disability, institutionalization, self-injury, injury to others, and property damage. Risk of crisis is high when impairment is severe, acting out behavior is intense, and operating stressors are many or powerful in character. Such stressors may include:

- Loss of someone who is close, especially after a long and emotional relationship, such as a spouse or parent.
- Loss of physical function. This may be natural with the aging. Sudden illness or injuries are another source.
- Residential change, including from a hospital or other institutional setting into the community.
- Change in one's social support system, which may affect employment, finances, and socialization opportunities.
- Change in legal status, including going from voluntary to involuntary treatment, involvement with litigation, and conservatorship.
- Social isolation or deprivation, having drawn into or been left in a withdrawn circumstance without appropriate stimulation.

Stressors may also be a result of happenstance, including giving birth, experiencing a failed love relationship, losing a job, pregnancy, and other flows and travails of life. Practitioners need to be prepared to respond, while also concurrently addressing more ongoing needs. Alertness for such events, and response to them, is an important aspect of the monitoring process.

The objective of crisis intervention is to provide emotional first aid through in vivo assistance (Parad, 1977). This entails relieving symptoms and enabling the client to return to a pre-crisis level of functioning. Parad, Selby, and Quinlan (1976) suggest four basic steps in practice:

1. Identify the precipitating event and closely explore its meaning for the client.
2. Examine the means the client employed in reacting to the event.
3. Search for alternative means of coping that will better serve the client.
4. Aid the client in implementing the new coping approaches.

In crisis intervention, there is an attempt to sharply delineate the problem by focusing on the most pressing aspect. Also, rather circumscribed time limits are set for seeking a solution. This allows the crisis to be resolved as quickly as possible, and serves also to mobilize the client's energies. Short-term parameters tend by necessity to call for a relatively active role by the practitioner. A positive aspect of these situations is that clients often are most susceptible to influence during crises, thereby opening up possibilities for the practitioner that were not available previously.

Crisis intervention reflects a perspective rather than a distinctive set of procedures. It draws eclectically on a wide range of existing techniques to implement a short-term mode of emergency assistance.

Counseling and therapy assume and draw on existing relevant community-wide supportive resources. The practice dovetails with the linking functions of the overall practice model. These functions require distinct perspectives and competencies that we will examine next.

REFERENCES

Austin, C. (1983). *Case management in long-term care: Options and opportunities.* Silver Springs, MD: National Association of Social Workers.

Baker, F. & Intagliata, J. (1982). Quality of life in the evaluation of community support systems. *Evaluation and Program Planning, 5*(1), 69–79.

Baker, F. & Weiss, R. (1984). The nature of case management support. *Hospital and Community Psychiatry, 35*(9), 925–928.

Ballew, J. R. & Mink, G. (1986). *Case management in the human services.* Springfield, IL: Charles C. Thomas.

Bandura, A. (1971). Psychotherapy based upon modeling principles. In A. E. Bergin & S. Garfield (Eds.), *Handbook of psychotherapy and behavior change* (pp. 653–708). New York: Wiley.

Basch, M. F. (1980). *Doing psychotherapy.* New York: Basic Books.

Basch, M. F. (1988). *Understanding psychotherapy.* New York: Basic Books.

Beck, A. (1976). *Cognitive therapy and the emotional disorders.* New York: International University Press.

Berger, D. M. (1987). *Clinical empathy.* New Jersey: Jason Aronson.

Blanck, G. & Blanck, R. (1974). *Ego psychology: Theory & practice.* New York: Columbia University Press.

Bowker, J. P. (Ed.). (1985). *Education for practice with the chronically mentally ill: What works?* Washington, DC: Council on Social Work Education.

Brill, R. & Horowitz, A. (1983). New York city home care project: A demonstration in coordination of health and social services. *Home Health Care Services Quarterly, 4*(3–4), 91–106.

Burack-Weiss, A. (Fall 1988). Clinical aspects of case management. *Generations,* 23–25.

Caragonne, P. (1983). *A comparison of case management work activity and current models.* Austin: Texas Department of Mental Health and Mental Retardation.

Craig, G. J. (1986). *Human development* (4th ed.). Englewood Cliffs, NJ: Prentice-Hall.

Downing, R. (1979). *Three work papers* (An exploration of case manager roles: Coordinator, advocate, and counselor; Issues of client assessment in coordination programs; and Client pathway). Los Angeles: University of Southern California, Social Policy Laboratory, Andrus Gerontology Center.

Downing, R. (1985). The elderly and their families. In M. Weil & M. Karls (Eds.), *Case management in human service practice* (pp. 145–167). San Francisco: Jossey-Bass.

Erikson, E. H. (1950). *Childhood and society.* New York: W. W. Norton & Company.

Ewalt, P. & Honeyfield, R. (1981). Needs of persons in long-term care. *Social Work, 26*(3), 223–231.

Fischer, J. (1978). *Effectiveness practice: An eclectic approach.* New York: McGraw-Hill.

Garvin, C. D. & Seabury, B. (1984). *Interpersonal practice in social work.* Englewood Cliffs, NJ: Prentice-Hall.

Golan, N. (1986). Crisis theory. In F. J. Turner (Ed.), *Social work treatment* (pp. 296–340). New York: The Free Press.

Goldstein, E. G. (1986). Ego psychology. In F. J. Turner (Ed.), *Social work treatment* (pp. 375–405). New York: The Free Press.

Greenberg, J., Austin, C., & Doth, D. (1981). *A comparative study of long-term care demonstrations: Lessons for future inquiry.* Minneapolis: University of Minnesota, Center for Human Services Research.

Greenson, R. R. (1960). Empathy and its vicissitudes. *International Journal of Psychoanalysis, 41,* 418–424.

Hogarty, G. (1979). Treatment of schizophrenia: Current status and future direction. In H. Pragg (Ed.), *Management of schizophrenia.* The Netherlands: Van Goreum, Assen.

Hogarty, G. (1981). Evaluation of drugs and therapeutic procedures: The contribution of non-pharmacological techniques. In G. Tognoni, C. Bellantvono, & M. Lader (Eds.), *Epidemiological impact of psychotropic drugs*. Amsterdam: North-Holland Biomedical Press.

Hollis, F. (1972). *Casework: A psychosocial therapy* (2nd ed.). New York: Random House.

Hollis, F. (1980). On revisiting social work. *Social Casework: The Journal of Contemporary Social Work, 1*, 3–10.

Kazdin, A. E. (1978). *History of behavior modification: Experimental foundations of contemporary research*. Baltimore, MD: University Park Press.

Kinard, E. (1981). Discharged patients who desire to return to the hospital. *Hospital and Community Psychiatry, 31*(11), 762–764.

Kolisetty, N. (1983). A study of case management systems in delivery of social services. *Dissertation Abstracts International, 20*(3), No. 1022.

Kurtz, L., Bagarozzi, D., & Pollane, L. (1984). Case management in mental health. *Health and Social Work, 9*(3), 201–211.

Lamb, H. R. (1980). Therapist-case managers: More than brokers of services. *Hospital and Community Psychiatry, 31*(11), 762–764.

Lamb, H. R. (1982). *Treating the long-term mentally ill*. San Francisco: Jossey-Bass.

Lazarus, A. A. (1981). *The practice of multimodal therapy: Systematic, comprehensive and effective psychotherapy*. New York: McGraw-Hill.

Leavitt, S. S. (1983). Case Management: A remedy for problems of community care. In C. J. Sandborn (Ed.), *Case management in mental health services* (pp. 17–41). New York: Haworth Press.

Levine, I. & Fleming, M. (1984). *Human resources development: Issues in case management*. Washington, DC: National Institute of Mental Health.

Liberman, R. P., Mueser, K. T., & Wallace, C. J. (1986). Social skills training for schizophrenic individuals at risk to relapse. *American Journal of Psychiatry, 143*, 523–526.

Linn, M., Klett, C., & Coffey, E. (1982). Relapse of psychiatric patients in foster care. *American Journal of Psychiatry, 139*, 778–783.

Meyer, C. H. (1987). Direct practice in social work: Overview. In *Encyclopedia of social work: Vol. 1* (18th ed., pp. 409–422). Silver Springs, MD: National Association of Social Workers.

Modrcin, M., Rapp, C. A., & Chamberlain, R. (1985). *Case management with psychiatrically disabled individuals: Curriculum and training program*. Lawrence: University of Kansas, School of Social Welfare.

Moxley, D. P. (1989). *The practice of case management*. Newbury Park, CA: Sage Publications.

Parad, H. J. (Ed.). (1965). *Crisis intervention: Selected readings*. New York: Family Service Association of America.

Parad, H. J. (1977). Crisis intervention. In *Encyclopedia of social work* (17th ed., pp. 228–237). Washington, DC: National Association of Social Workers.

Parad, H. J., Selby, L., & Quinlan, J. (1976). Crisis intervention with families and groups. In R. W. Roberts & H. Northen (Eds.), *Theories of social work with groups* (pp. 304–330). New York: Columbia University Press.

Patti, R. (1983). *Social welfare administration*. Englewood Cliffs, NJ: Prentice-Hall.

Perlman, H. H. (1957). *Social casework: A problem-solving process*. Chicago: University of Chicago Press.

Pinderhughes, E. (1983). Empowerment for our clients and for ourselves. *Social Casework, 64*, 331–338.

Raines, J. C. (1990). Empathy in clinical social work. *Clinical Social Work Journal, 18*(1), 57–72.

Rapp, C. (1985). Research on the chronically mentally ill: Curriculum implications. In J. Bowker (Ed.), *Education for practice with the chronically mentally ill: What works?* Washington, DC: Council on Social Work Education.

Reid, W. (1978). *The task-centered system.* New York: Columbia University Press.

Reid, W. & Epstein, L. (1972). *Task-centered casework.* New York: Columbia University Press.

Roberts-DeGannero, M. (1987). Developing case management as a practice model. *Social Casework, 8*(10), 466–471.

Sanborn, C. J. (1983). *Case management in mental health services.* New York: Haworth Press.

Schamess, G. (1983). Client/therapist interactions. In A. Rosenblatt & D. Waldfogel (Eds.), *Handbook of clinical social work* (pp. 362–366). San Francisco: Jossey-Bass.

Schinke, S. P. and Gilchrist, L. D. (1984). *Life skills counseling with adolescents.* Baltimore: University Park Press.

Schwartz, S., Goldman, H., & Churgin, S. (1982). Case management for the chronic mentally ill: Models and dimensions. *Hospital and Community Psychiatry, 33*(12), 1006–1009.

Siporin, M. (1983). The therapeutic process in clinical social work. *Social Work, 28,* 193–198.

Speigler, M. D. (1983). *Contemporary behavioral therapy.* Mountain View, CA: Mayfield.

Stein, L. & Test, M. (1980). Alternative to mental hospital treatment. *Archives of General Psychiatry, 37,* 392–397.

Watson, D. & Tharp, R. (1972). *Self-directed behavior.* Monterey, CA: Brooks/Cole.

Weick, A., Rapp, C., Sullivan, W. P., & Kisthardt, W. (1989). A strengths perspective for social work practice. *Social Work, 34,* 350–354.

Werner, H. D. (1986). Cognitive theory. In F. J. Turner (Ed.), *Social work treatment* (3rd ed., pp. 91–130). New York: The Free Press.

Wolf, E. (1988). *Treating the self.* New York: The Guilford Press.

Wolpe, J. (1973). *The practice of behavior therapy* (2nd Ed.). New York: Pergamon.

7
Linking Clients to Formal Organizations

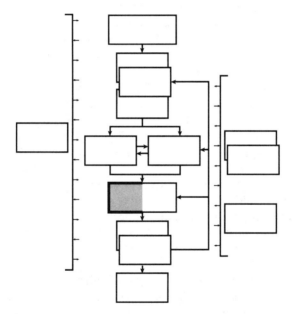

UNDERSTANDING THE FORMAL LINKING PROCESS

The Concept of Linking

From time to time life confounds intentions and everyone needs help. A social service agency can assist with perplexities about housing, job training, or family disruption. Ordinarily, people find organizations that they need by "taking a walk" through the yellow pages or asking for suggestions from a personal network of acquaintances.

Some individuals, though, are too green to use such resources. They are not in a position to know what services they actually need or how to access them. This includes the long-term mentally ill, the frail elderly, persons with physical or developmental disabilities, and dependent children—typical vulnerable clients. This is where the linking function comes into play.

The Random House Dictionary (1987) defines *link* as "anything serving to connect one part or thing with another; a bond or tie." Connecting clients to services is a fundamental part of comprehensive enhancement practice. Referral is also an aspect of most human service helping, but it often takes perfunctory or superficial form and is ordinarily a marginal consideration in defining professional competency. This is at variance with our practice model. "It is with this function that the role of the case manager departs most clearly from the typical role of the [service] professional" (Los Angeles County Department of Mental Health, 1985, p. 13). Highly vulnerable clients usually have multiple needs, requiring responses from a wide spectrum of service organizations. They often require assistance that is unavailable directly through the primary practitioner. For example, beyond direct counseling, an abused child and her family may require parenting classes, a "big sister," math tutoring, job training for a parent, and an after-school program. It is the practitioner's function to invoke a rounded configuration of community services that are appropriate for maintaining a decent quality of life for the client.

Professional linking does not consist of simply suggesting a referral. It also means making a good hook-up, including doing whatever is necessary to ensure that the client actually receives the needed aid. It calls for a wealth of knowledge about the community human services system: accurate, up-to-date information on policies, programs and procedures; contingencies and "loopholes"; and the costs and benefits of different options. The practitioner also needs to arrive at constructive working relationships with varied service agencies and institutions to actualize service outcomes.

Linking is not a one time event. Once clients have been connected with services their personal needs may change, requiring that they be tied in with other appropriate resources. For example, a discharged patient may be referred initially for emergency housing and to stabilize a medical condition. Once she makes progress with this, the practitioner could move toward linkage for job retraining, and then for job placement. Even when making a given agency connection, linkage is a process rather than a single action. A student intern comments:

> Even though my client has not actually received her first AFDC [Aid to Families with Dependent Children] check as yet, we have been involved with that agency for over a month. Without a helper to work things through, she might have been discouraged a few weeks ago and discontinued her application; she didn't understand what the worker was saying. There have been at least three instances in which she didn't receive a check because of different misunderstandings. Since I have been having weekly contact with her, I knew where she was in filing the application and how she was feeling each step of the way. I was also able to discuss problems with the AFDC worker and clarify the situation for both of them. This was a real catch-22 situation. The client was told she needed a green card to finish the application and get some money, but first she had to come up with seventy dollars to replace a lost card. To make a long story short, on Monday I spoke to the client's newly assigned AFDC worker, who said that the verification that I brought in would be sufficient to get the green card, after all. Why was I told a different story by every other staff member in person and on the telephone? I have had similar aggravations in dealing with other agencies.

Historical Perspective on Linkage

Early efforts at interagency coordination in the United States were through the social service exchanges established by the Charity Organization Societies in the late 19th century. Initially given the name "Registration Bureau," these units collected the names of individuals receiving services, the cash amounts allocated, and counseling provided (Levinson, 1988). The first annual report of the Associated Charities of Boston stated that the objective was "to secure an interchange of information and thereby detect imposture, discourage begging, distinguish the worthy from the unworthy, and promote economy and efficiency in the distribution of relief" (Woodberry, 1929). Intermingled here were philanthropy, social control, and fiscal constraint.

Subsequently, the name was changed to the Central Index. The focus encompassed aggregation of files of various agencies. Service agencies were encouraged to cooperate, ostensibly to meet all the needs of a client and develop unity among service providers (Woodberry, 1929). In practice, this meant that the Central Index was used by agencies to consult each other's records in overseeing clients. Issues of confidentiality, and genuine caring, took second place to cost efficiency in agency operations.

A national voluntary agency, Community Chests and Councils of America (later known as United Community Funds and Councils of America [UCFCA], and then the United Way), began establishing information and referral services in urban communities as early as 1921. Under the guidance of the UCFCA, community health and welfare councils shifted from client inventories to organized community resource files for information and referral services to clients, and for interagency planning and budget allocation (Levinson, 1988). These resource files were later made available to the general public in printed directories of community social services. Because they were in published form, these directories were often out of date and were less than an ideal tool.

Beginning in the 1960s, a variety of information and referral services were organized through federal governmental action. The development and evaluation of information and referral services was facilitated by the Community Health Services and Facilities Act of 1961 (providing grants for public health information and referral). Titles III and IV of the Older American Act of 1965 and the Older Americans Act Amendments of 1973 focused on development of a national network on aging. Other federal agencies, including the Social Security Administration, Federal Information Centers, the Department of Housing and Urban Development, and Office of Economic Opportunity, explored information and referral systems, but these efforts have had limited development.

During the 1970s, information and referral services expanded under Title XX legislation, which designated them a "social utility," and mandated such services for all citizens. The Administration on Aging, U.S. Veterans Administration, and the National Alliance of Information and Referral Services (AIRS) all helped to expand, train personnel, and establish standards for these services. Communication and coordination between information and referral providers, and public and voluntary sectors was encouraged.

Today, there is a multiplicity of information and referral programs. Their fragmentation and complexity have required new bodies to coordinate *even them*. A recent inventory of programs in North America was listed in the Directory of Information and Referral Services in the United States and Canada, published by the AIRS in 1984. According to this directory, there are some 600 specialized referral agencies of this type.

Despite the existence of these agencies and directories, making use of varied services and programs at the community level can be a baffling and frustrating experience for both clients and professionals. The availability of these references provides a resource, but one that often must be employed with considerable skill and determination.

The Practitioner's Role

When linking is conceived of as a simple information and referral task, separated from a broad practice approach, it does not call for much more than intelligent use of a telephone book or directory. Linking solely as information and referral, therefore, is sometimes conducted by para-professionals, interns, or case aides. Competency-based linking requires well-trained individuals who are not only familiar with the community services available and the procedures necessary for client access, but who can also determine and actualize the best possible service mix (Leavitt, 1983).

Highly vulnerable clients need more than a referral. If simply given a referral, with no additional encouragement and support from the practitioner, clients often will not engage services (Brindis, Bart, & Loomis, 1987). In a hospital study, Ritvo (1987) found that more than half of discharged patients either received no known post-hospital aftercare, or very little, when practitioners did not follow-up on the clients.

Initially, the practitioner can provide help to the client in overcoming emotional barriers of frustration and fear that stem from unfamiliarity with a new situation. The client may require additional concrete assistance such as referral letters, help with intake forms, and transportation to and from services. It may also be necessary to overcome barriers to service, such as a client's lack of funds, restrictive eligibility requirements, or biased policies.

Research studies shed further light on the linking role. Practitioners need to have available ample community resources in aiding clients (Brindis et al., 1987). If community services are not present, or are not considered reliable, practitioners are more likely to intervene solely through individual counseling (Fiorentine & Grusky, 1990; Baker, Intagliata, & Kirshstein, 1980). However, large caseloads can also increase the practitioner's reliance on linkage rather than intensive direct service (Fiorentine & Grusky, 1990; Baker, Intagliata, & Kirshstein, 1980). A high caseload inhibits the workers' performance because they devote less time to following through with referrals (Intagliata & Baker, 1983; Brindis et al., 1987). In addition to those with high caseloads, practitioners with limited experience also report that they do not have enough time to devote to completing linkages for their clients and rely more on individual counseling (Brindis et al., 1987).

Relationship to Other Functions in the Model

Our orienting model indicates that the functions interrelate in various ways. Some functions set the groundwork for the next step or function, while others loop back to earlier functions. The linking function, in this way, effects and is influenced by several others.

Connection with resource identification. For linkages to occur, community resources must be noted and appraised. This requires the identification of all programs available from local community and federal resources. The practitioner needs to be aware of what services exist in the community in order to begin the process of linking. If the resource identification area is weak, the linkage function is undermined.

Connection with monitoring. It is the practitioner's responsibility to confirm that the client enters into the service to which he or she was referred and to develop a monitoring plan. This monitoring plan will make it possible to receive information on and track the client's service situation and progress. As an aspect of linkage, monitoring assures the stability and consistency of the client's receipt of services.

Connection with advocacy. If a client is refused treatment, the practitioner must determine the reason. If it was an inappropriate referral, a new linkage needs to be made, and information regarding this resource has to be corrected. If the client is refused treatment due to errors or inequities in the intake process, the practitioner may then take on an advocacy role to ensure service. Advocacy may also be required if the agency is simply uncaring or overly bureaucratic (Minahan, 1987).

Connection with interagency coordination. Linkage is enhanced when favorable interagency agreements and policies have been arranged at the outset of the program. At the same time, successful linkage procedures can feed back and enhance the function and status of agencies in the community (Loomis, 1988).

Influencing Organizations

Making linkages involves both technical knowledge and interactional skills. It entails means of influencing organizational behavior.

Formal authority. In defining roles and responsibilities, formal arrangements may confer authority and control on the practitioner. The practitioner is the crucial catalyst in the client's progress, and authority can facilitate this wide-ranging responsibility. It can be acquired through a variety of means.

Several researchers have found that interagency linkage is facilitated by structural arrangements that have "intrusive influence" or "clout" (Cook, 1977; Frumkin, 1977; Grisham, White, & Miller, 1983; Miller, 1980; Perlmutter, 1977; Steinberg & Carter, 1983; Tarail, 1977; U.S. Department of Health and Human Services, 1986). This research indicates that requests and demands from the outside often upset organizations' regular patterns and sense of autonomy. As a result, organizations often do not collaborate voluntarily (Frumkin, 1977; Tarail, 1977).

To encourage community-wide coordination, in one situation, Cook (1977) found that a central agency with a dominant position over the other agencies was necessary. Some research indicates that only through a lead agency with control of resources and legal sanctions are programs able to form effective linkages. Grisham et al. (1983) also found that the authority to command resources and responsibility was a critical variable influencing the character and quality of interagency linkage. Through their study of case management in several California communities, these researchers noted a continuum of interagency relationships, including high to low levels of authority and responsibility. They include:

1. no linkage;
2. client needs assessment followed by information and referral;
3. some financial authority to purchase selected services;
4. control of prescreening for certain services (such as admission to private-service facilities) *or* of a percentage of funds. Control of a percentage of funds could include control over public funds for a range of specific services and population categories;
5. comprehensive service delivery on a capitation basis. This level provides all services and receives payment in capitation form (similar to the arrangements of a health maintenance organization).

There are clearly various sources of authority available to the practitioner. One involves *administrative authority,* based on established policy and procedures, or formal agreements. In this mode, the practitioner is given the mandate to control client linkages by virtue of the position. The outside agencies cooperate because of the policies of both agencies or through a contract prescribing given actions.

Through administrative authority a practitioner can integrate a decentralized network of providers, or he can work under the auspices of the umbrella of a *super agency,* such as a health maintenance organization, the Administration on Aging, or a mental health council. Departments of social welfare, rehabilitation, or medical services often rely on formal administrative authority.

Legal authority, or legislative mandates, forces responsibility and compliance on some agencies. This is especially true for child neglect and abuse services, which the courts officiate, and for chronically mentally ill clients, because local mental health services are mandated to monitor services. Child welfare departments and courts, for example, use practitioners to link abused and neglected children in their custody to counseling services, residential treatment facilities, or emergency group homes, to name a few. Many of these licensed facilities are obligated to provide services for these children, and licensing requirements are based in part on their compliance with these legal mandates.

Fiscal authority is the ability to purchase services on behalf of the client. In some instances, a practitioner may have fiscal authorization as the client's court-appointed conservator. A conservator is responsible for handling the client's finances when that person is deemed incompetent. The professional task, then, is to responsibly administer the funds for all aspects of the client's life. This includes identifying service costs and maximizing client benefits (Bertsche & Horejsi, 1980). Establishing fiscal contracts requiring providers to deliver services makes agencies strictly accountable to the practitioner.

A pilot study by the Mathematica Policy Research for the U.S. Department of Health and Human Services (1986) investigated fiscal factors. The traditional case management model uses voluntary relationships and a small amount of additional funding to coordinate the services of multiple providers. The Mathematica model expanded service coverage by establishing a pool of funds that individual case managers were authorized to use. Practitioners determined the amount, duration, and scope of fees for services. The financial control model increased both client satisfaction and involvement of community service agencies in patient care. There was also a reduction in unmet need. (However, no overall cost savings were found.)

Formal authority can explicitly define admissions criteria, specific provisions, and service arrangements. Agreements may exist on multiple levels, including program, regional, or state entities.

Informal Relationships

Informal modes or relationships call on the practitioner to develop a personal style to effectively reach and persuade others (Minahan, 1987). Informal relationships may be entwined with the formal arrangements previously discussed. Still, there are times when these formalities do not apply or create obstacles that can best be overcome through more subtle means. For example, the practitioner can make a referral to an agency, and if the client's eligibility is "on the borderline," contacts made through serving on a professional association committee may convince a provider to tip toward accepting the client for admission.

Informal connections can help speed up service, cut down paperwork, get a more qualified professional on the case, or reduce fees. Informal associations come about through frequent association, exchange of favors, outside professional contact, and simple courtesy and respect in dealing with others. If informal relationships are abused, through a dishonest representation of a client or a practitioner's lack of assistance during a client crisis at the outside agency, they may lose their effect.

Practitioners often cultivate agencies that are particularly useful to clients. As an example, the practitioner might typically refer physically handicapped adults to a core group of top-level job training agencies where good working relationships exist. From the job training agency's perspective, the practitioner has been helpful and cooperative in the past and has been frank and to the point when making referrals. It is on these kinds of relationships that the practitioner can rely when working with certain difficult-to-place clients.

Barriers to Effective Linkage

There are distinct barriers that practitioners often have to overcome in the linking process, growing out of the autonomous and fragmented nature of the human services system. The distance between the worker and the line clinician in another agency may hinder communication. This occurs if the line clinician thinks that a case manager is too far removed from the "actual work" to know the ropes: the client's true condition, his readiness level, or the pressures experienced by the other organization. This is a greater problem if the case manager lacks professional credentials, for example, when para-professionals are used to link clients.

Clients themselves may constitute a barrier. This may stem from low self-confidence, lack of awareness of eligibility requirements, or illiteracy. Persons who have experienced extended periods of institutionalization may have difficulty understanding or trusting the system, necessitating maximum use of the professional's counseling skills, teaching ability, and technical information in executing a successful linkage.

Agencies to which the client is referred may have constraining eligibility regulations and policies, or there may be informal resistance from agency personnel. This restrictive environment may include "creaming" during intake, i.e., selecting only those individuals who have the highest likelihood of success in the program. For example, it is relatively easy to find a job for a middle-class alcoholic with a history of steady employment. The prospects are slimmer for an alcoholic with a physical disability and no sustained employment history. The riskier client will not add to the agency's record for publicity or fund-raising purposes.

As already noted, a block may occur when practitioners do not control the mechanisms necessary to obtain services for a client, such as a legal mandate or funds to pay for certain provisions. Here the practitioner may have to fall back on informal relationship or work with a supervisor to gain official clout.

PRACTICE GUIDELINES FOR LINKING CLIENTS TO FORMAL ORGANIZATIONS

The practice of linking begins with a clear understanding of the nature of the overarching relationship with an external service agency. The practitioner needs initially to clarify whether there are existing interorganizational policies or agreements that bear on an intended transaction. Does a source of authority exist that strengthens the practitioner's hand? Is the sanction administrative, legal, or fiscal? What specific commitments of service has the external agency made and under what conditions? Does the practitioner have tools of compliance to encourage or enforce these? These broad, system-level factors provide the framework for the discussion that follows.

Linking a client to formal resources flows from the established intervention plan and the identification and indexing of resources, with the practitioner seeking a match between the client's needs and the available resources. The UCLA survey provided qualitative data on interagency relations with strong practice implications. All of the respondents, without exception, reported that they engage in linking clients to formal organizations. The action described fell roughly into a pattern of sequential steps for carrying out the function. We will list and describe those practice steps, based on the survey and supplementary data sources.

Clarifying Client Needs

Client needs have to be in focus for effective linkage to take place. This occurs early during assessment and goal determination. Here they must be brought forward clearly and pointedly. As one respondent in the UCLA study put it, "Linking starts with an understanding of client's ability to function. You have to have both a knowledge of the client and knowledge of available services."

Selecting Appropriate Resources

There should be on hand an index of working resources, including information on the availability, adequacy, appropriateness, acceptability, and accessibility of services. These matters were discussed in Chapter 5. A few key points will be mentioned in the current context: Does the client need a specialized or multipurpose agency? What level or quality of service is required? Does it provide well for clients with diverse ethnic backgrounds? What are the eligibility requirements? Is transportation available? Who is a good initial contact in the agency?

Matching the Client with Relevant Services

In the UCLA survey, linking was not a routine or casual task. It consisted of not only referring to a community agency, but also to the most uniquely suitable fit dictated by the client's situation. Field notes for one respondent convey this notion:

> If the client needs are for placement, and client qualifies based on my assessment of a board-and-care home, I call Continuing Care Services, which makes the placement.

> If client needs hospitalization, I make phone contacts to find hospitals that will accept on a voluntary basis.

> If client needs medication, he/she is referred by me to whomever actually makes the M.D. appointment for them at the facility.

> If client needs therapy, I make a follow-up appointment for them at the facility.

> If client lacks basics of life (food, for example), referral is made to the local mission or food bank.

> If client is relatively stable, I may refer to PROJECT RETURN [a socialization program run by the County Mental Health Association].

Respondents speak of matching this way:

> Linking involves much more than just getting a resource, one must understand and be able to use a resource appropriately. Some clients, more than others, have problems functioning and need special things (some have no friends, no ability to express themselves, etc., and have a very fragile alliance with reality); they also need help in following through with whatever they must do.

Matching very difficult clients with appropriate settings takes considerable diagnostic skill and interpersonal sophistication. One case manager depicts this vividly:

Resident managers all want *certain* people, and you soon know which! Once one gets to know them personally, this activity is less time-consuming. One residence, for example, takes my chronic people; another will freely accept drug abusers, very promiscuous people, old alcoholics (*very* difficult to place), violent people, fire starters. I found placement for a chronic fire-starter who was accepted there as a challenge! Women especially take on such placement challenges; one in particular runs her home like the military and is really successful with difficult cases!

Matching as a two-way process is brought home as follows:

Residence operators really want clients. The problems is that I don't have the right people for them, and clients are usually picky too (coed, age, location—there are many factors to consider). Residence homes usually are really not that structured, yet some clients really need a lot of structure. Instead, clients are pretty much independent in many situations.

At this point we separate, somewhat artificially because they overlap, practice roles with clients and with agencies.

Exercising Practice Roles with Clients

Involve the client.   Linking is not just acquiring resources *for* a client, it frequently involves acquiring resources *with* the client. A goal of linkage, to the degree possible, is to help the client develop independence and the ability to make his or her own linkages successfully. When possible, the client should be given an active part in choosing support resources. Options should be presented in an understandable and detailed way. Ballew and Mink (1986, p. 245) discuss this as follows:

When should we take over and rescue, and when should we offer support but, allow the client to find his own solutions? Our concern for the ultimate ability of our client to be competent suggests that we should most often choose to support rather than rescue, but at the same time we know that the discouragement of failure can destroy the client's confidence. It is sometimes necessary to provide our support by direct intervention when the demands and/or needs become overwhelming to the client. This should be done with the direct involvement of the client whenever possible.

A client that is unable to fully participate in linking or acquiring services may only benefit through being told which agency to attend and why. Practice with a significantly impaired individual might require this type of intervention. An adult client with the mental capacity of a young child is not in a position to make fine distinctions among services. In such a case, the practitioner will need to provide clear-cut direction for the client. Even so, the client can indicate a level of comfort in working with the assigned service providers.

Prepare the client. Survey respondents indicated that often clients need to visit an unfamiliar setting and may be apprehensive and confused. They frequently need to be given support in this new encounter. Respondents indicated that the client may be given information regarding the agency, a contact person in the agency, procedures that will be followed, and what follow-up assistance will be forthcoming. Some practitioners will coach the client about how to go through intake. Emotional support may be given about how to overcome anxiety or lack of confidence in going forward.

Some techniques described in previous chapters can be applied here. Modeling the actions necessary to link to services is a technique that can be used for clients who are not sure where to begin. The client can, perhaps, watch while the practitioner makes an initial telephone call.

Role-playing may help increase a client's ability to assume more responsibility. Coaching the client and rehearsing the first visit helps anticipate possible difficulties. It is a useful technique for clients that have the capacity to self-link but need to acquire the skills necessary to do so. The practitioner can begin by role-playing simple actions like inquiring at the local community center about recreation services or opening a bank account. Eventually, the client can be engaged in more complex role-plays such as a job interview or renting an apartment.

Initially, it is useful to clarify the purpose of a first visit. Make sure the client has the checklist of items to take and knows the name of the person to see. Then, the first visit might be role played so that the client becomes comfortable with the process.

Accompany the client if appropriate. On the day of the appointment, in some cases, it is beneficial to accompany the client. This may be the only time when the practitioner can observe the client in a new setting. The practitioner can also use the occasion to develop informal relationships with providers, or formalize relationships through scheduled case conferences.

If it is not possible to go with the client on a first visit, it may be helpful to arrange for someone close to the client (a relative or friend) to go along. Although some professionals think that escorting a client to an agency fosters dependence, it can sometimes be a great assistance in developing a client's independence, if used as a teaching opportunity.

Not all respondents in the survey escort the client to the facility. Some only give instructions. Others provide bus tokens. In other cases, they simply give the client a note.

For some respondents, client transport is a critical issue. They do not think it is realistic or fair to send an impaired person out alone to negotiate the complexities of the transportation system and then the service agency system.

Yet their agency, they believed, did not provide a means to offer clients sufficient transportation assistance. The issue was expressed as follows:

> The agency does not allow client transport; we are not allowed to take them in
> our own cars because of insurance problems. To use your own car, even in a
> case in which you feel it's essential to accompany that particular client some-
> where, is just too big a personal financial risk.

In some cases, arrangements for public transportation are inadequate:

> We have been unable to obtain bus tokens for outlying areas.

One result is that transportation is provided only to a few clients on a
selective basis:

> I used to take clients to day treatment, to vocational rehabilitation, etc. Now I
> do this only with clients who have language difficulties, or those who need
> additional support.

Or workers will take the matter into their own hands, at some risk:

> We are not supposed to transport clients in our own cars, but I do because I
> must. Clients do not have relevant skills in that area, and if the client does not
> show up, there is a drop in proper service on the part of the agency.

Review experiences with the client.   Activities the client performs solo
should be reviewed as appropriate. The practitioner should give positive
feedback whenever possible, even for incremental successes (Modrcin, Rapp,
& Chamberlain, 1985). Successes and failures can be discussed to determine
why they occurred. The practitioner should encourage the client to report the
strengths and weaknesses of the program that was experienced, using this as
an opportunity to monitor progress, provide additional support, and work
with any potential difficulties before they escalate. The trick is to strike a balance between providing too much assistance—leading to dependency, and
too little support—leaving the client immobilized and with low morale.

Exercising Practice Roles with Agencies

Determine the point of contact.   It is important to know whom to contact and at what level in the agency or system. This is important when using
an agency for the first time or when dealing with a special area of need (such
as job training resources for the developmentally disabled).

In linking a client to an organization, it is useful to identify a specific individual. One possibility is to call the agency directly and simply ask to speak to
an "intake worker." If it is not the type of organization that would have such a

position (such as a recreation facility), a functional title such as "Program Director" can be used. For large agencies, adding a descriptive prefix can elicit the proper person, for example: "Youth Services Program Director," "Health Services Program Director," or "Sheltered Care Program Director."

A contact at the administrative level may be necessary to clear the way for certain clients. The service provider may not be familiar with your agency and may have policies or admission criteria that are exclusionary, i.e., a recreation program does not allow blind persons to participate in activities or does not have scholarships available for those unable to pay. Only an executive director or assistant director may be authorized to deal with this (Modrcin et al., 1985).

If blocks persist, policy level contacts and advocacy actions may be required with board members or political leaders. More information about this level of activity is described in Chapter 10.

Initiate contact with the agency.   In the UCLA study, the initial contact with a relevant service was primarily by telephone. Information is obtained and given, appointments are made, and arrangements are agreed upon.

Respondents said that they try to present the client in a favorable light in order to gain acceptance, but that they also refrained from making false statements:

> I will make phone calls to agencies I'm linking clients to in anticipation of prob-lems that could come up. It's like putting in a good word for the client and pre-senting the situation realistically at the same time. It's sensitizing the agency to the patient. We try to sell our patient to the agencies. But you have to be honest above all. You have to keep a good inter-agency relationship and have some kind of credibility. I do not lie about clients. They know that I don't hold infor-mation back. It would be like cutting your nose off; you will never be able to place a client there again.

While the telephone is a quick and easy means of communication, it is not infallible:

> Sometimes I can't get people on the phone when I really need them (because they are out to lunch, at a meeting, etc.). But I usually need people *now* because the client is in my office just then. The most vexing of all is the Social Security Office—it is impossible. It is so hard to find out who is in charge there, they lose papers, and are *always* frustrating to me. Also, they deny *so* many applications, even if people are *clearly* disabled; what a waste of time to try to go through them.

It obviously helps in this process to know people beforehand, and have good rapport with them.

If the client will be undertaking the responsibility, the practitioner can clear the way. Making the initial telephone call for the appointment can be frightening or baffling for some clients (as we already discussed). Instead of making the appointment for the client, one strategy practitioners use is to call the service provider to let a contact person know that the client will be phoning soon. The client is then given the name of the contact person at the agency, sometimes with permission to "use my name."

To implement linkage, a considerable number of respondents stated they visit the agency (sometimes accompanying the client there). This visit has many of the purposes of the phone contact but carries them further: to prepare the agency to serve the client well, to observe the situation, to offer consultation, to arrange for follow-up evaluation, and to help the client adjust.

Complete necessary paperwork.   Intake procedures are complex at some agencies. The practitioner may want to prepare a checklist of the materials that are needed, such as social security number, birth certificate, special agency forms, proof of income, etc.

Respondents report that ordinarily a considerable volume of paperwork is needed to put through a referral. They tell of obtaining a release, compiling documentation, securing a psychiatric evaluation, and pulling together other forms—medical, social service, occupational, and criminal records, among others. The objective is, naturally, to protect the client, facilitate the link, equip the receiving agency to provide a smooth entry, and comply with existing regulations.

While this seems straightforward enough and appropriate, respondents indicate that it has its down side: "It requires lots of running around and a lot of time. Sometimes it takes hours to get a client to sign a consent form to release information, or to nail down an M.D.'s signature."

Negotiating Relationships with the Agency

Before discussing a client with another agency, the practitioner ought to have a consent form signed by the client. This promotes confidentiality and privacy. This form may specify that information be given only under particular conditions, or it may provide the practitioner with general discretion to selectively share information (Ballew & Mink, 1986). Before having a client sign an informed consent form, the practitioner needs to be sure the client understands the stipulations. The form needs to include: who will receive the information, why the information should be shared, and what specific information will be shared. It is usually best to provide only the minimum amount of information necessary for the referral as a way of optimizing confidentiality.

There has to be an agreement with the service provider about what is to be coordinated in the transaction. Do they want to develop a common treatment plan? Will common reporting forms be used? How will confidentiality be assured? After a client has completed a first visit at an agency, it is useful to make a follow-up telephone call. This is to confirm whether or not the linkage actually occurred, and to determine whether or not the referral was appropriate and effective. At this time, a monitoring plan can be agreed upon, including the scheduling of case conferences.

There is a range of coordinating procedures that can be worked out to guide interagency links. Steinberg and Carter (1983) have enumerated many of them:

- appeals committees
- assessment or care plan review teams
- co-location (sharing a facility)
- interagency central intake/standardized intake form
- interlocking governing bodies
- joint programs (pooling resources to provide a common service)
- loaned staff or jointly funded staff
- mandatory prescreening
- monitoring procedures
- out-stationing (locating workers from one agency on the premises of another)
- program review team
- purchase of service agreements
- referral agreements
- shared information system
- technical assistance
- contracts pertaining to services

Interagency contracts are typically negotiated by the policy-making administrators, but contracts can also consist of voluntary agreements among front-line service providers or purchase of service. Most often, agreements are made for specific clients (Weil, 1985). Client service contracts are sometimes developed to overcome problems associated with interagency cooperation; they specify services and reporting procedures. All agencies and professionals involved with helping the client should be involved in the contractual meeting and, if feasible, the client also.

Interagency contracts should specify the goals of the intervention plan and the services to be provided by each agency, including which person or agency provides which service(s), the cost, and a schedule, if appropriate. The higher the level of specificity, the easier the monitoring and evaluation of the program. It is useful to include procedures to ensure the practitioner can properly monitor the client's progress and the evaluation plan (Weil, 1985).

Examining Successes and Failures

The approaches that have been discussed are meant to increase the possibilities of successful linkage, but service systems are fluid and unpredictable. If the linkage fails, this indicates that either new service sources are needed, or better strategies for obtaining available resources are required. It is important to examine each unsuccessful effort to formulate a revised approach (Modrcin et al., 1985). This also promotes ongoing learning by the practitioner about how to optimize subsequent linkages.

REFERENCES

Baker, F., Intagliata, J., & Kirshstein, R. (1980). *Case management evaluation: Second interim report.* Buffalo, NY: Tefco Services.

Ballew, J. R. & Mink, G. (1986). *Case management in the human services.* Springfield, IL: Charles C. Thomas.

Bertsche, A. V. & Horejsi, C. R. (1980). Coordination of client services. *Social Work,* March, 94–98.

Brindis, C., Bart, R., & Loomis, A. (1987). Continuous counseling: Case management with teenage parents. *Social Casework, 68*(3), 164–172.

Cook, K. (1977). Exchange and power in networks of interorganizational relations. *The Sociology Quarterly, 18*(1), 62–82.

Department of Mental Health, Los Angeles County. (1985). *Human resource development: Issues in case management.* Los Angeles, CA.

Fiorentine, R., & Grusky, O. (1990). When case managers manage the seriously mentally ill: A role contingency approach. *Social Service Review, 64,* 79–93.

Frumkin, M. (1977). An exploratory study of service integration with organizations serving problem youth (Doctoral dissertation, Brandeis University). *Dissertation Abstracts International,* 77-15268.

Grisham, M., White, M., & Miller, L. (1983). *An overview of case management.* Multipurpose Senior Services Project Evaluation, University Extension, University of California, Berkeley.

Intagliata J., & Baker, F. (1983). Factors affecting case management services for the chronically mentally ill. *Administration in Mental Health, 11*(2), 75–91.

Leavitt, S. S. (1983). Case management: A remedy for problems of community care. In C. J. Sanborn (Ed.), *Case management in mental health services.* New York: Hawthorne Press.

Levinson, R. W. (1988). *Information and referral networks: Doorways to human services.* New York: Springer.

Loomis, F. J. (1988). Case management in health care. *Health and Social Work, 13*(3), 219–225.

Miller, P. (1980). An examination of interorganizational issues in coordination of human services (Doctoral dissertation, Ohio State University). *Dissertation Abstracts International, 16*(3), 1009.

Minahan, A. (1987) *Encyclopedia of social work* (vol. 1, 18th ed.). Silver Springs, MD: National Association of Social Workers.

Modrcin, M., Rapp, C., & Chamberlain, R. (1985). *Case management with psychiatrically disabled individuals: Curriculum and training program.* Lawrence, KS: University of Kansas School of Social Welfare.

Perlmutter, F. (1977). Interorganizational behavior patterns of line staff and service integration. *Social Service Review,* Dec., 672–689.

Random House Dictionary of the English Language. (1987). (2nd ed.). New York: Random House.

Ritvo, R. (1987). Coordinating in-patient and out-patient services: The need for action. *Social Work in Health Care, 13*(1), 39–50.

Steinberg, R. & Carter, G. (1983). *Case management and the elderly.* Lexington, MA: Lexington Books.

Tarail, M. (1977). A study of interorganizational relations: An exploration of interorganizational coordination among mental health organizations (D.S.W. dissertation, Adelphi University). *Dissertation Abstracts International, 38*(9-A), No. 5718.

U. S. Department of Health and Human Services. (1986). *The evaluation of the national long-term care demonstration final report.* Princeton, NJ: Mathematica Policy Research.

Weil, M. (1985). Professional and educational issues in case management practice. In M. Weil & J. M. Karls (Eds.), *Case management in human service practice* (pp. 357–390). San Francisco: Jossey-Bass.

Woodberry, L. G. (1929). *The central index.* NY: Social Service Exchange Committee of the Association of Community Chests and Councils.

8

Linking Clients with Informal Support Networks

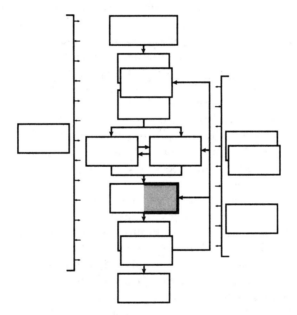

UNDERSTANDING INFORMAL LINKAGE

The Place of Informal Support

Everyone knows the old adage telling us that man's best friend comes from the canine world. Propaganda from the humane society aside, many men—and women—receive a great deal of aid and comfort from such humanoid representatives as a doting aunt, loyal roommate, and favorite teacher. Human service professionals refer to these helpers collectively as informal social support networks. These individuals have a special capacity to help clients cope with the daily demands of living. In one agency the staff mounted a poster reading: Friends Can Be Good Medicine. A client plaintively penciled in underneath, "If you have one."

In the UCLA survey of practitioners, there was general agreement about working intensively with informal networks. Survey respondents particularly emphasized contacts with the family. They described "increasing the involvement of family members" and "the solicitation of significant others to partake in tasks." One practitioner characterized the function more broadly as "establishing a network of helpful people one can draw on." This was not spoken of as a simple and automatic undertaking, rather "it requires knowing how to talk to people and obtain their cooperation."

In informal linkage, it is important to consider the network's pre-existing role in the client's life. The network members may already be helpers, and the practitioner needs only to oversee these supportive ties. Conversely, some network members may no longer be well connected with the client, for example, family members estranged from their relative or unaware of the need for help. Ties need to be reinstated. Other potential supportive resources in the client's environment may never have been tapped, such as distant relatives, self-help groups, or neighbors. Here, the practitioner can act to identify and then energize these inert sources of assistance.

Informal support systems are not a new phenomenon. The notion reflects a sociological reality: that family, friends, neighbors, and community members have traditionally been natural, and significant, helpers. Pearson (1990, p. 10) notes, "the concepts of social support and natural support systems have perennially occupied an important place in artistic and scholarly considerations of the human condition, though perhaps under different names and labels."

The theme of social support has surfaced throughout history. For example, biblical writings stress the importance of offering succor to neighbors, the poor, and strangers, as symbolized in the parable of the "Good Samaritan." In early social welfare policy, laws regarding governmental aid to families were based on the principle of family responsibility, viewed as a "legal obligation of support that adults had for their children, grandchildren, and aged parents" (Axinn & Levin, 1982, p. 15).

The use of natural supporters has been addressed differently across various disciplines. For example, sociobiological theorists view the extension of support (altruistic behavior, cooperation, and mutual protection) as an inherent human characteristic with group survival implications (Nelson & Jurmain, 1988). Psychologists and sociologists stress that the family and other close associations are uniquely able to provide a private haven of intimate companionship in an increasingly impersonal world (Coser, Rhea, Steffan, & Nock, 1983). The social work field, using a person-in-situation vision, has long sought to understand and treat clients by enhancing their interaction with others in their social circle (Hollis & Woods, 1981). The common thread between the various disciplines is that social support plays a vital role in promoting human well-being.

Members of ethnic communities traditionally seek help from the informal caregivers and voluntary associations of their culture, rather than from institutionally based professionals. For many people, help from informal sources is more accessible, culturally valid, and personally acceptable (Gottlieb, 1988). Research documents these differential patterns of social service use. For example, Hispanics turned mostly to their own informal systems for assistance, and used significantly fewer agency services than did a comparative group of Anglos (Greene & Monahan, 1984). Variations in use have also been associated with locality (i.e., urban or rural) (Jurkiewicz, 1980).

Functions of Informal Support

Informal support networks supplement the contributions of formal agencies; they can fill in gaps or enrich services. In addition, some needs of clients requiring intimate care can be satisfied as well or better by natural helpers than by professional workers. Currently the formal service sector must make do with shrinking resources, while the need for emotional and material support is increasing among some populations that rely on social services (Seltzer & Mayer, 1988). Taking advantage of supportive forces in the natural environment alleviates reliance on formal systems and professional experts. Recognizing the value of informal support, however, is not to advocate reduced public commitment to formal support for groups requiring it. There are limitations and difficulties within informal helping sources, as we will soon see.

Many of the functions of informal support networks described in the practice literature are confirmed by empirical research. Studies indicate the social networks provide "information, material assistance and emotional aid" (Grusky & Tierney, 1985). One study found a range of satisfactions from self-help activities, including sharing similar experiences, sharing information, receiving and giving advice, gaining comfort and reassurance, and even helping others (Taylor, Falke, Mazel, & Hilsberg, 1984). Kaye

(1985) sought the perspectives of formal home-care workers about the functions of informal networks. Respondents indicated provision of "material assistance," including telephoning, shopping, or bringing special treats, and of "emotional aid," including helping with emotional problems and offering general psychological support. Other research also emphasizes aid in meeting the immediate tasks of everyday living (Toseland, Rossiter, Peak, & Smith, 1990).

Studies have also confirmed that natural support systems are helpful in circumventing stressful events: social support plays an important role in buffering the deleterious effects of negative life-stressors (Beels, Gutwirth, Berkeley, & Struening, 1984). Findings indicate that "emotionally sustaining" roles are an important ingredient of natural support systems—caring, understanding, hope, and friendship—and that these facilitate patient recovery (Stefanik-Campisi & Marion, 1988). The type of support provided clearly varies and is systematized in the next section.

A Typology of Informal Support Functions

Informal support systems, among other things, provide *friendship and socialization.* They draw people into common interest relationships, thereby increasing a client's social interaction and companionship (Gottlieb, 1985). Some clients, such as the long-term mentally ill, lack social connections. The elderly commonly suffer from isolation and loneliness. A formal agency might send a nurse or aide for a few hours each day to alleviate the sense of isolation, thereby buoying the client's spirits sporadically. Yet the client may feel more genuine human connectedness when the help is given regularly by someone with whom there is a natural bond. Family, friends, and neighbors offer human connections that are typically deeper and more emotionally gratifying.

Another function that members of the informal network provide is *emotional support,* such as personal encouragement. This type of aid may engender a sense of having someone to rely on. Gottlieb (1984) refers to "emotionally sustaining discussions" in which the helping activity includes talk about stressful feelings and taking on tasks to lighten the other's feelings of overload.

Informal support networks often provide specific *practical assistance* for clients. There may be a need for help with tasks of daily living such as cleaning, grocery shopping, transportation, and assorted errands. Aid may include helping a client adhere to a treatment plan, such as following a medication schedule.

Informal networks can also give direct substantive *guidance and advice* to clients (Pearson, 1990). This can include assistance in decisions about planning for life transitions, such as taking a new job, getting married, or moving to another community.

These kinds of psychological and practical aids can, in consequence, *buffer the client against stressors* that occur in his or her life situation. While it is obviously impossible to block all negative effects of life-course events, such environmental supports can make the handling of stress easier. For example, the mentally ill are sometimes stigmatized and face prejudicial treatment. The client may have difficulty confronting detractors in daily activities, and a supportive companion can ward off discrimination. Or preventative actions can be taken (Biegel, Shore, & Gordon, 1984), as when a network member talks to a developmentally delayed child's teacher to encourage sensitive interaction with the pupil.

Social integration is another type of assistance, which incorporates some of the others. Informal helpers can assist with reintegration into the community after deinstitutionalization through making a job contact, being a cosigner for a loan, or providing a temporary place to live.

Types of Informal Support Networks

Different network members possess qualities that allow them to contribute differentially to caregiving. Here we examine the various types of helpers and their attributes.

Families. Families of clients are perhaps the most intimately exposed to the problems in living that confront their impeded relative and may be a rich source of aid. Because families are close at hand and permanent, they can offer help that is intense, timely, and sustained. The immediate family may include a spouse, adult children, siblings, and parents. "Kin" may include extended family such as aunts, uncles, and cousins. Ethnic groups often have extended families that include godparents and other non–blood-related individuals with very intimate ties, such as *compadres* and *comadres*. According to Kaye (1985), relatives typically take part in budgeting and planning, escorting outside the household, and speaking for the client at social service or welfare centers. These activities require the client to trust the caregiver as an honest, capable representative and advocate.

For the elderly, the family, primarily adult children, generally constitute the preferred source of care (Brody, 1978). Despite the public image of the abandoned and isolated elderly person, research by Brody and others indicates that the elderly are generally knitted into family life and continue to maintain close relationships with family members. The family, however, can not always be counted on to help because of physical distance, personal burdens, or disinterest.

A family member's contribution to the client's needs will depend on availability and willingness to participate. For example, families of the mentally ill often react with embarrassment and denial, distancing themselves from the impaired relative after the onset of illness (Gallagher, 1985). This withdrawal may stem from experiencing a sense of loss over their relative, fear of mental illness, and apprehension about coping with the new situation. In the case of abused children, a family tie remains a fundamental need for the young, but the particular family unit may be more destructive than beneficial. The gains and losses of family reunification in such instances need to be weighed.

Friends and neighbors.   Friends of clients are a prime source of social support. They may be individuals who the client has known for years or months. Those friends who live close to the client, naturally, are likely to be of greater assistance. Sometimes clients served by the same agency become friends and providers of mutual aid.

Neighbors are in a position to offer both practical and emotional assistance. Mutual aid arrangements frequently develop out of neighborhood, residential, and social contacts. If the helping relationship is reciprocal, giving assistance will not be viewed as an imposition or burden. For example, elderly neighbors may trade off tasks, such as shopping for one another and, because of their physical proximity, be a "valuable resource . . . in times of crisis" (Biegel et al., 1984, p. 21).

Sometimes a natural area such as a housing development or a set-apart city block can be fertile ground for informal networking. A field report to the author from an agency serving the elderly comments on this.

> Many of our clients lived in the senior housing complex next door to the agency, and thus were surrounded by people their own age who shared a common Chinese language and culture. The manager of the complex became very helpful to our agency, because she was often the first person to find out that a resident's health had deteriorated or a person was in crisis. She also told close neighbors about situations that needed a helping hand. Many of the clients lived alone in apartments that they had occupied for many years. Friendships of various kinds developed among these people. Also, they were able to socialize at teas during bingo and at other group activities in the building. The complex created a natural support system for the residents.

Community based groups.   A range of community based groups are sources of potential nurture. These groups can include ethnic societies, neighborhood associations, block clubs, and social, political, religious and fraternal organizations. Activities may include discussions, sharing recreational or cultural interests, field trips, and community involvement. Groups offer clients who are members such things as social contacts, ways of expressing interests, civic identity, and entertainment. Groups that engage in political advocacy and social action provide an outlet for attacking detrimental external factors impinging on the client and can foster a sense of personal empowerment.

Self-help groups. Self-help groups consist of individuals who are personally affected in common by a distressing psychological or social condition. Typical activities within self-help groups include fellowship, crisis assistance, mutual aid, self-development, and social action (Powell, 1975). While self-help groups sometimes are a formally organized means of support, they also often develop naturally without professional involvement.

A common affliction or difficulty generates quick and close bonding among members of self-help groups. Group members have a natural sensitivity for others, and their shared life experiences provide a basis for a mutual helping ethic. Group sessions lead individuals to realize that they are not alone, that others share in their problems and needs, and often cope successfully with the same issues.

Well known self-help programs are Alcoholics Anonymous, Parents Anonymous, and Synanon. Others include parents of mentally or emotionally handicapped children, AIDS or cancer groups, and support groups for the disabled.

Characteristics of Informal Networks

The characteristics of informal networks are important to consider in forging informal linkages. Different attributes meet different needs of clients.

Size. One characteristic is the network's *size*. The number of members included within a network will affect each member's role in caregiving. Distribution of the caregiving responsibilities among many network members will ease each individual's burden of support for the client. The social circles of severely mentally ill persons, for example, tend to be smaller in size than others because of the difficulty these clients have in forming personal relationships.

Helpfulness. The network members' *willingness to help* will be decisive in developing supportive ties (Segal, 1979). As mentioned earlier, some network members will be open to providing assistance while others may be estranged from the client. Some kinds of networks stress assertive aid-giving, such as self-help groups, and some churches. Another type of network may view a focus on helping individuals as an impediment to a higher priority goal, as for example in a home-owners association, where the overriding emphasis may be the external task of preventing high-rise development in the neighborhood. Network members may be unwilling to give assistance for a variety of reasons, i.e., the nature of the client's impairment may cause some network members to reject the disabled member. Pearson (1990, p. 84) asserts that "some individuals alienate the members of their natural support network so thoroughly that their supporters severely restrict their flow of assistance."

Intensity.   Another characteristic, *intensity*, or the frequency of contact between the members, will influence the extent and quality of available support. The members of a close-knit network, such as the nuclear family, will be able to communicate with each other readily and coordinate tasks in caring for the client. There can be more overlap and exchange in providing support than in a large group, where division of labor rather than integration may be called for.

Durability.   It is useful to consider the *durability* or the length of time of the network's existence. A long-term connection between the client and the network members is indicative of a more sustained level of social support. According to Gerhart (1990), acceptance of and sensitivity to a client's needs increases with the permanence of a network. Family members share a lifetime of experiences, and thus their relationships are typically described as deep and continuous. Certainly there are exceptions, and a durable relationship will not always be a supportive one. As already stated, some families are rife with conflict and members may be averse to providing assistance.

Accessibility and proximity.   It is also important to consider the *accessibility* of network members and their *proximity*. Both the network members' physical location as well as their openness in terms of availability of time and energy will affect the practitioner's ability to facilitate successful informal linkage. If the network members are physically close to the client, linkage will be logistically more feasible. Clearly, neighbors and community groups exist nearby and are at hand. Family, kin, and friends, say in the case of elders, sometimes reside in more distant places, rendering informal support linkage potentially problematic. However, frequent use of the telephone can serve to close the physical distance.

Reciprocity.   Other characteristics of the support network define the relationship between the network and the client, rather than the attributes of the network itself. One such characteristic is *reciprocity*—the flow of support between the client and the members of the network. A relationship in which both parties give and take is "reciprocal" because both sides benefit from the assistance they receive. Patterns of aid sometimes remain more stable if there is a norm of benefits exchange. Self-help groups incorporate this norm, and many families do also.

Some relationships between clients and the support network will be uni-directional; it is the client who basically receives favors and services, with network members giving more than they get back. Mentally ill individuals often have difficulty in reciprocating. While they can be generous, this help is sometimes sporadic and unreliable. Pearson (1990, p. 84) comments that "the paths of many unsupported persons are littered with relationships from which the other persons have withdrawn because they found the cost/benefit ratio was not running in their favor."

Network members may experience a heavy emotional or financial strain, "caregiver burden," when called on for ongoing one-directional support (Seltzer & Mayer, 1988). If the burden becomes too great, without reciprocation or relief, the network member may no longer be able to give. Literature on the elderly population commonly refers to caregiver anxiety and depression resulting from attempts to sandwich in the demands of a needy older relative and the needs of the helper's own children (Biegel et al., 1984).

Integration of Concepts

Table 8-1 presents a schematic summary of informal support network characteristics. This chart is useful in indicating to practitioners what kinds of networks to use for different purposes and circumstances. For example, if a client is reserved and private, a low or medium density situation might be preferred initially. If the client has a variety of different needs that have been carried out at different times and places, a large network with individuals who divide tasks may be the best choice. If the client is highly active and capable, a reciprocal arrangement might be called for. For each type of network helper, the table estimates the degree to which each characteristic is involved.

This chart is heuristically suggestive of the kind of diagnostic thinking that can go into planning network linkages. It is a working tool rather than a blueprint, and needs research to authenticate or refine these estimates.

Problems in Informal Support Linkage

In the UCLA field study, a large portion of responses pointed to problems in informal linkage. The following section summarizes the UCLA findings and related research.

Several practitioners referred to *burnout* in supporters as a common problem. Families often live with the client for long periods during which the stress of caring for a low-functioning individual slowly wears down the tolerance, patience, and understanding of kin. This experience is documented by Keating (1981) in a study of family attitudes toward deinstitutionalization of mentally retarded children. He found that families had difficulty in coping

TABLE 8–1 Characteristics of Informal Networks According to Type of Network

	FAMILY/ KIN	FRIENDS/ NEIGHBORS	SELF-HELP GROUPS	COMMUNITY GROUPS
Size	low	medium	medium/high	high
Willingness to help	high	medium	high	low
Intensity	high	medium	medium/high	low
Durability	high	medium	low	medium
Accessibility	high	high	medium/high	low
Reciprocity	high	medium	high	medium

if the child was older and had greater medical needs. Other research also documents that patients may place severe emotional and social strains on their families (Doll, 1976). Chronic mental health ailments tend to drain family caretakers of their emotional resources, especially if the impairment includes an element of danger. For example, the presence of children in the household may deter those responsible from keeping a client at home in order to avoid jeopardizing their safety.

Several practitioners in the survey indicated that the *lack of education, training, and understanding of the client's impairment* constitutes a major problem with informal support networks. For example, some family members lack the skills necessary to help the client follow treatment recommendations. Other research confirms this (Thompson & Barnsley, 1981). The family may perceive client needs differently than the client or than qualified professionals. Studies report that "families have been underprepared for the trauma of managing a deinstitutionalized relative" (Iodice & Wodarski, 1987, p. 122). One UCLA respondent commented that this deficit in the family's understanding and awareness of the client's problems and needs creates unrealistic expectations on the part of the family regarding the practitioner. Case managers in the UCLA study indicated that their caseloads typically do not allow time to adequately provide necessary information to families to win their understanding.

A few respondents reported experiences with overly meddlesome families who engage in *inappropriate interference* with the client's treatment and service plans. Families often want things done in a particular way and insist on specific service arrangements. In a few cases, respondents reported, the family reaction seemed extreme: "families scuttle treatment plans" and "they can really sabotage the case manager's work."

One respondent, reflecting the view of several, stated that in her experience *some families are "disorganized and destructive."* Scapegoating can pervade family interactions. Crotty and Kulys (1985), likewise, examined negative interaction between social networks and schizophrenic clients. They found that family frustration and impatience can cause the family to be not only nonsupportive but even hostile. Relatives serving as caregivers often unknowingly contribute to the stress felt by the patient. Thus, family involvement has been found sometimes to be problematic or erratic. Interactions with family members can be highly conflictual and may involve an unhealthy degree of overprotection of the patient, thus "contact with family members may be differentially beneficial" (Grusky & Tierney, 1985, p. 39). In some cases the family builds its life around a dependent member. Strengthening that member can throw off the thread of equilibrium, causing a parent, for example, to feel less needed and useful.

Families may also *neglect or abandon* their ill relatives, eschewing any level of support. Case managers in the UCLA field study noted a pervasive problem with uninterested and resistant families who disassociate themselves from the client's predicament. Families who refuse to work with the practitioners, and "dump" the client on them, set limitations on prospects for the client. A respondent noted that some families experience guilt and denial, which restricts their ability for supportive action. Other, more fragmented families, simply abandon their relative. According to several respondents, families fail to understand the client's impairment and reject the situation.

The UCLA survey also identified the family's *unwillingness to acknowledge a client's ailment* as a problem in dealing with families. The stigma of the impairment exacerbated family anger, disappointment, and frustration in coping. Some study respondents indicated that family members exhibit the same symptoms the clients do. One practitioner observed that in mental health settings "the family can be just as sick as the client!" These issues, combined with the family's unrealistic expectations, render informal linkage an often arduous practice task.

The field study was conducted in a mental health context, and family difficulties may be more pronounced in that setting. With other clients, such as the aging, there may be similar manifestations, but at a less intense level. Nevertheless, these data warn that informal social supports are no panacea in the realm of social services. It is fruitless to bank on them to somehow replace public services and magically wave away the costs of helping people in need.

PRACTICE GUIDELINES FOR INFORMAL LINKAGE

This section presents methods for the practice of informal linkage. The topics covered include: defining the network; selecting key helping sources; making linkages between clients and informal helpers; strengthening existing networks; and evaluating linkage strategies.

Defining the Network

One fundamental activity in informal linkage is an analysis of the client's personal network. A preliminary step in assessment is to identify all the natural helping sources, their attributes, and their potential. Two main approaches to this are common: taking a self-report from the client or interviewing other informed individuals, such as family members, friends, and relevant professionals. Service data can also be reviewed for clues.

The following points are useful:

- Interviews can be conducted in an informal or a formal manner.
- Relevant information can be obtained through questionnaires, checklists, and interviews.
- The same interview or questionnaire questions can be used for both the client and network members, with the phrasing adjusted accordingly.

Maguire (1983) proposes certain basic questions as an aid to developing an informal support profile for a client.

1. Who are the people in your life who would be really helpful for the types of problems we have discussed? Please list them.
2. For each person, please define your relationship to him or her as either relative, friend, neighbor, work colleague, professional helper, or other (please define).
3. How often do you see or talk to this person (daily, weekly, twice monthly, monthly, yearly, less than yearly)?
4. Who usually initiates the contact?
5. How far does this person live from you in minutes, using your usual mode of transportation?
6. Do you feel you give more than you get, get more, or that the relationship is fairly even?
7. How long have you known this person?
8. Now, can you diagram for me which of these people know each other?
9. List the organizations with which you are currently or recently involved, including clubs, church groups, unions, ethnic organizations, or community activities.

The practitioner should be closely attuned to the client's ethnic identity and personal and cultural preferences in exploring sources of support.

Information about groups that offer potential aid might have to be gathered independently by the practitioner. It is important to include:

1. the group's goals or objectives;
2. its membership criteria, that is, who gets in, in terms of the type of problem or concern, as well as whether there are any guidelines or restrictions based on age, race, sex, income, marital status, political or sexual orientation;
3. its meeting times and places;
4. its format for meetings (certain groups have rather rigid rules for how meetings are to be conducted, and others are responsive to the changing needs of its members);
5. its dues or membership costs;
6. its sponsorship, if any (e.g., a church, social service agency, etc.);
7. whether professionals are allowed or encouraged to be involved in any capacity.

It is often advantageous to employ mapping through diagrams and charts to depict the network of helpers once information has been gathered. A useful example of the mapping technique has been presented by Germain and Patterson (1988, p. 64):

> Mrs. Martin, Caucasian and 62 years old, came to the local agency with complaints of loneliness, depression, and anxiety. She had been widowed two years earlier and continues to live alone on the family farm. As a life-time resident she knew almost everyone. Yet, she could name only a few persons to whom she felt close, exchanging supportive help:
>
> > · Her daughter, age 38, married with four school-age children, drives Mrs. Martin regularly to town for shopping, medical care, postal services, and so on. Mrs. Martin, in turn, babysits for her daughter and also listens to her complaints about her marriage.

· Her son, age 41, married with two children, owns a dry goods store and keeps the books for his mother's farm. She babysits for him and his wife, but complains that he insists she sell the home place and move into town.
· Two women described as "best friends" from high school days. Mrs. Carson, a recent widow, demands much of Mrs. Martin's time every day to express her grief and worries. Mrs. Dean, on the other hand, exchanges recipes, meals, and gossip with Mrs. Martin. They go on shopping jaunts, and provide emotional support to each other in respect to problems with their children.
· A neighbor, Mr. Rich, three miles down the road, comes twice a year to plow up the garden. Other neighbors, Mr. and Mrs. Johanson, stop by regularly to help Mrs. Martin fertilize and weed the garden, pick apples and peaches in season, or just to visit. Mrs. Martin shares her home-canned fruit and vegetables with them.

This information is mapped in Figure 8–1.

Selecting the Most Appropriate Support Units

Sketching out or mapping an individual's informal social network is an essential step in activating natural support, but it is not a sufficient one. The network may be too extensive to use in its entirety; not all the elements may be beneficial; and the client may have selective preferences about assistance. A next analytical or diagnostic task is necessary, one that entails identifying specific individuals or groups that will become the focus of attention.

Specifying client needs and helping resources. As already stated, it is important to elicit the client's view about who might be most helpful, who the client is most comfortable with, and who has assisted in the past. To this should to be added professional judgment about what the client most needs and who can provide it—a judgment that should systematically be colored by the input of relevant family members and service providers who know the client well. An amalgam of client perspectives and practitioner perspectives (informed by others) will likely generate the optimal informal helping team.

A guide to this selection process can be based on the discussion of the functions of social support in the first section of this chapter. These functions mesh with client needs—for example, the socialization function addressing the need for companionship. The set of functions can be contracted to four key types: *friendship and socialization; emotional support; practical assistance; guidance and advice.* There is some overlap among these (socialization accompanied by emotional support), but the functions also have some discrete identity. Guidance and advice relates to the kind of cues a neighbor who is experienced and wise in dealing with the social security bureaucracy can

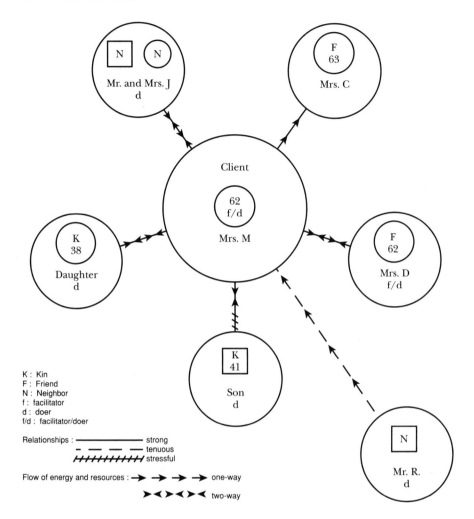

FIGURE 8–1   Map of informal network

pass over to an elderly client, as distinct from counseling provided by a professional.

One means of proceeding is to pinpoint the types of supports that a client needs and the available sources for providing these. A need–support worksheet may be used for doing this kind of analysis. For each function, the worksheet asks for an assessment of the extent of this need. All social supports that can provide this particular need are listed, together with an estimate of the degree to which each support unit is capable of delivering the needed support to the client (see Figure 8–2).

FIGURE 8-2 Need-support worksheet

Need For Friendship and Socialization			Need For Emotional Support			Need For Practical Assistance			Need For Guidance and Advice		
Extent of Client Need (Circle) High M Low			Extent of Client Need (Circle) High M Low			Extent of Client Need (Circle) High M Low			Extent of Client Need (Circle) High M Low		
Individual Support (Family, friends, neighbors) List		Group Support (Community groups, self-help groups) List	Individual Support (Family, friends, neighbors) List		Group Support (Community groups, self-help groups) List	Individual Support (Family, friends, neighbors) List		Group Support (Community groups, self-help groups) List	Individual Support (Family, friends, neighbors) List		Group Support (Community groups, self-help groups) List
H* M L		H* M L	H* M L		H* M L	H* M L		H* M L	H* M L		H* M L
H M L		H M L	H M L		H M L	H M L		H M L	H M L		H M L
H M L		H M L	H M L		H M L	H M L		H M L	H M L		H M L
H M L		H M L	H M L		H M L	H M L		H M L	H M L		H M L
H M L		H M L	H M L		H M L	H M L		H M L	H M L		H M L
H M L		H M L	H M L		H M L	H M L		H M L	H M L		H M L
H M L		H M L	H M L		H M L	H M L		H M L	H M L		H M L

*Degree of potential for meeting the need: high, medium or low. Circle one.

Assessing the potential of help-giving sources. The capacity or potential for each support unit to deliver assistance is influenced by a variety of factors. An assessment scheme for appraising help potential of units can flow from the discussion of support network characteristics in the first section. To accomplish this a separate card can be made out for each support unit (individual or group), using a check-list format for quickly estimating the helping potential for that unit. The dimensions that are appraised for the unit include: *willingness to help; frequency (intensity) of contact; proximity; accessibility; durability (or continuity) of helping; and expectation of reciprocity for assistance (which might be considered a cost).* Proximity and accessibility overlap in part but are not identical: some people who live in close proximity are not easily accessible because they are busy or self-involved, while others who are at a distance are easily and quickly accessible by telephone.

A sample helping unit assessment sheet is provided in Figure 8–3. It would be possible to attach scores of 3, 2, and 1 to the categories of high, medium, and low support, respectively, thereby yielding a global support rating of 0 to 18 for each support unit (the six categories of support in aggregate). This would be a rough and rather mechanical procedure. Probably a clinical "eyeballing" approach would be most advisable until such a format is further refined.

FIGURE 8–3   Helping unit assessment sheet

1. Helper (individual or group)   _____
2. Relationship or connection   _____

TYPE OF
HELPING POTENTIAL   *COMMENTS*

                    Circle
            (High, Medium, Low)

Willingness to help   H M L _____

Frequency of contact   H M L _____

Proximity   H M L _____

Accessibility   H M L _____

Durability   H M L _____

Reciprocity expected   H M L _____

Making and Maintaining Linkages

Linking clients with informal networks involves bringing connections into operational form. The following are guidelines for energizing linkage after the appropriate individuals and groups have been selected:

- the practitioner should seek to personally meet the network members to discuss the situation, determine interests, and orient them to their new caregiving role;
- during this initial meeting the practitioner should share information about the client's needs and preferences and encourage the potential member to express personal perspectives and intentions;
- these linking tasks can also be done by telephoning network members. With the practitioner's guidance, network members can also phone each other to coordinate caregiving tasks;
- linking should be activated through obtaining specific commitments, pinpointing tasks, and setting definite appointment times;
- the practitioner should act as a continuing liaison by maintaining close and recurring contact with key persons;
- through observation and input from both the client and helpers, the practitioner should assess the arrangement and make any necessary adjustments;
- the practitioner should meet as required with the network members or be in touch by telephone to provide encouragement, new directions, and problem-solving assistance.

Informal linkages involve sensitive relationships with people who do not have professional experience and skills in providing human services. Understanding and motivation needs to be engendered. Confidentiality has to be weighed and explained. There is also the question of continuity and consistency of help-giving and the possibility of discouragement and burnout. All of these matters implicate each linkage. Having established an informal help-giving system, the next step is to upgrade its potentials.

Enhancing Helper Capabilities

An important role in informal linkage is strengthening the helping capabilities of network members. After the initial analysis of the network the practitioner might move, if necessary, to improve the quality of potential helpers. Education and support efforts are well established ways to buttress the capability of helpers. Several organized projects illustrate means by which this can be accomplished.

One example is the "Family Support Project," a 9-week skills training project in Tucson, Arizona. This program actively taught informal supporters specific skills through direct instruction, modeling and role playing, behavior rehearsal, coaching, social reinforcement, performance feedback, and homework assignments (Ferris & Marshall, 1987). Family members learn how to cope both practically and emotionally with their impeded relative, and they also widen their circle of support through new contacts.

The *family intervention program* consists of five specific phases, which can be adapted for new applications:

1. A crisis oriented 2-hour weekly group helps families who are either having their first encounter with the impairment or who are in a crisis for which they need additional support for a short period.

2. An education class teaches families how the world is perceived through the eyes of the client; how to improve social functioning or manage relatives' behavior; and how to use a new vocabulary to better communicate with the impaired individual.

3. A skills training course teaches skills in communication, assertiveness, behavior management, and problem solving.

4. A long-term support group in which families are able to meet once monthly provides encouragement and information.

5. A task group in which families work together for problem solving and education fosters the group cohesiveness necessary for families to continue to move forward as a unit.

Another program of interest emphasizes aftercare treatment for mental patients living at home and also focuses on family members (Iodice & Wodarski, 1987). The program provides information and management skills at the time of a relative's discharge from the mental hospital. The *psychoeducational model* described can be applied readily in other settings.

Phase I: Connection. The goals of the first phase include connecting with the family and enlisting cooperation with the program, decreasing guilt, coping with emotions and negative reactions to the illness, and reducing family stress. The techniques used are joining; establishing treatment contact; discussing crisis history and feelings about the patient and the illness; and making specific practical suggestions that mobilize concerns into effective coping mechanisms.

Phase II: Survival skills workshop. The goals here are to increase understanding by the family of the patient's illness and needs, continue reduction of family stress, and enhance social networks. The techniques are multiple: family education and discussion, concrete data on the disability, concrete management suggestions, and basic communication skills.

Phase III: Re-entry and application. The goals of the third phase include maintaining the patient in the community, strengthening marital and parental coalition, increasing family tolerance for low-level performance and dysfunctional behaviors, and the resuming of responsibilities by the patient gradually. Techniques include reinforcing boundaries (generational and interpersonal), taking task assignments, and participating in low-key problem solving.

These programs are suggestive of the kind of educational and supportive input that can be provided to network members in structured programs or by individual actions by the practitioner. Many of the areas covered and methods used can apply to friends and neighbors as well as to family members.

Evaluating Linkage Strategies

Evaluation of informal linkages will help determine the adequacy of supportive connections that were made and what changes to consider. The following points can be addressed in an assessment of informal network effects:

> How many contacts were there in the relationship between the client and natural helpers?
> Was there an increase in help to clients?
> How often was the network's advice useful or used?
> Was the client's level of functioning improved?
> Was the client's feeling of well-being or satisfaction improved?

To evaluate aid to caregivers, appropriate questions include:

> Was there an increase in knowledge, skill, and morale?
> Was the burden to caregivers decreased?
> How satisfied were the caregivers with education and support actions?
> Was their participation sustained?

As an aid to evaluation the practitioner can join in or "follow along" with the client and the network members in helping episodes (Weissman, Epstein, & Savage, 1980).

This discussion has touched on some key practice roles in informal linkage. It is clear that informal support networks can provide nurturing aids for severely vulnerable clients that are broad and numerous. As we saw, a range of different sources of informal support exist and differentially affect client care. Practitioners have available to them a variety of means for carrying out this linking function, thereby maximizing the opportunities for clients to live and seek satisfaction in natural community settings.

REFERENCES

Axinn, J. & Levin, H. (1982). *Social welfare: A history of the American response to need.* New York: Longman.

Beels, C., Gutwirth, L., Berkeley, J., & Struening, E. (1984). Measurements of social support in schizophrenia. *Schizophrenia Bulletin, 10*(3), 399–411.

Biegel, D. E., Shore, B. K., & Gordon, E. (1984). *Building support networks for the elderly.* Beverly Hills: Sage.

Brody, E. M. (1978). The aging of the family. *The Annals of the American Academy of Political and Social Science,* July, 13–27.

Coser, L. A., Rhea, B., Steffan, P. A., & Nock., S. L. (1983). *Introduction to sociology*. New York: Harcourt Brace Jovanovich.

Crotty, P. & Kulys, R. (1985). Social support networks: The views of schizophrenic clients and others. *Social Work, 30,* 301–309.

Doll, W. (1976). Family coping with the mentally ill: An unanticipated problem of deinstitutionalization. *Hospital and Community Psychiatry, 27*(3), 183–185.

Ferris, P. A. & Marshall, C. A. (1987). A model project for families of the chronically mentally ill. *Social Work, 32,* 110–114.

Gallagher, D. E. (1985). Intervention strategies to assist caregivers of frail elders: Current research status and future directions. In C. Eiserdorfer (Ed.), *Annual Review of Gerontology and Geriatrics* (pp. 249–280). New York: Springer.

Gerhart, U. C. (1990). *Caring for the chronically mentally ill.* IL: F. E. Peacock.

Germain, C. B. & Patterson, S. L. (1988). Teaching about rural natural helpers as environmental resources. *Journal of Teaching in Social Work, 2*(1), 73–90.

Gottlieb, B. H. (1985). Assessing and strengthening the impact of social support on mental health. *Social Work, 30,* 293-200.

Gottlieb, B. H. (1988). (Ed.), *Marshaling social support.* Beverly Hills: Sage.

Greene, V. & Monahan, D. (1984). Comparative utilization of community based long term care services by Hispanic and Anglo elderly in a case management system. *Journal of Gerontology, 39*(6), 730–735.

Grusky, O. & Tierney, K. (1985). Social bonding and community adjustment of chronically mentally ill adults. *Journal of Health and Social Behavior, 26,* 49–63.

Hollis, F. & Woods, M. E. (1981). *Casework: A psychosocial therapy.* New York: Random House.

Iodice, J. D. & Wodarski, J. S. (1987). Aftercare treatment for schizophrenics living at home. *Social Work, 32,* 122–128.

Jurkiewicz, V. (1980). An exploratory descriptive study of interorganizational and case coordination programs for the multiproblem, frail, and minority elderly (D.S.W. Dissertation, University of California, Los Angeles). *Dissertation Abstracts International, 42*(5), 2294-A.

Kaye, L. W. (1985). Home care for the aged: A fragile partnership. *Social Work, 30,* 312–317.

Keating, D. (1981). Deinstitutionalization of the mentally retarded as seen by parents of institutionalized individuals (Ph.D. Dissertation, Temple University). *Dissertation Abstracts International, 42*(6), 2505-B.

Maguire, L. (1983). *Understanding social networks.* Newbury Park, CA: Sage.

Nelson, H. & Jurmain, R. (1988). *Introduction to physical anthropology.* New York: West Publishing.

Pearson, R. E. (1990). *Counseling and social support: Perspectives and practice.* Newbury Park: Sage.

Powell, T. J. (1975). The use of self help groups as supportive reference communities. *American Journal of Orthopsychiatry, 45,* 97–102.

Segal, S. P. (1979). Community care and deinstitutionalization. *Social Work, 24*(6), 521–527.

Seltzer, M. M. & Mayer, J. B. (1988). Families as case managers. *Generations,* (Fall), 26–29.

Stefanik–Campisi, C. & Marion, T. R. (1988). Case management follow-up of a chemically impaired nurse. *Perspectives in Psychiatric Care, 24*(3–4), 114–119.

Taylor, S. E., Falke, R. L., Mazel, R. M., & Hilsberg, B. L. (1988). Sources of satisfaction and dissatisfaction among members of cancer support groups. In B. H. Gottlieb (Ed.), *Marshaling social support: Formats, processes, and effects.* Beverly Hills: Sage.

Thompson, A. & Barnsley, R. (1981). Personal crisis: A report from the people. *Canada's Mental Health, 29*(3), 21–27.

Toseland, R. W., Rossiter, C. M., Peak, T., & Smith, G. C. (1990). Comparative effectiveness of individual and group interventions to support family caregivers. *Social Work,* May, 209–216.

Weissman, H., Epstein, I., & Savage, A. (1980). *Agency-based social work: Neglected aspects of clinical practice.* Philadelphia: Temple University Press.

9
Monitoring, Reassessment, and Outcome Evaluation

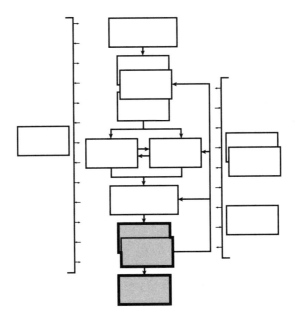

OVERVIEW

The word *monitoring* has a bad connotation for many of us. It evokes the image of that kid in elementary school who snitched to the teacher when we mouthed an off-color word or cheerfully shoved our best friend. The monitor was the teacher's pet or the class bully, enlisted to be her snoop when she was otherwise occupied. Even if we ourselves were lucky enough to be appointed monitor one year, we hated the kid who got the job the next year.

The dictionary gives monitoring a somewhat more neutral tone: "to watch, observe . . . to keep track of, regulate." In comprehensive enhancement practice this translates into following up on an intervention plan to make sure it is carried out and that it brings about the helpful results that were intended.

In monitoring, the practitioner sees to it that the agencies accepting clients actually provide the needed services, that aid from family or friends is forthcoming, and that the client carries out tasks that were agreed upon. It also is a means of tracking the practitioner's own intended performance. Facilitative and trouble-shooting activities also accompany monitoring to expedite the established plan.

Monitoring is closely intertwined with reassessment because looking at a process in action automatically provides feedback about how the process is playing out and with what consequences. Reassessment, therefore, implicates possible redesign of the intervention plan. This dual aspect is conveyed in the dictionary notions of both observing and regulating or, in more jaunty parlance, assaying and replaying.

Outcome evaluation is ostensibly different from reassessment in that it applies to an end-state, a more or less final effect. Highly vulnerable clients are typically enmeshed in long-term problematic situations and, thus, evaluation takes place at some point in a service program that is indeterminate. Evaluation and reassessment are ordinarily congruent, in that the task of gauging results with these clients is ongoing. Only infrequently do the frail elderly, chronically mentally ill, or severely disabled improve sufficiently to allow for full independence and total termination from service, necessitating a discharge evaluation. In any case, the tools and methods used in reassessment and terminal outcome evaluation are the same.

This chapter focuses on monitoring. Reassessment is treated more briefly, as the earlier examination of assessment covered most of its essential features. Outcome evaluation, by and large, is merged into the reassessment discussion.

MONITORING

UNDERSTANDING MONITORING

Definition and Purpose

The goal of practice is to help the client to establish as satisfactory and satisfying a life as possible within the community. The goal of monitoring is to ensure that community supports are provided and that they enable the client to lead such a life. One major task of monitoring, therefore, is to witness the service-delivery process—a passive-sounding role. Actually, "monitoring and maintenance" would be appropriate terminology, as the function also includes actively guiding service delivery to maintain the client in the community. Monitoring is a fluid, extended process lasting as long as the client remains in the system (Morris & Fitz-Gibbon, 1978b; Patton, 1987). It calls for systematic attention to the client, to the informal support network, and to formal provider actions.

A macroscopic byproduct of monitoring goes to the assessment of the efficacy of the agency program system itself (Levine & Fleming, 1985). Information gathered in the process of evaluating the individual intervention plan, in aggregate, yields a basis for evaluating how well clients in the agency overall are being served.

In studies of practice, monitoring has been found to be a basic component of case management (Gerhart, 1990; Stein & Test, 1980; Wolkon, Peterson, & Rogowski, 1978). In the UCLA survey of practitioners, the preponderance of respondents reported they engage in monitoring. Austin (1983) reports that a group of researchers at the Andrus Gerontology Center at the University of Southern California examined case coordination in programs for the vulnerable elderly across the nation and found that some form of follow-up with the client was used by all participants, and most reported some monitoring functions with service providers. Caragonne (1983) reports that following service was a core activity of the line-service workers in her study. Without adequate follow-up, clients are at risk of getting lost in the system. Wolkon et al. (1978) found in a study of psychiatric day-hospital clients that regardless of the intervention, over one-third "dropped out." This confirms the need for continuing follow-up.

The literature suggests that an important purpose of monitoring is to prevent and respond quickly to disruptive occurrences in a client's life. Baker, Burns, Libby, and Intagliata (1985) conducted a study aimed at determining those crisis points where client's needs could be anticipated to increase or change. They focused on life events that vulnerable clients perceived as stressful. The most commonly reported events were changes in structured daily activities (whether day treatment, work, school, leisure activities, or social organizations), anticipated or actual change in residence, and physical health problems. The authors suggest that by monitoring such events the practitioner may be able to provide preventive intervention so that the situation does not escalate into a full-blown crisis. The researchers also found that pawn events (events judged not to be under one's control), even positive ones, are more likely to be associated with psychological disturbance than are events attributed to one's own purposeful efforts. They advise practitioners to track such events in order to move in quickly before the situation escalates. Practitioners "should make special efforts to learn from their clients about the occurrence of events that the clients believe are outside their control . . . [and] should be particularly sensitive to the role such events may play in relapse and possible rehospitalization" (Baker et al., 1985, p. 301). This area is further discussed in the practice section.

The Unique Place of Monitoring

Monitoring, while a prominent feature of case management approaches, has been a rather insignificant aspect of traditional methods in the helping professions. When this area does get addressed in traditional practice, the term "follow-up" is ordinarily used to describe the activity. Major works on clinical practice, casework, or psychotherapy do not include follow-up, or only touch on it peripherally (Corsini, 1979; Hackett & Cassem, 1978; Maxmen, 1985; Nurcombe & Gallagher, 1986; Whittaker & Tracy, 1989; Woods & Hollis, 1990). In a review of a wide range of treatment methods by Turner (1986), follow-up never appears in the index. Turner's review covers such areas as psychoanalytic theory, transactional analysis, gestalt theory, the task-centered approach, existential treatment, psychosocial treatment, and others.

The reason for this void can be found, as previously noted, in the way the problem situation is viewed in the typical practice modes, and the theoretical posture that is brought to bear. The presenting problem or difficulty is commonly seen as acute and emergent, as an interference with the normal functioning of the individual. Or there may be a longtime blockage that thwarts the individual's inherent potential to lead a normal life. The task is to cure or substantially reduce the difficulty through providing greater insight, coping skills, or personality restructuring, so that the client may return or rise to a normal state.

Furthermore, because the acquisition of a normal state should be self-sustaining, a termination should be clean and decisive, leaving the client no room for continued dependency on the therapist. Continued involvement by the helper in the client's life is viewed as counter to the objective of fully autonomous self-direction and self-determination.

The circumstances are vastly different with long-term vulnerable client groups, where difficulties and impairments are ongoing or even progressive and where, ordinarily, there does not exist the possibility of return to a previous "normal" state. It is the obligation of the practitioner to stay involved with the client in a supportive role that enhances without "curing." This perspective mandates a monitoring function; traditional clinical theory does not allow for it.

There are some exceptions to this. Behavioral therapy, with its learning theory base, does incorporate a follow-up aspect. The follow-up is geared to determining whether sufficient learning has taken place and is maintained. Bloom (1990, pp. 118–119) describes the approach in this way:

> . . . let's say that there is a mutual decision to terminate services. What remains is to conduct a follow-up contact (or contacts) with the clients, both to assess the long-term staying power of the changes that have occurred and to provide "booster shots" as needed. The very understanding that the worker will be calling the clients every once in a while as a friendly check to see how things are going may help the clients to rehearse what they have learned so as to be ready for that call.

Learning, apparently, has a more open-ended outlook than does recovery.

Fischer (1978, p. 292) incorporates follow-up into practice, but he views it as preceding rather than following termination. He visualizes an elongated process of termination: ". . . it is neither wise nor necessary for the termination to be an abrupt one. The frequency and amount of contacts should be gradually decreased. Particularly, follow-ups should be planned on a progressively diminishing basis. . . ."

It might be said that monitoring in psychotherapy is concurrent with treatment and involves the client's verbal indication of progress. Monitoring in case management forms of practice takes place during and following specific interventions and is cyclical. It involves not only client reports, but direct observation and engagement in "hands-on" fashion.

Client Involvement

We have maintained that the client should be involved as far as possible at all stages of the practice process. Therefore, as an important part of monitoring the client's progress, the client's reactions to the service program need to be purposively elicited. Because the end result is personal and subjective, evaluative feedback from the client is especially relevant in determining the impact of the service plan. Clients are the basic consumers of services, and their reactions and feelings are an important component of the overall monitoring process (Scott & Cassidy, 1981). Client's rights and prerogatives are maximized in this way, particularly as their personal circumstances and community agency service patterns change.

In addition, it is important that the client perceive the helper as acting beneficially on a continuing basis, rather than in either a detached or intrusive manner. The practitioner should be seen as someone who, by attending to the client, tries to make sure that real problems are being resolved along the way.

Examples of the value of client input may bring these points out further. A frail elderly client may need help with activities of daily living because of physical limitations. The professional perceives the service to be delivered in a timely and efficient manner. However, the client may believe that the service provider acts as though there are mental impairments present as well as physical ones, making the experience a demeaning one. With this feedback from the client, the practitioner can take steps to make the situation more satisfactory.

A mentally ill client may think that a day-treatment center is providing good service but that side-effects from medications are not tolerable. The client may not be able to convince the attending physician to try something different. By listening closely, the practitioner can learn why the client is non-compliant about taking medications and can probably gain the attention of the physician more readily than the client is able to.

Dynamics of Monitoring

Both the practice and research literature reveal there are multiple aspects to monitoring.

Multiple sources of information. Practitioners in the UCLA study indicated that monitoring of client functioning can be accomplished by drawing on information from numerous sources—including initiatives by others in providing information to the practitioner—and need not be direct or intrusive. For example, besides the obvious direct route of speaking personally with the client, monitoring is also accomplished at times by consulting informally with a residence operator or staff members involved in the client's daily activities (such as day-treatment groups or vocational trainers), and occasionally by speaking with family members who may be involved with the client day-by-day.

Intertwining of functions. Intermingling of functions was found to exist in the UCLA study when certain practice activities fulfill multiple objectives. Monitoring a client's ongoing status and counseling that client or that client's collateral outside parties may often go on simultaneously. A study respondent noted a client whose history included long stable periods interrupted by occasional jaunts, in which he simply left to go traveling for a few months and used up meager finances needed for basic survival. There were hints that another such leave-taking might soon occur. Faced with this possibility, the practitioner initiated a stepped-up schedule of contacts with the client and the residence operator. This served the dual functions, simultaneously, of providing opportunities for closer monitoring of this client's activities and also informally counseling him (and others concerned with his well-being) about difficulties inherent in this potentially harmful trip.

Multiple actions.   Monitoring service delivery quality, timeliness, and appropriateness to client needs are all vital tasks. In this context, monitoring was said by study respondents to take many different forms in implementation.

Monitoring was confirmed to include concrete actions and also "stand by" or anticipatory periods. Sometimes a client's current problem situation demands vigilance and readiness to intervene—although on a moment-to-moment basis no actual intervention takes place. One practitioner described her work as analogous to a physician on-call, in that the situation may or may not, unpredictably, require overt interventions and yet readiness to respond is mandatory.

Not only are there a variety of monitoring techniques, but they vary in degree of intensity from a penetrating and time-consuming visit to a facility to receiving a phone call from another person. There is a great deal of individual discretion involved in constructing and carrying out a monitoring program. This is illustrated in a comment by a practitioner.

> I get to see nearly all of my clients four times a week, because most of them are members of the day-treatment center I help run. Others, I get to interact with once every couple of weeks, and usually only via telephone. The latter group is functioning rather well in the community and most have some ongoing informal support or caregivers. Occasionally, one of them calls me about a particular need, and usually I can meet it fairly simply and expediently.

Multiple bases for decisions.   Occasional conflicts and differences of opinion have been observed regarding the locus of decision in the monitoring process. Hennessy (1989) analyzed actual or potential conflict between staff decisions regarding frail elderly clients served by a community-based multi-service program and the clients' wishes. The study found that the wishes of the elderly client were moderated by the extent to which a particular course of action would threaten the client's medical or functional stability or manageability within the program (i.e., risk management). The data suggested there are trade-offs in balancing the wishes of clients, the judgments of professionals, and the sensibilities of the organization.

Variations by Client Populations

While the goals and purposes of monitoring are general and applicable across various populations, identifiable differences of emphasis exist. For example, monitoring with the elderly can involve a wide span of agencies and services touching on almost every facet of living: physical health, daily routine activities, social support, social participation, economic status, and mental status, including emotions and cognitive functioning (Downing, 1985). This requires a broad sweep of observations and communications. Also, in working with the elderly, changes in life are progressive, perhaps necessitating more frequent reassessment. This contrasts with the physically disabled, whose services and resources tend to cluster around the physical dimension. Here, there is more concentrated interface with medical service providers than is true with some other client groups, such as dependent children.

When working with abused children the types of agencies and persons one must confront are also varied, but the configuration is different than with the elderly. They include police, protective services, courts, schools, and public health nurses (Wells, 1985). There is heavy emphasis on work with parents and foster parents. In the setting of child welfare, monitoring is especially crucial in order to see that a dependent child does not get lost in the complex delivery system. Good record keeping and regular follow-up are important. While gerontology and physical rehabilitation services lean toward contacts with medical institutions, child welfare often requires many relations with legal institutions.

Some aspects of monitoring may be more predictable than others. For example, with the elderly we can anticipate that there will be physical and mental loss over time. At certain age thresholds there is likely to be impairment in hearing, sight, and reaction time. Anticipation of change is true also for young children who progress developmentally to increasing capability over time. With the mentally ill, however, sporadic, unanticipated crises may occur with no particular expectation or forewarning. Monitoring, therefore, contains predictable and unpredictable elements, which vary for different client populations. This discussion of variations in intervention tasks for different client populations is expanded in the practice section.

Special Problems in Monitoring

Even when the role of the practitioner is clear, it is not always easy to effectively carry out all monitoring functions. There is challenge in overseeing the work of diverse staff in other agencies and programs. Authority may be necessary to see that a physician or nurse follows through on a particular treatment or to ensure the city housing department provides a client with an apartment. There may be disagreements and status jockeying among professionals over client loyalty and strategies for problem solving. The practitioner may be viewed as a threat to a community agency's prerogatives and judgment. Requests for extraordinary service are often resisted and sometimes promised routine services are neglected.

Turf issues in the monitoring process arise primarily because of overlapping or confusion of roles within organizations and because practitioners may be employed in settings that are directed by professionals of other backgrounds. For example, social workers in health settings often find their functions and tasks overlapping with the nurses; with so much blurring, nurses and social workers are used interchangeably or on a team basis.

Questions of professional turf and autonomy arise because many professionals in host agencies are concerned with similar activities and interventions related to clients' welfare. Although these problems are not new in host agencies, there is growing concern and discussion about the increased role blurring in work with psychosocial aspects of the client's life (Dane & Simon, 1991, p. 211).

While this is a disadvantage, it can also be seen as an opportunity to clarify and extend the scope of the professional function (Gitterman & Miller, 1989).

With the increase in managed health care, primary care physicians are increasingly called on to perform case management tasks such as needs assessment and linkage. "Physicians have neither the knowledge of community resources nor the human relations training to make them ideal for the role of brokering service" (Kane, 1985, p. 194). In such cases the physician's involvement too often ends with the referral—and the monitoring function, which could be crucial to favorable outcome, is overlooked entirely. Practitioners with a comprehensive orientation become frustrated in dealing with such situations.

Turf issues exist not only among professionals within the same organization, but also among different organizations. This may be highlighted when a patient who has been followed by a community-based practitioner is ready for discharge. Often the discharge planner in the hospital or mental hospital (be it nurse, social worker, or other) completes arrangements, and the transfer is made before the community-based practitioner is informed about it and is able to develop a community service plan. A child welfare worker who is assigned to a foster child may have a jurisdictional mix-up with a practitioner in a school-based family center. Other turf issues arise over which agency in the community should take prime responsibility for service functions when a client receives assistance at more than one agency.

There are, of course, difficulties in working with the clients during monitoring as well as with support systems. Some clients fail to follow through—and miss appointments or do not take medications. Sometimes the client misunderstands what is expected, particularly those with impaired hearing, memory lapses, or developmental disabilities. In addition, confidentiality must be protected when dealing with several different agencies and the informal support system. The practitioner has to maintain a balance, being adequately informed but not being too intrusive in obtaining or sharing information. These issues are discussed further in the next section.

PRACTICE GUIDELINES FOR MONITORING

Using Formal and Informal Means

Monitoring takes place formally and informally. Formal monitoring is more structured and standardized; instruments (forms, rating scales, questionnaires, checklists) are used as are standardized assessment scales against which to measure service results. The practitioner may also choose to use some of these monitoring tools to obtain an initial baseline for comparing with data collected at intervals thereafter. The decision to use formal monitoring instruments may be mandated by the agency or program. Examples of forms follow.

Informal and qualitative monitoring involves the judgment of the practitioner and is more impressionistic. Here the practitioner serves personally as an instrument of monitoring. It is a less attenuated process and may be more feasible when time is a limiting factor. Techniques include correspondence, casual meetings, talks with the clients, everyday observation, telephone contacts with members of the support network, and scanning case records.

The practitioner can choose, of course, a combination of both formal and informal techniques aimed at different phenomena and outcomes.

Using Different Levels of Monitoring

Monitoring focuses on the client, the informal network, and the formal service system.

The client level.   Bellow and Mink (1986) point out that monitoring clients inextricably brings the practitioner into service provision roles, and vice versa. While monitoring, the practitioner must tinker and adjust in order to execute the established plan. This can include providing a helpful interpretation of what is happening, or taking additional linking actions that keep the client productively connected to the formal and informal helping networks.

Regular contact with the client will give clues to the client's emotional state in the situation. A common problem is a feeling of despair with doubt about the wisdom of the intervention plan. To help overcome this, the practitioner can offer well-chosen words of encouragement and express empathy. Any client effort or accomplishment, no matter how small, might be rewarded by positive strokes in order to increase the likelihood of continued effort.

Two kinds of interpretation can assist the client. One is to help clients understand agency regulations and the necessary bureaucratic red tape in order to successfully navigate the system. If the client can understand the reasons for regulations, this may go a long way to relieving frustration and hostility emanating from encounters with an impersonal entity.

The second type of interpretation is a reframing technique in which the meaning of events is recast into a less odious light. For example, a teenage mother may see the occupational therapist as controlling and domineering, causing her to skip appointments. If the practitioner reframes this in the context of the client's strongly expressed wish to walk again, the client could perhaps become more responsive.

There are occasions when the client becomes overwhelmed and needs direct crisis help. One common situation is a breakdown in secondary services such as the client's car needs repair, child care arrangements fall through, or funding for a program is cut off. Often the client is unaware of alternative resources, and the case manager can be instrumental in finding a solution.

The level of informal helpers.   This includes family, friends, neighbors, church members, and others who have been worked into the service plan. Telephone calls, visits, notes, and casual contacts are ways of keeping in touch with such individuals.

The practitioner may go further in tracking and ask informal network members themselves to keep logs or diaries detailing their support activities. Rating tools can record the frequency of support activities, and structured feedback questionnaires filled out by network members can surface problems encountered in support effort.

Informal helpers tend to offer aid how and when they can, not necessarily on a regular basis. They freely use their own styles in relating to the client, which may at times create friction or engender anger and anxiety. One common complaint from clients is that informal helpers are too controlling. The practitioner needs to use special tact, patience, and diplomacy in dealing with such interpersonal tensions to alter the way these individuals give voluntary help.

For effective service there needs to be a free exchange of information among all members of the support network. But there is a need for confidentiality: *personal information about the client is not to be revealed to anyone except on a limited basis.* This creates a dilemma for the practitioner, who is often the conduit of information to the client's whole network, and is a particularly sensitive issue in working with informal helpers. How much and what kind of information should be communicated and to whom? Natural helpers need a certain amount of information in order to be effective. Also to feel appreciated they need to know when their efforts have been helpful. However, the client may not want information of a personal nature conveyed to certain family members or acquaintances. Having the client sign a consent form conferring permission to share information gives the client some control and also protects the practitioner should there be a question of a breach of confidentiality.

In working within the informal network the practitioner needs to be aware that there are some natural helpers who can be taught to keep confidences and others who cannot. Decisions will have to be made on an individual basis. As a general rule, the practitioner and the client, together, insofar as the client is capable, should determine who ought to be entrusted with personal information.

The formal system level.   This includes all other professionals included in the service plan: collaterals in the practitioner's own agency (physicians, psychiatrists, nurses, lawyers) or staff in other agencies and organizations in the community. These are spelled out in the service plan.

Formal or quantitative monitoring of professional caregivers aids accountability. The practitioner needs to ensure that accurate and consistent records are kept by both the employing agency and other service providers. Specific tools include:

1. official milestone meetings during which services are reviewed and evaluated;
2. systematic oversight of records focusing on types of services, length of interaction, adequacy, and client progress;
3. structured instruments that require service providers to self-evaluate their contributions to client care and support. (Moxley, 1989, p. 121)

Comments from the practitioners in the UCLA survey provide valuable information about relevant practice methods. Telephone communication with the agency was the main method of contact for this group. The general approach is expressed by comments such as the following:

· Telephone next day or same day to see if client arrived.
· Check a week later to see if client is continuing to receive needed services.
· Check to see if all information that was necessary for client to receive services is available and in the correct form for the agency's requirements.

Telephone monitoring is aided, respondents indicated, if the practitioner has a specific personal contact in the agency, if good interpersonal relationships are established, if the paperwork has been completed in good order, and if the agency knows that regular monitoring will be carried out as follow-up. The personal quality was described by one practitioner as follows:

I visit three board-and-care homes on a regular basis, which fosters a personal attachment, and by just chatting I give advice and support to the operators. One keeps calling me at the office here to extend some of those conversations.

Visits are the most frequent mode of monitoring following telephone contact. A monitoring visit can turn up a great deal of information if the worker is alert to seeing the totality of the client's situation.

When I go out to agencies I have to check on a wide variety of services. Mostly I'm concerned with residential placement. By being there on the premises, talking to patients, making my own observations, I'm able to see whether there are enough beds, if the food is decent, or if there is anything that doesn't look right.

Sometimes visitation situations can be acrimonious in nature:

Residence managers are sometimes lying and deceitful, in the sense that they misrepresent their facility in order to get more funds—they tend to have an "impaired cash flow." Take the worst pit and the operator will tell you it has a great program! So, to get more accurate information on the quality of board-and-care homes, I make frequent site visits and confer with co-workers.

Problems with Agencies

Problems in agency performance and turf issues that emerge during monitoring can be dealt with in several ways. The role calls for coordination between agencies, and in this role the case manager may need authority to perform effectively. In the same way authority may be essential in linking, it can be crucial in monitoring. Even access to observe or contact the client can be difficult in some cases. Authority may be required to cut through regulations, to set up more responsive procedures, to modify how agencies relate to each other, and to change how agencies relate to the client. Such authority can include control of funds or a mandate from the administration of the external agency.

If there are problems with service providers, such as reports not being sent on time or complaints from the client about the service, the practitioner must decide whether to deal personally with the professional involved or to use more formal channels. As the chapter on advocacy states (Chapter 10), it is generally best to discuss the matter directly with the person involved before going to the person's supervisor. This serves to preserve good working relationships. A well-formulated service contract between agencies will explicitly state what to do in the case of disagreements.

Most often professional helpers receive feedback only when mistakes are made. However, when the work is particularly good, the case manager should consider sending a note of appreciation to the worker's supervisor. This can promote current goodwill between agencies, and also increases the likelihood that the client (and others) will receive continued appropriate services in the future. The practitioner can also provide consultation to the external agency in areas of particular expertise, and involve the agency in deciding on changes in the plan for the client.

When service is impeded because of poor communication or turf conflicts, the *case conference mechanism* can be employed. The case conference is a time-honored method used in case management, wherein members of the client's formal support network meet face-to-face in order to resolve disputes or expedite processes. Case conferences have certain obvious advantages: sharing information that is mutually beneficial in making decisions; promoting trust and understanding; arriving at congruent goals; and adjusting the configuration of services.

The major drawback to case conferencing is the high cost it requires in time and personnel. Therefore, the practitioner needs to be sure that there is a compelling reason to call a conference. Valid reasons, as suggested above, include eliminating or minimizing frictions; clarifying resources; and distributing responsibilities.

Forms to Aid Monitoring

By having convenient forms and set procedures for looking at the entire caseload, the practitioner can oversee client progress in a timely and systematic manner. A useful device was created in a child protective services setting (*Highlights, Champaign, Illinois, Region* v. *Child Welfare Training Center* [1980]). This procedure involves using two simple index cards, which are punched and placed in a binder. One card contains client background data, problems, goals, and tasks (Fig. 9-1). The second card is used for keeping track of all contacts made with the client and the client's support network (Fig. 9-2). Additional cards can be inserted to make notes about the contacts if desired. These cards are reviewed at the end of each month and serve as a reminder of the client's current status. The notes can be useful in updating the client's case file and planning future contacts.

Ballew and Mink (1986) suggest that a monthly review of the caseload be made using a monthly caseload activity sheet as a prompting procedure. There are four cases to each letter-size sheet of paper so that an entire caseload can fit into a file folder, facilitating the monthly review. Each case review sheet includes the following information: client's name, goals, activities, who is responsible for the activity, and the completion date. To use the system they suggest specific steps:

(1) Every month each case is reviewed using the previous month's data. A record is made of activities that were completed and those in process. Points of uncertainty prompt the manager to review the client's case more thoroughly. In this way glitches in the plan are detected early. (Some practitioners prefer to review their caseloads every 2 weeks instead of monthly.)
(2) If no interventions are indicated, the practitioner should probably note that a monitoring contact ought to be made within the month.
(3) The practitioner should go from the form to scheduling monitoring activities in an appointment book or work schedule.

When an activity or particular service is terminated, it is useful to evaluate the effectiveness and quality of the intervention with more quantitative tools. One such monitoring instrument used to evaluate the outcome of planned interventions is the *goal attainment scaling* method (GAS). It is useful for evaluating the individual client as well as a research instrument. With the GAS one "can tell at a glance what the goals of treatment for each client are, whether they were attained, and whether they exceeded or failed their expectations" (Gerhart, 1990, p. 215). Each goal is specified and five possible outcomes are described ranging from "much less than expected," (–2), to "much better than expected," (+2). It is an objective, behavioral tool in measurable terms. An example of a GAS used in an outpatient community mental center is shown in Fig. 9-3 (Gerhart, 1990, p. 215).

This overlaps significantly with reassessment, the next phase of the process. While it is difficult, if not impossible, in actual practice to totally separate monitoring and reassessment, for the purposes of our analytical discussion they are considered separately.

FIGURE 9–1   Client contact card

Name: _____ Case number: _____
Type of contact: _____
Contact support: _____
_____
_____
_____
_____
_____

Goal of contact: _____
_____
_____

Monitoring tasks: _____
_____

Results: _____

Follow-up: _____
_____

FIGURE 9–2   Visiting record (indicate dates)

HOME VISITS TO CLIENT	OFFICE VISITS BY CLIENT	TELEPHONE CALLS TO CLIENT	COLLATERAL CONTACTS

FIGURE 9–3 An example of a goal attainment scale used in an outpatient department of a community mental center

Client's name: _____

Date of goal negotiation with client: _____

Check ( ) goal levels for above date.

Follow-up dates: _____

	GOALS		
ATTAINMENT LEVEL	*1 HOUSING*	*2 SELF-CONTROL*	*3 APPOINTMENTS*
Much less than expected (–2)	Client is homeless	Daily temper tantrums	Fails to keep all appts.
Less than expected (–1)	Has to share room and cannot afford the rent	Temper tantrums twice a week	Is late for all appts. but keeps half
Expected level of goal attainment (0)	Has own room, within means	Can control tantrum, only 1 per month	Can keep 4 of 5 appts. on time
Better than expected (+1)	Own housekeeping apartment within means	Only one, brief outburst of temper, once every 2 months	Can keep 8 out of 9 appts.
Much better than expected (+2)	One-bedroom apartment, within means, in nice part of town	No more uncontrolled, unexpected, and unjustified outbursts of temper	Can keep all appointments on time

Anticipating Critical Events and Projecting Time Lines

Monitoring programs should anticipate needs and provide means to serve clients during crisis periods. A study by Baker et al. (1985, p. 301) identifies life events that the chronically mentally ill perceived as emotionally disturbing. This information is useful for planning early intervention or preventive action. By anticipating and monitoring these occurrences "case managers may be able to provide the kind of intensive social support that earlier research has suggested can buffer the negative consequence of stressful life events." (See also Cassell, 1974; Cobb, 1976.) Stressful events include changes in regular daily activities, residential moves, and physical health problems. Also, events that are perceived as not under the client's control are viewed as stressful.

One method to anticipate stressful life events or transitions is to formulate a time line and project into the future critical events and transitions that may reasonably be expected. This enables the practitioner to help prepare the client and kin for these events, and perhaps lessen the intensity of the crisis. It also directs the practitioner's attention to activities or events that need to be monitored.

Time lines graphically chart the client's past history (Quam & Abramson, 1991). The client and worker can graph significant life events by age and date. Such events as births, deaths, marriages, separations, hospitalizations, occupational shifts, and legal involvements can be included, as well as other events the client considers momentous.

The worker can then, according to Quam and Abramson (1991, p. 29), use this social history data to "identify gaps in developmental patterns and age-appropriate tasks that were thwarted or obliterated by illness, family disruption, or lack of opportunity." These authors illustrate as follows:

Events	Mother died	Was hospitalized	Was hospitalized	Moved to apt.	Lived with sister	Was hospitalized	Lived in group home
Age	9	18	25	32	45	53	57

It may be desirable to use large sheets (butcher paper, shelf paper, or computer paper) for more space or detail. Colored pens can be used to highlight aspects of the client's life (childhood, young adulthood, middle age, past and future times), happy or sad events, or events that involved a relationship with others (birth of a child, divorce) as opposed to events that relate only to the client (menopause, illness).

Time lines are used effectively in a retrospective way and have implications for counseling or therapy. However, the same means can anticipate life transitions for purposes of monitoring and negotiating future troubled times. An illustration may be useful. Sarah was 11 years old when she first entered treatment. She was the youngest of five children; she had two brothers (ages 24 and 22 years) and two sisters (ages 19 and 17 years). Her mother died of cancer when she was 7 years old. Shortly before the mother's death she requested that the girls not live with their father, as she was aware that he had sexually molested the 17 year old and there was some question as to whether he had molested the 19 year old as well. Prior to that time this information had not been reported to the children's protective service. After the mother's death, the children went to live with a cousin. The worker made a time line listing significant events in Sarah's life to date, followed by a projection (double line).

Events:	Birth 4/79	Mother dies/ placed with aunt	Placed with cousin	Enters therapy	Court grants greater visitation rights	Jr. High/ puberty	High School	College/ trade school	Marriage/ career
Age	0	7	9	11	12	13–15	15–18	18	20+

The practitioner should be monitoring the transition to junior high school, including the client's academic performance, her social adjustment, and attitudes at school. In high school she will need to negotiate the troubled waters of adolescence and relationships with boys. Career planning will become important. When she is 18, she will be out of the system but will need someone to help her to make decisions about college, trade school, or a job.

Using Management Information Systems

Management Information Systems (MIS) is defined as "an organized set of data gathering and processing procedures designed as a supportive tool for managers" (Gruber, 1981, p. 236). Computers and their usages have proliferated in recent years. Their applications are becoming more widespread in all industries and in the social services field. Typically, computers are effective for generating statistical data and quantitative comparisons. Reports can be prepared displaying how many clients are on each caseload and how many different kinds of contacts were made in toto or during different time periods (i.e., in person, telephone contacts, visits to clients, contacts with informal supports, and professionals).

A caution is necessary here. Such information, while extremely useful, can be misleading if the data are interpreted to imply that those practitioners with the highest statistics are the most efficient, and a standard by which others should be measured. Quantity output may mean that the practitioner is working superficially for many clients, rather than providing purposive service to those actually seen. Quantitative data need to be interpreted with the knowledge that they are only part of the picture.

Computers are able to shorten the time it takes for recording contacts and generating reports. When case notes can be entered directly into the computer, valuable time is saved, and information from various sources becomes available almost instantly. Problems in implementing the service plan can be identified quickly, leaving the practitioner more time for finding solutions.

Tracking clients.   Systems that are interfaced between agencies so that information can be shared immediately can be highly efficient. "Where interactive computer systems are operating in several agencies participating in the case management program, they can greatly assist service monitoring and troubleshooting, speed up the process of feedback, and provide the timely information needed to take corrective action to deal with problems in service delivery for clients" (Weil, 1985b, p. 63). For instance, a practitioner in one agency may call up a particular client's file on the screen and discover that she hasn't attended her day-treatment program (conducted in another location) for over a week, didn't pick up her last prescription, and the last contact the agency had with her was 4 days ago when she called in sick. With this monitoring information, the practitioner may follow up on this client immediately, starting with an inquiry about her illness. Similarly, if the practitioner calls the next client's file to the screen and finds that she has been attending day treatment regularly, picking up medications regularly, and keeping her appointments with the psychiatrist, this suggests recontacting the client at a later date and turning to cases that have a more urgent quality.

MIS can help track clients through the system and ensure that follow-up contacts are made on a regular basis and when the client's status changes in an important way. For instance, if the first client mentioned above were to enter the hospital, the practitioner would know from a routine checking of her case load on the screen that this client is being discharged from the hospital and may need assistance with medications or contact with her employer.

Drawbacks of MIS. Computers, however, have their drawbacks. State-of-the-art systems may not be attuned to the particulars of the service approach for vulnerable populations. There is the issue of confidentiality in easily accessible information. How to safeguard the privacy and legal rights of clients, and yet take full advantage of the benefits the MIS can offer, is a matter needing careful scrutiny. Current technology has serious drawbacks. Programs often add to the workload rather than streamline effort. Kane (1985, p. 191) comments, "Program staff complain that they are inundated with paperwork and that they rarely receive timely and useful displays of data from the system." The rapid changes occurring in the technology will probably address these types of questions in the near future.

Using Monitoring with Different Client Populations

In the first section of this chapter it was stated that monitoring may be applied differently in the specifics with different client groups. With the mentally ill one can anticipate occasional psychotic crisis episodes that will need to be addressed. With the elderly it is important to be on the watch for physical or mental deterioration and to keep track of Medicare and insurance requirements. In child welfare, legal requirements may effect monitoring, including rulings of the court. The child welfare context is further discussed to illustrate differences in the dynamics of monitoring practice.

Epstein (1988) states that court orders may dictate monitoring in some populations, for example, foster care, probation and parole, legal protective guardianship, and child welfare. Time limitations are crucial in child welfare work, especially in permanency planning. Efforts to reunite a child with his or her family can be thwarted without vigilance in monitoring:

> Foster care drift refers to the endless wandering of a child through the foster care system without a plan to return the child to her home and without prospects for adoption. Losing the child in the system is often the result of fuzzy planning, inadequate record keeping, and a lack of a means to monitor children who enter foster care (Wells, 1985, p. 123).

This emphasizes the importance of formulating a monitoring scheme and establishing time frames for effort.

The worker needs to be in contact with the parents frequently and regularly. Documentation of these contacts needs to be scrupulously maintained, as records may be used as evidence in court. Persons working in child welfare should know the laws relating to children, court procedures, and methods of presenting testimony.

Timeliness is important in efforts at family reunification. It needs to be taken into account through the entire process: the time between when a report of suspected child abuse is received and the initial investigation, the time between the first contact with the family and the beginning of treatment, and also the total time the case is in process (Berkeley Planning Associates, 1977; Stein, Gambrill, & Wiltse, 1978).

Monitoring in child welfare ideally involves once-a-week contact rather than the once-a-month contact often recommended with other populations (Wells, 1985, p. 134).

> Evaluation of progress and reassessment occur continually. Case review, one tool for evaluation, consists of reviewing the cases of children in placement at specified time intervals. Case review may be done within the agency, by juvenile court, by a professional board, or by a citizen's review team. The case review is usually done within three months after the initial placement and every three to six months thereafter. Cases determined to require long-term foster care may be reviewed less often. Public Law 96-272 is one example of legislation that mandates periodic reviews.

Because records become legal documents, formal monitoring using written, standardized instruments is a higher priority than informal monitoring. Written contracts and established indicators of desired client behavior guide the monitoring function. In areas where the county purchases service contracts from private agencies to provide child welfare services, monitoring takes on a particular significance. Payment for services may be contingent on evidence of services so these cases must be carefully tracked and documented (Ten Broek, 1980).

The particulars of monitoring differ for other client populations. This discussion of child welfare suggests the kinds of contextual factors to look for that may influence the process.

REASSESSMENT AND OUTCOME EVALUATION

Tasks and Objectives

No matter how precisely an intervention plan is structured and closely monitored, clients and their supports are supremely unpredictable and emergent in their ways of behaving. The social scientist and human service practitioner are driven back recurrently to the drawing board. We ought to celebrate this instinct for freedom in the human personality, while muttering about the trouble it causes us.

The California Assembly Select Committee emphasized reassessment as necessary because client circumstances change over time. Therefore, "a community survival plan must shift emphasis with the person's development and needs" (Bronzan, 1984, p. 8). Key questions that have to go into such an evaluation are posited by Weil (1985a, p. 349): "Whether the client is making the expected progress toward individual goals, . . . whether the service plan should be continued or modified, and whether the client is ready to be terminated from the case management program."

In the introduction to this chapter it was noted that reassessment and evaluation involve identical procedures, but the first assumes further assessments and the latter assumes a culmination or termination of service. Highly vulnerable clients do not ordinarily present the typical acute symptomology that permits a cure or return to "normal" ways of functioning. Speaking from a mental health perspective, Honnard and Wolkon (1985, p. 111) put the issue as follows:

> The problem of defining when a client completes or should complete a case management program is unclear. Usually the target group of case management programs are the chronically mentally ill. These are patients for whom a lifetime of treatment of one kind or another is the best prognosis . . . if case management is a lifelong program, how can the outcome be measured? What constitutes an after study? Few case management programs have criteria for discharge from the program; what criteria do exist vary from program to program. . . .

While discharge/outcome evaluation occurs occasionally and is represented in the model guiding this book, the broken lines in the diagram of the model suggest its subordination to the perspective of evaluation as reassessment.

In reassessment/evaluation of a client's circumstances and condition the following factors are examined.

Implementation of the treatment or service plan.   Were the service activities that had been designated actually put into practice? This is analogous to process evaluation or input evaluation in more formal program evaluation research. It is sometimes referred to as "effort."

Progress toward goal attainment.   What advancement was made toward the specific goals that had been designated? What discrepancy exists between intended and actual achievement, and what further work is needed? This concern is referred to as "adequacy" in program evaluation.

What specific outcomes or changes were brought about?   This concerns factors such as social functioning (examined with respect to role enactment or task management), quality of life, or client satisfaction with current circumstances. These questions are at the heart of traditional outcome evaluation research.

Validity of the intervention plan.   The question here is whether the plan for client progress, and the strategy underlying it, was appropriate for the intended aims. Weiss (1972) indicates that when a program fails in its aims, this may reflect a failure of program implementation, or there may be a failure of theory. Did the program basically fail because it was not carried out properly? That matter was discussed under the first two factors. The criterion stated here examines the *match* between the strategy and the situation it is applied to. Did the program fail because the theory of what kind of intervention was required is erroneous? In that case, a new approach or strategy has to be designed, rather than applying more energetic efforts to actualizing the original plan.

Instruments

Assessment instruments of various kinds were discussed in Chapter 4 and these same tools apply as well to reassessment and outcome evaluation. The original assessment of the client provides a baseline against which to measure progress, using the same type of observations and measurements as before.

We will not examine assessment tools in depth here. There are numerous books that offer a wide variety of assessment/evaluation methods for appraising practice (Bloom & Fischer, 1982; Powers, Meenaghan, & Toomey, 1985). There are specific procedures for examining service implementation (Epstein & Tripodi, 1977) and outcome assessment related to social functioning and role performance (Bergner, Bobbit, Pallard, Martin, & Gilson, 1976), task enactment (Kane, Kane, & Arnold, 1985), and client satisfaction (Reid & Gundlach, 1983). Means are available to examine the match between the intervention or program strategy and client needs, particularly with shifting or emergent needs (Stufflebeam & Shinkfield, 1986). Any of the goal attainment scales can be used for appraising the extent to which goals are reached and the remaining gap, either through measuring segmented goals (Morris & Fitz-Gibbon, 1978a) or by a global assessment (Endicott, Spitzer, Fleiss, & Cohen, 1976). A sample goal attainment scaling procedure was shown earlier in the chapter.

In the same way that client input contributes to monitoring, it can be extremely valuable in reassessment. Clients are in immediate touch with their circumstances and needs. Only they can provide a subjective appraisal of their living reality. Some tools specifically elicit client judgments on their satisfaction and performance; others rely on more objective sources, such as case records. However, even when instruments are not based on client perspectives, it would be sensible to informally draw out the client's personal views regarding the factors being measured.

Key Aspects

The nature of the reassessment process and issues related to putting it into practice were brought out vividly in the UCLA practitioner survey. Reassessment was a function carried out by most of the respondents in the survey. It was described as follows:

> I do evaluations periodically. I read all the records, assess progress made, eliminate old goals, and set new ones. This is a formal part of my activities.

> I primarily examine my own effectiveness in meeting the goals set for the client. I determine if short- and long-term goals are being met and if treatment needs to be altered to deal with new situations in the client's life.

There was a great deal of variation reported among respondents regarding reassessment. Their comments reflected the following approaches.

Formal and prescribed v. informal and emergent. Some respondents conduct official reassessments with set forms on a monthly, 3-month, or 4-month basis. Quarterly and semi-annually mandated summaries are referred to frequently.

Other people approach reassessment as an informal "constant, ongoing, continuous" process, which is responsive to ever-changing client needs, and involves "sitting and talking." Some staff use both formal and informal means.

Variations in frequency. Some workers engage in frequent reassessment and others do it sporadically. Some talk of almost daily reassessments, others engage in the activity "occasionally," "when things are not going well," or when the patient has "accomplished a goal and it is time to move on to something else."

Client and staff participation. One respondent stated, "This is not done with the client—only with the residential home staff." Most specifically carry out reassessment in direct interaction with the client—considering goals and functioning and the modifying of goals. Other relevant individuals are involved. One respondent had discussions with the client, agency staff, the physician, and board-and-care staff. Another approach was through the weekly staff meeting, which involves input from the full staff and sometimes the family.

Marginal activity for some. For some, reassessment is an expendable activity. For example, one view was that "patients are chronic and can't change," therefore reassessment is not necessary. Another respondent acknowledged that reassessment is an expected, formal activity, "but I can't get to it."

While there is much variation, most people do engage in reassessment and lean toward the ongoing concept, using both formal and informal means. Most involve the client and others in the reassessment process.

Obstacles

While re-evaluation is a basic component of the work, a variety of obstacles hinder its execution. Comments by the respondents highlight these:

Lack of Client Motivation

If the patient has no motivation to pursue additional goals, i.e., going back to school, I get frustrated. I will continue to help, but I am not as motivated. Also, re-evaluation is difficult with dependent individuals who want to be taken care of or don't want to get well. Sometimes the system rewards clients' helplessness.

Loosely Formulated Goals

It gets in the way if you have no clearly defined concrete goals in terms of what you're aiming for.

Client Resistance

"No shows" are a real problem. If the client doesn't come around or is sporadic, you can't monitor progress. Or if a client comes around but holds back information, it makes reassessment impossible. Also, some clients discharge themselves prematurely.

Unsteady Client Progress

Sometimes it is difficult to measure improvement. If the patient is oscillating up and down, results depend on when you reassess the patient. You always need to show success for justification of program. If the patient is unstable, the case manager feels obliged to find a new treatment need.

Uncooperative Agencies

A big problem is nonresponse by agencies, or responses that do not come quickly enough. In such cases, my information is sketchy (and my credibility with clients drops radically). I have known of as long as a 2-year wait. Lack of documentation, generally, is a problem.

Time Limitations and Work Pressures

This is very time-consuming. If we are asked to do x, y, and z, then we must put some things aside to respond to the mandated tasks. Usually it is the quiet patients who are set aside. A hindrance is also the excessive paperwork involved—I guess it is needed, but it is hard to keep up with it. This takes our energy and time away from service delivery. Yet, if you continue performing well, the administration thinks it can be done.

The Matter of Discharge Evaluation

In the survey, respondents were asked about evaluation as well as reassessment. Few thought of evaluation in terms of full discharge from further service activity and a return to independent living. In general, evaluation overlapped or was equated with reassessment. This confusion is associated with clients who are in a "continuing care" context. The decisions that were related to evaluation generally considered whether the client was ready for a more enriched intervention plan, or if an alternative course of action was needed in achieving the initial short- and long-term objectives. Clients were viewed as requiring some ongoing form of intervention. It was a question of more, less, or different.

Decisions about the reassessment/evaluation and implications for further service were made variably, including: an independent decision by the practitioner; a combination of the practitioner and his or her supervisor; or a broad review panel consisting of the practitioner, the supervisor, other personnel in the agency, and staff from external agencies. However, for the most part this was a principal activity of the primary practitioner.

Evaluation suggests a termination of the practice process, and reevaluation implies some new beginning in the cycle of service. At this point our analysis has covered all the functions in the practice model that are involved in either conception. What we have not discussed in detail as yet are contextual factors, including organization and community influences. These are extremely important and will be considered next.

REFERENCES

Austin, C. (1983). Case management in long term care: Options and opportunities. *Health and Social Work, 8*(1), 16–30.

Baker, F., Burns, T., Libby, M., & Intagliata, J. (1985). The impact of life events on chronic mental patients. *Hospital and Community Psychiatry, 36*(3), 299–301.

Bergner, M., Bobbitt, R. A., Pollard, W. E., Martin, D. P., & Gilson, B. (1976). Sickness impact profile: Validation of a health status measure. *International Journal of Health Services, 6*, 393–415.

Berkley Planning Associates. (1977). Evaluation of child abuse and neglect demonstration projects, 1974–1977. *Quality of the case management process* (Vol. 6). Springfield, VA: U.S. Department of Commerce.

Bloom, M. (1990). *Introduction to the drama of social work.* Itasca, IL: F. W. Peacock.

Bloom, M. & Fischer, J. (1982). *Evaluating practice: Guidelines for the accountable professional.* Englewood Cliffs, NJ: Prentice-Hall.

Bronzan, B. (1984). *Preliminary findings of the Assembly Select Committee on Mental Health.* Sacramento: California Assembly Select Committee.

Caragonne, P. (1983). *A comparison of case management work activity and current models of work activity within the Texas department of mental health mental retardation.* Austin: Texas Department of Mental Health and Mental Retardation.

Cassell, J. (1974). An epidemiological perspective of psychosocial factors in disease etiology. *American Journal of Public Health, 64*, 1040–1043.

Cobb, S. (1976). Social support as a mediator of life stress. *Psychosomatic Medicine, 38*, 300–314.

Corsini, R, (Ed.) (1979). *Current psychotherapies.* Itasca, IL: F. E. Peacock.

Dane, B. O. & Simon, B. L. (1991). Resident guests: Social workers in host settings. *Social Work, 36*(3), 208–213.

Downing, R. (1985). The elderly and their families. In M. Weil, J. M. Karls, & associates (Eds.), *Case management in human service practice* (pp. 145–169). San Francisco: Jossey-Bass.

Endicott, J., Spitzer, R., Fleiss, J., & Cohen, J. (1976). The global assessment scale: A procedure for measuring overall severity of psychiatric disturbance. *Archives of General Psychiatry, 33,* 766–771.

Epstein, I. & Tripodi, T. (1977). *Research techniques for program planning, monitoring and evaluation.* New York: Columbia University Press.

Epstein, L. (1988). *Helping people: The task-centered approach* (2nd ed.). Columbus: Merrill.

Fischer, J. (1978). *Effective casework practice: An eclectic approach.* New York: McGraw-Hill.

Gerhart, U. C. (1990). *Caring for the chronic mentally ill.* Itasca, IL: F. E. Peacock.

Gitterman, A. & Miller, I. (1989). The influence of the organization on clinical practice. *Clinical Social Work Journal, 17*(2), 151–164.

Gruber, M. L. (Ed.) (1981). *Management systems in the human services.* Philadelphia: Temple University Press.

Hackett, T. P. & Cassem, N. H. (1978). *Massachusetts general hospital handbook of general hospital psychiatry.* Saint Louis: C. V. Mosby.

Hennessy, C. H. (1989). Autonomy and risk: The role of client wishes in community based long-term care. *Gerontologist, 29*(5), 633–639.

Honnard, R. & Wolkon, G. H. (1985). Evaluation for decision making and program accountability. In M. Weil & J. M. Karls (Eds.), *Case management in human service practice* (pp. 94–118). San Francisco: Jossey-Bass.

Kane, R. A. (1985). Case management in health care settings. In M. Weil, J. M. Karls, & associates (Eds.), *Case management in human service practice* (pp. 170–203). San Francisco: Jossey-Bass.

Kane, R. A., Kane, R. L., & Arnold, S. (1985). *Measuring social functioning in mental health studies: Concepts and instruments.* Washington, DC: U.S. Government Printing Office.

Levine, I. S. & Fleming, M. (1985). *Human resource development: issues in case management.* Washington, DC: National Institute for Mental Health.

Maxmen, J. S. (1985). *The new psychiatry.* New York: William Morrow.

Morris, L. & Fitz-Gibbon, C. (1978a). *How to measure achievement.* Beverly Hills, CA: Sage.

Morris, L. & Fitz-Gibbon, C. (1978b). *How to measure program implementation.* Beverly Hills, CA: Sage.

Moxley, D. (1989). *The practice of case management.* Newbury Park, CA: Sage Publications.

Nurcombe, B. & Gallagher, R. M. (1986). *The clinical process in psychiatry: Diagnosis and management planning.* New York: Cambridge University Press.

Powers, G. T., Meenaghan, T. M., & Toomey, B. G. (1985). *Practice-focused research: Integrating human service practice and research.* Englewood Cliffs, NJ: Prentice-Hall.

Quam, J. K. & Abramson, N. S. (1991). The use of time lines and life lines in work with chronically mentally ill people. *Health and Social Work, 16,* 27–33.

Reid, P. & Gundlach, J. H. (1983). A scale for the measurement of consumer satisfaction with social services. *Journal of Social Service Research, 7*(1), 37–53.

Scott, R. & Cassidy, K. (1981). *The case management function: A position paper.* Unpublished manuscript.

Stein, T. J., Gambrill, E. D., & Wiltse, K. T. (1978). *Children in foster homes: Achieving continuity of care.* New York: Praeger.

Stein, L. & Test, M. (1980). Alternative to mental hospital treatment. *Archives of General Psychiatry, 37*(4), 392–397.

Stufflebeam, D. & Shinkfield, A. (1986). *Systematic evaluation.* Boston: Kluwer, Nijhoff.

Ten Broek, E. (1980). *The family protection act—It can work.* Paper presented at the 25th Child Welfare League of America, Western Region Training Conference, Pasadena, CA.

Turner, F. J. (1986). *Social work treatment: Interlocking theoretical approaches.* New York: The Free Press.

Webster's ninth new collegiate dictionary. (1989). Springfield, MA: Merriam-Webster Inc.

Weil, M. (1982). Research on issues in collaboration between social workers and lawyers. *Social Service Review, 56,* 393–405.

Weil, M. (1985a). Adopting case management to specific programs and needs. In M. Weil, J. M. Karls, & associates (Eds.), *Case management in human service practice* (pp. 317–356). San Francisco: Jossey-Bass.

Weil, M. (1985b). Key components in providing efficient and effective services. In M. Weil, J. M. Karls, & Associates (Eds.), *Case management in human service practice* (pp. 29–71). San Francisco: Jossey-Bass.

Weiss, C. H. (1972). *Evaluation research: Methods of assessing program effectiveness.* Englewood Cliffs, NJ: Prentice-Hall.

Wells, S. J. (1985). Children and the child welfare system. In M. Weil, J. M. Karls, & associates (Eds.), *Case management in human service practice* (pp. 119–144). San Francisco: Jossey-Bass.

Whittaker, J. K. & Tracy, E. M. (1989). *Social treatment: An introduction to interpersonal helping in social work practice.* (2nd ed.). New York: Aldine DeGruyter.

Wolkon, G., Peterson, C., & Rogowski, A. (1978). The implementation of a psychiatric continuing care program. *Hospital and Community Psychiatry, 29*(4), 254–256.

Woods, M. E. & Hollis, F. (1990). *Casework: A psychosocial therapy.* (4th ed.). New York: McGraw-Hill.

10
Advocacy

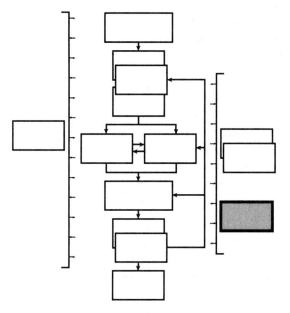

UNDERSTANDING ADVOCACY

The Concept of Advocacy

There are times when a rational argument presented in a highly civil manner does absolutely no good. As an illustration, recall the saying that there is no problem with adolescents that reasoning with them will not aggravate. From time to time in the natural course of events, determined and forceful action may be required of us, even if it runs against the grain. William James commented, "We are all ready to be savage in some cause." He went on to qualify, "The difference between a good man and a bad man is the choice of the cause." There are occasions in practice when advocacy on behalf of a client is an imperative, especially for vulnerable individuals with compelling needs. Professional integrity sometimes calls for taking sides, vigorously.

Advocacy figures prominently in almost all discussions of case management. Indeed, Lanoil (1980) identifies it as one of the two distinctive ingredients, along with social support. Fischer (1978, p. 21) observes that it is one of the important roles in professional helping generally, and states that the field of social work began "as an attempt to mediate between individuals and societal institutions. Gradually, however, this role became submissive to the clinical role of casework . . ."

This approach in the human services was given impetus for a time during the social upheavals of the 1960s. Advocacy planning came to the fore in the field of urban planning (Davidoff, 1965). The National Association of Social Workers established an Ad Hoc Committee on Advocacy (1969), which vigorously endorsed the advocacy role as a practice imperative deriving from the NASW Code of Ethics. The War on Poverty relied on advocacy as a prime weapon.

Advocacy and Case Management

There has been limited research on the use of the advocacy function within case management. However, empirical studies have been undertaken on advocacy in related areas that hold interest for comprehensive enhancement practice.

One study suggests that the proportion of professionals who entertain the advocacy function and are willing to "stand up to its demands" may be relatively small. Based on a national study, Rees and Wallace (1982, p. 162) conclude that clients "have valued negotiations and advocacy on their behalf" but workers "have not considered such roles to be important." A study of members of the American Psychological Association reached similar conclusions (Fairbank & Jarrett, 1987). Respondents significantly favored professional concerns (licensure, public image, and training) over social advocacy (human rights and community education).

Not all the research supports this view. For example, in the UCLA study, most of the practitioners said they engage in some form of advocacy—

only seven of the 48 did not. The matter of internal agency advocacy was examined by Patti (1980). Most of the 59 human service professionals he studied reported engaging in some form of internal advocacy during a recent 2-year period—only six indicated no such involvement. The highest percentage of responses (29%) related to seeking improvement in client well-being through new or modified service and programs. Efforts of this nature were also directed at changing procedures for processing clients and obtaining new facilities and resources. Some of the efforts were more intraprofessional or career oriented, such as dealing with work flow, personal practices, and communication.

External advocacy was examined in another study. In a survey of 105 professionals in Michigan (Epstein, 1981), more than two thirds of the advocates (71%) reported encountering obstacles in their own agencies. This was in addition to the extensive external blocks, which were reported by 90%. The worker may pay a personal price for taking on this responsibility. Forty percent experienced burnout as a moderate or great problem as an aftermath. This suggests the need to provide greater support to those who engage in advocacy.

Purpose of Advocacy

Taking a psychosocial or ecosystems perspective, advocacy signifies the occurrence of a problematic person-in-environment fit. Ordinarily the environment, or a relevant part of it, will manifest one of three alternative responses to the entreaties of a person: positive, neutral, or negative. Sosin and Caulum (1983) visualize this interaction in terms of allies, neutrals, and adversaries. If the external stance is positive, the individual need only make a routine request in order to be accommodated. If neutral, calling attention to the matter forthrightly or providing convincing information may suffice to gain the desired ends. However, when the environment is negative, pressure of an adversarial nature may be required. Advocacy is an instrument for bringing about a more satisfactory person-in-environment fit for individuals seeking a given benefit from a recalcitrant system.

Advocacy typically comes into play when clients are denied service. Some clients may be perceived by agencies to be unattractive, to not match up with overly rigid service categories (Johnson & Rubin, 1983) or to behave in ways deemed inappropriate. Clients with dual diagnoses or persistent impairments often experience such rejection. For example, Lamb (1976) observed a pattern of resistance to meeting the needs of long-term mental patients, and this group has been characterized as a low-priority population (Los Angeles County Department of Mental Health, 1985).

Advocacy involves the use of strong influence or pressure to compel a target entity to engage in behavior sought by the advocate. More specifically, in the human service field, the advocate serves as a professional spokesperson or agent who pursues the interests of a client treated unfairly by community institutions where the client, because of impairment or dependency is unable to achieve a remedy alone. Thus, advocacy may involve resolution of conflict or confrontation aimed at inducing desired change in the institution.

Human service professionals may naturally shrink from using advocacy tactics, preferring discussion, cooperation, and collaboration. When confrontation is necessary, there has to be deliberate and disciplined use of self on behalf of clients, similar in principle to the clinical context. One may need to go against one's own proclivities and regroup internally.

Characteristics of Advocacy

There are certain core elements of advocacy, according to Sosin and Caulum (1983): *change effort;* focus on *a specific decision* to be influenced; involvement of *three social actors* (the advocate, the client, and a decision maker); *an imbalance of power;* and *potential for a positive outcome* in affecting the decision. The authors put these pieces together defining advocacy as follows (p. 36):

> An attempt, having a better than zero probability of success, by an individual or group to influence another individual or group to make a decision that would not have been made otherwise and concerns the welfare or interests of a third party who is in a less powerful status than the decision maker.

In the UCLA field interviews, practitioners characterized the role as "guardian for the client," being a "client representative," and "demanding services." Sosin and Caulum mention champion, defender, supporter, and reformer.

Advocacy theory may be approached from a legal perspective. Social welfare services are assumed, in contemporary Western societies, to constitute a form of property that is obligated to particular classes of people as an entitlement (Reich, 1964). Social welfare institutions in their operations, however, often place their own corporate interests above the rights of their designated beneficiaries. Clients under those circumstances need protection and representation.

McGowan (1974) found that outcomes were affected importantly by two variables: the resources mobilized by the advocate and the receptivity of the target. In addition, positive outcomes were associated with use of communication and mediation rather than power. One way to interpret this is that advocacy operated best when relatively moderate means were used in situations involving moderate conflict.

Diverse Applications

Advocacy cuts across different client populations and service settings. It has appeared prominently in such areas as public welfare, children's services, the elderly, and mental health. In a special issue on this subject, the *Practice*

Digest (Sancier, 1984) applied the concept broadly across family advocacy, adoptive parents, Vietnam veterans, the women's movement, and an industrial union.

In addition to its application in various settings, advocacy can take place at most any point in the intervention process. It can comprise a vigorous form of monitoring to see that agreed-upon services are actually implemented, or may coincide with linking to assure that a client's right to be offered a given program is not denied. Alternatively, it may occur during intake when it is learned that an older client has been locked out of his apartment and is undergoing elder abuse. In an important sense, the practitioner is acting as a vigorous supporter of the client in every step of the process, and intercedes with individuals and organizations on behalf of the client while performing functions other than advocacy. What makes advocacy distinctive is its forthright character among the many choices of action open to the worker. Advocacy is often the final action, the last arrow in the practitioner's quiver.

Advocacy may be directed at the internal system or at outside agencies (such as Social Security or board-and-care homes). It maybe directed to the original organization level at which a problem appeared or be elevated to a higher level. For example, the practitioner may go to the supervisor of the offending party in the other agency or may pass the issue up to his or her own supervisor to pursue with the other body.

Client Involvement

Several studies have examined the issue of inculcating self-advocacy skills in clients. One of these surveyed the views of patient education managers concerning the skills they believed were necessary to develop in clients for them to act on their own behalf (Bartlett, 1986). Three sets of such advocacy competencies were delineated:

1. general advocacy skills and strategies, e.g., developing effective personal relations, developing knowledge, self-confidence, and savvy, listening and negotiating;
2. preparation skills and strategies, e.g., gaining access to administration, clarifying the role of the patient education manager, setting reasonable goals, and learning the rules of the game;
3. implementation skills and strategies, e.g., being concrete in explaining patient education, establishing quality assurance policies, and *persistence* (thought to be extremely important by all participants).

The potential for clients to acquire and use such skills is addressed by Sievert, Cuvo, and Davis (1988). Focusing on mildly disabled clients, they produced a handbook instructing clients on how to redress violations of their legal rights in personal, human service, consumer, and community areas. Findings indicated that clients could learn and retain such information over a 3-month period, which was the time frame of the study. Self-help advocacy guides were also employed by Seekins, Fawcett, and Mathews (1987) with clients having physical disabilities. They found that clients were able, with reasonable effectiveness, to apply three focal skills: presenting brief personal testimony, writing letters to the editor, and writing to public officials. Training clients for empowerment was supported by these studies as a feasible advocacy function.

A student comments on a previous experience with client involvement and empowerment:

> An exciting example of group advocacy by clients occurred 2 years ago during one of the governor's infamous budget-cutting bouts. Massive reductions in mental health and social services were being proposed, and at our small agency one full-time professional was in danger of being eliminated. We were able to get a few clients involved in self-advocacy by discussing the situation with them, helping them prepare a statement, and doing some necessary translating. We then helped arrange transportation to a hearing that was scheduled, and encouraged them to speak for themselves about why such drastic cuts should not be made. There were other clients from other agencies also, and their personal stories and pleas made the advocacy very meaningful and empowering. In this case, empowerment included both self-direction and social change, and as a result the staff position in our situation wasn't cut out.

A study on forms of *group advocacy* identified two typical modes of organizational activity: forming issue-oriented alliances grounded on shared grievances, and using existing social networks based on friendship (Cable, Walsh, & Warland, 1988). Another investigation examined *case advocacy* in public welfare agencies where grievance machinery existed. It was found that clients were more likely to make use of these due process procedures when a legal representative was available to them (Hagen, 1983). A role for the practitioner is suggested, providing access to such representation as a facet of the advocacy function. Other studies have found that the propensity to use advocacy measures or to heighten their intensity is associated with reactions of targeted authorities in closing off communication or responding repressively (Obershall, 1969). (This is related to McGowan's finding that advocacy is affected by the degree of receptivity by the target.) With this awareness, the practitioner may be able to predict circumstances in which he or she is more likely to escalate to intensive advocacy, or when client groups are prone to be motivated to take collective action.

Modes and Tactics

Advocacy can take a micro or macro perspective, comprising case advocacy or social advocacy (Moxley, 1989; Terrel, 1967). The terminology varies somewhat, broker advocacy vs. group advocacy, or client advocacy vs. system advocacy, but the concept is the same. Case advocacy indicates actions on behalf of a single individual, social advocacy entails concern for an aggregate population of clients.

As indicated above, the advocacy concept is sometimes expanded to include the notion of client empowerment through self-advocacy (Weil & Karls, 1985). Here clients are provided with the ability and the confidence to engage in advocacy by themselves on their own behalf. The practitioner advocate takes on a training role, transferring the capabilities of advocacy from the professional to the client. Such empowerment may relate either to individual clients or to groups of clients, who then engage in collective action. Two examples from the field of aging illustrate different forms of group empowerment. In New York City the Joint Public Affairs Committee for Older Adults has engaged the elderly in the development of needed public policy and legislation related broadly to income, health, and social services (Duhl, 1983). At the Cambridge Nursing Home in Massachusetts, a political campaign model was employed among the local residents, wherein they take responsibility to act on their own behalf in upholding a residents' bill of rights (McDermott, 1989). The immediate focus of professional attention and the skills employed differ in the indirect form of professional advocacy reflected in empowerment.

Empowerment viewed broadly has two dimensions: training clients to act on their own behalf as discussed, and changing the environment directly so that the rights and entitlements of the client are protected and experienced. In either of these ways, the life of the client is enriched and the capacity for fulfillment is enhanced. The power of the client to attain maximum self-fulfillment is increased.

The value of empowerment has been described by a practitioner as follows:

> Very concrete advocacy skills, once developed and employed by clients, can be highly empowering. For instance, one of my clients was upset over how a bus driver had treated him. When the client arrived at the clinic in the morning, he told me that he thought that he should report the driver, having taken the step of marking down the driver's name and badge number. I encouraged him to go ahead with that, and made my telephone available to him. I also sat near him, giving support but not direct assistance. After reporting the incident to a transport representative, the client felt much better and proud of himself, and shared this new-found skill with other clients. He was a superstar that day in the clinic.*

A continuum of intensity in forms of advocacy is portrayed in the UCLA study. The mildest form involves *discussion* (65% of the responses): providing information, explaining, giving reminders, and joint problem-solving. The next level entails *persuasion* (42% of the responses): recommending, urging, repeating, and reasoned argumentation. Greater intensity involves *prodding* (21% of the responses): here one "pushes" the other party

---

*Personal communication to the author (1993).

into compliance by mild threats ("I'll go over your head," "you wouldn't want that decision to be known all over town") and calling a meeting on the subject. Still another degree of assertiveness is indicated by *coercion* (25% of the responses): taking legal action, releasing a story to the press, having an advocacy group mount a campaign, cutting off the flow of clients or funds, and contacting a legislator. Respondents did not confine themselves to only one level of intensity in their work. Intensity levels are made clearer through examples from the field interviews:

> **Discussion.** I advocate by speaking to supervisors at other agencies. I also send letters explaining the referral. If agencies withhold service, I explore with them why they did it and try to understand their criteria. I consult with them and I inform them of the special circumstances of my client. Just making people aware of the problems helps. They think they're doing a great job and don't realize what the situation is like from the client's point of view.

> **Persuasion.** Of course I advocate. Maybe not the legislative kind, but if someone turns down a client of mine, I challenge them! And I am *very* persistent, and explain the situation completely. I usually get *some* results; I may say "just sign this person on temporarily until you have a personal interview."

> **Prodding.** I do advocacy all the time. Outpatient facilities aren't even following their own guidelines and if someone is thrown out for misbehavior, they don't want to accept him back again. So you get on the phone with the outpatient facility, and the cops as a lever, and you try to negotiate. Also, putting the complaint in writing exerts a lot of pressure. People hate to look bad on paper. Organizations don't want anything detrimental in writing, so if you get it down on paper, that really moves them into action.

> **Coercion.** If the patient is denied a service, often by Social Security, I must find a way for the patient to receive the service. This may involve getting legal help through specialized legal clinics. I show the client how to get an appeal. I will write letters or actually go with the patient to a particular agency to represent him, or I'll attend a hearing. Advocacy is hard—it is always a bear. I have limited knowledge of the legal system, therefore, I must call in a consultant or do my own research. This is very time-consuming.

The single most popular form of advocacy was of low intensity, although a wide range of degrees of intensity was reported, and practitioners did not restrict themselves to one mode. There appeared to be a substantial amount of activity even at the highest level of intensity. Other ways of conceptualizing forms and levels of advocacy are presented in the practice section.

Sometimes different forms of advocacy are used in combination or sequence with a particular client, even over a short time period. A student intern described her work with a chronically mentally ill client.

Since the day when the case was transferred to me, I have engaged in advocacy for this client, primarily focused on obtaining financial aid through AFDC. This particular client is easily confused and intimidated by fast-talking bureaucrats. As a result, one of the first tasks I helped her with was her initial application. After she went down to the AFDC office on her own, she came back to the clinic saying that they had turned her away. They said that she did not have sufficient evidence that she was a legal resident. When I called the AFDC office to inquire about her case, I was told that she should not have been turned away because she has 30 days to provide them with proof of residency.

The client had to go through the process of applying again, but this time I went with her so I could advocate on her behalf. I had to use various tactics with the many different workers that I dealt with in order to complete her application that day. With most of the workers, "persuasion" worked fairly well, and they helped me after I calmly repeated my requests. Although "discussion" would have been a more ideal place to begin, the workers I met that day were not open to discussion. In fact, with one particular worker who was giving us a hard time, "prodding" was necessary, and as soon as I asked to speak with her supervisor, she began to cooperate as much as she could.

Constraints on Use of Advocacy

There does not always exist a clear field for carrying out advocacy. The feasibility of the advocacy function has been questioned by some writers in the case management field who maintain that practitioners are faced with a conflict of interest: the needs of their clients versus the wishes of their employers (Wolowitz, 1983). Professionals are seen to occupy a middle position, with a "double-agent" task. It is suggested that practitioners in this bind seek to preserve their job, and tend to identify more with the interests of the agency. For this reason, according to Wolowitz (1983, p. 82), practitioners may be compromised in exercising "zealous advocacy" on behalf of their clients. He suggests a number of solutions, including turning the advocacy function over to a third-party organization, building long-term funding into contracts so that withdrawal of funds cannot serve as an instrument of conformity over workers, and reaching firm prior understandings with the sponsoring agency about the place of advocacy. The role of ombudsman has been examined as an alternative formulation, and found to be more neutral and intra-organizational in the way it is implemented (Blazyk, Crawford, & Wimberly, 1987). While more stable in some ways, it is not a substitute for vigorous and partisan assertion on behalf of clients.

There are also constraints that derive from professional ideology. Some human service writers equate advocacy with "doing for" the client, an obnoxious form of paternalism. Others believe it drives a wedge between the client and the agency, thereby doing injury to the cooperative and holistic values of the human service field. While some professionals distance themselves from advocacy because it is too radical, others think case-by-case advocacy, in particular, individualizes problems that have broad social ramifications, and this inhibits fundamental system reform. These viewpoints notwithstanding, advocacy remains an established and highly regarded function, at some level, within the human services.

Influence Base for Advocacy

There remains the question of the means available to practitioners to engage viably in advocacy: what are their sources of influence and power when confronting recalcitrant organizations? The bulk of these resources lies in the practitioner's knowledge and skill in organizing and manipulating the human service environment. Because of the complex and multi-layered aspects of advocacy its exercise requires diversified knowledge of the following:

(1) the client,
(2) the originating service organization,
(3) the community service network,
(4) the workings of other specific agencies, and
(5) broad community resources (Weissman, Epstein, & Savage, 1983, p. 164).

Moxley (1989, p. 105) groups the practitioner's influence resources into five power categories:

1. *Authority.* Use of formal authority to enforce access to services and standards of care. This authority may derive from legislative, legal, or administrative mandate.
2. *Human resources.* Encouraging cooperation from other professionals, organized consumer groups, and watchdog organizations.
3. *Skill and knowledge.* Using detailed knowledge of eligibility, licensing, and standards to induce services.
4. *Social psychological factors.* Being charismatic, influential, or having an exemplary reputation in a way that enlists support for one's clientele.
5. *Material Resources.* Having funds to purchase services from providers, using these funds to assure service to a client by paying for the service or by withdrawing funds if the agency is not forthcoming.

PRACTICE GUIDELINES FOR ADVOCACY

This discussion concentrates specifically on the performance of advocacy functions. Some points from the previous sections will be examined and new information will be introduced to illuminate implementation of the adversarial process.

Framework for Advocacy Planning

Because of complex and interactive variables that are at play, advocacy needs to be approached carefully. McGowan (1987) has proposed a mode of analysis that can be used to aid advocacy planning. Her delineation of the key factors follows.

Problem definition. Does the problem arise because of a special client need, a maladaptive relationship between the client and the service system, a structural or personnel deficiency in a service agency, an inter-organizational difficulty, or a dysfunctional social policy?

Objective. Is the objective to secure or enhance an existing service, resource, or entitlement; to develop a new one; or to prevent or limit client involvement with dysfunctional service system?

Target system. Is the target of intervention some component in the worker's own organization (internal advocacy) or in another institution (external advocacy)? What is the service rendered by the organization? Is the relationship between advocate and decision maker one of allies, neutrals, or adversaries (Sosin & Caulum, 1983)?

Sanction. What gives the worker the right or authority to intervene in a system that has not requested help? Does this derive from a client's legal right, an administrative entitlement, a discretionary benefit, or a professional assessment of client need?

Resources. What assets does the advocate possess or have access to that could be used in the proposed intervention? Assets might include knowledge of a client's situation, organizational and political dynamics, and community resources; influence with members of the target system or community power sources; communication and mediation skills; and assistance from a client's natural support system, professional colleagues, or agency officials.

Potential receptivity of target system. What is the likelihood that the significant decision makers in the target system will be receptive to the advocate's request? Will the advocate's role and request be viewed as legitimate?

Level of intervention. At what level should the intervention be carried out? Can the objective be achieved by the action of an individual decision maker in the target system or does it require administrative or policy change (Davidson & Rapp, 1976)?

Object of intervention. With whom should the advocate intervene to secure the change needed? The object of intervention might be a line staff member, supervisor, or administrator in the target system; a policy-making or funding body; a public official; an independent service organization or community group; or an adjudicatory or legislative body.

Strategy of intervention. What approach and means should be used to achieve the desired objective? Should the advocate assume a collaborative, mediatory, or adversarial strategy? What actual modes of intervention should be employed: intercession, persuasion, negotiation, pressure, coercion, or indirect action—for example, preparing a client to take independent action, organizing a community or client group, asking an outside party to intervene?

Outcome of prior advocacy efforts. What can be learned from prior efforts to address the identified problem? Were there any unanticipated obstacles or consequences? Have new resources or problems emerged? Is there any need to reassess the problem, renegotiate the client contract, or revise the plan of intervention based on prior experience?

Determining When to Use Advocacy

Determining the circumstances and timing for use of advocacy is crucial. This includes the following considerations:

- Advocacy is an available tactic when community service organizations fail consistently to provide legitimate services to clients.
- Advocacy involves measures reflecting pressure and conflict. There are varying degrees of intensity of conflict that can be applied within an advocacy context.
- Generally speaking, it is a wise approach to use the principle of "least contest" (Middleman & Goldberg, 1974, p. 73), meaning applying the minimum degree of conflict that will bring about the desired results.
- Controlled escalation of the intensity of advocacy allows optimal outcome for minimal expenditure of strategic resources.

The adversarial initiative contains within it potentially powerful forces of inducement. It also involves risk. The tactic often evokes counterattack, retaliation, resistant "digging in" of organizational heels, or negative and hostile attitudes that persist over time and go beyond particular matters at issue.

Given these factors, a disciplined strategy would combine the principle of least contest with the concept of controlled escalation in planning an advocacy action. A good rule of thumb is to start with the mildest appropriate form of advocacy and move up stepwise to more confrontational forms. There are several advantages to this. Stronger advocacy represents a heavier energy and emotional drain on the case manager than milder advocacy. Therefore, if a milder form will achieve the goal, that is preferred. This notion of least contest has been expressed with plain reason in the following way, "If you can persuade someone, then why mediate? If you can mediate, then why fight with them?" (Weissman, Epstein, & Savage, 1983, p. 105).

This can relate back to Epstein's research in which he found many intra-agency blocks to advocacy actions. Lower intensity advocacy is less likely to bring about disapproval from within one's own organization. Also,

McGowan's study suggests that moderate intensity might be the most effective level of confrontation.

Advocacy is appropriate when there is an imbalance in power and resources. One common approach to advocacy is to create win–win situations, i.e., those that are mutually beneficial to all parties (Weissman, Epstein, & Savage, 1983). A helpful tactic may be to present a problematic situation as an exchange relationship to the target agency, i.e., you take our clients and we will give yours special consideration. The exchange may involve resources, time, assistance, or simply rewarding cooperative staff. The major underpinning at the bargaining table is that each party invests in the relationship and hopes for a payoff. If this type of advocacy is to be successful, the rewards must outweigh the costs. But keep in mind that the benefits and costs are affected by what the problem is, the procedure employed to present it, and methods used to obtain it.

Unlike some other approaches, advocacy may contain a mutually exclusive feature as a strategy. Many practice methods can be used concurrently in combinations that jointly maximize objectives. For example, in linking with agencies it is possible to emphasize interdependence by demonstrating potential instrumental gains for both. At the same time, the practitioner can draw upon an existing informal relationship of friendship with a key staff member. With advocacy, however, all additional options may become closed out by the antagonistic spirit that is generated. Put another way, "One cannot be in continual disagreement and conflict on one set of issues and expect others to cooperate on others" (Weissman, Epstein, & Savage, 1983, p. 148).

Advocacy in a given situation may be the valid and compelling way to proceed, and if so it should be carried out without flinching. But it needs to be considered with reference to effects on strategic mixtures that would be useful over time. When the continuance of an amiable working relationship is important, advocacy may not be the strategy of choice.

Selecting Targets

All of these areas could be discussed at length, however, one matter particularly deserves further consideration: the identification of the target of adversarial action. There is an amorphous quality to large formal organizations and urban communities. If appropriate power centers are not identified, much effort can be expended with little result.

It is important to be attuned to organizational variables in defining the target. Who has the power or responsibility to make the decision? Is it an individual or a group? At what level of the organization is the target located: a clerical person who processes forms at the base; a program professional who delivers services; a supervisor who oversees a program area; an administrator who implements policy; a board that enacts or changes policy at the apex of the institution? Who is above the target in the organization? Is an individual or group decision necessary? To what kind of influence or pressure is each individual or group subject? For example, the clerk at the reception window might be "gotten to" through an immediate supervisor in the agency, but the administrator might only respond to external exposure through the media.

Selecting Tactics

Tactics were examined earlier when results of the field study were presented. Responses fell into certain conceptual categories: discussion, persuasion, prodding, and coercion. The analysis of advocacy tactics is expanded here through a more detailed set of techniques. These will be grouped according to the degree of conflict intensity involved. Three levels of intensity are delineated (low, moderate, and high) because of the utility of that formulation for intervention planning. The principles of least contest and controlled escalation can be applied readily within this framework.

Low Conflict Intensity: Discussion and Persuasion

>Contact provider
>Make the need known
>Use nonaccusatory firmness
>Coach client
>Accompany client
>Use special knowledge of the agency's policies and procedures

Moderate Conflict Intensity: Prodding

>Negotiate and bargain with organizational actors
>Invoke legal mandate of your agency
>Appeal to external ombudsman
>Use target's grievance procedures
>Use your knowledge and authority robustly
>Make assertive requests
>Appeal to a higher authority in the target

High Conflict Intensity: Coercion

>Appeal to target's funding sources
>Seek community media exposure
>Mobilize organized consumer groups
>Use the courts
>Use outside authority (political leaders, state bureau)
>Invoke a licensing or regulatory agency
>Inform a government agency that had contracted for the service being sought

This listing is suggestive, not exhaustive. One way to use it is to apply a series of tactical questions to the set.

- Which of these options is most likely to induce the desired response from the target?
- Do I have the skills to carry it out (hard bargaining, public speaking, organizing demonstrations, etc.)?
- Do I have the sanction from my agency to use this tactic? (You may want to go ahead anyway in deference to the interests of your client. But it is better to know beforehand that you are not likely to get your supervisor's support than to be taken aback and become disoriented at a crucial time.)
- Do I have access to resources necessary to implement the tactic (contacts with the media, legal knowledge or available consultation, an understanding with relevant advocacy groups, etc.)?

The UCLA field study identified a variety of techniques through which advocacy roles are exercised (Table 10-1). Six techniques (above the dotted line) are used by at least five respondents and perhaps merit attention: phoning, writing letters, preparing other written documents, listing the agency, getting legal aid, and referring the matter to a higher authority in the agency.

Using Tactics

The field study indicated that influence can be exerted in some instances by accentuating, with exaggerated bureaucratic fanfare, the advocate's agency and position. This means using all the trappings of formal status and authority. In one field report it was noted that a client came to the practitioner with

TABLE 10–1 Advocacy Activities Reported by Case Managers

ACTIVITY	*NO. OF TIMES REPORTED*
I phone the agency, provide information, problem solve, mediate, persuade, etc.	21
Write letters, give information	8
Visit the agency to give information, "raise a stink" if necessary	8
Get legal help through a legal clinic	6
Refer to my supervisor	5
Write reports: psychiatric verification, court documents, etc.	5
Show client how to self-advocate—get an appeal	4
Support or use clients' rights organizations	3
Contact Congressman, City Council members, Board of Supervisors	3
Attend hearings	3
Let agencies know of issues at community meetings	2
Negotiate (get on phone with the police and the facility)	2
Help the family to be competent to advocate for the client	2
Go above someone's head	1
Call to account those who are rude to clients	1
Use constant follow-up procedures	1

a mysterious but official notice about an arrest warrant and fines that were due, but with no knowledge of what his crime was or how to interpret and deal with the frightening situation. Advocacy in this situation required the practitioner to determine the facts. Once it had been ascertained that the "crime" involved several unpaid jaywalking tickets the client had no memory of receiving, she successfully intervened. This was done by submitting a formal letter in response: using agency letterhead, the professional's title, and as much officialese as possible in a respectful-though-strongly-worded request of the warrant holder that the action be dismissed as inappropriately demanding of this psychologically disabled client. Luckily, this use of official pomposity was successful in altering the situation in favor of the client—the tickets, warrants, and all fines were dismissed and the client was freed from the legal limbo into which he had fallen.

When large and powerful bureaucracies inhibit client well-being, advocacy may also require pronounced exercise of technical proficiency. This was indicated in field notes on dealing with the Social Security Administration. One practitioner stated flatly that "the SSI report is where I always have to advocate for the client," noting further that "... these reports are classic examples of when advocacy can really matter ... and of the *way* you present information can make a critical difference." In the agency report it was necessary to document the need for services clearly and with designated categories and language so that when the report is later forwarded to the Disability Evaluation Facility they will not disallow benefits simply because of incomplete or ambiguously presented client information, including precise documentation of impairment. It seems that the length of presentation counts also as this case manager indicated "the longer the form is—the more you write out—the better they like it." In this instance, it was meticulous and thoroughgoing attention to technical factors that served as a tool of advocacy.

This same target agency revealed additional observations about advocacy. The process of securing SSI monies for a client was sometimes exceedingly lengthy (spanning several years if there are application denials and appeals for re-evaluation). This provides an example of combining the function of advocacy and the function of linkage to formal organizations within the practice model. Such mixtures are not uncommon. In working to effect a successful linkage of a client to an appropriate funding source (and thereby access to additional services the client could not otherwise afford to receive), practitioners were called on to advocate recurrently over time in various ways on the client's behalf through an extended linking process.

Field reports showed that in carrying out advocacy activities practitioners with experience in a given location were at an advantage in being familiar with the workings and reactions of various organizations. This type of worker knew immediately how to deal with situations as they arose. Personal history will suggest which organizations are responsive and which are passive, which are flexible and which are rigid, which can be "reached" by friendly persuasion and which are closed off. The degree of assertiveness to be applied in various instances was relatively evident. Also, the quality of relationships that were formed with key members of the external organization had an effect on whether advocacy or normal linkage was required, and the level of intensity that might be necessary within the advocacy strategy. This suggests that some degree of longevity in the job is useful, and that newer workers should take advantage, collegially, of those with longer tenure.

Reisch (1990) studied advocacy in a cross section of human service agencies, examining factors that distinguished the more successful from the less successful organizations. The more effective of the 150 units he looked at structured their organizational efforts as follows:

> used a designated planning board,
> involved staff in key decision-making roles,
> used clear and formal means of internal communication,
> used established goal-setting procedures,
> involved women in key leadership roles,
> pursued consistent goals over time,
> sought to influence legislation and public opinion, and
> engaged in coalitional activities.

In general, groups that are well organized and that employ planned and controlled advocacy processes do better than groups that rely on informal means of action.

Applying Psychological Pressure

Social–structural elements have been covered through concepts such as targeting, escalation, and strategic mix. Emotional and cognitive processes in the target also can materially affect the results, to wit:

> *Go outside of the experience of your target.* This involves shifting the play to your own turf, a domain that makes the target feel unsure, insecure, and vulnerable. If you are dealing with a routine-driven bureaucracy, bring salient professional elements strongly to bear. With a professional agency, couch the encounter around community politics; however, these crossovers are not always the tactic of choice. Sometimes you can best outpoint the target on his own home grounds. Maybe embarrass the professional agency by dramatizing a section of the professional code of ethics that is being violated.
>
> *Lead your target to believe that you have power.* Put your best foot forward in magnifying your potential threat. (Dropping a few names of individuals from the United Way might give the impression that you are better placed there than is the case. The target's perception of your power is as good as the real thing. But don't overextend yourself—

beware of loss of credibility. Evident failure to deliver nullifies the weapon of threat.)

Use your target's own norms against him. Exposure of violations of an organization's own code of conduct is a potent tool. (This means gaining access in one way or another to the rule book, and either mastering it or having an insider provide intimate guidance in the area at issue.)

Keep the pressure on. Maintaining pressure results in the issue remaining open and the target remaining off balance. Large formal organizations may be able to respond to immediate pressures or disruptions, but they cannot easily tolerate extended instability. (By remaining resolute in pursuing the issue, the advocate can pass through the target organization's allowable time period of self-defense and into a phase when it wishes relief from a sustained, routine-disturbing intrusion. This necessitates application of valuable time, energy, and emotional resources on the part of the case manager. As Epstein's 1981 research showed, burnout is a common consequence of advocacy intervention. The cost/benefit element has to be weighed.)

This discussion has by no means exhausted examination of the use of confrontational methods on behalf of clients. The entire legal profession rests on this orientation as its foundation; however, what has been presented suffices for an overview of this available, and sometimes necessary, means of promoting client empowerment.

REFERENCES

Ad Hoc Committee on Advocacy. (1969). The social worker as advocate: Champion of social victims. *Social Work, 14*(2), 16–22.

Ballew, J. R. & Mink, G. (1986). *Case management in the human services.* Springfield, IL: Charles C. Thomas.

Bartlett, E. E. (1986). Advocacy skills and strategies for patient education managers. *Patient Education and Counseling, 8,* 397–405.

Blazyk, S., Crawford, C., & Wimberly, E. T. (1987). The ombudsman and the case manager. *Social Work, 32*(5), 451–453.

Cable, S., Walsh, E. J., & Warland, R. H. (1988). Differential paths to political activism: Comparisons of four mobilization processes after the Three Mile Island accident. *Social Forces, 66*(4), 951–969.

Davidoff, P. (1965). Advocacy and pluralism in planning. *Journal of the American Institute of Planners, 31*(4), 331–337.

Davidson W. and Rapp, C. (1976). Child advocacy in the justice system. *Social Work, 21,* 225–232.

Duhl, J. (1983). An advocacy coalition of older persons. *Journal of Jewish Communal Service, 60*(1), 44–47.

Epstein, I. (1981). Advocates on advocacy: An exploratory study. *Social Work Research and Abstracts, 17*(2), 5–12.

Fischer, J. (1978). *Effectiveness practice: An eclectic approach.* New York: McGraw-Hill.

Hagen, J. L. (1983). Due process and welfare appeals. *Social Work Research and Abstracts, 19*(3), 3–8.

Jarrett, R. B., & Fairbank, J. A. (1987). Psychologist's views: APA's advocacy of and resource expenditure on social and professional issues. *Professional Psychology: Research and Practice, 18*(6), 643–646.

Johnson, P. J. & Rubin, A. (1983). Case management in mental health: A social work domain? *Social Work, 28 (1)*, 49–55.

Lamb, H. R., & Associates (1976). *Community survival for long-term patients.* San Francisco: Jossey-Bass.

Lanoil, J. (1980). The chronic mentally ill in the community—case management models. *Psychosocial Rehabilitation Journal, 4*(2), 1–6.

Los Angeles County Department of Mental Health. (1985). *Human resources development: Issues in case management.* Los Angeles, California.

McDermott, C. J. (1989). Empowering the elderly nursing home resident: The resident rights campaign. *Social Work, 34*(2), 155–157.

McGowan, B. G. (1974). Case advocacy: A study of the interventive process in child advocacy. Unpublished doctoral dissertation, Columbia University.

McGowan, B. G. (1987) Advocacy. In A. Minahan (Ed.), *Encyclopedia of Social Work.* National Association of Social Workers.

Middleman R. & Goldberg G. (1974). *Social service delivery: A structural approach to social work practice.* New York: Columbia University Press.

Overschall, A. (1969). *Group violence: Some hypotheses and empirical uniformities.* Paper presented at American Sociological Association Conference, San Francisco.

Patti, R. (1980). Internal advocacy and human service practitioners: An exploratory study. In H. Resnick and R. Patti (Eds.), *Change from within: Humanizing human service organizations* (287–301). Philadelphia: Temple University Press.

Reich, C. (1964). The new property. *Yale Law Journal, 73*(5), 733–787.

Reisch, M. (1990). Organizational structure and client advocacy: Lessons from the 1980s. *Social Work,* January, 73–74.

Sancier, B. (Ed.). (1984). A special issue: Advocacy. *Practice Digest, 7*(3).

Seekins, T., Fawcett, S. B., & Mathews, R. M. (1987). Effects of self-help guides on three consumer advocacy skills: Using personal experiences to influence public policy. *Rehabilitation Psychology, 32*(1), 29–38.

Sievert, A. L., Cuvo, A. J., & Davis, P. K. (1988). Training self-advocacy skills to adults with mild handicaps. *Journal of Applied Behavior Analysis, 21*(3), 299–309.

Sosin, M. & Caulum, S. (1983). Advocacy: A conceptualization for social work practice. *Social Work, 28*(1), 12–17.

Weil, M. & Karls, J. M. (Eds.) (1985). *Case management in human service practice.* San Francisco: Jossey-Bass.

Weissman, H., Epstein, I., & Savage, A. (1983). *Agency-based social work.* Philadelphia: Temple University Press.

Wolowitz, D. (1983). Clients' rights in a case management system. In C. J. Sandborn (Ed.), *Case management in mental health services* (81–90). New York: The Haworth Press.

11
Interorganizational Coordination and Agency Access

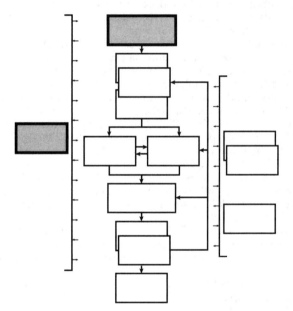

OVERVIEW

There is an ideal-type quality to the proposed model of intervention. It is a "normative" guidepost steering the practitioner of comprehensive enhancement toward exemplary performance. In *Walden*, Thoreau comments about that kind of mental stretch, "If you have built castles in the air, your work need not be lost; that is where they should be. Now put the foundations under them." For the practitioner to move forward with specific clients, a platform has to be put in place involving system-level functions, largely carried forward by administrators and policy makers.

These initial functions entail groundwork in establishing interorganizational policies and relationships, and providing access to the case-managing professional for clients in the community. An interorganizational menu of varied services has to be worked through before the program begins and any clients are seen. This is a given if any meaningful "comprehensive" service delivery is to take place. This function is also intermittent, in that revised and innovative interorganizational arrangements have to be forged over time as conditions and client needs change and new information and understandings emerge.

Also, before the practitioner can engage with a client, the client first has to know about the program and find a way into the lead agency. Without such access, programs exist merely as good intentions or symbols. Providing access can be seen as both a precursor to service generally and the first step in direct service to a specific client. The discussion that follows treats these underpinning functions in sequence.

INTERORGANIZATIONAL COORDINATION

UNDERSTANDING INTERORGANIZATIONAL COORDINATION

The Place of Interagency Coordination

During a particular spell of frustration and pique, the author in a conference paper penned some wistful comments about case management. The essential purpose of case management, he enunciated, is to wheedle services for clients in situations that are devoid of funds and agency will. An agency with no services to provide hires a specialized employee to assist clients to link with other community agencies that also believe they have no services available to provide. Thereby, many clients who are bored, lethargic, or homebound are given the exhilarating benefit of passing time away and seeing various parts of the city they would not ordinarily have an opportunity to visit. Experts assure us that circumstances are not quite that bleak, even though they sometimes seem to be. At any rate, that flight into satire emblemizes the need for a forceful interorganizational function in aiding highly vulnerable clients.

Not only is the interorganizational task vital under prevailing conditions, it is also a first order activity that paves the way to service generally.

> Interorganizational relations must be considered from the earliest point in planning a case management system. . . . Most case management programs depend on other agencies to see that clients get access to and receive needed services. Even before the case management program begins, most proposed programs need the backing of service network leaders [and] . . . will depend on the collaboration of the service network. (Weil, 1985, p. 347)

Aspects of Coordination

The issue of organizational collaboration remains a prime concern in the literature of case management, regardless of field of practice or client population served. Intensive discussion of the subject is found in the diverse areas of health (Ryndes, 1989), mental health (Turner, 1979), developmental disabilities (Stedman & Weingerink, 1979), child welfare (Downing, 1979), the physically handicapped (Bowe, Jacobi, & Wiseman, 1978), and the elderly (Kirwin, 1988).

Through the exercise of this function, interorganizational understandings and procedures are formulated about the flow of clients and the forms of aid they receive. This may involve the concurrence of an agency to accept all of a certain number or a particular type of client referred to it. It may entail fiscal inducements through contracts, per capita payments, and other means. It could involve an exchange of clients or a sharing of facilities. The arrangements may be official and even legally bound, or they could be basically informal, arrived at by a verbal acknowledgment or a routine memorandum. The arrangements may come about at any point in the case management process, and may be revised or expanded recurrently throughout the process.

Many human service professionals, guided by an altruistic and rationalistic orientation, assume that cooperation among agencies is natural and expected. This is more a wish than a sober appraisal of reality. Social agencies in the American tradition are fiercely individualistic, autonomy-minded, competitive for funds, and committed to voluntarism as a modus operandi. This puts a premium on self-directed action and a constraint on coordination. Agency interests largely dominate over community interests in day-to-day operations. From a sociological perspective, coordination involves certain agency-perceived costs: less freedom of action; use of resources for matters that are of lower priority; and pressures to respond to a variety of newly emerging problems.

Researchers have identified obstacles of various kinds that can stand in the way of productive collaborative relationships among organizations. The political and social climate in the community can induce competition and stress that inhibits mutual respect (Harbin, Eckland, Gallagher, Clifford, & Place, 1991; McCann & Gray, 1986). Often this is on top of a prior history of poor relationships, which serves as another deterrent (Bierly, 1988; Davidson, 1976; Rist, Hamilton, Holloway, Johnson, & Wiltberger, 1980). Insufficient funds may result in minimal resources to support coordination efforts and lead to unfriendly jockeying for position (Alaszewski & Harrison, 1988; Means, Harrison, Jeffers, & Smith, 1991).

The tone of relationship among agencies is another potentially disruptive factor. For example, when there is an absence of open communication (Agranoff & Lindsay, 1983), or few informal linkages among members of different organizations (Horwitch & Prahalad, 1981), the propensity for collaboration is reduced. The same holds when organizations have procedures or attitudes that are inflexible and prevent adaptability (Horwitch & Prahalad, 1981; Isles & Auluck, 1990).

Structurally, coordination is difficult if no steering group emerges that is perceived as holding a position of leadership in the community (Coe, 1988). Likewise, there needs to be a convener with the special skills required for integrating the activities of disparate groups that may not understand their interdependency and the advantages of mutual aid (Kagan, Rivera, & Parker, 1990).

This discussion naturally impinges on a related subject, linking clients individually to agencies in direct practice, in that both concern interorganizational association. There is some overlap in chapters, but the emphasis here is on general system-level tasks by administrative people, while the other discussion concentrates on the individualized activities of line service practitioners.

FACTORS EFFECTING COLLABORATION

Understanding and fostering interagency coordination entails a high level of complexity, not only because the internal structure and process of each organization is often perplexing, but because a number of these multifarious organizations have to be brought together concurrently and synthesized. A range of contextual variables impinge on the propensity of organizations to interrelate. We focus on the task environment and exchange relationships within it.

The Task Environment

Hasenfeld (1983) indicates that each agency's task environment bears on its need or willingness to gear itself to other organizational units. Five relevant features of the environmental situation were identified involving characteristics of organizations in the community that in various ways affect a particular agency's capacity to function. These community agencies are providers of desirable assets, and fall into the following categories.

Providers of fiscal resources. Every agency needs funds in order to carry out its mission. The vast majority of agencies are not fiscally self-sufficient, lacking such niceties as a substantial and steady endowment. They need grants, contributions, fees, material donations, and similar aid. Key organizations in the environment can provide such financial resources, and an agency is likely to interrelate actively and positively with these potential benefactors. For example, a local mental health center may seek monetary relationships with the National Institute of Mental Health (NIMH), health insurance companies, the state department of mental health, or a relevant county commission.

Providers of legitimacy and authority. Agencies often need external social acknowledgment, approval, and authorization to conduct their work and are handicapped if they are not able to achieve support from other organizations that grant such approbation. Governmental agencies, such as public welfare departments, derive their authority from legislative statutes at the federal, state, and local level and have their work monitored by personnel in these external organizations. The basic mandate to function is conferred by these outside institutions, and that mandate needs to be sustained through appropriate contact with these entities to assure them of compliance with expectations. Voluntary agencies receive their sanction in a less tangible way through relationships with respected and prestigious community groups such as churches and synagogues, business elites, civic associations, political leaders, and professional associations.

Providers of clients. Human service agencies need clients to carry out their missions. Annual reports and evaluation statistics are expected to reflect the number of clients who benefitted and the extent of aid they received. Clients represent the raw material of the human services industry, and all agencies depend on an adequate flow of clientele. Some agencies automatically get all the clients they can handle (such as the public schools), but others are dependent on various groups and organizations in the community for referrals (such as community hospitals depending on physicians for patients).

Providers of complementary services. The case management agency typifies a human service organization needing program assistance from other service providers. But many other agencies, including those that case management agencies rely on, also benefit from complementary service support. For example, a drug treatment center may lean on a nearby hospital for detoxification of its clients, a family court may use a mental health facility to diagnose some of its cases, and a nursing home may take advantage of a community recreation center to round out the lives of its residents.

Competing organizations. These are organizations that vie with any given service agency for resources and clients and can therefore influence that agency's access to these necessities. For example, if one mental health organization receives a high budgetary allotment from the United Way, that may reduce the allocation available to another mental health service. Agencies as a matter of course will find it necessary to decide on ways to relate to their competition in the community, whether that involves co-optation, collaboration, or conflict.

An agency may have varied relations with a range of such external groups, relying on one for funding, another for clients, and others for complementary services. In addition, a single external organization may be a source for a number of these accoutrements and resources at the same time, making the need for a positive association with that unit all the more imperative.

An example of organizations involved in a task environment is given by Hasenfeld (1983) with reference to the juvenile court. Providers of fiscal resources could include the county government and the state public welfare department. Authority and legitimation come from the state supreme court, public prosecutor's office, and child interest groups. Client referrals might originate from the public schools, police, and hospitals. Complementary services might be provided by child and family service agencies, the youth service bureau, and a drug treatment center. Competing organizations would include other courts, child advocacy programs, and the public defender's office. These comprise the "organizational set" of the juvenile court and suggest a framework for establishing a formalized interagency network.

Interdependence and Domain Consensus

A valuable concept in analyzing interorganizational relations is exchange theory or interdependence, as discussed in classic works by Blau (1964) and Levine and White (1974). Interdependence conveys the notion, already suggested, that organizations must consider each other in order to attain their purposes—acts of one affect the performance of the other in a material way. This indicates that organizations are more likely to cooperate if they are interdependent. Levine and White (1974, pp. 547–548) note that all formal organizations are task-driven:

> In order to achieve its specific objectives, however, an agency must possess or control certain elements. It must have clients to serve; it must have resources in the form of equipment, specialized knowledge, or the funds with which to procure them; and it must have the services of people who can direct these resources to the clients. Few, if any, organizations have enough access to all these elements to enable them to attain their objectives fully. . . .

> Although . . . an organization limits itself to particular functions, it can seldom carry them out without establishing relationships with other organizations of the . . . system. . . . Interorganizational exchanges are essential to goal attainment.

Not only must a condition of interdependence exist, but there must be awareness of this interdependence among the parties for a *de facto* exchange relationship to come into being (Litwak & Rothman, 1970). Often representatives of human service organizations are brought together to discuss the desirability of coordination, but nothing substantial happens. It may be either a lack of real interdependence, or the absence of sufficient awareness that that interdependence exists, that contributes to the many aborted attempts to increase agency cooperation.

Good working relationships and exchanges are facilitated when the parties form *domain consensus*. This means that the agency of interest has gained the recognition of other organizations about its mission and program. Without this agreement, other organizations may challenge its legitimation and hold back needed resources of various kinds. The consensus ordinarily entails, also, the agency's parallel recognition of the domain of others, a willingness not to encroach, and an indication that the other parties will also benefit from the mutual relationship. Levine and White clarify (1974, p. 555).

> The domain of an organization consists of the specific goals it wishes to pursue and the functions it undertakes in order to implement its goals. In operational terms, organizational domain . . . refers to the claims that an organization stakes out for itself in terms of (1) [problem] covered, (2) population served, and (3) services rendered. . . . Exchange agreements result upon prior consensus regarding domain . . . to the extent that parts of the system will provide each agency with the elements necessary to attain its ends.

Forming a domain consensus encompasses a process of negotiations, compromises, and exchanges between an organization and the elements of its task environment that reflect their respective calculations of the costs and payoffs to be derived. Thus, the domain of an organization is not static, but is subject to political and economic changes in the task environment. Domain consensus is affected by several elements in the situation: stability of the units involved, their homogeneity or similarity, the resource endowment of the broader environment, and the condition of turbulence (or tranquility) of that environment.

Linking Mechanisms in Coordination

When agencies form cooperative relationships, they do so in a variety of different ways, using an array of linkage mechanisms. These linking mechanisms may involve administrative devices or program procedures, and include fiscal considerations that may vary in scope and intensity. A useful summary of these mechanisms has been given by Lauffer (1978) and will provide the basis for this discussion.

Each of the coordinating approaches can be viewed as a means used by the lead agency to influence another agency—providing something the other may need (such as funds, manpower, or expertise) through a particular exchange structure. In return, the lead agency receives from the other agency cooperation and service provision for its clients. The mechanisms are tools that fuel and expedite exchange relationships when interdependency exists between agencies. They are the medium for receiving and giving supportive elements needed by agencies to conduct their programs.

Fiscal arrangements. These are exchanges that involve the use of funds as an incentive. As in other spheres of social interaction, monetary mechanisms are highly potent, probably offering the maximum clout for drawing forth desired responses from others. Initiatives with intrusive impact (clout) have been found to maximize desired responses by other organizations (Platman, 1982; Schwartz, Goldman, & Churgin, 1982; Weil & Karls, 1985).

Purchase of service. This is a familiar and self-explanatory way of eliciting service. An agency simply buys what it needs or wants from another organization, ordinarily through a legally constructed contractual arrangement. Mental health centers typically are equipped to fund housing for clients released from state institutions, and vocal rehabilitation counselors have funds to pay for job training and prostheses for physically disabled clients. Homemaker assistance, diagnostic workups, and educational programs are other frequently paid for aids. This procedure is attractive to contracting agencies because it is a means to expand their financial base and increase the number or types of clients they can include in their service net.

Joint funding and joint budgeting. These are less prevalent than the purchase arrangement, but merit mention. In joint funding several agencies together finance a program, bringing to bear resources that would be beyond the capability of any one of them. Sometimes this involves concurrent funding from an outside source, which is matched by the agencies through monetary or in-kind contributions. Each agency, thereby, benefits in the extent of coverage provided to its clients. Sometimes joint budgeting for a common service program offers a way to obtain outside matching funds. The budgeting might be carried out through an external unit, such as the United Way or a planning council.

Joint administrative procedures. In some instances efficiencies in operation and program expansion can be achieved by dovetailing administrative operations among agencies. Several examples follow.

Information management. The use of common and standardized record-keeping forms and procedures facilitates the exchange of information among organizations. These data may be needed to increase effectiveness within an organization in serving its own clientele, or it could lead to efficiencies in operation through eliminating cross-agency duplication or delay. Collaboration could also include joining in the processing of this information, when one or another organization possesses equipment or technical personnel of high capability. This could involve, at least on a partial basis, the purchase or subsidizing of these arrangements.

Publicity and public relations. Agencies can assist one another by collaborating in providing information to the public, or in promoting more favorable community attitudes regarding a client group for whom they have mutual concern. This could include interpretation of the role and importance of the services they provide, and might involve the recruitment of volunteers or clients.

Joint research.   Sometimes agencies conduct conjoint research or participate together on a study committee that has responsibility for such activities. When organizations have an overlap in clientele or operations, common research activities can have cross-cutting benefits. Combining resources in terms of technical staff, volunteer interviewers, or data processing can make the job easier and more substantial. Several different types of projects are possible.

Conducting studies. These might include opinion surveys about services or client groups. Community attitudes can be an important input for restructuring services to make them more appropriate or acceptable.

Needs assessment and related studies. This is another means of shaping services to best conform to realistic community requirements. Occasionally demonstration or experimental studies are carried out jointly to probe for a better understanding of common problems and intervention issues, sometimes in collaboration with university faculty.

Accountability audits. This constitutes another form of agency research, focusing on administrative matters. Agency records are examined in regard to expenditures, program activities, staffing, and distribution of resources. An outside agency is frequently useful in assuring an objective, impartial review, and attaching legitimacy to the conclusions that are reached.

Joint staffing.   Outside of finances, a human service agency's most important and substantive need is for staff, particularly professional personnel. Exchange relationships that allow for an increment in manpower offer a great incentive. These may take several forms.

Loaner arrangements. One agency may assign a staff member to another agency that is serving the same kind of client. The loaning agency gains in that it is able to provide its service without having to incur all the usual overhead costs. The receiving agency simply gains additional personnel to carry out its mission. The loaner staff member does the work of the organization to which he or she is assigned, in a way that is identical to other staff members in that situation, although paid by another organization. In this arrangement, matters of authority, supervision, and the chain of command have to be clearly defined at an early point.

Out-stationing. Here the staff member is ordinarily on site in another agency, but continues to be directed and supervised by the original assigning agency. Outreach staff who operate in one or another agency facility to make better contact with targeted clients operate on an out-stationing basis. It can be said that the on-site agency is loaning its clients to the other agency. Here, again, firm understandings have to be reached about the control of the staff member and the activities that are undertaken. Otherwise, turf problems and program confusion are a distinct risk.

Liaison teams and joint use of staff. In this arrangement the agencies together oversee staff members and deliver the service. Often the procedure is employed because a set of different skills and competencies is required, which can only be aggregated when agencies representing different disciplines combine forces. Each member of the liaison team holds loyalty to the team entity, although paid externally by one of the constituent agencies. Supervision can be provided by an independent professional hired by the agencies to oversee the program, or one agency can provide team-based supervision, with the agreement of the other participating agency units.

Joint programming.   Joint programming involves two or more agencies coming together to design and carry out a new service approach. There may be efficiencies involved in working in combination, there may be expanded scope of coverage of clients, or greater creativity can be achieved through the interplay of different perspectives and competencies. A few types of joint programs are discussed.

Pilot and demonstration projects. Often agencies do not have the resources and energy to undertake something new, or they may be too set in their ways to be able to conceive a highly innovative way of carrying out a program. Pilot projects provide a means by which only a small input is required from several different agency sources, and there can be an interplay of different ideas from among these agencies in designing a new thrust. Implementing pilot and demonstration projects may make use of different funding and staffing procedures already discussed.

Loaning or sharing facilities. Here an agency makes available to another agency physical facilities rather than staff. This could be a room in which to do interviewing, a lounge in which to conduct a day program, a kitchen in which to prepare meals, or a gymnasium for conducting a recreation program for children. The facility may be one that has been underutilized, or the arrangement may provide a basis for diversifying the use of the facility. This arrangement has some overlap with the out-stationing concept.

Serving special client groups. Certain clients have needs that are complex and emergent, for example, dual diagnosis clients who are mentally ill and are also substance abusers. Other clients "fall between the cracks" because their difficulties are novel or because no specific agency seems to have taken on responsibility for them. Runaway adolescents and AIDS babies and their families are two groupings that at one time fell into the latter category. Collaborative exchange relationships are a means for gaining leverage in these situations, to each agency's advantage.

Joint client processing. There is a level of cooperation by agencies concerning common clients that involves less than joint programming. It includes sharing information about mutual clients, doing some mutual decision making, and taking on specific agreed-upon tasks in serving clients.

Case conferences and ad hoc *case coordination.* Here each agency is providing different services to the same client group. Staff members of the agencies come together at regular intervals (biweekly, bimonthly) to review cases. Individuals may be tracked through the service process to determine points of deficiency or duplication, and decisions are made about how to handle the trouble spots. The participating staff members agree about treatment plans, division of labor, and who should take responsibility for specific functions. Sometimes such conferences are called solely on an *ad hoc* basis when specific needs arise. This is because case conferencing has sometimes been criticized as being too time-consuming and because it causes staff-layering (too much staff concentration on simple client situations).

PRACTICE GUIDELINES FOR INTERORGANIZATIONAL COORDINATION

Practitioner Experiences in Coordination

This section begins with comments by practitioners interviewed in the UCLA survey regarding activities they engage in that are geared to structuring interorganizational relationships. As expected, respondents reported that they do little in this area: the majority (30 of 48) answered "no" to an inquiry about their involvement in the function and instead referred to actions by administrators. Even those who said they had some activity apparently misconstrued the question to mean working out accommodations for an individual client rather than developing general policies or agreements for categories of clients. It was identified as one of the functions to which little time was given.

Among the respondents who declared involvement in the function, three levels of activity were reported: referring policy issues to higher levels of the organization; monitoring agencies to ascertain that policy is properly executed; and making informal interagency program agreements.

Referring policy matters to higher levels. A number of respondents made explicit that interorganizational policy development is the responsibility of those occupying positions of greater authority than exist in the case manager role. For example:

> Usually my supervisor handles this task. I will coordinate services for a client but ordinarily general agreement and cooperation has been obtained beforehand, and there are long-standing policies, channels of communication, and funding mechanisms that channel my work.

In some cases respondents indicate that they would like to have more responsibility in this area: "My supervisor insists on doing this task, and I resent it." Others criticize the way the policies are developed and apparently do not envision having a personal role in influencing this. One complaint is that arrangements involve too much red tape and other bureaucratic blocks to smooth interactions. Another view is that policies are unclear regarding what each agency's tasks are. The lack of clarity, it is said, may derive from a failure to inform line staff appropriately when new decisions are made, and some policies inherently prevent effective work. One person put it this way:

> There are Catch 22 situations that make your life difficult. Policies don't work but they are rigid and can't be changed. An example of this is in trying to assist someone with financial grants. If the person has a high level of motivation to continue with vocational rehabilitation or work, this hampers them from getting into the system of financial assistance. These things keep you going around in circles.

Monitoring policy execution. A larger number of respondents indicate they have a direct part to play in ensuring the implementation of policy. There are two aspects to this. One involves a surveillance and advocacy role wherein the manager makes sure that the outside agency holds to its agreements:

> These agreements are obtained by administration and skillfully defended at the clinical level. If the hospital discharges a client early, it is up to the line worker to tell the hospital that it is too early. We police the activity and fight back if agreements are disregarded.

The other role is that of a policy executor and refiner. In playing this part the case manager works out the details of how the policy is carried out at the field level.

> I become involved in the process by carrying out agreements that have already gotten started. I interact with other clinics, Public Welfare, private hospitals, public hospitals, SSI. If we have an agreement, I hammer out what it is and what we need to do to see that it doesn't fall apart. We make sure it's being carried out.

Education is identified as an aspect of monitoring implementation, and it can be used with either of the two previous roles. Often failure to implement agreements is located at the lowest echelons of the other organization. Apparently, clerks have a key gatekeeping role that can be restrictive and frustrating:

> There are no "good" agreements with SSI, Public Welfare, or the Public Guardian's Office. Clerks at these offices do not understand client limitations and view clients as just noncompliant. Patients may be hallucinating and can't give the truth. They repeatedly become frustrated with the system. Financial agencies seem to be the worst in this.

Chapter 10 (Advocacy) has suggested some means of dealing with such situations.

Making informal agency agreements. Not all agreements between agencies are on an official basis. Some can be arranged through discussion and negotiation at the line level. The agreement can be concluded with a nod of the head, a handshake, letter of understanding, or a memorandum. Typically, such arrangements are *ad hoc* or involve an agreement between two service professionals about how to accommodate a particular set of clients. The agreement is not at the system or policy level, but rather it is personal and programmatic. This process, and the difficulties in carrying it out, are described in the following comment:

> Case management takes a lot of negotiating! Some of the weight of this is on my shoulders, but a lot of the weight is nowhere! We need more collaboration and less screening out. I am forced to establish my own network and try to negotiate arrangements with agency staff. This is not always possible because the system is so cold and callous.

Developing Strategy for Interorganizational Exchange

Since interorganizational policies are typically developed at the system level rather than practitioner level, the remainder of this discussion treats actions that are the responsibility of administrators and policymakers. We will present a comprehensive analytical scheme for planning steps to enhance cooperation by community organizations, drawing on concepts from the previous section.

Identifying resource agencies

1. First of all, it is important for the lead agency to delineate with some degree of specificity exactly what it is that clients need. Needs assessment techniques described later in the chapter can assist with this.

2. Next, it is important to clarify definitively what the lead agency can offer directly in terms of counseling, program services, and material aid.

3. As counterpoint, other client requirements that do not fall within the agency's domain and have to be obtained elsewhere need to be identified.

4. For each of these unattended needs, agencies and community organizations that can provide relevant support should be explicated concretely. (Informal sources of support cannot ordinarily be approached similarly on a policy level, but rather have to be tailored individually for each client by the practitioner.)

Through this process, a substantive listing is made of relevant community agencies, together with designated support that each can provide to the client population. The priority agencies and supports would be flagged at this point in order to focus and sequence further actions.

Assessing modes of influence

5. The lead service agency should proceed to determine what incentives having "clout" it possesses to influence responses by the relevant community organizations. Fiscal and authoritative sanctions are prime among these. A lead agency may have program or discretionary funds available for purchase of services. If not, it may be able to obtain such funds through legislative advocacy; federal, state, county, or municipal grants; United Way allocations; and foundation grants, sometimes through collaborative proposals with counterpart organizations. These possibilities should be explored, because often more opportunities exist than are obvious to agencies mired in the pressures and routines of everyday operation. Freeing the time of designated staff to concentrate on this task is a way to give it the attention it may require.

Authoritative sanctions to be promoted can include legislative policies, judicial rulings, or administrative regulations at a higher level of an organization, typically federal or state. These sanctions can direct or allow community organizations to respond to referred clients in a prescribed way, and can come from superordinate hierarchical echelons (the state department of social welfare to a local child welfare program), or an external source (the municipal court). In examining such possibilities, staff or consultants with technical competencies, either legislative or legal, need to be involved. Professional or civic advocacy groups in the community might have to be mobilized to exert pressure. A point to consider here is whether it is important to have ongoing cordial relationships with some or all of the external service agencies, in which case a high conflict advocacy approach would be inappropriate and counterproductive. For example, an external agency might be providing other more important services on a voluntary basis and would withdraw these if they felt put upon.

6. Where financial incentives and authoritative sanctions are not available or appropriate, voluntary interdependency relations can be emphasized. For each priority agency an analysis should be conducted: What resources or benefits does the lead service agency possess that would be advantageous to the external agency for furthering its program? These can include, among others:

political support
legitimacy in the community
clients
technical assistance
manpower
information
training
public relations
facilities
liaison or brokering assistance
complementary services

In making such an assessment, it is important to determine the amount of energy and resources the lead agency has accessible, so that the exchange does not calculate to a detriment to its overall program, or that a good deal more is given out than is gained for its clients.

Initiating the relationship

7. In arranging exchange relations, careful planning has to be done about an initiating strategy. At what level of the other organization should contact be made—executive, board, or program supervisors? Through what level in the lead agency should the approach be made? What kind of bearing should negotiators bring: formal (persons with appropriate authority) or informal (who has previous positive relations, who is viewed as prestigious, professionally respected, trustworthy, or socially powerful)? Should the contact be through an official written communication or a personal overture? Should neutral outsiders be used to clear the way? What means of influence should be used: providing information, persuading, modeling positive examples, showing the downside of noncooperation, or using threats?

8. In addition to attending to the concrete elements of exchange, it is important to make existing interdependency explicit and tangible. The specific benefits to the other organization(s) may need to be surfaced in an overt, though appropriately delicate, way. Domain consensus needs to be worked through.

Using appropriate mechanisms of coordination

9. The use of the most suitable mechanisms of coordination should be considered and applied. Some procedures that have been previously mentioned and could be established include:

joint funding or budgeting procedures,
combined information management techniques,
publicity and public relations programs,
conducting surveys and other studies,
conducting a needs assessment,
conducting accountability audits,
providing specific loaner staff,
out-stationing specific staff,
setting up liaison teams and joint staffs,
conducting pilot and demonstration projects,
loaning or sharing physical facilities,
serving special or emergent client groups, and
organizing case conferences and other case coordination procedures.

As in all exchange relationships, two-way benefits are implicit in each of these mechanisms. Specific commitments, expectations, tasks, responsibilities, communicating and reporting procedures, and timing have to be worked through to assure implementation. There is a substantial administrative and organizing element involved that cannot be minimized or neglected. Interorganizational relationships are complex and navigating them is demanding. Because of the weight of these involvements, managing the process by sequencing it, from higher priority clusters to lesser priority clusters, is advisable.

Once the framework of an interorganizational support network has been set in place, service is ready to begin. First, though, clients have to be informed and engaged.

ACCESS

UNDERSTANDING ACCESS

Components of Access

There is a famous story about the boy scout leader who meets one of his young charges at a shopping mall. "How are you, Tim?" he asks. "Just fine, Mr. Sterling," comes back the shy reply. "And have you done any good deeds this week?" inquires the watchful scoutmaster. "Yes, me and the rest of the troop helped an old lady across the street." There is a pause. "Why did it take the whole troop to help one old lady across the street?" A longer pause. "Well, uh, she didn't wanna go."

The story illustrates a key element of meaningful access—locating the right client. Without that step, there may be more access than the client bargained for or, as in the more usual scenario, the specific people needing services are overlooked or neglected. Weil (1985, p. 31) comments, "Any case management program must first identify its target population and individual clients within the population." This suggests an assessment of need so that underlying problems are understood and those people affected by them are put into focus. Following identification, targeted clients have to be informed about the service, or even persuaded to make use of it. The service agency may have to reach out to those affected in a vigorous manner. In addition, a pathway through the community into the agency has to be provided in some instances to expedite the service trans-action. This is sometimes referred to as *channeling*. From a broader person-in-environment ecological perspective, access establishes the link between the vulnerable individual in a community setting and a source of aid and support in a responsive organization. The major difficulty in providing access to vulnerable populations is that clients often do not know about the relevant sources of help, or they lack the capacity or motivation to connect with them (Turner & TenHoor, 1978). "Yet, those who are incapable or unwilling to do so may be most in need of case management assistance" (Weil & Karls, 1985, p. 10).

The three main components of the access function, as suggested above, include:

(1) need assessment and client identification,
(2) outreach and social marketing, and
(3) channeling.

We will come back to that threefold formation as the discussion proceeds.

Access has been interrelated with other concepts. Caragone (1985) makes a distinction between service availability and service accessibility. Availability connotes that a service has been put in place and that it exists for potential use. Accessibility relates to actualizing the potential use: Is the client aware of it, can it be reached, and is it reasonably convenient and affordable?

According to Kane and Kane (1987, p. 83), access, quality, and cost are highly correlated factors that need to be considered jointly. "Service should be of acceptable quality, however defined; those who need the services should have reasonable access without financial or other barriers; and the cost should be affordable by individuals and society." The authors think that all three factors need to be incorporated, but recognize that achieving a satis-factory balance among them is both "difficult" and "murky."

From the client's viewpoint, agencies that genuinely wish to serve often are not perceived in a favorable way. The climate and procedures may not broadcast cultural or social class compatibility or genuine interest. Social sta-tus and ethnic background have been found to be associated with who uses services, how, and in connection with what problems (Greene & Monahan, 1984; Hollingshead & Redlich, 1958). Agencies, on their part, however, frequently see the problem as originating with clients. A study of family service organizations concluded that many clients are distracted from engaging in service because they have "insufficient motivation or [are] under stress of temporary crisis or other outside pressure" (Beck, 1963).

According to Kahn (1967), there is a kind of social darwinism involved in such thinking, allowing us to abandon clients to fend for themselves in the harrowing marketplace of human services. He is disturbed by "a large reservoir of the unserved," who are left to struggle unsuccessfully in the quest for succor.

Access, when neglected by the service agency, may be promoted externally by client advocacy organizations. Lobbying and clients' rights groups of varying kinds have come to look out for the prerogatives of clients in these circumstances, sometimes vigorously goading agencies to be responsive and open up their entrenched boundaries. The Independent Living Movement, Alliance for the Mentally Ill, Children's Defense Fund, and Gray Panthers typify such substitute purveyors of the access function.

The threefold breakdown of the access function indicated earlier provides the structure for the presentation that follows.

Identifying Needs and Targeting Clients

In dealing with access, need assessment plays a significant role. Need assessment methods are used to identify pertinent client groups, to clarify their characteristics, and to pinpoint the specific types of needs that require a response. This often entails an analysis of the current service pattern, including gaps and inadequacies in the program. Need assessment results signal to the agency who it should endeavor to bring within its service net. These assessment tools also act as a basis for planning, setting priorities, and defining program development in greater detail. Needs assessment methods are described in the subsequent section on practice application.

In a classic study, Scott (1974) highlighted the importance of explicitly clarifying client needs, using as an example the circumstances of the blind. Scott indicates that the prevailing assumption is that programs should be geared to client needs. However, welfare organizations often allow considerations of organizational survival and of efficiency and cost to predominate in determining who is sought for service. Likewise, public opinion, and especially that of the financial contributors to and benefactors of welfare programs, profoundly influences which clients are pursued.

Scott found, demographically, that the majority of blinded individuals were elderly (66% between the ages of 55 and 80), and only 2% were children under the age of 18. Two thirds of the blind were in age groups where retirement was a reality or pending, and only a small minority were in age categories where employment or education was a realistic prospect.

Still, only 9% of the relevant agencies nationally targeted their services to the elderly blind; 67% aimed their programs at children and employable adults. A systematic review of journals in the field revealed that some 70% of the blind population (the older group) were discussed in only 2% of the articles, while the 30% of the blind population comprising children and employable adults were examined in 98% of the articles analyzed. Scott (1974, p. 490) concluded that at that time there was a "systematic bias of work for the blind in favor of young blind children and employable blind adults, and the corresponding neglect of older blind persons."

His further analysis of the fund-raising campaigns of organizations aiding the blind revealed some of the reasons for this discrepancy. The campaigns used appeals that catered to cultural stereotypes among the public, associating blindness with youth, work, and hope. The images of blind people that were projected in the campaigns portrayed educable children or young, employable adults who with help could master a serious handicap and become productive in a material way.

Because money-generating potential was associated by them with what would appeal to the public, agencies competed with one another to seek out the relatively few blind people who had the requisite personal attributes. Access was promoted for a small proportion of the affected population, while many others fell outside of the targeting apparatus. Access, in this instance, was distorted and determined by criteria other than need. Sociologically speaking, a powerful lesson of this study was that agencies need to be alert to the dangers of goal displacement, resulting in a focus on organizational self-enhancement instead of client service requirements.

Needs arise other than from internal detriments of individuals. Taking account, again, of an ecosystems person-in-environment perspective, the environment rather than agencies or clients may designate need and determine who constitutes a client. The environment often generates the problems that result in the difficulties experienced by individuals. For example, social trends that increased family tension and breakdown and fomented widespread substance abuse have contributed to a greater prevalence of child abuse. This suggests looking not solely at *troubled persons* but also at *troubled environments* in assessing needs and planning interventions.

The environment in other ways shapes what problems should be addressed and who should be brought into the service system. Legal mandates requiring the scrupulous reporting of possible child abuse have promoted agency attention to this problem, as has the intensive coverage in the media (with resulting political embarrassments and pressures) when children have been discovered to be severely harmed by their parents. For this reason, an energetic approach to clients often occurs in this context, involving engagement with clients who may be disinterested or even hostile. Another example of environmental shaping of clienthood is found in shifting public concepts of mental illness, including what type of behavior is considered tolerable within the community.

Client Outreach

A core aspect of access provision involves informing potential clients about the availability of services. This approximates the marketing function in the commercial realm. In the human services field, engagement with consumers can be at two levels: a *response mode* to inputs to the agency or an *extension mode* involving agency outreach. Each mode in turn can be either on a routine basis or in an assertive fashion. The routine response mode is probably most common and consists of taking action when another agency (such as family service or the "Y") refers an individual, or a family member or community participant (such as a clergyman or a neighbor) initiates a contact, or the client self-refers. The assertive response made involves a rapid reaction to incoming information, such as when a worker or team goes out to a home when a case of alleged child abuse is reported.

Routine extension involves such things as distributing printed pamphlets in the community or putting up notices on bulletin boards in schools or service agencies. It relies on use of media. Assertive extension has greater intensity, emphasizing personal contact. Levine and Fleming (1984) characterize this as an "aggressive and creative" activity and give examples of outstationing staff to make contact with individuals in soup kitchens or social security offices.

Some agencies and programs make imaginative use of the extension mode to become known in the community and interest potential clients. Of course, if there is an overabundance of clients and even waiting lists, client identification and outreach may be down played. Some clients, such as mentally disabled individuals discharged from state hospitals, are, by law or common practice, regularly directed into public mental health agencies. Agencies experiencing service pressures from such a continual flow of clients often take a passive stance, prioritize or narrow service scope, or shift their efforts toward resource development in order to increase their capacity to serve the heavy volume of clients they encounter.

Outreach targeting is a critical aspect of the accessing process, in the view of Kane and Kane (1987, p. 371), in that it can operate as "a gatekeeper who can control the flow of resources." It can operate to tune up or tone down the flow pattern. Said differently, there can be an element of rational distribution of services involved in a finely modulated and controlled access process. In the absence of a workable outreach arrangement, Kane and Kane discuss the use of a rationing procedure for delivering medical and nursing home care to the burgeoning elderly population. Certain allocation criteria for service could be applied, such as attaining a certain age, or being eligible for certain services that are found to be most efficacious. The authors, however, point out pitfalls of resorting to mechanistic rationing schemes. A related procedure that has been used for Medicaid-financed services is centralized preadmission screening for persons in a region or state who are at risk of being placed in a nursing home (Iverson, 1986). All individuals who are eligible for Medicaid in the geographical area are considered part of a common pool and are screened using similar criteria.

Channeling

Informing targeted clients about services is not the end of the access transaction. There often remains the task of making sure clients use the information to actually enter the service agency and receive the help they need. Kahn (1969) describes this as channeling and characterizes it as "system linkage," which includes *steering-advice-referral*. Clients have to have a pathway through the community into the service agency, a pathway that is paved through such things as giving tailored information about hooking up with the services, generating motivation, and making sure the service is convenient (hours of operation of the program, adequate transportation, geographic location of agency, and multilingual staff if necessary).

In Kahn's view, channeling grows out of client identification and case finding, and he indicates that the absence of proper steering of clients results in a considerable amount of "case loss." The consequences of this can be substantial, not only to the client, but to the community itself. "There is a large element of injustice and community foolishness in permitting inadequate channeling to reserve resources for those sufficiently informed, motivated, or culturally pre-conditioned to make use of them. Furthermore, a large price tag is paid in social pathology, disorganization, and loss for that collective ignorance of the scope of real need that permits a channeling maze to decrease effective demand" (Kahn, 1969, p. 266).

Some number of experimental community-based programs have been established to test varying means of channeling and to evaluate their effectiveness. The most extensive of these has been the National Channeling Demonstration, geared to long-term services for the elderly. The Demonstrations were conducted in a basic form, which used information as the key ingredient in steering clients into services, and a complex form, which included use of funding mechanisms to facilitate channeling (Haskins, Capitman, & Bernstein, 1984; Kemper, Braun, & Carcagno, 1986).

One of the most well-known local projects aimed at effective channeling is ACCESS, located in the Rochester, New York area (Eggert & Brodows, 1984). It is a centralized, free-standing steering organization for all individuals 18 years of age or older who reside in the surrounding county and have long-term care needs. Medicaid and Medicare funds are used to energize the program through a waiver formula. A preadmission assessment form (PAF) is used by an outreach community health nurse from the health department or a visiting nurse association for physically disabled or elderly persons who come to be known to require extended care. The early assessment by the initial contact nurse provides the basis for firmly channeling the client into service. ACCESS is an example of "a high-volume program that has saturated an urban area" (Kane, 1969, p. 186).

Kahn advocates several other community-based mechanisms to provide channeling. One of these is the Citizen's Advice Bureau approach that has been developed in Great Britain. A network of neighborhood-level offices has been established to provide both information and advice to all residents about the broad array of governmental and private aids that are available to them. The existence of the CABs is widely broadcast to the populace. The CABs provide no sustained direct services themselves, but are highly visible and assertively service-oriented in their role of broker into programs. Another interesting approach is found in the French *polyvant* (multipurpose) worker, who is a line social worker (*assistante sociale*) based in various local agencies. A "permanence" is established, whereby a set place and time in the community is announced when the *assistante sociale* is available to offer comprehensive brokerage assistance. The permanence is not a designated independent office, as in the case of the CABs, but rather a designated time and place within an otherwise ongoing program where citizens can receive skilled consultation about access to diverse services.

In the absence of such community-centered means of providing access for clients, human service agencies are left to take upon themselves responsibility for the access function. We will discuss implementation of that task in the next section.

PRACTICE GUIDELINES FOR FACILITATING ACCESS

Roles in Providing Access

Providing access is a largely macro-level activity carried out by administrators and planners. However, some direct service workers take part in a variety of ways. In the UCLA study of practitioners, 25% (12 of 48) reported that they engage in access functions, but stated that the approach was largely passive and responsive ("we are cautious, because we are short-staffed"). Examples of specific responsive activities include the following:

> We do this very little because we have referrals and a waiting list until August. Patients hear of us by word of mouth. At the time we see patients we give them our brochure and tell them about our services. Lawyers will refer patients because they have heard about us through the grapevine.

I may be called out to help if a very marginal person, very needy of help, refuses help. Also, if I see my own patients at a residential facility, people come up to me and ask, "Will you be my social worker?" I am also approached at meetings, because I am bilingual; I even get calls from the newspaper and the police for that reason.

To the degree extension-type outreach takes place, it is largely through visits to other agencies. This is sometimes by giving a talk and sometimes by serving as a liaison to that agency on a continuing basis. Agencies may include the county department of children's services, drug rehabilitation centers, police departments, churches, juvenile court, health agencies, or community-based crime organizations. Some examples include:

We link with health services by going out and speaking with them. We let them know of our services and what we offer. We also have brochures and let staff know of us through conferences.

I go to board-and-care homes that have recently placed persons (these could come from anywhere) as part of our established liaison, to assess these new people's needs and screen them for case management eligibility and suitability.

Those case managers who do assertive extension work use a wide variety of different methods, any one of which is cited only by a small number of individuals: circulating brochures, giving talks at conferences, phoning potential clients, and making door-to-door visits.

A few case managers used highly intensive outreach, for example, going to places where mentally ill congregate, like parks, street corners, and bus benches, and approaching police regarding homeless people they know. These assertive approaches seem to be related to special projects, such as one on engaging the homeless.

Targeting the Client Population

A useful framework has been developed by Rapp and Poertner (1992) for relating need, the definition of client groups and issues of access. First, one has to discern the *general population,* the relevant universe from which the agency draws its service clientele. This includes everyone living in a political jurisdiction or catchment area. Statistical social indicators are important here. If a child welfare agency was the focal program entity, data would be sought on families and children in the area, family composition, economic status, housing accommodations, and similar variables.

Next, there is the task of determining the *at-risk population,* those clearly in need. Here a sub-group is delineated who are especially vulnerable to the problem being addressed, with attention to the number of people so affected and their characteristics. If child abuse is of special concern, poverty, unemployment, substance abuse, spouse abuse, and contact with the police and courts are factors that may help identify this group, leaning on social indicators and rates-under-treatment data.

Agencies further narrow down a particular *target population* within those who are at risk and for whom outreach efforts are made. The range of needs assessment methods can be applied here. These are individuals who are eligible to receive service and have clearly discernible needs that are relevant to the service agency. Agency policies and objectives, legislative statutes, court mandates, and funding regulations also bear on who is specifically targeted for service. Some agencies focus in on those in greatest need, the most serious cases. Others seek those with the greatest potential of success, seeing this as the most effective way to use limited resources. (Sometimes these are referred to as "good apples versus bad apples" strategies.) Or the target group may be people who are most clearly identifiable and ready to engage. For example, a child protection agency may reach out actively to mothers who are in the early recovery phase from substance abuse, having completed a treatment program.

The *client population* comprises that portion of the target population who actually come to use the services provided by the agency. These are the people who actually gain access, because of agency outreach combined with willingness to respond, or because of their own initiative. Rapp and Poertner depict these various sub-groups in the "population funnel" (Figure 11–1) reproduced below.

FIGURE 11–1   Population funnel

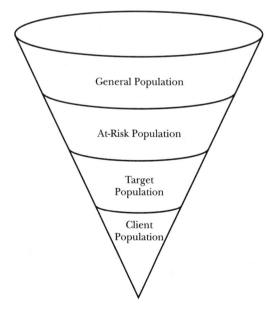

Employing Needs Assessment Techniques

Earlier we noted that needs assessment methods are an important aspect of the access function. While direct service professionals may rarely be responsible for designing and conducting such assessment projects, they often participate as team members, in advisory roles, or as consumers and implementers of the resulting findings. For this reason, it is useful for them to be aware of the main methods and procedures employed in needs assessment studies.

A cogent overview of methodologies has been set forth by Warheit, Bell, and Schwab (1984). We will draw on their formulation in order to summarize the main approaches. The authors delineate five basic means of gauging needs:

> key informant
> community forum
> rates-under-treatment
> social indicators
> field survey

A brief encapsulation of each will suffice for our purposes here.

Key informant.   The key informant approach elicits information from individuals who, through their background and experience, are assumed to be acutely knowledgeable about the needs of particular client populations. Informants can include involved professionals, community leaders, selected clients and their families, scholars and researchers, administrators of human service agencies, neighborhood activists, clergymen, and teachers. The approach involves identifying informants related to the problem under consideration, making sure that the sample selected is relevant and cross-sectional, so that bias in any direction is mitigated.

The next step involves constructing a questionnaire or interview schedule that will include the specific questions that need to be asked (like what individuals or groups are affected by a particular problem, identifiable subgroups, demographic features of the population, what current services are provided, and what limitations or gaps in these exist). The information can be gathered through face-to-face interviews, mailed questionnaires, or telephone interviews, each of which has different strong points. Person-to-person contact allows for in-depth exploration, while mailed questionnaires offer clear benefits regarding ease in tabulating and analyzing the data. After the data have been summarized, the key informants are sometimes brought together to give their reactions to the conclusions and to make suggestions about intervention.

Advantages of the key informant approach are numerous. It is fairly simple and inexpensive to carry out, and it focuses on the input of people who are keenly knowledgeable about the issues. The procedures do not require personnel with highly technical competencies, as the analysis is often qualitative in nature. And the ability to bring all respondents together to review the results can result in comprehensive conclusions that are reality-based and interactive. This feature can engender enthusiasm and commitment on the part of participants concerning follow-up program steps.

A major disadvantage is that the technique can reflect a bias in that only a relatively small number of selected individuals provide the data. People who are especially informed are by definition a special or biased slice of a general population and may present a distorted picture.

Community forum.   Here a somewhat larger and more diverse group of people are called together to give their opinions about needs and services, responding to similar queries as in the previous approach. One or more public meetings are scheduled, during which the participants are encouraged to share their views and their recommendations about action. Or one large meeting can be held at which the issues and questions are posed, and then break-out smaller gatherings are conducted in which participants provide their input.

Some specific tasks in this approach include selecting participants who will be able to reflect accurately on the problem; designating one or more convenient meeting places; announcing the meeting(s); fostering active participation; and making arrangements for people to lead the discussions and record the information that is forthcoming. An agenda or discussion guide has to be prepared in advance, incorporating the kinds of questions that would ordinarily go into an interview schedule.

The community forum is relatively inexpensive to conduct and easy to arrange. Another advantage is that it has a flexible quality, allowing input from any member of the community who is willing to attend a "one-shot" meeting. The discussion procedure can stimulate thinking about the problem and increase the number of responses and their quality. It provides an opportunity to identify individuals who are resources for later implementation activities, and can be a basis for organizing a citizen action group. The method constitutes a plus for agencies with limited financial resources in that it does not require hiring highly paid experts with strong technical competencies.

But the civic forum has a number of disadvantages. The people who are contacted and decide to attend a forum meeting may not necessarily be representative of the community as a whole. The more active participants, whose comments are recorded, may not reflect the views of all those attending, or they may sway the thinking and contributions of more passive participants in nongenuine ways. In addition, the responses emitted in an open meeting are somewhat unruly. The analysis is usually qualitative and impressionistic, and hard to set down and summarize in systematic or "scientific" fashion. There is also the danger that the meetings can become bogged down as grievance sessions, and unrealistic expectations of those attending can lead to later confusion or dissatisfaction when implementation proceeds.

Rates-under-treatment.   Here the objective is to gather service data from agencies and organizations that deal with clients experiencing the problem of concern. This involves a descriptive enumeration of people who have partaken of the programs of human service agencies in the community. It is assumed that aspects of need in the community can be extrapolated by examining the experiences of those who have received treatment or care for their difficulties. It is essentially an epidemiological type of analysis of the prevalence of disabilities and disorders. Typically the variables that are examined include: sociodemographic characteristics of clients; presenting problems; type, frequency, and duration of services; referral sources; and outcomes that are achieved.

To conduct this analysis a range of relevant agencies serving the designated clientele have to be identified. It is necessary to determine what data are in the public domain and how they can be accessed, and agencies having private data have to be solicited actively to make them available. A worksheet needs to be designed for systematically recording the information that is gathered, and statistical procedures have to be applied to produce summary tables, descriptive tendencies, and associations among variables.

An advantage here, especially when official information is publicly available, is the ease and low cost of obtaining such secondary data. The steps are rather straightforward and encompassable. The approach yields a broad portrait of the variety of relevant services provided in the community, as well as of those individuals who avail themselves of the services. It can also result in better intelligence and communication among service agencies.

There are, however, drawbacks. Issues of confidentiality and anonymity can surface and close out access to data. Some clients are seen concurrently by numerous agencies, and figures on them could distort or inflate the results. Some agencies may not be willing to cooperate by sharing their service data, or the data may be recorded in categories that are not compatible for aggregate analysis among agencies. Finally, there may be significant differences between disabled persons who seek help and those who do not, thus putting into question the rationale of generalizing from one group to the other.

Social indicators.   This approach relies on information, largely statistical, that is reported in public records as a matter of course, particularly governmental documents pertaining to the population census: health, education, housing, mental illness, and crime. The data can illuminate such matters as population trends, social behavior, quality of life, and social conditions. The assumption is that by analyzing statistics describing social phenomena, estimates can be made of the social well-being of the population, including deficits requiring attention. Social indicators, if properly treated, thereby become need indicators.

Documents are obtained from the U.S. Government Printing Office, Bureau of Census, county mental health centers and health departments, the Department of Commerce, local school boards, and similar institutions. One looks for mortality and morbidity rates, arrest records and crime patterns, differential income distribution, and changes in employment. The trick is to select the type of data that will best illuminate the need that is being addressed.

An important task in this process is selecting the right unit of analysis, and a consistent one. For example, in using census records, it is possible to make an analysis according to census track, larger enumeration districts, small block groupings, or minor civil divisions. The scope and detail of data will vary, based on the unit chosen to work with, and one of these will be more useful than another for different purposes. Carefully constructed worksheets need to be designed for transferring a large volume of data from document sources in an organized fashion. The analysis is typically highly statistical, involving tables, correlations, graphs, and transparent overlays of geographic areas.

There are some decided advantages to using social indicators. Large pools of data are already in place in the public domain and often easy to obtain. A broad base of information can be brought together, rather inexpensively, and can include data from several different sources simultaneously. The information typically has a high degree of legitimacy regarding scientific validity and public acceptance. There is comparability with other studies, and longitudinal trends can be discerned.

On the negative side, social indicator studies can be highly complex and costly. There is often a need for computers and other equipment, skilled analysts, and other arrangements for conducting a substantial research undertaking. Also, data used as indicators are indirect rather than direct indicators of need. For example, high-density housing conditions may indicate the existence of poverty and social disorganization for one group, but can reflect cultural patterns and preferences for a particular ethnic population. Obtaining access to data from voluntary organizations can become sticky, making it difficult to supplement governmental statistics and obtain a well-rounded picture. An additional complication is that figures are kept by different units of analysis by different organizations and jurisdictions (i.e., inconsistent clustering of census tracts to signify community composition), making aggregation of data problematic.

Field survey. The survey is perhaps the approach most familiar to the general public. This involves asking for information from a large set of respondents, either an entire population in a small area or a sample of a larger population. These informants are individuals who are immediately affected by problems and who can articulate their needs in a direct way. Through careful sampling procedures a representative sample of the population can be drawn, and rather firm generalizations about an entire group can be drawn. The public opinion poll or consumer survey are familiar analogues.

The survey uses a formal questionnaire or schedule (with either a structured or unstructured format), and it can be conducted in person, through the mail, or by telephone. The approach requires tasks such as selecting a valid sample; constructing a reliable instrument that will bring forth from respondents accurate information about their needs; training interviewers; organizing the field operation; editing, coding, and processing data; and performing rather complicated statistical analyses.

The survey can produce probably the most accurate, direct, and scientifically sound gauge of needs. At the same time it offers a great deal of flexibility in the manner in which questions can be framed, which particular groups and sub-groups are included, and how data is cross-roughed in the analysis. The results can be very rich and highly suggestive of intervention.

Nevertheless, the undertaking can be costly, lengthy, and complex with respect to staffing, training, organizing, and computing. If the core staff is not sophisticated, erroneous conclusions can easily result. There also can be a variety of troublesome field problems, including a high refusal or non-return rate among the sample.

This discussion has just touched the surface in treating these needs assessment methodologies. It has, however, suggested alternatives that can be used, and highlighted factors that have been considered in carrying any of them forward. For further details, see the previous Warheit et al. citation.

It is evident that although assessment attempts to gain objectivity in analyzing and understanding a problem, total truth is evasive. Surveying clients reveals how the problem feels to them. Speaking to professionals offers expert insight and experience. Consulting social indicators displays facts on the basis of data that are somehow available, but may be slanted. The analyst must decide which of these approaches (or sources) is most critical in a given situation or what combination might best illuminate the client need. Even with an aggregate approach there remains the problem of interrelating and weighting the various streams of information.

Engaging in Outreach and Social Marketing

The practices geared to contacting and steering potential clients go under several different terms: outreach, information and referral, community relations, increasing agency visibility, and several others. Some prefer the notion of social marketing, which carries over the strategies and activities that have been finely honed in commercial marketing to the sphere of non-profit organizations and social causes (Kotler and Zaltman, 1973; Lazar and Kelley, 1973; Rothman et al., 1983; Solomon, 1981). We discuss outreach practice from the perspective of social marketing in this presentation as it offers a useful framework for the planning of actions.

Social marketing builds from needs assessment (which, however, falls under the rubric of market research in that field). One starts by obtaining a clear concept of what needs and desires exist, and who the pool of potential consumers (clients) are. This provides the basis for constructing a profile of the consumer pool (its demographic characteristics, geographic dispersion, etc.) and for dividing it into clusters that have similarities (people living in particular locales or having particular interests or needs). This effort is termed *market segmentation,* and is predicated on the assumption that the different clusters of people may require different outreach strategies.

A widely recognized formulation for designing an effective program has been propounded by McCarthy (1968), comprising the *Four P's* of marketing: *product, promotion, place,* and *price.*

Product.   This projects the notion that what is offered to consumers should closely match their needs and wishes. It assumes that a competent needs assessment was conducted, and that the offering matches up with "where the consumer is," that it is "buyable." In other words, the step prior to outreach is again brought into focus. The "product" catch word alerts us to making sure that the service program we have developed to serve clients is responsive to their real needs and concerns.

Promotion.   Here we come more concretely into the realm of outreach tasks—communication and persuasion that will make the service familiar, understandable, acceptable, and desirable. Four different types of promotional activities are suggested.

Advertising. Using mass media and other nonpersonal means (paid or donated) to reach clients (newspapers, television, cable television, ethnic newspapers, radio, brochures, posters, flyers, etc.). There are matters of choosing the right slant or appeal, designing attention-capturing copy, pitching the material at the appropriate language level, choosing the media that your target group will be tuned into, and having the right timing.

Personal contact (selling). This involves some of the direct contact activities that were described by the practitioners in the UCLA survey, including visits to agencies, homes, and places where potential clients congregate. The outreach workers need to be oriented to knowing how to communicate directly with people, to handle follow-up questions, and to foster motivation.

Publicity. Here a variety of media are employed to tell the story of the program as news, rather than as sponsored and pre-prepared information. It is nonpaid and noncontrolled information and, of course, runs the risk of being inaccurate or slanted. News releases, public service announcements, and feature stories are typical examples. Cultivating contacts with particular people in various media outlets greatly facilitates this component.

Promotional events. This entails conducting special events that intersect with the public. Examples are a health fair, a conference on senior services, a concert for the physically disabled, an exposition on mental hygiene, or even a contest or lottery.

Kotler and Zaltman (1973, p. 62) are aware of the issue of tone and ethics in the marketing process. They observe, "Many persons mistakenly assume that marketing means hard selling. This is only a particular style of marketing, and it has its critics both inside and outside of the profession." They note that some firms use marketing methods consistently with taste and sensitivity, including Hallmark, Xerox, and Container Corporation. It is clear that any human service agency that makes use of the procedures of marketing must be alert to these considerations.

Place.   This concerns the place where the product is obtained (the location of the service). There is typically a physical facility where the transaction being promoted occurs. This "outlet" needs to be positioned so that it can be used with relative ease—not at too great a distance, where transportation is available, and at convenient hours.

Price.   Here the emphasis is on the costs to consumers to obtain the service. Cost in money is highlighted in the commercial realm and may be prominent in human service provision as well. But social marketing highlights other costs to clients that are also very important: opportunity costs, energy costs, and psychic costs. Choosing to use a given service may preclude doing some other useful or pleasurable thing, or could mean being closed out from some other service. The time and effort it takes to get there, wait in the reception room, and fill out a ream of forms may be draining, especially for older people or those with health problems. And then there is the psychological wound of having to admit you are dependent and to be treated like a "welfare case."

In one study described by Kotler and Zaltman (1973), it was found that patients preferred going to private clinics that charge a fee rather than to free hospitals. At the hospital, patients on each visit had to wait for a long time to be seen, talk first with a social worker, submit to a series of questions about income in order to prove eligibility, and see several other staff members for a series of required tests, during which income again came up for discussion. Finally the patient visited with the doctor, who could decide that she really needs to see a specialist who will not be available for 2 weeks. The cost of the free service proved to be too high for many of these people. This should underline for us that the price we ask of our clients comes in many different forms, and that all of these have to be taken into account in our planning for access.

The marketing orientation tells us that clients often do a cost/benefit analysis in deciding whether to avail themselves of a service they learn about. When the configuration of costs we impose outweighs the benefits they calculate, they may well opt out. A social marketing perspective calls for carefully designing a "marketing mix" of all the factors discussed above, targeted to specific sub-groups through market segmentation, so that clients will be reached and the benefit-over-cost ratio perceived by them will be favorable. When that happens, the direct practice of giving help can commence, beginning with intake, assessment, and goal-setting functions for individual clients and their families.

REFERENCES

Agranoff, R. & Lindsay, V. (1983). Intergovernmental management: Perspectives from human services problem-solving at the local level. *Public Administration Review* (June) 227–237.

Alaszewski, A. & Harrison, L. (1988). Literature review: Collaboration and co-ordination between welfare agencies. *British Journal of Social Work, 18,* 635–647.

Beck, D. F. (1962). *Patterns in use of family agency service.* New York: Family Service Association of America.

Bierly, E. W. (1988). The world climate program: Collaboration and communication on a global scale. *The Annals, 495,* 106–116.

Blau, P. M. (1964). *Exchange and power in social life.* New York: John Wiley & Sons.

Bowe, F. G., Jacobi, J. E., & Wiseman, L. D. (1978). *Coalition building.* Washington, DC: American Coalition of Citizens With Disabilities.

Coe, B. (1988). Open focus: Implementing projects in multi-organizational settings. *International Journal of Public Administration, 11(4),* 503–526.

Davidson, S. (1976). Planning and coordination of social services in multiorganizational contexts. *Social Service Review, 50,* 117–137.

Downing, R. (1979). An exploration of case manager roles: Coordinator, advocate, and counselor. In *Three Working Papers.* Los Angeles Social Policy Laboratory, Percy Andrus Gerontology Center, University of Southern California.

Eggert, G. M. & Brodows, B. (1984). Five years of ACCESS: What have we learned? In R. Zawadski (Ed.), *Community-based systems of long-term care.* New York: Haworth.

Green, J. W. (1982). *Cultural awareness in the human services.* Englewood Cliffs, NJ: Prentice Hall.

Harbin, G., Eckland, J., Gallagher, J., Clifford, R., & Place, P. (1991). *Policy development for P.L. 99-457, part H: Initial findings from six case studies.* Chapel Hill, NC: Carolina Institute for Child and Family Policy, University of North Carolina.

Hasenfeld, Y. (1983). *Human service organizations.* Englewood Cliffs, NJ: Prentice Hall.

Hasenfeld, Y. & English, R. A. (Eds.). (1974). *Human service organizations: A book of readings.* Ann Arbor: The University of Michigan Press.

Haskins, B., Capitman, J., Bernstein, J., et al. (1984). *Report. Evaluation of coordinated community-oriented long-term care demonstration projects.* Berkeley, CA: Berkeley Planning Associates.

Hollingshead, A. B. & Redlich, F. C. (1958). *Social class and mental illness.* New York: John Wiley & Sons.

Horwitch, M. & Prahalad, C. K. (1981). Managing multi-organization enterprises: The emerging strategic frontier. *Sloan Management Review, 22(2),* 3–16.

Isles, P. & Auluck, R. (1990). Team building, inter-agency team development and social work practice. *British Journal of Social Work, 20,* 165–178.

Iverson, L. H. (1986). *A description and analysis of state preadmission screening programs.* Minneapolis, MN: InterStudy, Center for Aging and Long-Term Care.

Kagan, S. L., Rivera, A. M., & Parker, F. L. (1990). *Collaboration in practice: Reshaping services for young children and their families.* New Haven, CT: The Bush Center in Child Development and Social Policy, Yale University.

Kahn, A. J. (1969). *Theory and practice of social planning.* New York: Russell Sage Foundation.

Kane, R. A. (1985). Case management in health care settings. In M. Weil, J. M. Karls, and Associates (Eds.), *Case Management in Human Service Practice* (pp. 170–203). San Francisco: Jossey-Bass.

Kane, R. A. & Kane, R. L. (1987). *Long-term care: Principles, programs, and policies.* New York: Springer.

Kemper, P., Braun, R. S., Carcagno, G. J., et al. (1986). *The evaluation of the national long-term care channeling demonstration.* Princeton, NJ: Mathematica Policy.

Kirwin, P. M. (1988). The challenge of community long-term care: The dependent aged. *Journal of Aging Studies, 2(3),* 255–266.

Kotler, P. & Zaltman, G. (1973). Social marketing: An approach to planned social change. In W. Lazer & E. J. Kelley (Eds.), *Social marketing: Perspectives and viewpoints* (pp. 52–69). Homewood, IL: Richard D. Irwin.

Lauffer, A. (1978). *Social planning at the community level.* Englewood Cliffs, NJ: Prentice Hall.

Lazer, W. & Kelley, E. J. (Eds.). (1973). *Social marketing: Perspectives and viewpoints.* Homewood, IL: Richard D. Irwin.

Levine, I. S. & Fleming, M. (1985). *Human resource development: Issues in case management.* Rockville, MD: National Institute for Mental Health.

Levine, S. & White, P. E. (1961). Exchange as a conceptual framework for the study of interorganizational relationships. In Y. Hasenfeld & R. A. English (Eds.), *Human service organizations: A book of readings.* Ann Arbor: The University of Michigan Press.

Litwak, E. & Rothman, J. (1979). The impact of organizational structure and linkage on agency programs and services. *Strategies of Community Organization: A Book of Readings* (pp. 249–262). Itasca, IL: F. E. Peacock.

McCann, J. E. & Gray, B. (1986). Power and collaboration in human service domains. *International Journal of Sociology and Social Policy, 6(3),* 58–67.

McCarthy, E. J. (1968). *Basic marketing: A managerial approach* (pp. 31–33). Homewood, IL: Richard D. Irwin.

Means, R., Harrison, L., Jeffers, S., & Smith, R. (1991). Co-ordination, collaboration and health promotion: Lessons and issues from and alcohol/education programme. *Health Promotion International, 6(1),* 31–39.

Platman, S. R. (1982). Case management of the mentally disabled. *Journal of Public Health Policy,* 302–314.

Rapp, C. A. & Poertner J. (1992). *Social administration: A client-centered approach.* New York: Longman.

Rist, R. C., Hamilton, M. A., Holloway, W. B., Johnson, S. D., & Wiltberger, H. E. (1980). *Patterns of collaboration: The CETA/school linkage, an analysis of inter-institutional linkages between education and employment/training organizations.* Ithaca, NY: Interim Report #4, Youthwork National Policy Study, Cornell University.

Rothman, J., Teresa, J. G., Kay, T. L., & Morningstar, G. C. (1983). *Marketing human service innovations.* Beverly Hills: Sage Publications.

Ryndes, T. (1989). The coalition model of case management for care of HIV-infected persons. *Quality Review Bulletin, 15(1),* 4–8.

Schwartz, S. R., Goldman, H. H., & Churgin, S. (1980). *Manpower issues in the care of the chronically mentally ill.* Sacramento: Department of Mental Health, State of California.

Scott, R. A. (1967). The selection of clients by social welfare agencies: The case of the blind. In Y. Hasenfeld & R. A. English (Eds.), *Human service organizations: A book of readings.* Ann Arbor: The University of Michigan Press.

Stedman, D. J. & Wiegerink, R. (1979). Future of service delivery systems for handicapped individuals. In R. Wiegerink & J. W. Pelosi (Eds.), *Developmental disabilities, the DD movement.* Baltimore: Paul H. Brookes.

Turner, J. C. & TenHoor, W. J. (1978). The NIMH community support program: Pilot approach to a needed social reform. *Schizophrenia Bulletin, 4,* 319–348.

Warheit, G. J., Bell, R. A., & Schwab, J. J. (1974). *Planning for change: Needs assessment approaches.* Rockville, MD: National Institute of Mental Health.

Weil, M. (1985). Key components in providing efficient and effective services. In M. Weil & J. M. Karls (Eds.), *Case management in human service practice.* San Francisco: Jossey-Bass.

Winston, W. J. (Ed). (1985). *Marketing strategies for human and social service agencies.* New York: The Haworth Press.

III
Systemic Factors

12

Community and Organizational Issues

OVERVIEW

"A part of the main," is the way poet John Donne described the relationship of the particular to the general. "No man is an island entire of itself," he wrote, people and things interconnect and profoundly affect one another. This applies pertinently to the subject matter we are exploring.

We have concentrated on how practice within an agency can radiate and affect help-giving processes and possibilities in the environment. We have not given proportional attention to the converse—how elements of the social context, the community and organizational setting, make their mark on the way practice is put into effect. According to Intagliata (1982, pp. 657, 670), practice with highly vulnerable clients has a distinct structure: "The specific meaning of case management, however, depends on the [service] system that is developed to provide it. In turn, the particular characteristics of the system are shaped by the context in which it is expected to operate. . . . Case managers' actual activities are shaped ultimately by the constraints of the environments within which they work, not by their formal job descriptions."

The context, we found in the UCLA survey, has a pronounced influence on the nuances of practice implementation. We examine context with respect to two system components, community and lead agency, discussing them in sequence. In carrying out that analysis, we draw heavily on data from interviews with practitioners in the survey, bringing the survey now into the forefront substantively rather than using it in large measure as background to provide intermittent concepts and illustrations. As an aspect of context, we examine the question of effectiveness of case management as a service modality. The confidence of community leaders and agency administrators in case management, and their willingness to underwrite it, depends in part on research evidence about its efficacy.

In the survey, interviewers probed in depth about contextual factors, asking the 48 agency respondents to draw on their specific experiences in practice as a basis for their views and conclusions. Respondents provided information about community and employing agency influences and the problems these created for their practice, and also made recommendations about how they thought the contextual situation might be modified and improved.

Because the study was conducted in one community, although an enormously diverse one, it does not provide definitive generalizable findings. Also, one vulnerable client group, the mentally ill, was involved, not the range of vulnerable populations. The data are largely qualitative in character—rich in heuristic notions and reflective of the atmosphere of practice, with examples from on-the-line engagement. They offer a repertoire of ideas rather than a treatise propounding conclusions. For this reason, trends rather than statistics are given emphasis in the presentation, and where numbers are provided they are meant to be suggestive. Nonetheless, what the practitioners report here is highly consistent with the literature in the field, including the comprehensive synthesis of pertinent research that was compiled through the UCLA project (Rothman, 1992). The survey materials serve to give real-world detail, supplementing the research literature.

THE COMMUNITY CONTEXT

The community is the environmental setting in which clients (and practitioners) live, and in which the lead service agency must function and gain sustenance. The community provides a resource base and a service network that can make a difference in respect to the form and quality of practice in that locale. The point has been made as follows:

> While the activities are relatively standard, case management may take on dramatically different shades of emphasis depending upon such factors as: the richness and nature of services available in a specific locale; how the inventory of services is controlled; the geography of the area in which case management operates; the existence of other case management systems; and the value system which informs the behavior of case managers" (National Conference on Social Welfare, 1981, p. 20).

The values and attitudes existing in the community also impact such things as whether group residential homes can be established in neighborhoods, and the extent and type of informal social support available to draw upon (Fleming & York, 1989; Hereford, 1989; Johnson, 1980). Johnson found that public support is rather unstable and varies from community to community and in different time periods. Variations in type of media treatment can have an effect on fears and misconceptions among community residents about impaired populations, and can lead to differences in the nature of support (Johnson & Beditz, 1981). In situations of low community support, practitioners, it was found, devote a greater proportion of their practice time to creating or directly providing these supplemental services, and they spend proportionally less time in expediting formal agency linkage for clients (Intagliata, 1982).

The unique composition of the agency network in the community affects service in another way; it shapes the pattern of exchange and competition. Accordingly, "Turf issues arise. . . . Any designation of a lead agency disrupts the balance of organizational power in the region . . . the question of who controls the purse strings takes on added importance" (Kane, 1985, p. 195). These factors determine which community agencies the practitioner can draw upon for support and what kinds of linkage strategies have to be applied differentially.

A range of related community factors are at play and were identified by practitioners interviewed in the survey. The remainder of this discussion relies on their observations.

COMMUNITY ASPECTS AND PROBLEMS

Aspects of Community

To explore community matters, the practitioners were asked two specific questions: "Is there something distinctive about [this geographic region] that gives case management a unique form here? Why is it unique—what makes it different?"

All 48 practitioners we interviewed stated that their work was influenced by contextual factors. A multiplicity of community influences were identified as important in shaping practice in the locale. These cluster into three basic categories: population aspects, economic aspects, and aspects related to the geographic layout of the community. These are not discrete, but rather overlap; for example, an economically depressed community may have a relatively high specialized homeless population. As ideas about types of influence are the important issue here, frequencies of response are not emphasized.

Population Aspects

Three aspects of population composition are noted by respondents:

(1) mixed ethnic groupings and other heterogeneous populations;
(2) ethnic homogeneity, as in a community dominated by a particular race or nationality; and
(3) special vulnerable populations that have relevance for service, such as drug abusers.

Ethnic heterogeneity. This matter is described by one practitioner as follows: "We have a very mixed population; we're the original melting pot. There is a myriad of clients with numerous needs due to their cultural and ethnic backgrounds."

Multiethnicity seems to affect case managers in a number of different ways. As suggested in the quotation, several respondents speak of having to understand and respond to diverse needs. It is therefore more difficult, they say, to predict or anticipate needs. Others specify having to carefully take cultural issues into account in their work. Language is a consideration, "We have to establish bilingual programs, i.e., Korean, English, Japanese, Chinese, Cambodian, and Laotian. We use bilingual volunteers." Some workers think that this makes the job more difficult; others think it adds a lot of interest and variety, contributing to professional growth.

Population heterogeneity also overlaps with the clustering of several different types of special client groups, "We have pockets—gay pockets, drug abuse pockets, black pockets." Each of these requires tailored services, and some clients are especially difficult to serve.

Ethnic homogeneity. Respondents refer to single ethnic concentrations, such as a "dense population of Filipinos." Other concentrations named are Indo-Chinese, African–Americans, and Latinos.

Cultural features must be addressed in a focused way. For example, regarding Indo-Chinese:

> We don't deal with patients initially as mentally ill—that conflicts with their culture. They come in with physical symptoms and we work on that basis. Later on, the clients come to realize that there is a mental problem and we are ready to help in that way.

Special populations. Special population groups that were named include: homeless, gays and lesbians, drug abusers, refugees, and young adults. There are also stable versus transient populations. Some groups are identified as "dangerous," including drug abusers and the homeless.

These special populations are hard to work with and to link to services that are both relevant and willing to respond. Stable populations are easy to track and relate to; transient populations are often associated with crime and drugs and need a quick response because they live in a continuing crisis environment.

Economic Aspects

Here the reference is to the economic level of the community, usually low versus middle socioeconomic status.

Lower economic level. Some of the points made about a low socioeconomic community include a greater need for help, few resources, and more dual-diagnosis patients. More linkages have to be made, while at the same time clients in the inner city need more help in completing linkages. There is also an acute housing shortage for these people.

Higher economic level. Residence in communities having higher economic levels can be a disadvantage because there are generally fewer public facilities and resources available in the immediate area. For example, often there is no bus system. Also, the community is less tolerant of personal deviation, such as acting-out behavior. However, family support systems with available resources and more organized advocacy groups are likely to be at hand and can be engaged readily by the practitioners.

Geographic Aspects

The physical layout of the area is another influential aspect. Three ecological matters were pointed to: geographic spread, physical isolation, and number of governance units.

Geographic spread. This notion is described well as follows:

> The community is suburban, but rather sprawling. That makes networking very hard. And once you make contact with an agency on a client's behalf, the client may not be able to get to the place.

Both communication with services and mobility for clients are problematic in expansive areas.

Geographic isolation. The isolated community is described as follows:

> Because of our location and the distances involved, there is isolation of our workers from other agencies. This leads to high client drop out rates because it is hard to coordinate services for them. Clients lose interest and motivation to follow through. They show up again 2 or 3 months later and we have to start from scratch.

Other similar comments refer to client separation from senior centers, ethnic programs, and low-cost pharmacies.

Number of governance entities. If there is only one governmental entity to relate to, the practitioners said, this enhances the work. An excerpt from field notes makes the point:

> This is one city, with one police force, public welfare department, and so on. You only have to deal with one bureaucracy and that makes it easier to learn what resources are available to do your job.

Another respondent put it somewhat differently:

> This is a fairly well-defined community—we have a stable population. We have a low turnover of staff and can provide continuing services to clients.

General Community Problems

Practitioners were asked "What are some of the main problems you face in doing case management?" and were requested to relate these to five different spheres that impinge on intervention: the *practitioner*, the *client*, the *client's family*, the *agency*, and the *community*. We felt these spheres provide a comprehensive inventory of the major arenas of difficulty encountered by practitioners. Experience with the field interviews demonstrated that this frame did actually encompass all the problems respondents wished to raise.

The main problems at the community level include both attitudinal and material issues:

> depreciation and stigmatization of clients,
> lack of services and poor coordination with other agencies, and
> misunderstanding the case management role.

Negative attitudes toward clients.   Practitioners are dismayed by negative community attitudes toward their clients. They indicate that the basic causes of the stigma are ignorance about clients and of their circumstances. The major result of this is discriminatory behavior directed toward clients; for example, people reject having group homes in their neighborhoods. At the agency level, many programs show intolerance toward highly vulnerable clients and do not want to provide them with services. One response is illustrative:

> It's hard to make referrals for volunteer work or to place clients in job settings. The community lacks understanding that these people are human beings and need the opportunity to prove themselves. It would be helpful if community people could be educated.

Another response makes a similar point:

> Some of the community agencies don't even try to work with us, and kick out anybody who acts strangely. If they are not willing to provide services to people who are dependent or sometimes behave in an unusual way, that puts the whole burden back on us.

Other responses dealt with community apathy and indifference toward the homeless or abused children, or noted that the community does not recognize the legal rights of clients. For example, certain ethnic groups in the community do not view harsh disciplining of children (constituting child abuse) as against the law. A respondent said, "In their country of origin it is their prerogative to punish their children in any way they view as appropriate. This ethnic community doesn't understand it when we take action on behalf of the child."

Lack of services and poor coordination. Several practitioners lamented a general lack of services in the community. One stated, "It's completely impossible to find placement for people with double diagnoses . . . a mentally ill person with AIDS no one will touch." Problems of transportation, they said, compound the problem of service gaps. (Because of the importance of ancillary services, the specific matter of service gaps in the community is treated separately shortly.)

A series of difficulties in obtaining services for clients was detailed; for example, the problem of setting up medical examinations for clients. Due to homelessness and transportation problems, it is often difficult for some clients to be punctual. If clients are late for an appointment, they are turned away. High turnover in other agencies makes it difficult to maintain a relationship with a key contact person who is cooperative and understanding. A problem with the licensing agency for board-and-care homes is another concern, "Complaints are made and the licensing agency acts slowly and unpredictably."

Misunderstanding case management.   Several replies pointed to lack of public understanding of case management. Community members and community agencies expect the practitioner to "take troublesome clients away and provide for all their needs." One respondent explained that the community does not understand that "it is not against the law to be crazy or disabled."

Service Gaps in the Community

Because of its importance as a barrier to good practice, we asked in a separate item on the questionnaire for practitioners to specifically tell us the main service gaps they experienced in the community. They indicate three main lacks: special services, shelter and housing, and hospital beds, plus a few others.

Lack of special services.   There was high concern about the absence of programs for those clients with dual diagnoses or special needs. The majority of these clients have chemical dependencies. Other combined problem situations include clients who are illegal aliens, homeless women with children, clients with AIDS, violent clients (e.g., homicidal, suicidal, self-abusers), and hearing- or sight-handicapped clients.

Other respondents mentioned a lack of structured socialization programs (e.g., day-treatment programs) and long-term residential treatment and transitional living programs. Medical care services for low-income people are also deficient.

There is also a clear need for more sheltered workshops where clients can work on a limited basis for payment. "This experience is especially important to restore a sense of meaning in clients' lives." Responses indicate that discrimination in the community toward vulnerable clients results in a scarcity of employers who are willing to offer this type of opportunity.

Lack of shelter and housing.   A number of practitioners indicate that there is a shortage of low-income housing, especially for the elderly on SSI. Board-and-care homes often do not have day activities and good quality care. Respondents suggested that it is especially difficult to find placement opportunities for younger, severely mentally ill individuals in board-and-care homes.

Hospital bed capacity.   Lack of hospital beds to accommodate clients in a sheltered environment also received a high number of mentions. The need is especially acute for homeless clients, young children, potentially violent individuals, and adolescents.

Access to funds (SSI, or Supplementary Security Insurance).   SSI funding criteria are too rigid and the funding amounts are too small. In addition, delays in obtaining funds (i.e., 3- to 4-month processing time) result in clients' basic life needs going unmet.

Transportation.   Absence of adequate ways to transport clients to needed services presents difficulties. A client might have to travel long distances to see a doctor who takes Medi-Cal. The medical condition is compounded with the client's inability to get to the service and to get there on time. Although many clients do get bus passes from the city, sometimes this process takes a long time. In suburban jurisdictions the bus lines do not accept the bus pass. In other instances, a client with an acute need does not have enough time to obtain a bus pass.

Miscellaneous.   Sundry additional community deficiencies include lack of meals, police support, English-as-a-second-language classes, self-help support groups, and child care for adult clients with small children.

Problems with Service Providers

In order to delve more deeply into the dynamics involved in linking with service providers, staff members were asked an additional question about the nature of problems they experienced in dealing with other agencies. The main ones mentioned include:

> overburdened providers,
> rigid policies and procedures, and
> negative attitudes of service providers toward clients.

Overburdened providers.   Other service providers have large case loads already and are generally overworked and short-staffed. There are long waiting lists in many places. Service providers do not return phone calls and fail to offer feedback on service provision. It was also stated again here that high staff turnover results in the loss of important contacts. The general tenor is that problems named exist or are intensified because other service providers often are dealing with more than they can handle.

Rigid policies and procedures.   Our informants point to rigid admission requirements and "hyperselectivity" on the part of other service providers. A typical response is, "You have to be a certain sex, a certain age, and have a certain diagnosis to be accepted into an agency." Limited agency hours and strict appointment schedules present special problems for impaired individuals, who often have transportation problems. "Agencies claim they provide a lot in the beginning when they are trying to get established. Later on, they get picky and don't want troublesome clients."

Negative attitudes of service providers.   There is also an inappropriate level of intolerance and discriminatory behavior by providers. They show apathy and indifference toward highly dependent individuals and have an inaccurate view of the role of the lead agency. "They believe we should take care of the complete needs of the clients."

RECOMMENDATIONS FOR IMPROVING THE COMMUNITY CONTEXT

In this section we focus on potential solutions that were suggested regarding problematic community strictures. These derived mainly from the question, "What recommendations would you make to strengthen the case management process and program in the department?" Three main directions of amelioration were suggested:

   increase resources and special services,
   provide education on client conditions, and
   enhance interagency networking.

Seeking increased resources and providing community education received highest mention. Expanding community services was addressed, both in general and targeted to particular ethnic groups. Many respondents thought that education of the public was essential to decrease stigma toward client conditions and to inform the community about the functions and limitations of case management. Better interagency networking was a desired goal, in particular, fostering coordination of community agencies. This was seen as a way to increase, or at least make more accessible, agency services in the community. Practitioners also encouraged effort to foster a more favorable political climate.

More concrete initiatives were suggested when the practitioners were asked what could be done specifically about gaps in service. Solutions fell into the following categories:

locate or develop new providers,
advocate for clients,
provide creative alternatives,
use administrative channels, and
pursue solutions persistently.

Locate or develop new providers.   Most of the answers focused on the direct service workers making more effort to find new service providers by contacting different agencies. Typically, "I keep calling around; I try everything I can think of and ask others for ideas. I guess I aim to be creative." Some practitioners indicated that searching for private providers of care who accept Medi-Cal, or treat indigent clients, is an ongoing area of effort, and one response refers to using a specialized staff community developer at the agency headquarters to locate or help establish new services. The overall thrust was advice to "know your resources."

Advocate for clients.   Some practitioners speak for a vigorous advocacy role, and they themselves attempt to prod rejecting agencies to accept clients. This may include calling "to beg" for special allowances, helping clients to compile all the needed documentation to increase the probability of acceptance, writing appropriate letters and reports, and attending court hearings. One person noted that clients who are experiencing difficulties with service providers can be referred to a clients' rights advocacy program in the community.

Provide creative substitutes.   One group of respondents suggested searching out a service substitution, such as sending clients to private restaurant owners who are known to be kind enough to provide a meal to the hungry. Another example is using one's own car to transport a client to an off-site agency. Or the practitioner might actuate informal social support in a unique way, such as training the family to carry out special activities in the absence of a service provider. The overall impression is that service substitutions are difficult to establish and are highly irregular at best. Many times they involve bending or breaking the agency rules in order to serve a client in a flexible and innovative way.

Use administrative channels.   The point here is to use administrative channels to inform "higher-ups" about service gaps. For example, committee meetings at the local facility were used to assemble information about holes in service, put the information in writing, and send a report to the executive office. This is no panacea. One respondent commented, "It doesn't necessarily do much good, but we document the problems in writing and send reports off anyway. We keep hoping something will change."

Pursue solutions persistently. Some case managers talk about the need to keep working away on the problem at any level that seems feasible. Actions have included: monitoring waiting lists for clients; working with families in the AMI (Alliance for the Mentally Ill); moving family members to engage in political action; campaigning for sympathetic candidates; and persevering so a client does not wind up with an inappropriate referral. The suggestion is that the practitioner not give up, but chip away relentlessly at community obstacles. Other practitioners were less optimistic and resilient, taking the view that there was nothing they could do to overcome these systemic conditions.

Overall, it is evident that to tackle community system problems the lead agency needs to examine, concertedly, what it can do from an administrative and policy standpoint to forge linkage arrangements with vital agencies in the community, develop new community services, educate the public, and cultivate political support. These are functions that are generally beyond the scope of the individual service practitioner and require the resources and authority that reside in the organizational system. Direct practitioners also have some leverage on these issues. They can actively locate and sometimes develop community service resources, engage more intensively in advocacy, seek out alternatives and substitutes in a creative way, and resolutely keep probing for solutions. There are concrete implications here for graduate education and in-service training within agencies; practitioners have to be helped to acquire or deepen these skills.

THE ORGANIZATIONAL CONTEXT

The agency constitutes a social system and a context that is immediate and often determinate. It generates policies, directives, regulations, norms, and expectancies that mold the form, constraints, and opportunities of professional intervention. Zald (1987, p. 244) refers to such organizations as polities and observes, "Whatever the practitioner's activity, he is guided by the structure, aims and operating procedures of the organization that pays the bills."

When there is an appropriate match between practice requirements and the organizational context, there will likely be optimal outcomes. Weil (1985, p. 319) observes:

> The case management function must be suited to the organization as well as its clients. That is, the case management system must fit the organizational system and support desired patterns of organizational behavior. For example, case management systems designed for large, bureaucratic, multisited or nested systems, such as state mental health programs or public child welfare settings, will be different in scale, complexity, design, and sophistication from those of small voluntary agencies or a newly developing program such as a center for independent living.

Weil goes on to discuss specific organizational variables that have a bearing on intervention. These include, among others, the clarity of goal definition, and of procedures to implement goals; the degree to which these are attuned to client need; the funding and resource level in the program; the number and composition of staff; and the forms of support available to assist staff. Rubin (1987) adds several additional factors: the size of assigned case loads, clarity versus ambiguity of role definitions, and the type of physical and technical facilities in the program. The "culture" of the organization is still another consideration (Levine, 1979), and may include such human relations factors as cooperation and teamwork arrangements; the openness of communication; and the opportunity structure for participation by staff in decision making. Other elements of structure and process can be added, but this covers many of the important ones—as we will see shortly in the comments from the field survey.

The discussion of organizational variables is similar in format to the one on community, concentrating on problems and recommendations. The presentation relies on comments by the practitioners who participated in the UCLA survey, based on a similar set of items in the questionnaire.

The interviews were conducted in a very large public agency in a major urban center, and a proper analysis of the responses about organizational variables requires keeping that feature firmly in mind. Public services in the Ronald Reagan and George Bush presidencies experienced severe fiscal constriction, together with client pressures for expanded services. Federal policies and regulations zigged and zagged unpredictably, and programs associated with "welfare" were under high suspicion and close scrutiny—with concomitant demands for elaborate accountability procedures and documentation by the agencies. The operating climate of big city human service organizations given responsibility for large populations of highly dependent or disabled clients became characterized as complex, stressful, and turbulent. These trends are reflected in the survey responses in this local agency, and are best understood as a particularized expression of a more generic pattern within a class of agencies.

ORGANIZATIONAL PROBLEMS

Six areas of organizational problems come to the fore in practitioner comments:

    Work overload (paperwork, case load)
    Deficiencies in field operations
    Lacks in organizational coherence and stability
    Inadequate staff development and support
    Inadequate client centeredness
    Lack of funding and resources

Work overload.   Sixty percent of those interviewed mentioned work overload issues. A high volume of paperwork and client responsibility in tandem seem to be overwhelming many workers. Some of the respondents think there is an excessive emphasis on documentation of service, which interferes with the quality of service. Several supported documentation, but believe that the paperwork becomes dysfunctional when case loads are too high. The issue is intensified, some say, by staff shortages. The image of a staggering paperwork burden comes through over and over again, both in the number of responses and the intensity of expression by practitioners.

Deficiencies in field operations.   There was concern expressed about inadequate physical arrangements at local facilities (e.g., not enough space to do group counseling, not enough privacy, and drab surroundings that are hard on client and staff morale). Some local facilities are professionally short-staffed or lack clerical support.

Lacks in organizational coherence and stability.   A substantial set of responses cite frequent changes in policies, administrative procedures, and program guidelines. ("Things are always in a state of flux.") One statement typifies the flavor of these comments, "General turnover in operations is high and every time a new administrator comes along she brings a new policy. On some issues administrators go back and forth constantly." A related comment is that programs are implemented without adequate guidelines, "which is why they are weak and often fail." Many staff members find there is insufficient opportunity for their input in policy formation and policy changes. Policies that impede practice were noted: obstacles to off-site work with clients (i.e., accompanying a client to another agency for a required service) and a maximum 72-hour hospitalization hold time for certain clients who might require a longer stay. Additionally, the case management role and its functions are too vaguely defined. This creates uncertainty for practitioners as well as other staff members.

Inadequate staff development and support.   Policies often do not enhance professional functions: "They took our wheels away, I have no power to do my job." A few respondents claimed that professional benefits are not up to par and that there are not enough incentives for promotion. A final set of responses here criticized the level of in-service training and supervisory help. One stated:

> The organization does not provide enough training to teach you techniques about discovering how other agencies in the system work. For example, they gave a real short seminar on SSI. It's too much information in too short a time period. And this makes it hard for you to educate the client. So if we don't know how the system works and can't adequately explain it to a client, the client is doomed to fail.

Inadequate client-centeredness. Some respondents think the agency is not client-centered enough to fulfill its obligations, "It is sometimes more concerned about units of service, documentation, and routines than about the real needs of the clients."

RECOMMENDED ORGANIZATIONAL IMPROVEMENTS

There were a considerable number of recommendations to improve organizational functioning, related to problems previously identified:

> obtain more funding and resources,
> increase staff,
> reduce case loads and time pressures,
> decrease paperwork and red tape,
> streamline management and improve human relations,
> clarify and enhance the case management role,
> improve physical facilities and operations in the field, and
> give more support to coordinating community services.

Increase funding and resources. A strong recommendation was that the agency take more assertive responsibility for obtaining funding and bringing more resources to the program. Practitioners acknowledge that the agency itself does not have control over such resources, but believe it should be more aggressive in interpreting needs to those who serve as gatekeepers for these resources. One comment placed the matter in broader context, "In essence we need more money for the human services system. But this is difficult. These things are way down there compared to Star Wars or overseas intervention." But still, "We should not back away from putting political pressure on the county board of supervisors. We should really lobby hard for funding."

Increase staff. An aspect of resource expansion should be adding more staff. Sentiment for increased resources appeared to be aimed primarily at expanding manpower in order to reduce work overload and time pressures and to improve quality of service.

Reduce case loads and time pressures. Respondents spoke of job stress, time pressures, and excessive case loads. They advocated reducing case loads as an important means of making the job more manageable. The following comment captures the view of many:

> With the present levels of overwork people suffer many stress disabilities. This loss of staff and absenteeism due to stress further increases the stress on those on the job. There is very low morale due to tremendous demands. It is important to set realistic case loads and job standards.

Decrease paperwork and red tape. Reduction of paperwork, forms, and red tape came up constantly in the interviews. This comment is representative, "The level of bureaucracy and red tape is overwhelming. Staff should be relieved of a huge paperwork burden. For example, record keeping for mileage is much too complicated."

These recommendations seem to form a cluster of related ideas. Those that follow are somewhat different in form.

Streamline management and improve human relations. Recommendations on managerial matters covered several areas:

1. It is important to aim for a suitable level of organizational equilibrium, "There should be greater stability on the part of the department."
2. Specific goals and delineated priorities are necessary, "Administrators have to define goals, procedures and services more clearly." Examples of useful cookbook-type manuals were mentioned several times, always positively.
3. Management people should be in close touch with program issues and field operations:

All supervisors and directors need to know every aspect of practice activity. But they do not. They are not aware of problems we face or of field needs. They should understand the complexities—that you may have to spend an entire day with one client. On paper this doesn't look good, of course. They should ask for our input about these things.

4. There should be a pattern of free exchange within the organization, "We need to have more open communication and greater sharing of information." The respondents noted that agency atmosphere or degree of social comfort influences their performance. Atmosphere was viewed as an important system variable subject to control by the agency management.
5. Practice is enhanced when agency staff members work as a team and combine efforts to improve one another's productivity. It is also helpful when staff identify one another as competent, successful professionals. Teamwork is especially beneficial when we face understaffing and limited resources. Positive influences were also reported when agency personnel included multilingual and multiethnic representatives on staff. In a team framework, they are readily available for consultation on client issues.

Clarify the practice role. The position of case manager should be clarified and upscaled, "There has to be a clear message on the part of the agency as to what our role and responsibilities are to be. The position of case manager should be upgraded. Right now there are no job specifications or job classifications that are appropriate."

There was a call for heightened client-centeredness in the organization, "Goals have to be clear and the rules especially have to be adjusted to make the client a real priority rather than a second thought."

Enhance physical facilities and field operations.   Several suggestions were made to improve field operations. Providing better physical facilities was one of these. Establishing a local unit computer capability to compile and keep data on community service resources was another. It was also recommended that specialized staff such as physicians and psychiatrists be available on a regularly scheduled basis to assist clients with assessment and treatment. More generally, there was a suggestion that local units or regions have greater responsibility in the use of resources, and that decision making be more decentralized.

Bolster coordination among community services.   Practitioners indicated that one of their central functions is linking clients to varied community services, but that many agencies are uncooperative, "There is a need for better coordination and integration of services. The agency should try on the policy level to increase resources in the community, and should provide better media coverage." This same point was discussed in the community section, but here the emphasis was more on what needed to be done internally and administratively.

Summary of Systemic Factors

The discussion has touched on a wide range of problems and related approaches for structuring and improving services. A few of the key points coming from the field are listed below. The solutions seem valid and obvious; implementing them presents a daunting challenge.

Problem	*Practitioner Recommendations*
Negative attitudes toward clients	Provide public education to improve understanding of clients.
Lack of support services, lack of coordination	Promote more resources for new programs; foster more interagency coordination and development.
Lack of understanding of case management	Conduct public education programs and clarity role definition.
Excessive paperwork and case loads	Reduce documentation demands and increase the staff/client ratio.
Lack of organizational coherence and stability	There should be specific goals and minimal policy change; administrators should be closer to field operations; there should be open communication and teamwork.

Lack of support for staff	There needs to be ample in-service training and clarification of the staff role within the organization.
Lack of funding and resources	Administrators should actively seek ample funds and resources.
Inadequate client-centeredness	Client well-being should be a clear and explicit priority.
Inadequate field services	Ample local facilities should be developed, possibly decentralize decision making.

The discussion has conveyed some of the flavor of practice as affected by community and organizational factors, especially in the large-city context. The ideas that were presented are suggestive of actions to consider on a broad policy basis (such as gaining more substantial funding for community supports), or in selected agency situations (such as strengthening teamwork).

EVALUATION OF SERVICES AND SOCIAL SYSTEM ENDORSEMENT

To carry out comprehensive enhancement practice, a baseline of social system endorsement is essential, including an appropriate level of funding and available facilitating services. The extent of community commitment is contingent on the degree of confidence the public has in the effectiveness of the service. "Does case management work?" is a valid question asked by community leaders and agency executives.

While contemporary case management is relatively new and not yet well researched, some number of evaluation studies have been conducted that shed light on its utility for the community. Much of that research was synthesized in the course of the UCLA studies (Rothman, 1992), and we draw on that compendium to provide a brief summary.

Such a review is impeded because of a lack of uniformity in measurement instruments, operational definitions, and outcome criteria. Also, research designs are often weak in experimental rigor. Replication is rare (Curry, 1981; Field & Yegge, 1982; Graham & Birchmore-Timney, 1989; Intagliata, 1982; McCoin, 1988; Muller, 1981; Rapp, 1983).

Evaluations of case management have tended to focus on either the social adjustment or quality of life of the client in the community, or the capacity of the client to remain in the community without being reinstitutionalized. Some studies have examined both of these variables. The majority of these studies arrived at positive assessments of case management in both dimensions, though a smaller set of studies found a negative association between case management and these outcome variables.

Evaluation in the field of aging has relied heavily on systems appraisals rather than outcomes for individual clients. Much of the funding for research has been sponsored by the United States Health Care Financing Administration, which has been concerned with Medicare/Medicaid performance and funding. For this reason the focus has been on prevalence of hospitalization and on costs. For example, the extensive Multipurpose Senior Services Program of California was evaluated in terms of "increasing efficiency" (Miller, 1988), defined as the number of days clients were able to function without a hospital stay and the dollar savings that accrued. Kane and Kane (1987) indicate that studies of long-term care of the elderly generally are concerned with quality, access to the system, and program costs. Quality issues they identify pertain not to client lifestyles, but to the performance levels of service organizations: licensing considerations, certification to receive governmental payment, inspection of care, and regulation of personnel.

Mental health research has emphasized evaluating effects on individuals, without eliminating systems considerations. Conversely, gerontological research has leaned toward evaluating systems. The preponderance of studies we review are drawn from the mental health field and focus on outcomes for individuals. This also is the orientating service perspective of this book.

POSITIVE OUTCOME STUDIES

Case management programs have been found to positively affect client adjustment to life in the community and to reduce the occurrences of reinstitutionalization (Bigelow & Young, 1983; Blume & Sovronsky, 1981; Bond et al., 1989; Brown & Learner, 1983; Bruce & Buehler, 1973; Byers, Cohen, & Harshberger, 1978; Curry, 1981; Dickstein, Hanig, & Grosskopf, 1988; Field & Yegge, 1982; Freddolino, Moxley, & Fleishman, 1989; Goering, Farkas et al., 1988; Goering, Wasylenki et al., 1988; Hammaker, 1983; Land, 1980; Lannon, Banks, & Morrissey, 1988; Madiasos & Economou, 1988; Modricin, Rapp, & Chamberlain, 1985; Modricin, Rapp, & Poertner, 1988; Morrow, 1984; Muller, 1981; Rapp, 1983; Rapp & Chamberlain, 1985; Rapp & Wintersteen, 1989; Silber, Braren, & Ellis, 1981; Smith & Smith, 1979; Stein & Test, 1980; Wasylenki et al., 1985; Wright, Heiman, Shupe, & Olvera, 1989; Yordi, 1982).

Provision of case management services has frequently been associated with improvements by clients on "quality of life" indices (Bigelow & Young, 1983; Caragonne, 1980; Curry, 1981; Field & Yegge, 1982; Goering, Farkas et al., 1988; Goering, Wasylenki et al., 1988; Modricin, Rapp, & Poertner, 1988; Muller, 1981; Rapp, 1983). Stein and Test (1980) have provided evidence of case management effects within a community-based, comprehensive service program intended to address the needs of chronically mentally disabled adults. This project addressed outcome measures to areas including client symptomatology, self-esteem, social functioning, life satisfaction and quality of life, and the burdens of clients to family or community. Numerous results across these areas indicate that the "case managed" approach to service delivery succeeds. Independent confirmation of these results is provided in work reported by King, Muraco, and Wells (1984). Their quasi-experimental design and relative rigor in the project's implementation foster a measure of confidence in their study's results.

Positive effects were also noted by Rapp (1983) in case management evaluation conducted at a community mental health center. In this study, case management services were administered and monitored for a group of 19 clients over a 7-month period. Case management effectiveness was assessed through levels of goal attainment clients achieved, clients' satisfaction with services, rehospitalization rates, and other measures. Case managers and clients negotiated goals as part of their involvement with each other, and these goals were categorized into one of nine identified life domains. Rapp reports that 61% of the established goals were achieved and 16% of the goals were partially achieved. The highest rates of goal attainment were found in the areas of medical/nutritional status, transportation, family life, and finances. None of the clients was rehospitalized during the intervention period.

Two studies (Bigelow & Young, 1983; Field & Yegge, 1982) included the effect of case management services on clients' quality of life, using both a common subject population and the same instrument for assessment of outcomes. Both projects examined quality of life for chronically mentally disabled adults, and measured outcome by comparing scores obtained at different times with the Oregon Quality of Life Questionnaire. Neither study assigned subjects randomly to groups; however, Bigelow and Young (1983) did include a control group of clients, thought to be comparable, who were not receiving case management services. In Field and Yegge's (1982) work, case management was left undefined and appears to have been one of a continuum of services possible during the intervention phase. In Bigelow and Young's (1983, p. 10) report, case management is "an intensive, systematic provision of services which otherwise exist informally and to a lesser extent in the human service system."

Field and Yegge (1982) pretested 106 clients and included 151 in the posttest phase that followed their 9-month intervention in case-management service provision. Although they report that there was little change on the posttest as measured by the Oregon Quality of Life Questionnaire, other life adjustment indices did improve. Improvements were noted in clients' employment and social activities, while self-reports indicated clients perceived their basic needs as being met more completely and to their greater satisfaction.

These favorable results need to be viewed cautiously because of methodological uncertainties, exceptions, and variations. For example, client improvements may disappear after intervention terminates (Freddolino, Moxley, & Fleishman, 1989) or results may differ for different types of clients, such as older versus younger client populations (Lannon et al., 1988).

Studies have demonstrated the positive effects of case management on the ability of the client to remain in a natural community setting without requiring a return to an institutional site (Anthony, Buell, Sharratt & Althoff, 1972; Claghorn & Kinross-Wright, 1971; Curry, 1981; Johnson, 1987; Land, 1980; Rapp, 1983; Wasylenki et al., 1985; Zolik, Lantz, & Sommers, 1968).

Positive results on maintaining clients in community settings were reported in work by Curry (1981). Three groups of chronically disabled clients were examined for comparison, and rehospitalization rates were linked to hospitalization rates in previous years for each client in the study. Seventy-one clients were given case-management services. Curry reported a 47% drop in hospitalizations overall for this group, and the length of hospitalization decreased from an average of 83.2 days per year to 49.9 days per year. Although case management was not explicitly defined in the study, the direct service aspects of the case manager's role were clarified. Case management was seen as a role incorporating skills in conversation, modeling, monitoring, information-giving, and listening, and these were quite obviously effective in producing dramatic decreases in institutionalization when offered within a format of aftercare planning and service delivery.

Hammaker (1983) reported a decline in both the recidivism and the lengths of hospital stays by chronically mentally ill adults after community support services were initiated. Hammaker tracked a random sample of 400 discharged state hospital patients after a community help program was begun. He used the patients' previous records of service consumption as the basis of comparison.

Some related evidence suggests that perhaps case management can function preventively for even a first hospitalization. According to Bruce and Buehler (1973), comprehensive case management services can potentially supplant hospital care entirely, or at least for some individuals who would previously have required hospitalization. They assessed community-agency assistance in aiding assimilation and community re-entry of all residents released from state mental hospitals in a California county during a 2-year study period. They suggest that some patients may not have needed treatment in a hospital setting at all, given appropriate community services. Brown and Learner (1983), in another service field, found that community-based services can prevent unnecessary admission of the elderly to nursing homes.

Case management service provision has been shown to enhance quality of life and reduce reinstitutionalization. Several studies show simultaneous attainment of these outcomes (Bigelow & Young, 1983; Bond et al., 1989; Rapp, 1983; Rapp & Wintersteen, 1986, 1989; Silber, Braren, & Ellis, 1981; Smith & Smith, 1979; Wright et al., 1989).

Smith and Smith (1979) evaluated 130 mental patients discharged to the community from two state hospitals, examining indices for family and living situation, educational/vocational plans and competencies, specific aftercare needs, and successful community readjustment and rehospitalization. Discharged patients were assigned to social workers who recorded patient progress in these areas. Clients' lowered recidivism and more positive community adjustment were significantly influenced by case management service and the availability of appropriate community resources.

Rapp and Wintersteen (1986) studied 155 young-adult, chronically mentally ill clients in seven different settings, each with different sets of personnel. The project was interesting in that an explicit aim of the work was to test a particular model of case management, and the multiple sites provided a way to permit systematic replication. Results were almost uniformly positive with respect to clients' success in avoiding rehospitalization and achieving numerous life quality-enhancing goals. Perhaps more impressive was that six of seven client groups manifested improved outcomes on all posttest measures and demonstrated the potential of the developmental-acquisition case management approach.

A parallel comprehensive review of relevant research studies aimed at assessing efficacy is worth examining. Solomon (1992) reviewed 20 studies that included a range of different case management approaches. That review concluded that case management is particularly effective in reducing the number of rehospitalizations and contracting the length of stay. Stated differently, it served to maintain clients in community living. It also improved quality of life and garnered a high level of treatment satisfaction from clients. Emergency room use and contact with the criminal/legal system had fewer positive outcomes. There were also limited results in the clinical realm of social functioning and symptomatology. The author notes that the service is community and system oriented, "Therefore it is not surprising that case management appears to affect system outcomes, e.g., rehospitalization, more than clinical outcomes" (Solomon, 1992, p. 177).

NEGATIVE SERVICE RESULTS

Although there is a body of evidence indicating the efficacy of case management, a smaller number of studies indicate lack of association between case management and positive client outcomes (Byers, Cohen, & Harshberger, 1978; Callahan, 1989; Coulton & Frost, 1982; Franklin et al., 1987; Wasylenki et al., 1985).

Byers and her coworkers (1978) investigated community case management service provision and recidivism rates of all patients discharged in a 2-year period from a large state mental hospital. This was a sophisticated, well-designed study that used multiple-regression statistical techniques and produced unusually firm and specific conclusions. Byers and colleagues found that case-management services alone were not sufficient to produce positive client outcomes. Their effect depended significantly on the quality and quantity of resources and needed services that were available in the community.

Similarly negative assessments appear in work by Johnson and Rubin (1983), who ultimately conclude that though case management does not appear to be harmful, there is no definitive evidence that it enhances outcomes for clients.

Strong negative evidence was reported by Franklin and associates (1987), who indicated that their case-managed clients differed unfavorably from non–case-managed controls in several ways, including more frequent rehospitalizations, more service consumption, and larger fiscal expenditures, as well as no concomitant improvements in quality of life indicators. This particular study is worthy of note because of the rigorous design and careful procedures that were attempted.

Coulton and Frost (1982) found that receiving case management services had no effect on the extent to which elderly clients used or declined mental health services. In a broad review of existing research, Callahan (1989) concluded that case management for the elderly is not a "panacea," and that the research fails to affirm its effectiveness.

COST-EFFECTIVENESS

Cost-effectiveness is another important aspect of evaluation that has come into prominence as budget reductions and service cutbacks have infiltrated the human services. This makes it more difficult to draw firm conclusions as evaluating cost-effectiveness in case management studies is even newer than evaluating service outcome effectiveness.

Studies have shown that there are favorable economic correlates of case management. For example, Wright and associates (1989) reported a reduction in hospital days and events, jail incarcerations and charges, and billings per patient in a program for severely disturbed mental patients. A study of elderly patients showed that those receiving long-term care avoided unnecessary institutionalization and defrayed Medicaid and Medicare expenditures (Brown & Learner, 1983). Similar findings are reported by Dickstein, Hanig, and Grosskopf (1988).

Franklin and associates (1987) found, however, that clients under case management showed worse progress at higher costs. An analysis of elders having managed-care service found few differences in comparison with clients not in the demonstration project, except that project patients made more visits to health clinics and had longer hospital stays for medical procedures at higher costs (Wan, 1989). Borland, McRea, and Lycan (1989) discovered in a group of thought-disordered patients that hospital cost-savings were offset by increased community-care expenditures.

Clearly results are not final on the cost dimensions of case management. Methodological aspects of cost-effectiveness research, perhaps an issue in these results, were discussed previously in Chapter 1. Even though dollars are more tangible and accessible to analyze than service outcomes, such as quality of life, there are concerns about the weakness and lack of agreement on measurements and methodology. For the time being, the cost-effectiveness of case management is an open question with evidence supporting both sides. Tentative assumptions and exploratory program development are warranted.

The studies suggest that case management can be effective, and point to a number of variables that can potentially enhance effectiveness. Communities can have a reasonable degree of confidence about the approach, but should not be sanguine. A positive but exploratory outlook seems justified.

PANACEA VERSUS COP OUT: A SUMMING UP

Two opposing views of case management are described by Austin (1992) in a thought-provoking paper. One position seems to view case management as a panacea for the problems of the highly vulnerable. The approach has been compared to a silver bullet, "Like the Lone Ranger's ammunition, [it] is expected to eliminate serious problems in a single shot, with no extra costs and few unintended secondary consequences" (Brecher & Knickman, 1985, p. 245). Political leaders and professionals who spearheaded the deinstitutionalization movement sometimes lauded the community-based service approach in ecstatic terms, seeing it as a humane and liberating antidote to suffocating backwards and custodial guardhouses. This is reflected vividly in *One Flew Over the Cuckoo's Nest*, by way of Kesey's vision of clients who thrive when set loose from the fetters of a mental hospital.

Others discount case management as a gimmick and a cop out, seeing it mainly as a convenient device to save money by emptying out large and expensive physical facilities and dumping clients on the streets without ample service back-up. According to this view, case management is used by canny politicians to protect the public coffers while giving the illusion of meeting the needs of people—echoing Henry Cabot Lodge's plaintive query to Theodore Roosevelt during the 1902 coal strike, "Is there something we can appear to be doing?"

It is evident from the formidable enumeration of problems outlined earlier in the chapter that the case-management approach is no cure all. At the same time, it is a considered response to the compelling needs of vulnerable groups, with justification provided by evaluation studies as well as illustrations from practice throughout this book. It is also a response to the failure of the human services system to tackle those needs, and in some ways is "an indictment of existing organizational and interorganizational patterns" (Rose, 1992, p. vii).

The rationale and thrust of comprehensive enhancement practice seems to hold promise and merit encouragement. Intrinsic to the rationale is the fundamental assumption that there will be a baseline of community resources to support the linking function of the practice. Without that reality, case management can be an instrument contributing to the abandonment of the dependent, disabled, and deinstitutionalized in the service of fiscal exigency. Serious professionals may, with reason, lend themselves to this service thrust, but with an eye toward not being used in cynical ways that diminish society's commitment to the most needful. Professionals should take care to not participate in "appearing to do something."

The path of wisdom surely would be to fight on various fronts and levels for the range of necessary community resources, while continuing to aid people in the existing case-management framework. If all else fails, the path instead might be to refuse to collaborate in a faulty and potentially corrupt enterprise and to seek other means to cope with this set of critical human needs. A valid immediate objective is to mount a true test, involving competent and cogent implementation of the practice paradigm undergirding case management, buttressed by ample community support resources. From that vantage point, further directions can be plotted in an informed and constructive way.

REFERENCES

Anthony, W., Buell, G., Sharratt, S., & Althoff, M. (1972). Efficacy of psychiatric rehabilitation. *Psychological Bulletin, 78,* 447–456.

Austin, C. D. (1992, February). *When the whole is more than the sum of its parts: Case management issues from a systems perspective.* Paper presented at The First International Conference on Long-Term Care Case Management, Seattle, WA.

Bigelow, D. & Young, D. (1983). *Effectiveness of a case management program.* Unpublished manuscript, University of Washington, Graduate School of Nursing, Seattle.

Blume, R. & Sovronsky, H. (1981). Establishing a countrywide community support system for mental health care. *Hospital and Community Psychiatry, 32,* 633–635.

Bond, G. R., Witheridge, T. F., Wasmer, D., Dincin, J. (1989). A comparison of two crisis housing alternatives to psychiatric hospitalization. *Hospital and Community Psychiatry, 40,* 177–183.

Borland, A., McRea, J., & Lycan, C. (1989). Outcomes of five years of continuous intensive case management. *Hospital and Community Psychiatry, 40,* 369–376.

Brecher, C. & Knickman, J. (1985). A reconsideration of long-term care policy. *Journal of Health Politics, Policy and Law, 10*(2).

Brown, T. & Learner, R. M. (1983). The South Carolina community long term care project. *Home Health Care Services Quarterly, 4,* 73–78.

Bruce, D. & Buehler, R. (1973). Post state hospital adjustment and community service utilization of persons released after July 1, 1973. *Exchange, 1*(6), 26–31.

Byers, E., Cohen, S., & Harshberger, D. (1978). Impact of aftercare services on recidivism of mental hospital patients. *Community Mental Health Journal, 14*(1), 26–34.

Callahan, J. J. (1989). Case management for the elderly: A panacea? *Journal of Aging and Social Policy, 1*(1/2).

Caragonne, P. (1980). An analysis of the function of the case manager in four mental health social service settings (Doctoral dissertation, University of Texas). *Dissertation Abstracts International, 41,* 3262A.

Claghorn, J. & Kinross-Wright, J. (1971). Reduction in hospitalization of schizophrenics. *American Journal of Psychiatry, 128,* 344–347.

Coulton, C. & Frost, A. (1982). Use of social and health services by the elderly. *Journal of Health and Social Behavior, 23*, 330–339.

Curry, J. (1981). A study in case management. *Community Support Service Journal, 2*, 15–17.

Dickstein, D., Hanig, D., & Grosskopf, B. (1988). Reducing costs in a community support program. *Hospital and Community Psychiatry, 39*, 1033–1035.

Field, G. & Yegge, L. (1982). A client outcome study of a community support demonstration project. *Psychosocial-Rehabilitation Journal, 6*(2), 15–22.

Fleming, M. L. & York, J. L. (1989). The community support system concept: Implementing a community support system in an urban setting [Special issue]. *Psychosocial-Rehabilitation Journal, 12*(3), 41–53.

Franklin, J., Solovitz, B., Mason, M., Clemmons, J., & Miller, G. (1987). An evaluation of case management. *American Journal of Public Health, 77*, 674–678.

Freddolino, P. P., Moxley, D. P., & Fleishman, J. A. (1989). An advocacy model for people with long-term psychiatric disabilities. *Hospital and Community Psychiatry, 40*, 1169–1174.

Goering, P. N., Farkas, M., Wasylenki, D. A., Lancee, W. J. et al. (1988). Improved functioning for case management clients. *Psychosocial-Rehabilitation Journal, 12*(1), 3–17.

Goering, P. N., Wasylenki, D. A., Farkas, M., Lancee, W. J. et al. (1988). What difference does case management make? *Hospital and Community Psychiatry, 39*, 272–276.

Graham, K. & Birchmore-Timney, C. (1989). The problem of replicability in program evaluation: The component solution using the example of case management. *Evaluation and Program Planning, 12*, 179–187.

Hammaker, R. (1983). A client outcome evaluation of the statewide implementation of community support services. *Psychosocial-Rehabilitation Journal, 7*(1), 2–10.

Hereford, R. W. (1989). The market for community services for older persons. *Pride Institute Journal of Long-Term Home Health Care, 8*(1), 44–51.

Intagliata, J. (1982). Improving the quality of community care for the chronically mentally disabled: The role of case management. *Schizophrenia Bulletin, 8*(4), 655–674.

Johnson, C. A. (1987). Readmission to the mental hospital: An indicator of quality of care? *Journal of Mental Health Administration, 14*(1), 51–55.

Johnson, P. (1980). Community support systems for the mentally ill: A study of the general public, mental health workers, and board members in Leon County, Florida, 1979–1980 (Doctoral dissertation, Florida State University). *Dissertation Abstracts International, 41*, 1216A.

Johnson, P. & Beditz, J. (1981). Community support systems: Scaling community acceptance. *Community Mental Health Journal, 17*, 153–160.

Kane, R. (1985). Case management in health settings. In M. Weil & J. M. Karls (Eds.), *Case management in human service practice* (pp. 170–203). San Francisco: Jossey-Bass.

Kane, R. A. & Kane, R. L. (1987). *Long-term care: Principles, programs and policies.* New York: Springer.

King, J., Muraco, W., & Wells, J. (1984). *Case management: A study of patient outcomes.* Columbus: Ohio Department of Mental Health, Office of Program Evaluations and Research.

Land, D. (1980). Evaluation of community support system development in New York State: A preliminary review. *Community Support Service Journal, 5*, 3–6.

Lannon, P. B., Banks, S. M., & Morrissey, J. P. (1988). Community tenure patterns of the New York State CSS population: A longitudinal impact assessment. *Psychosocial-rehabilitation journal, 11*(4), 47–60.

Madiasos, M. G. & Economou, M. (1988). Preventing disability and relapse in schizophrenia: II. Psychosocial techniques and working with families: Negative symptoms in schizophrenia: The effect of long-term, community-based psychiatric intervention [Special issue]. *International Journal of Mental Health, 17*(1), 22–34.

McCoin, J. M. (1988). Adult foster care, case management, and quality of life: Interpretive literature review. *Adult Foster Care Journal, 2,* 135–148.

Miller, L. S. (1988). Increasing efficiency in community-based, long-term care for the frail elderly. *Social Work Research and Abstracts, 24*(2), 7–14.

Modricin, M., Rapp, C. A., & Chamberlain, R. (1985). *Case management with psychiatrically disabled individuals: Curriculum and training manual.* Lawrence: University of Kansas, School of Social Work.

Modricin, M., Rapp, C. A., & Poertner, J. (1988). The evaluation of case management services with the chronically mentally ill. *Evaluation and Program Planning, 11,* 306–314.

Morrow, H. (1984). Functional change in the elderly: Results of the multipurpose senior services project (Doctoral dissertation, University of California, Berkeley). *Dissertation Abstracts International, 20,* 1050.

Muller, J. (1981). Alabama Community Support Project evaluation on the implementation of initial outcomes of a model case management system. *Community Support Service Journal, 2,* 1–4.

National Conference on Social Welfare (1981). *Case management: State of the art* (Grant no. 54-P-71542/3-01). Washington, DC: Administration on Developmental Disabilities, U. S. Department of Health and Human Services.

Rapp, C. A. (1983). *Community mental health case management project: Final report.* Lawrence: University of Kansas, School of Social Work.

Rapp, C. A. & Chamberlain, R. (1985). Case management services for the chronically mentally ill. *Social Work, 30,* 414–422.

Rapp, C. A., & Wintersteen, R. (1989). The strengths model of case management: Results from twelve demonstrations. *Psychosocial-Rehabilitation Journal, 13*(1), 23–32.

Rose, S. (1992). *Case management and social work practice.* New York: Longman.

Rothman, J. (1992). *Guidelines for case management: Putting research to professional use.* Itasca, IL: F. E. Peacock.

Rubin, A. (1987). Case management. In A. Minahan (Ed.), *Encyclopedia of Social Work* (pp. 212–222). Silver Springs, MD: National Association of Social Workers.

Silber, B., Braren, M., & Ellis, C. (1981). Rehospitalization rates and function levels of patients discharged to a comprehensive community support system. *Journal of Mental Health Administration, 8*(2), 24–29.

Smith, C. J. & Smith, C. A. (1979). Evaluating outcome measures for deinstitutionalized programs. *Social Work Research and Abstracts, 15*(2), 23–30.

Solomon, P. (1992). The efficacy of case management services for severely mentally disabled clients. *Community Mental Health Journal, 28*(3), 163–180.

Stein, L. & Test, M. (1980). Alternative to mental hospital treatment. *Archives of General Psychiatry, 37,* 392–397.

Wan, T. T. & Weissert, W. B. (1981). Social support networks, patient status, and institutionalization. *Research on Aging, 3,* 240–256.

Wasylenki, D. A., Goering, P. N., Lancee, W. J., Ballantyne, R., & Farkas, M. (1985). Impact of case manager program on psychiatric care. *Journal of Nervous and Mental Disease, 173,* 303–308.

Weil, M. (1985). Adapting case management to specific programs and needs. In M. Weil & J. M. Karls (Eds.), *Case management in human service practice* (pp. 317–356). San Francisco: Jossey-Bass.

Wright, R. G., Heiman, J. R., Shupe, J., & Olvera, G. (1989). Defining and measuring stabilization of patients during 4 years of intensive community support. *American Journal of Psychiatry, 146,* 1293–1298.

Yordi, C. (1982). Service integration: The impacts of a comprehensive continuum of services for the frail and elderly on the quality and cost of long-term care (Doctoral dissertation, University of California, Berkeley). *Dissertation Abstracts International, 16,* 1085.

Zald, M. N. (1989). Organizations as polities: An analysis of community organization agencies. In F. M. Cox, J. L. Erlich, J. Rothman, & J. E. Tropman (Eds). *Strategies of community organization: Macro practice* (pp. 243–254). Itasca, IL: F. E. Peacock.

Zolik, E., Lantz, E., & Sommers, R. (1968). Hospital return rates and pre-release referrals. *Archives of General Psychiatry, 18,* 712–717.

Appendix

METHODOLOGY OF THE UCLA STUDY

OBJECTIVES AND GENERAL DESIGN

The study commenced with representatives of the University of California, Los Angeles, School of Social Welfare and the Los Angeles County Department of Mental Health coming together to consider the possibility of initiating a collaborative research and development project. The School, through its newly formed Center for Child and Family Policy Studies, offered its research capabilities to support systematic knowledge development and informed problem-solving. The Department offered access to a significant social agency grappling with fundamental urban problems of concern to academic researchers with human service interests. After deliberation, both parties agreed that the collaborative effort would go forward, and the Department indicated its desire to have case management constitute the focus of study.

There were several reasons for this choice. Nationwide, there has been a lack of clarity about definitions of the case management role, and this was reflected in the Department as well, including the existence of several different modes of practice. The California state-level case management program (Office of Mental Health Social Services) had recently been shifted over to county mental health departments, creating a problem of organizational integration. In addition, despite the best efforts of service programs, long-term clients in most urban areas, including Los Angeles, were escaping the web of service. Many clients placed extreme pressures on their families, and some wandered the streets, expanding the ranks of the homeless. Others exhibited bizarre behavior that sometimes posed a danger to themselves or a threat to innocent citizens. These circumstances had negative ramifications, both professional and political.

In response to these issues, the research project sought both to obtain data and to formulate an intervention design that would provide a more systematic framework for service. With the concurrence of the Department, an initial intervention research study plan was developed, composed of the following elements.

1. *A comprehensive meta-analytical synthesis of existing research findings was performed in order to assemble what was known nationally about case management.* The research staff systematically derived implications from this knowledge pool of some 135 studies for the purpose of intervention design.

2. *A written questionnaire census was taken of all staff in the Department identified as carrying out case management functions.* A profile of such staff was developed initially, including personal demographic factors, job-related factors, such as years in the position, and case load factors.

3. *A survey involving intensive field interviews with 48 case managers was conducted, drawing the sample from the census data.* The survey sought practitioner views of the functions of case management, how they are carried out, typical problems encountered, and recommendations for enhancing service effectiveness.

Through these diverse activities and data sources a new empirically based model of practice would be devised, specifying intervention functions and the sequence and dynamics of implementing them. It was hoped that a triangulation approach encompassing several sources of data would be especially useful in clarifying a human services role that is emergent, amorphous, and has limited professional consensus.

After an initial model of practice was constructed, a panel of experienced practitioners, who were rated as highly competent, reviewed it and suggested refinements. This working model was then pilot-tested for implementability by a small group of practitioners in a typical agency setting. Support has also been obtained from the National Institute of Mental Health (NIMH) for a projected study to evaluate outcomes with clients through use of the model.

Because the methodology of the meta-analytic research synthesis aspect and of the procedure used in the pilot test of the initial practice model has been reported elsewhere (Rothman, 1980; Rothman, Damron-Rodriguez, & Shenassa, 1993; Rothman & Tumlin, 1993), this discussion focuses on the field survey of practitioner views and experiences.

The overall approach followed an intervention research design and development methodology (Rothman & Thomas, 1993), also variously termed *developmental research* (Thomas, 1984), *social R&D* (Rothman, 1980), *experiential social innovation* (Fairweather, 1967), *behavioral community research* (Fawcett, 1990), and *modal development research* (Paine, Bellamy, & Wilcox, 1989). A chief purpose is to create or improve human service interventions through use of systematic research procedures. Both knowledge about aspects of intervention and the concrete development of intervention technology are advanced through this approach.

THE SAMPLE

Design of the interview study suggested inclusion of approximately 50 case managers in the sample. Three case management roles were identified in the agency census. The number of initially proposed interviewees for each of these is listed below:

Professional continuing-care workers carrying mainly case manager functions	20
Professional primary therapists with 20% or more case manager functions	20
Paraprofessional workers with 20% or more case manager functions	5 to 10

The objective was to obtain a purposive, stratified sample of the main case manager roles in the organization.

The approach was to select respondents by facility to ease data collection. Interviews were held at a subset of the sites that previously responded to the initially mailed case manager questionnaire survey that was used to do a census of staff. For the continuing-care group, there were 15 facilities, from which we retained a core group of ten sites in the sample. Those eliminated duplicated or overrepresented important variables (ethnicity, geographic location, clientele, staffing). In selected sites we aimed for two case managers per facility, giving us our sample of 20. Because results of the previous census indicated that all continuing-care workers predominantly do case management, we were able to sample participants randomly from within these facilities.

Thirteen primary therapy facilities were in the census data, and following elimination of overrepresented sites (according to the same criteria), ten sites remained in the sample. Again, we sought two workers from each facility to obtain the required 20 primary-therapist case managers. Interviewee selection was more complicated here, however, as the census suggested that only a portion of these workers carried substantive case management functions (20% or more of their time). In this instance, therefore, we sought additional information from potential interviewees during our initial telephone contacts with them to make appropriate interviewee selections and appointments. From a random listing, the first ones to meet the work criterion were selected.

Overall, two respondents were sought from each of the ten continuing-care facilities, and the ten primary-therapy outpatient centers. A few facilities with a greater or lesser proportion of appropriate professional staff had a slightly weighted selection. When the total staff in a facility was particularly large, one or two workers were added above the standard two. Similarly, when staff was particularly small, the standard two were reduced by one in a few instances.

As the census results indicated that there were very few paraprofessional workers in the agency, the final number of these to be included for in-depth interviews was left open, and it was planned that, if possible, we would interview the universe of those who worked in the 20 sample sites. In the end, eight were identified and included.

In initial calls, if a case manager was unavailable, refused to be interviewed, or had schedule conflicts, the next person on the sampling list was contacted. Serious recruitment problems never developed. This required flexibility and patience in terms of the time of appointments, conditional arrangements, and rescheduling.

FIELD PROCEDURES

A top administrator in the County Department of Mental Health addressed a letter to practitioners in the selected sites. This letter informed recipients that the research project was continuing beyond the mailed questionnaire census and into a second phase, and that more in-depth data would now be collected. Recipients of this letter were encouraged to participate and were informed that UCLA staff would soon contact them with details about involvement in the next phase of the study.

Subsequent to this, a letter from the project director at UCLA was sent to case managers at the 20 facilities. The letter described the upcoming field interview phase, and indicated that a member of the project staff would call personally to arrange an interview. The notions of confidentiality and voluntary participation were emphasized in this letter, and time allotment for an interview (approximately 2 hours) was clearly indicated.

As a follow-up measure, a member of the research project assigned to the facility contacted sampled staff in order to make necessary arrangements for field interviews. Four individuals served in a field interviewer capacity, and each one conducted about 25% of the interviews. Assignments of these staff members were divided evenly across all facility locations to achieve balance among them. All four interviewers were advanced graduate school students from UCLA's School of Public Health, and all had previous research experience and prior training in survey and interview techniques.

Before data collection ensued, several training sessions were held, and each staff member was observed by the other project staff as they conducted a practice interview to familiarize themselves with procedural requirements and to standardize the work. Established instructions for conduct of field interviews were also formalized, put in writing, and thoroughly discussed by the group. Interviewing guidelines directed project staff to do the following:

> Write as much as necessary during the interview, but not more.
> Do the final write-up as soon as possible after the interview.
> Get word-for-word quotations whenever someone makes a particularly striking or clarifying remark.
> Keep the interview on track, at the same time leaving room for flexible responses and follow-up questions as necessary.

A standard format for introducing the interview was also developed, as was a script for preliminary telephone appointments in which invitations to participate were initially extended to the sample. All interviews were completed within approximately 8 weeks.

DATA COLLECTION AND ANALYSIS

The specific interview format that was followed made use of a 24-topic, semi-structured instrument containing primarily open-ended probe items, but including also a small number of forced-choice or check-listed questions. *The form is reproduced at the end of this Appendix.* The questionnaire focused on the following:

> functions and tasks performed as a case manager;
> obstacles and problems encountered in role performance; and
> recommendations for facilitating role implementation.

As is evident, the study was designed specifically to gather data on case management functions that are performed by practitioners in the field as perceived and reported by them. These would later be collated conceptually with a meta-analysis of case management research studies. Field interviews were conducted in person, at the interviewee's work site, and in conformance with specific scheduling needs or restrictions. Each of the 48 interviews that were ultimately completed lasted at least 2 hours, although a few continued for a 3-hour period.

Data analysis techniques were relatively simple and straightforward. The quantitative items were tabulated routinely and there was, primarily, use of means, medians, and ranges in analyzing responses.

Qualitative measures involved identifying basic concepts or themes inductively from the open-ended responses, going back and coding all responses within these categories, and then quantifying these in terms of means.

Three common training and practice sessions were held for three analysts in order to encourage uniform interpretations and approaches in the analytic task. The project director added reliability across analysts by reviewing and responding to all analytic work, thus serving as a second collaborating analyst.

Quotations from respondents are meant to be as exact as possible in reflecting the thoughts and specific words of those interviewed, but, because of the length and complexity of the interviews, these comments may not be absolutely identical to the original language. The reader should be aware of this potential minor discrepancy.

While there was an initial assumption that the three roles of continuing care, primary therapist, and paraprofessional might yield distinctly different patterns of response, this generally did not occur. For the purposes of the project it was considered most useful to combine the categories and present an aggregate or cross-cutting profile of practice among this cohort of staff.

The study is largely qualitative and heuristic in nature. It was intended to assist in formulating a model of practice, which would be systematically field-tested in a subsequent development stage.

REFERENCES

Fairweather, G. (1967). *Methods for experimental social innovation.* New York: John Wiley & Sons.

Fawcett, S. B. (1990). Some emerging standards for community research and action. In P. Tolan, C. Keys, F. Chertok, & L. E. Jason, (Eds.), *Researching community psychology: Integrating theories and methodologies* (pp. 64–75). Washington, DC: American Psychological Association.

Paine, S. C., Bellamy, G. T., & Wilcox, B. (1984). *Human services that work: From innovation to standard practice.* Baltimore, MD: Paul H. Brookes.

Rothman, J. (1980). *Social R & D: Research and development in the human services.* Englewood Cliffs, NJ: Prentice-Hall.

Rothman, J., Damron-Rodriguez, J., & Shenassa, E. (1993). Systematic research synthesis: Conceptual integration methods of meta-analysis. In J. Rothman & E. J. Thomas (Eds.), *Intervention research: Design and development of human services.* Binghamton, NY: Haworth Press.

Rothman, J. & Thomas, E. J. (Eds.). (1993). *Intervention research: Design and development of human services.* Binghamton, NY: Haworth Press.

Rothman, J. & Tumblin, A. (1993). Pilot testing and early development of a model of case management. In J. Rothman & E. J. Thomas (Eds.), *Intervention research: Design and development of human services.* Binghamton, NY: Haworth Press.

Thomas, E. J. (1984). *Designing interventions for the helping professions.* Beverly Hills, CA: Sage Publications.

STUDY QUESTIONNAIRE

UCLA/DEPARTMENT OF MENTAL HEALTH
CASE MANAGEMENT STUDY INTERVIEW FORMAT

Date of Interview: Interviewer:
Facility: Case Manager:

THE CASE MANAGEMENT PROCESS

In this interview I will be speaking with you about your activities and views concerning case management. First we will look at the tasks involved in the case management process.

FUNCTIONS

This sheet (*let the interviewee have a copy of the sheet*) lists a set of functions that have sometimes been associated with case management. (*The sheet is at the end of the questionnaire.*)

1. Based on your own experience in the Department of Mental Health, would you *eliminate* any functions from this list? Which ones?

2. Would you *add* any functions, again based on your experience? Which ones?

3. Would you *re-arrange* the chronological order in any way, using the new set of functions?

Now let's go back to the *first function* on the new list.

4a. Do you perform this function as part of your case management role?

4b. What are the main things you do in carrying this out? What activities are necessary to implement it?

4c. Is there anything that facilitates your performing this function?

4d. Is there anything that hinders your performing this function?

4e. Is there anything else that it would be useful for me to know about this function?

4f. In a typical week, how many hours do you spend doing this function?

Now, let's go on to the second function. (*Repeat the set of questions for the listed functions.*)

5a. Would you like to devote more time to some of these functions? Which ones? Why?

5b. What keeps you from doing that?

6a. Do you work part time or full time?

6b. What percentage of your time do you give to case management? ___%

6c. Is that work on your own or on a team or group basis? Explain.

EFFECTIVE CASE MANAGEMENT

7. Tell me what you think is required for effective case management to occur. In other words, what do you think is the secret of good case management?
   [Practitioner(s) (including self), clients, families, the Department (including local facility), community] [Probe for definition of effectiveness]

8a. What has been the most successful part of your experience as a case manager?

8b. How do you define or measure success?

9. To what do you attribute your success?
   [Practitioner(s) (including self), clients, families, the Department (including local facility), community]

COMMUNITY AND ORGANIZATIONAL INFLUENCES

10a. Is there something distinctive about _____ (specify the geographic region) that gives case management a unique form here?
   [Practitioner(s), clients, families, the Department, the community]

10b. Why is it unique and what makes it different?

11a. Is there anything specific about _____ (indicate the name of the local facility where the respondent works) that gives case management a unique form here?

11b. Why is it unique and what makes it different?

PROBLEMS

12. What are some of the main problems you face in doing case management? (Probe for each.)
    Practitioner(s), including self:

    Clients:

    Families:

    The Department, including local facility:

    The community:

13. What are some of the main service gaps you encounter in working with clients?

14. When there is such a service gap, are there any things you do? (Probe for locating or developing new providers, or activating the Department.)

15. What problems do you have with service providers, particularly agencies in the community that are essential to your clients?

16. What problems do you have with informal social support networks, including the family?

17. What administrative problems do you encounter in your daily work?

18a. What are some crisis situations you typically face with clients?

18b. What are some things you typically do when these crises arise?

18c. Can you generally handle these situations in an adequate way?

Yes   No

18d. How could you be enabled to deal with crisis situations more adequately? (Probe for Department, the community)

I would like to ask you about the client group that is hard to handle, requires frequent acute services, recurrent hospitalization, and sporadic emergency treatment.

19a. A board-and-care home calls you to state that a client of yours in this category is having hallucinations that are causing behaviors threatening to other clients. What do you consider your most therapeutic intervention, given no limitations on resources?

19b. If the patient were living at home with the family, would you do anything differently?

20. What can case managers do to optimize maintaining hard to handle patients in board-and-care facilities or with their families?

RECOMMENDATIONS

21. What recommendations would you make to strengthen the case management process and program in the Department? [Probe for each]

Practitioner(s):

Clients:

Families and informal support networks:

The Department (including local facility, administrative arrangement, and procedures):

The community, including service providers, gaps, etc.:

22. Since you started working in this program, have you initiated any major changes in the way you do things or in the procedures?

                                                Yes   No

    What are they?

    Why did you make them?

    Have other staff adopted the change(s)?

23. If you could design a case management program from scratch, based on your experience here, what changes would you make?

24. What advice would you give to a new case manager coming into this agency?

INITIAL LIST OF CASE MANAGEMENT FUNCTIONS

1. Client Identification and Outreach
2. Intake
3. Psychosocial Assessment
4. Goal Setting
5. Resource Identification and Indexing
6. Getting General Agreement by Community Agencies
7. Direct Treatment (Therapy)
8. Service Planning
9. Counseling
10. Linking Clients to Needed Services and Supports
11. Monitoring Service Delivery
12. Reassessment
13. Advocacy
14. Client Evaluation

Subject Index

Page numbers followed by t and f denote tables and figures, respectively.

Acceptability, of intervention plan, 104
Access, 233–249
  components of, 233–235
  facilitation of, practice guidelines for, 239–249
  interrelationship of, 234
  roles in providing, 239–240
  understanding, 233–239
ACCESS [channeling project], 238–239
Accessibility
  agency, 26, 95
  of informal network, 158, 166
Accountability, for assessment, 70
Accountability audits, 226
Activities of daily living, assessment of, 72,
  76t–77t, 78, 79f
Adaptive balance, 43
Addams, Jane, 40
Administration on Aging, 136, 139
Administrative authority, 139
Administrative channels, use of, 264
Administrative procedures, joint, 225–226
Advertising, 247
Advice, provided by informal network, 154,
  163–164
Advocacy, 32, 53, 199–217. *See also* Self-advocacy
  and access issues, 235
  applications of, 202–203
  case, 204
  and case management, 200–201
  characteristics of, 202
  and community context, 264
  concept of, 200
  connection to linking, 137–138
  constraints on, 207–208
  external, 201
  forms of, 205–207, 212
  group, 32, 204
  influence base for, 208
  internal, 201
  modes and tactics for, 204–207, 212–215, 213t
  practice guidelines for, 208–216
  psychological pressure in, 215–216
  purpose of, 201–202

  successful, guidelines for, 215
  target of, 209, 211–212, 215–216
  timing of, 210–211
  understanding, 200–208
Advocacy planning, framework for, 208–210
Advocate, role of, 201–202, 205
Agency(ies). *See also* Interagency coordination
  accessibility of, 26, 95
  and assessment, 69–71
  competition among, 223
  contact with, for linkage, initiation of,
   146–147
  fees, 95
  interdependence of, 223–224, 232
  key characteristics of, identification of,
   94–96, 96f
  linking clients to. *See* Formal linkage
  problems with, during monitoring process,
   184
  resource, identification of, 231
  uncooperative, 195
  visibility, promotion of, 246–249
Aggression, excessive, intervention planning
  for, 106–107
Aging. *See* Elderly
AIRS. *See* National Alliance of Information
  and Referral Services
Alcoholics Anonymous, 157
Alliance for the Mentally Ill (AMI), 235, 265
American Psychological Association, 200
Andrus Gerontology Center, University of
  Southern California, 174
Antecedents, 119
Appraisal. *See* Assessment
Appropriateness, of service, determination
  of, 61, 102
Assertive extension, 237
Assertiveness, low, intervention planning for,
  105–106
Assessment, 27, 68–80, 85–86. *See also*
  Reassessment
  activities, frequency of, 68t, 69
  agency/community factors in, 70–71

Assessment (*Cont.*)
  basic components of, 68–70
  of formal agency support, 73–78
  framework for, 71
  of informal support, 73
  information gathered during, integration of, 80, 83
  practice guidelines for, 71–78
  of practice relationship, 71
  purpose of, 68
  of specific needs, 71–73
  tools for, 78–80
  understanding, 68–71
Associated Charities of Boston, 135
Atmosphere, agency, 269
At-risk population, 240, 241f
Attainment, of treatment-service plan, high potential for, 99
Attitudes
  client, addressed during intake interview, 63
  community, 256–257, 260, 270
Audits, accountability, 226
Authority
  for advocacy, 209
  and effective linking, 138–139
  and interagency coordination, 222, 231–232
  and monitoring procedures, 179–180, 184
Availability
  around-the-clock, 15
  of service, 95

Barriers
  to advocacy, 207–208
  to formal linkage, 140–141
  to interagency coordination, 220–221
  language, 37, 258
  to reassessment, 195
  to treatment-service plan, 100
Behavioral approach, 119–120, 176
Behavioral functioning, assessment of, 73, 74t–75t
Behavioral rehearsal, 108, 119
Behavioral techniques, 125–126. *See also* Modeling; Role playing
Blind, organizations aiding, access analysis of, 236
Boundary-spanning approach, 14
Buddy system, 106
Budgeting, joint, 225
Bureau of Census, 245
Burnout, 201
  avoidance of, 15, 27
  in informal network, 159–160

CAB. See Citizen's Advice Bureau
California Assembly Select Committee, 192
Cambridge Nursing Home, 205
Capacity, for independent functioning, assessment of, 73

Caregiver burden, 159
Case advocacy, 204
Case conferences, 184, 228
Case coordination, ad hoc, 228
Case history, 60
Case loss, 238
Case management. *See also* Comprehensive psychosocial enhancement
  and advocacy, 200–201
  cost-effectiveness of, 276–277
  evaluation of, 271–272
  general, 16
  public understanding of, 261
  summary of, 277–278
Case management agency, and interagency coordination, 222–223
Case management programs, positive outcome studies of, 272–275
Caseload
  monthly review of, 185
  reduction of, 268, 270
Caseload activity sheet, monthly, 185
Causality, transactional, 43–45
  examples of, 44–45
Census records, 245
Central Index, 135
Challenges, versus stressors, 50
Channeling, 26–38, 234, 238–239
Charity Organization Societies, 40, 135
Child welfare field, 4
  monitoring in, 191
Children's Defense Fund, 235
Chronic pain, intervention planning for, 107
Citizen's Advice Bureau, 239
Clerical support, lack of, 267
Client(s)
  attitudes of, addressed during intake interview, 63
  basic information about. *See* Intake
  channeling of. *See* Channeling
  and circumstances, 5
  empowerment of. *See* Empowerment
  evaluation of. *See* Evaluation; Reassessment
  negative feelings of, 50–51, 63, 65
  newly constituted, 3–9
  practitioner's knowledge of, 123
  preparation of, for formal linkage, 144
  processing of, joint, 228
  progress of, unsteady, 195
  resistance, 195
Client-centered support systems, coordination of, 13–14
Client-centeredness, need for, 268, 270–271
Client contact card, 185, 185f
Client level, monitoring at, 181–182
Client motivation, 123–124
  lack of, 195
Client participation, 15. *See also* Self-advocacy
  in formal linkage, 143–144

Client participation (*Cont.*)
 fostering of, 124–125
 in goal setting, 81–82, 85
 in monitoring process, 176
 in practice process, 15, 117–118
 in reassessment, 193–194
Client population, 241, 241f
 and access issues, 240–241
 and intake procedures, 66
 and monitoring procedures, 178–179,
  190–191
Client-practitioner contract, 108–109, 117
Client-practitioner relationship. *See* Practice
  relationship
Client transportation, 144–145
 assessment of, 72
 problems of, 261–262
Climate, service, 95
Coercion, 206, 212
Cognitive functioning, assessment of, 73
Cognitive methods, of change, 108
Cognitive orientation, 120
Cognitive restructuring, 120
Coherence, organizational, lack of, 267, 271
Collaboration, organizational. *See* Inter-
  agency coordination
Collection, of data, 68
Communication, in support network, 182
Communication problems, due to language
  barriers, 37, 258
Community, definition of, 256
Community based groups, support provided
  by, 156. *See also* Informal linkage
Community-based mechanisms, of channel-
  ing, 238–239
Community Chests and Councils of America,
  135
Community context, 256–265
 improvement of, 263–265
 problems with, 260–262
 significance of, 255–256
Community coordination, lack of, 260–261, 270
Community education, promotion of, 14
Community factors, 18, 257–259
 in assessment, 70–71
Community forum, 243–244
Community Health Services and Facilities
  Act of 1961, 136
Community impulses, versus policy
  impulses, 19
Community living, support for, emphasis on,
  115–116
Community living educational program,
  125–126
Community living objectives, 10
Community meetings, advocacy, 32
Community relations, 246–249
Community relationship, multicultural con-
  siderations for, 37

Community services, 12
 connecting clients with, 13. *See also* Linking
 coordination of, 270
 positive outcome studies of, 273–274
Competence, 46–47
Competition
 agency, 223
 professional, and monitoring procedures,
  179–180, 184
Complimentary services, and interagency
  coordination, 222–223
Comprehensive psychosocial enhancement, 16
 professional standards needed for, 20
Comprehensive psychosocial enhancement
  practice
 alternative models for, 36
 implementation model for, 23–38
Comprehensive service delivery, 100–101, 110
Computers, monitoring with, 189–190
Confidentiality, need for, 182
Conflict intensity, 212
Conflict situation, self-instructions for, 107
Consent form, for formal linkage, 147
Contact
 for linkage, initiation of, 146–147
 point of, determination of, 145–146
Contextual factors, 18
Contingency analysis, 119
Continuity of care, 11
 assurance of, 101–102, 110
Contract
 interagency, 148, 230
 practitioner-client, 108–109, 117
Control, sense of. *See* Self-direction
Coordination. *See also* Interagency coordination
 of client-centered support systems, 13–14
 community, lack of, 260–261, 270
Coping
 definition of, 50
 difficulties with, 7, 51
 functions of, 50–51
Coping skills
 for chronic pain, 107
 development of, 13, 49–51
Cost-effectiveness, 276–277
Counseling/therapy, 31, 113–132. *See also* Psychotherapy
 differences between, 32, 114–115
 fundamental tasks of, 121–122
 individual, versus linking, 137
 long-term versus short-term, 31
 practice guidelines for, 121–129
 understanding, 114–121
 use of, 115–116
Court orders, monitoring dictated by,
  190–191
Creaming, 141
Crisis events, 29

Crisis events (*Cont.*)
anticipation of, 187–189
assessment in, 69
definition of, 128
Crisis intervention, 120–121, 128–129, 181
basic steps in, 129
Crisis services, time-limited, 121
Crisis theory, 120–121
Critical events, anticipation of, 187
Cross-sectional service, 11–12
Cultural considerations
in community context, 257–258
in empowerment, 53
in informal linkage, 29, 153, 155, 162
in intervention planning, 101
for service paradigm, 36–38
Culture, organizational, 266, 269

Data base, compilation of, 62, 64
Data collection, during assessment, 68
Defense(s), unconscious, 51
Defense mechanisms
development of, 119
maladaptive, 119
Deficits, 7–8
Deinstitutionalization, 18
and social integration, 155, 274
Demonstration projects, 227
Denial, 119
of service, and advocacy, 201
Department of Commerce, 245
Department of Housing and Urban Development, 136
Development, Erikson's stages of, 118
Diagnostic and Statistical Manual of Mental Disorders, 78
Direct practice
key components of, 116–117
supportive/skill development emphasis in, 12–13
Directory of Information and Referral Services in United States and Canada, 136
Disabilities
nature of, 5–7
understanding of, in informal network, 160–161
Disability Evaluation Facility, 214
Discharge evaluation, 195–196. *See also* Termination
Discreetness, of goals, 82
Disempowerment, and vulnerability, 52–53
Documentation, of monitoring process, 191
Domain consensus, 223–224
DSM-III-R. *See Diagnostic and Statistical Manual of Mental Disorders*
Durability, of informal network, 158, 166
Duration, of disabilities, 6

Ecological perspective, 39–55
history and professional values, 39–42
Economic aspects, of community context, 258–259
Education
for advocacy, 32
assessment of, 73
community, promotion of, 14
lack of, in informal network, 160
in monitoring implementation, 230
Educational program, community living, 125–126
Effectiveness, of intervention plan, 103–104
Efficacy, 46–47
of case management approaches, 275
Ego adaptability, 119
Ego psychology, 118–119
Ego supportive techniques, 119
Elderly, 4
family support for, 155
field of, evaluation in, 272
interviewing of, guidelines for, 66–67
Eligibility, determination of, 61, 64, 95, 102
Emotional functioning, assessment of, 73
Emotional support, 154, 163
for problem solving, 51
Empathic listening, 128
Empathic understanding, 122
Empathy, 15, 122–123
versus sympathy, 123
Employment
assessment of, 72
need for, 261
Empowerment, 27. *See also* Self-advocacy
dimensions of, 205
and intervention planning, 101, 110
value of, 205
Encouragement, importance of, 47
Engagement, 62–63
techniques of, 64–65
English as second language, 37
Enhancement, 13. *See also* Comprehensive psychosocial enhancement
objectives, 10–11
Environment. *See also* Community context; Organizational context
people and. *See* Holism; Person:environment relationship
service, 95
social support, 8–9
task, and interagency coordination, 222
Environmental intervention, 13–14
Environmental resources, 50
Erikson's stages of development, 118
Ethnic communities. *See also* Cultural considerations
informal networks in, 153, 155, 162
Ethnic heterogeneity, 257–258

Evaluation, 30
  multicultural considerations for, 38
  outcome, 191–196. *See also* Reassessment
  service, 271–277
  for termination, 30, 175, 192, 195–196
Expectations, unrealistic, 63
Exploitation, of power, by dominant groups,
  52–53
Extension mode, 237
External advocacy, 201
External informants, for assessment, 69

Facilities
  enhancement of, 270
  loaning/sharing of, 227
Family
  assessment of, 27, 29
  support provided by, 155–156, 160. *See also*
  Informal linkage
Family as case manager service concept, 36
Family intervention program, 168
Family members, assessment information
  from, 69
Family reunification, 191
Family Support Project, 167
Feasibility
  of intervention plan, 103
  practice, 35–36
Federal government, information/referral
  services organized by, 136
Federal Information Centers, 136
Fees, agency, identification of, 95
Field operations, inadequate, 267, 270–271
Field survey, 245–246
Financial situation, of client, determination
  of, 61
Fiscal authority, 139
Fiscal resources, and interagency coordination, 222, 225
Flexibility, of comprehensive enhancement
  practice model, 33
Flexner, Abraham, 39–40
Follow-up. *See* Monitoring
Formal linkage, 28–29, 133–150
  assessment of, 73–78
  barriers to, 140–141
  concept of, 134–135
  evaluation of, 182
  historical perspective on, 135–136
  and influencing organizational behavior,
    138–140
  interrelationship of, 137–138
  practice guidelines for, 141–149
  practitioner's role in, 136–137
  success of, 148–149
  understanding, 134–141
Formal monitoring, 180–183, 191

Formal reassessment, versus informal, 194
Friendship, 154, 163
  support provided by, 156. *See also* Informal
  linkage
Friendship skills training, 106
Funding
  access to, 262, 268, 271
  joint, 225

GAS. See Goal attainment scaling
General population, 240, 241f
General systems theory, 41
Genuineness, 15
Geographic aspects, of community context,
  259
Gerontological research, 272
Goal(s)
  clearly defined, in treatment-service plan, 99
  long-term, 82–84
  loosely formulated, 195
Goal attainment, progress toward, evaluation
  of, 192
Goal attainment scaling, 185, 187f
Goal displacement, 236
Goal setting, 27, 80–86
  client and professional inputs, 81–82
  criteria for, 82–83
  key aspects of, 80–81
  practice guidelines for, 83–85
  understanding, 80–83
Goal statements, 83–84
Governance entities, number of, 259
Government, federal, information/referral
  services organized by, 136
Great Society, 8
Grey Panthers, 235
Group advocacy, 32, 204
Guidance, provided by informal network,
  154, 163–164

Health care, assessment of, 72
Hearing limitations, 67
Helpfulness, of informal network, 157
Heterogeneity, population, 257–258
High conflict intensity, 212
Holism, 42–43, 45. *See also* Person:environ-
  ment relationship
Hospital bed capacity, 262
Housing
  assessment of, 72
  lack of, 262
Hull House, 40
Human relations, improvement of, 269
Hyperselectivity, 263

IADL. See Instrumental Activities of Daily
  Living
Imitative learning, 119

Impediments, internal, 123–124
Implementability, of intervention plan, 104
Impulses, policy versus community, 19
Income, assessment of, 72
Independent functioning, capacity for, assessment of, 73
Independent Living Movement, 235
Indexing, resource. *See* Resource identification/indexing
Individual counseling, versus linking, 137
Individualization, of services, 100, 110
Influence, modes of, assessment of, in interagency coordination, 231–232
Influence base, for advocacy, 208
Influencing techniques, organizational, for formal linkage, 138–140
Informal interagency contracts, 230
Informal interagency relationships, and linking, 140
Informal linkage, 29, 151–171
    assessment of, 73
    evaluation of, 169, 182
    functions of, 153–155, 163
    identification of, 94
    place of, 152–153
    practice guidelines for, 161–169
    understanding, 152–161
Informal monitoring, 181
Informal network(s)
    analysis of, 161–163
    capabilities of, 166, 166f, 167–169
    characteristics of, 157–159, 159t
    depiction of, with mapping techniques, 162–163, 164f
    making and maintenance of, 167
    selection of, 163
    types of, 155–156
Informal reassessment, versus formal, 194
Informant(s)
    external, for assessment, 69
    key, 242–243
Information
    assessment, integration of, 80
    basic. *See* Intake
    lack of, 7
    versus linking, 136
    monitoring, sources of, 177
    practical, provision of, 125–126
    provision of, 108
Information broker role, 126–127
Information management, 225–226
Informed consent, 147
In-service training, need for, 267
Instrumental Activities of Daily Living, 78, 79f
Intake, 26, 60–68, 85
    components of, 60–62
    early steps in, 64
    during linkage, helping clients with, 147

practice guidelines for, 64–68
    timing factors with, 63–64
    understanding, 60–64
Integration, social, 155
Intensity
    of advocacy, 212–213
    of informal network, 158, 166
    of practice relationship, 14–15
Interagency contracts, 148
    informal, 230
Interagency coordination, 30–31, 219–233
    aspects of, 220–221
    barriers to, 220–221
    and community context, 263
    connection to linking, 138
    early efforts at, 135
    factors effecting, 221–223
    and informal relationships, 140
    initiation of, 232–233
    linking mechanisms in, 224–228
    and monitoring process, 179–180, 184
    negotiation of, 147–148
    place of, 219–220
    practice guidelines for, 228–233
    procedures for, 148, 233
    strategy for, 230
    understanding, 219–228
Interdependence, agency, 223–224, 232
Interdisciplinary involvements, 11–12
Interference, inappropriate, by informal network, 160
Internal advocacy, 201
Internal impediments, 123–124
Internal linkage, in comprehensive enhancement practice model, 34
Interpersonal relations, during engagement phase, 62–63, 65
Interpersonal relationships, assessment of, 72–73, 75t
Interpretation, 181
Intervention
    advocacy, 209–210
    components of, 9–15
    environmental, 13–14
    organizational variables affecting, 266
    requisites, 9–21
    schematic model of, 24–26, 25f
Intervention plan, components of, 99–100
Intervention planning, 27–28, 97–110
    basic principles of, 100–102
    criteria for, 102–104
    definition of, 97
    diagram of, 98f
    implementation of, 107–110, 192–193
    practice guidelines for, 102–110
    for specific problems, 104–107
    strategic and procedural aspects of, 98–99
    treatment and service aspects of, 28, 97–98
    understanding, 97–102

Interview, first, 62–64
in linkage process, accompanying client on, 144–145
Interview format, UCLA study, 290–294
Interviewing, of elderly, guidelines for, 66–67
Isolation
geographic, 259
social, 106, 154

Joint administrative procedures, 225–226
Joint budgeting, 225
Joint funding, 225
Joint programming, 227–228
Joint Public Affairs Committee for Older Adults, 205
Joint research, 226
Joint staffing, 226–227

Key informant, 242–243

Language barriers, 37, 258
Language function limitations, 67
Least restrictive environment, 10
Lee, Porter, 40–41
Legal assistance, assessment of, 72
Legal authority, 139
Legal considerations
in advocacy theory, 202
in monitoring process, 190–191
Legitimacy, and interagency coordination, 222
Leisure activities, assessment of, 72
Liaison teams, 227
Life events, unanticipated, stressors generated by, 49
Life History Questionnaire, 64
Life situation, client's, intake form for, 67
Life skills counseling, 125–126
Life stressors. *See* Stressors
Life transitions
anticipation of, 187–189
stressors generated by, 49
Linear causality, 43–44
examples of, 43–44
Link, definition of, 134
Linking, 28–32. *See also* Formal linkage; Informal linkage
and advocacy, 214
of clinical and community roles, 117
in comprehensive enhancement practice model, 34
versus individual counseling, 137
versus information, 136
and interagency coordination, 224–228
versus referrals, 134, 136
Listening, empathic, 128
Loaner arrangements, 226–227
Loaning, of facilities, 227
Longitudinal service, 11

Long-term goals, 82–84
Long-term therapy, versus short-term, 31
Los Angeles Department of Mental Health. *See* UCLA study
Low conflict intensity, 212

Macro practice perspective, 14
Mainstreaming, 10
Maintenance program, 27
Management, streamlining of, 269
Management Information Systems, 189–190
Mapping techniques, depiction of informal network with, 162–163, 164f
Marketing, social, 246–249
Market segmentation, 247
Mastery, client's sense of, 124
Matching, of client and services, 142–143
Mathematica Policy Research, 139
Medical assessment. *See* Assessment
Mental health, assessment of, 72
Mental health research, 272
Mental limitations, 67
Micro practice perspective, 14
MIS. *See* Management Information Systems
Misuse, of power, by dominant groups, 52–53
Model presentation, 107–108
Modeling, 117–120, 125–126, 144
Moderate conflict intensity, 212
Monitoring, 29, 174–196
client participation in, 176
with computers, 189–190
connection to linking, 137
definition and purpose of, 174–175
with different client populations, 190–191
dynamics of, 177–178
formal and informal means of, 180–181
forms and set procedures for, 184–185, 186f
and interagency coordination, 184
key aspects of, 183
levels of, 181–182
overview of, 173
place of, 175–176
of policy execution, 229–230
practice guidelines for, 180–191
problems with, 179–180
purpose of, 29
understanding, 174–180
Motivation, client, 123–124
lack of, 195
Multicultural practice, criteria for, 37–38
Multiethnicity, 258
Multipurpose Senior Services Program of California, 272

NASW Code of Ethics, 200
National Alliance of Information and Referral Services, 136
National Channeling Demonstration, 238

National Conference of Charities and Corrections (NCCC), 39–41
National Institute of Mental Health, 222
Needs
  definition of, 70
  scope of, 6–7
  specific, screening, 71–73
Needs assessment
  and access issues, 235–237
  for effective linkage, 141
  and informal network, 163–164
  and interagency coordination, 226
  techniques for, 242–246
Need-support worksheet, 164, 165f
Negative attitudes
  of community, 256–257, 260, 270
  of service providers, 263
Negative feelings
  about seeking help, 63, 65
  regulation of, 50–51
Negative service results, 275–276
Neighborhood, support provided by, 156. *See also* Informal linkage
Network. *See* Informal network(s)
NIMH. *See* National Institute of Mental Health
Normalization, 10–11

Office of Economic Opportunity, 136
Older Americans Act Amendments of 1973, 136
Older Americans Act of 1965, 136
Ombudsman, 207
Operational tasks, identification of, 109
Oregon Quality of Life Questionnaire, 273
Organization(s). *See* Agency(ies)
  coherence/stability of, lack of, 267, 271
  influencing, 138–140
Organizational context, 18, 265–271
  improvement of, 268–270
  problems with, 266–267
  significance of, 255–256
Organizational culture, 266, 269
Outcome(s), rewarding, 124
Outcome evaluation, 191–196. *See also* Reassessment
  overview of, 173
Outcome evaluation studies
  negative, 275–276
  positive, 272–275
Outreach, 26, 227, 237–240, 246–249
Out-stationing, 227
Overload, work, 263, 266–267

PAF. *See* Preadmission assessment form
Pain, physical, intervention planning for, 107
Paperwork
  burden of, 266–267
  reduction of, 269–270
  for referrals, 147

Paraprofessional format, 36
Parents Anonymous, 157
Parsimony, 101, 110
Participation. *See* Client participation
Peer acceptance, 106
Permanence, of informal network, 158
Permanency planning, 11
Personal care skills, assessment of, 73, 74t
Personal contact, 247
Personal feelings, of practitioner, toward client, 123
Personal helping, alternative theoretical approaches to, 118–121
Personal preferences, in informal linkage, 162
Personal resources, 50
Person:environment relationship, 42
  assessment of, 70–71
Person-in-environment, 14, 97, 121, 201, 234, 236–237
Person-in-situation reflection, 119, 153
Persuasion, 205–206, 212
Physical functioning, assessment of, 73, 74t
Physical layout, of community, 259
Physical pain, intervention planning for, 107
Physically disabled, 4
PIE. *See* Person-in-environment
Pilot projects, 227
Place, 248
Planning. *See also* Intervention planning
  advocacy, 208–210
  permanency, 11
Point of contact, determination of, 145–146
Policy(ies)
  changes, system-wide, promotion of, 14
  execution of, monitoring of, 229–230
  rigid, 263, 267–268
Policy impulses, versus community impulses, 19
Policy issues, referral of, to higher levels, 229
Political factors, 18–19
  and community context, 263, 265
Polyvant worker, 239
Population aspects, of community context, 257–258
Population funnel, 241, 241f
Population group differences
  and access issues, 240–241
  and intake procedures, 66
  and monitoring procedures, 178–179, 190–191
Positive outcome studies, 272–275
Positive regard, unconditional, 15
Positive reinforcement, 126
Power, misuse of, by dominant groups, 52–53
Practical assistance, provided by informal network, 154, 163
Practice(s)
  direct, supportive/skill development emphasis in, 12–13
  feasibility of, 35–36

Practice(s) (*Cont.*)
intensity, 14–15
micro and macro perspectives, 14
multicultural, criteria for, 37–38
new paradigm for, 15–17
Practice Digest, 202–203
Practice relationship
assessment of, 71
establishment of, 122–123
style of, and cultural considerations, 36–37
Practice roles
with agencies, 145–147
clarification of, 267, 269–270
with clients, 143–144
in client's self-direction, 48–49
in human relatedness, 46
in linking process, 136–137
Practitioner, personal feelings of, toward client, 123
Practitioner-client contract, 108–109, 117
Practitioner-client relationship. *See* Practice relationship
Preadmission assessment form, 239
Preparation, of client, for formal linkage, 144
Price, 248–249
Primary care physicians, monitoring functions of, 180
Principles, intervention planning, activation of, 109–110
Problem, clarification of, 60, 209
Problem solving, 50–51
and monitoring procedures, 179
Problem-solving roles, 13
Problem statements, development of, 65–66
Prodding, 205–206, 212
Product, 247
Professional competition, and monitoring procedures, 179–180, 184
Professional factors, 19–21
Professional sensitivity, empowering and ethical considerations with, 53
Professional standards/values, 20, 39–41
Programming, joint, 227–228
Progressive Era, 40
Projection, 119
Promotion, 247–248
Promotional events, 248
Proximity. *See also* Accessibility
of informal network, 158, 166
Psychoeducational model, 168
Psychological aspects, of support, 127–128
Psychological assessment. *See* Assessment
Psychological centrality, and self-esteem, 48
Psychological pressure, in advocacy, 215–216
Psychosocial enhancement. *See* Comprehensive psychosocial enhancement
Psychosocial practice, 14
Psychosocial rehabilitation center approach, 36
Psychotherapy
monitoring in, 176

skills, 20
value of, 115–116
Public relations, 226
Publicity, 226, 247–248
Purchase, of service, and interagency coordination, 225

Qualitative monitoring, 181
Quality of life indices, 272–274
Quality of service, 95
Quantitative monitoring, 180–183, 191

Rapid assessment instruments (RAIs), 78
Rapid early assessment, 69
Rates-under-treatment, 244
Reassessment, 30, 191–196
client participation in, 193–194
factors hindering, 30
formal versus informal, 194
frequency of, variations in, 194
instruments for, 193
key aspects of, 194–195
obstacles to, 195
overview of, 173
tasks and objectives of, 191–193
Reciprocity, of informal network, 158, 166
Recreational activities, assessment of, 72
Red tape, 266–267
reduction of, 269–270
Referrals, 26, 34
versus linking, 134, 136
and monitoring procedures, 180
paperwork for, 147
Reframing technique, 181
Registration Bureau, 135
Reinforcement, positive, 126
Reinforcement theory, 119
Reinstitutionalization, 274
Relationship(s)
community, multicultural considerations for, 37
interagency. *See* Interagency coordination
interpersonal, assessment of, 72–73, 75t
practice. *See* Practice relationship
Relaxation exercises, for chronic pain, 107
Reliability, of service, 95
Research, joint, 226
Residential treatment, long-term, lack of, 261
Resistance, client, 195
Resource(s)
for advocacy, 209
appropriate, selection of, 142
community support, connecting clients with, 13. *See also* Linking
environmental, 50
and goal setting, 84
personal, 50
specification of, and informal network, 163–164
understanding and using, 90–96

Resource agencies, identification of, 230
Resource aggregation methods, 91–93
Resource identification/indexing, 27–28, 90–96
  connection to linking, 137
  definition and context of, 90–91
  diagram of, 98f
  and organizational context, 268, 271
  problems with, 93–94
Respect, for client, 122
Response mode, 237
Rewarding outcomes, 124
Risks, 129
Role(s). *See also* Practice roles
  of advocate, 201–202, 205
  case management, definition of, need for, 267
  clarification of, during intake, 63
  information broker, 126–127
  problem-solving, 13
  in providing access, 239–240
Role playing, 108, 117, 119–120, 125–126, 144
Routine extension, 237

Scapegoating, 160
Self-advocacy, 203–205
Self-attributions, and self-esteem, 48
Self-change, by clients, 120
Self-concept, development of, 48
Self-direction, 48–49
  promotion of, 117–118
Self-esteem, 47–48
  low, 7–8
Self-help groups, support provided by, 157. *See also* Informal linkage
Self-sufficiency, emphasis on, 117–118
Self validation, 122
Selling, 247
Sensitivity, professional, 53
Service(s). *See also* Community services
  appropriateness of, determination of, 61, 102
  availability/accessibility of, 95
  cross-sectional, 11–12
  denial of, and advocacy, 201
  eligibility for, determination of, 61, 64, 95, 102
  evaluation of, 271–277
  individualization of, 100, 110
  lack of, 260–261, 270
  longitudinal, 11
  matching client with, 142–143
  multicultural, criteria for, 37
  needed, development of, 13
  purchase of, and interagency coordination, 225
  quality of, 95
Service climate, 95
Service delivery
  comprehensive, 100–101, 110
  monitoring of, 178
Service goals, establishment of. *See* Goal setting
Service planning, 28, 97–98
  implementation of, evaluation of, 192
Service providers. *See* Agency(ies); Practitioner
Service settings, client's experience of, 124–125
Service substitution, 264
Service system, tangled arrangement of, 91, 92f
Settlement house workers, 40
Severity, of disabilities, 5–6
Shaping, 125–126
Sharing, of facilities, 227
Shelter
  assessment of, 72
  lack of, 262
Sheltered workshops, need for, 261
Short-term therapy, versus long-term, 31
SILS. *See* Social and independent living skills modules
Skill deficiencies, 7
Skill development, emphasis on, in direct practice, 12–13
SLOF. *See* Specific Level of Functioning Scale
Social acceptability, assessment of, 73, 75t
Social and independent living skills modules, 126
Social assessment. *See* Assessment
Social comparisons, and self-esteem, 48
Social connections, lack of, 154
Social context. *See* Community context; Organizational context
Social darwinism, 235
Social indicators, 244–245
Social integration, 155
Social isolation, 154
  intervention planning for, 106
Social marketing, 246–249
Social Security Administration, 136, 214
Social support
  environment, 8–9
  importance of, 153
  and negative life-stressors, 154
  networks. *See* Informal network(s)
Social system endorsement, 271–277
Social work, history and professional values, 39–41
Social-emotional support, 154
  for problem solving, 51
Socialization, 154, 163
Socialization programs, lack of, 261
Societal forces, new clientele created by, 3–5
Specific Level of Functioning Scale, 78
Specificity, of goals, 82–83
SSI. *See* Supplementary Security Insurance
Stability, organizational, lack of, 267, 271
Staff, assessment information from, 69
Staff shortages, 263, 267
Staffing
  increase in, need for, 268, 271
  joint, 226–227
Standards, professional, 20, 39–41

Steering-advice-referral, 238
Strengths, 8
  assessment of, 70
  emphasis of, 127
Stress inoculation program, 107
Stress-coping paradigm, 49–51
Stress-coping skills, for chronic pain, 107
Stressors, 49–51, 129
  anticipation of, 187–189
  versus challenges, 50
  negative, and social support, 154–155
Success
  client's sense of, 124
  criteria for, 21
Super agency, 139
Supervising staff, advocacy issues for, 32
Supervisory help, need for, 267
Supplementary Security Insurance, 262
Support. *See also* Social support
  importance of, 47
  psychological aspects of, 127–128
Support systems
  client-centered, coordination of, 13–14
  linking clients to. *See* Linking
Supportive care model, 36
Supportive emphasis, in direct practice,
    12–13
Survival skills, teaching of, 125
Sympathy, versus empathy, 123
Synanon, 157
System linkage, 238

Target population, 241, 241f
Target system, for advocacy, 209, 215–216
  selection of, 211–212
Targeting
  and access issues, 235–237, 240–241
  outreach, 237–238
Task(s)
  operational, identification of, 109
  specific, of treatment-service plan, 99
Task environment, and interagency coordination, 221
Task planning, 109
Task strategies, 13
Teaching, 117
Telephone monitoring, 183
Termination
  in comprehensive enhancement practice
    model, 33
  evaluation for, 30, 175, 192, 195–196
Therapist-case manager model, 36, 117
Therapy. *See* Counseling/therapy; Psychotherapy
Time element
  in comprehensive enhancement practice
    model, 33
  with intake efforts, 63–64
  of treatment-service plan, 100, 102

Time limitations, 195
Time-limited crisis services, 121
Time-limited planning, 102
Time lines, projection of, 187–189
Time pressures, reduction of, 268
Title XX legislation, 136
Tracking systems, 189–190
Traditional practice, versus new practice
    paradigm, 16–17
Training
  in-service, need for, 267
  lack of, in informal network, 160
  multicultural considerations for, 38
  for self-advocacy, 203, 205
Transactional causality, 43–45
  examples of, 44–45
Transitional living programs, lack of, 261
Transitions, life
  anticipation of, 187–189
  stressors generated by, 49
Transportation, 144–145
  assessment of, 72
  problems of, 261–262
Traveling companion, 29, 144–145
Treatment planning, 28, 97–98
  implementation of, evaluation of, 192
Treatment-service plan, 99–100
Turf issues, and monitoring procedures,
    179–180, 184
Turnaround time, 26
Turnover, administrative, 267

UCFCA. *See* United Community Funds and
    Councils of America
UCLA study, 23
  of access facilitation, 239
  of advocacy, 200–202, 205–206, 213
  of assessment procedures, 69
  of client participation, 118
  of counseling and therapy, 114–116
  of formal linkage procedures, 141–142,
    146
  of goal setting procedures, 80–81
  of informal linkage procedures, 152,
    159–161
  of intake procedures, 61t, 61–62, 65–68
  of interagency coordination, 228
  interview format, 290–294
  methodology of, 285–294
  of monitoring procedures, 174, 177, 183
  of organizational context, 266
  of reassessment procedures, 194
  of resource identification/indexing, 91
  of service evaluation, 271
  of social context issues, 255–256
Unanticipated life events, stressors generated
    by, 49
Unconditional positive regard, 15
Unconscious defenses, 51

Understanding
  empathic, 122
  of impairment, lack of, in informal network, 160–161
Unemployment, intervention planning for, 105
United Community Funds and Councils of America, 135
United Way, 135, 215, 223, 225, 231
University of California, Los Angeles Center for Child and Family Policy Studies. *See* UCLA study
University of Southern California, Andrus Gerontology Center, 174
U.S. Government Printing Office, 245

Validity, of intervention plan, evaluation of, 193
Values, professional, 20, 39–41

Veterans Administration, 136
Vision limitations, 67
Visiting record, 185, 185f
Visits, monitoring, 183
Voluntary agencies, and interagency coordination, 222
Vulnerability, and disempowerment, 52–53

Waiting lists, monitoring of, 265
War on Poverty, 8, 200
Willingness to help, of informal network, 157, 166
Withholding, of power, from vulnerable groups, 52
Work overload, 263, 266–267
Work pressures, 195
Working assessment, 69

Name Index

Abramson, N. S., 188, 197
Ad Hoc Committee on Advocacy, National Association of Social Workers, 200, 215
Agranoff, R., 221, 249
Ainsworth, M. D., 47, 54
Alan, 47
Alaszewski, A., 221, 249
Althoff, M., 274, 278
Anderson, C. M., 51, 53–54
Andrasik, F., 107, 111
Anthony, W., 274, 278
Arnold, S., 193, 197
Asher, S. R., 106, 111
Auluck, R., 221, 250
Austin, C. D., 70, 86, 114, 122, 130, 174, 196, 276, 278
Aviram, U., 10, 18, 21, 22
Axinn, J., 152, 169
Azrin, N. H., 105, 110

Bagarozzi, D. A., 69, 87, 114–115, 131
Baker, F., 12, 21, 64, 82, 86, 115, 123, 127, 130, 137, 149, 174–175, 187, 196
Ballantyne, R., 272, 274–275, 280
Ballew, J. R., 8, 21, 62, 64, 82–86, 122–124, 127–128, 130, 143, 147, 149, 181, 185, 212, 215
Bandura, A., 119, 130
Banks, S. M., 272, 274, 279
Barber, T. X., 107, 110
Barnsley, R., 160, 171
Bart, R., 136–137, 149
Bartlett, E. E., 203, 215
Basch, M. F., 122–123, 130
Beardsley, C., 12, 21
Beck, A., 120, 130
Beck, D. F., 235, 249
Becker-Haven, J. F., 105, 111
Beditz, J., 257, 279
Beels, C., 154, 169
Behn, J. D., 37–38
Bell, R. A., 242, 251
Bell, S. M., 47, 54

Bellack, A. S., 78, 87
Bellamy, G. T., 286, 294
Berger, D. M., 122–123, 130
Bergner, M., 193, 196
Berkeley, J., 154, 169
Berkeley Planning Associates, 191, 196
Bernstein, J., 238, 249
Bernstein, L., 88
Bertsche, A. V., 70, 86, 139, 149
Biegel, D. E., 155–156, 159, 169
Bierly, E. W., 221, 249
Bigelow, D., 272–274, 278
Birchmore-Timney, C., 271, 279
Blanck, G., 118–119, 130
Blanck, R., 118–119, 130
Blankertz, L., 5, 7–8, 10–12, 14–15, 21
Blau, P. M., 223, 249
Blazyk, S., 207, 215
Bloom, M., 66, 86, 176, 193, 196
Blume, R., 272, 278
Bobbit, R. A., 193, 196
Bond, G. R., 272, 274, 278
Borland, A., 276, 278
Bowe, F. G., 220, 249
Bowker, J. P., 115, 130
Bowles, D. D., 53–54
Brager, G., 53–54
Braren, M., 272, 274, 280
Braun, R. S., 238, 250
Brecher, C., 276, 278
Brightman, A. J., 4, 21
Brill, R., 115, 130
Brindis, C., 136–137, 149
Brodows, B., 238, 249
Brody, E. M., 79, 87, 155, 169
Bronzan, B., 192, 196
Brown, T., 272, 274, 276, 278
Bruce, D., 272, 274, 278
Buehler, R., 272, 274, 278
Buell, G., 274, 278
Burack-Weiss, A., 8, 21, 62, 64, 66, 83, 86–87, 122, 124, 130
Burnett, K. F., 105, 111
Burns, E., 41, 54

Burns, T., 64, 86, 174–175, 187, 196
Byers, E., 272, 275, 278

Cable, S., 204, 215
Caires, K. B., 86
Callahan, J. J., 275–276, 278
Camp, B. W., 106, 110
Capitman, J., 238, 249
Caragonne, P., 114, 130, 174, 196, 234, 272, 278
Carcagno, G. J., 238, 250
Caro, F. G., 4, 21
Carter, G., 36, 38, 138, 148, 150
Cassell, J., 187, 196
Cassem, N. H., 175, 197
Cassidy, K., 176, 197
Caulum, S., 201–202, 208, 216
Chamberlain, R., 84, 87, 122, 124, 131,
    145–146, 148–149, 272, 280
Chaves, J. F., 107, 110, 112
Chesney, M. A., 107, 111–112
Churgin, S., 16, 22, 114, 132, 225, 251
Claghorn, J., 274, 278
Clemmons, J., 275–276, 279
Clifford, R., 221, 249
Cnaan, R. A., 5, 7–8, 10–12, 14–15, 21
Cobb, S., 187, 196
Coe, B., 221, 249
Coffey, E., 115, 131
Cohen, J., 193, 197
Cohen, M. B., 63, 65, 86
Cohen, S., 272, 275, 278
Colligan, R. C., 81, 86
Cook, K., 138, 149
Cooper, L. B., 53, 55
Coopersmith, S., 47, 54
Corbin, J. M., 53–54
Corcoran, J. J., 78, 86
Corsini, R., 175, 196
Coser, L. A., 153, 170
Coulton, C., 275–276, 279
Cox, D. J., 107, 111
Coyne, J. C., 49, 54
Craig, G. J., 118, 130
Crawford, C., 207, 215
Crotty, P., 160, 170
Curry, J., 271–272, 274, 279
Cuvo, A. J., 203, 216

Dahlem, N. W., 106, 110
Damron-Rodriquez, J., 65, 286, 295
Dana, R. H., 37–38
Dane, B. O., 180, 196
Davidoff, P., 200, 215
Davidson, M., 81, 86
Davidson, S., 221, 249
Davidson, W., 208, 215
Davis, P. K., 203, 216
DeJong, G., 4, 21
Devore, W., 53–54

Diagnostic and Statistical Manual of Mental Disorders, 78, 86
Dickstein, D., 272, 276, 279
Dincin, J., 272, 274, 278
Doll, W., 160, 170
Doth, D., 114, 130
Downing, R., 86, 101, 111, 114–115, 130, 178,
    196, 220, 249
Dubos, R., 46, 54
Duhl, J., 205, 215

Easton, K., 13, 21
Eckland, J., 221, 249
Economou, M., 272, 280
Eggert, G. M., 238, 249
Ellis, C., 272, 274, 280
Endicott, J., 193, 197
Epstein, I., 61, 88, 118, 169, 171, 193, 197, 201,
    208–210, 215–216
Epstein, L. H., 69, 86, 107–108, 111, 116–117,
    132, 190, 197
Erikson, E. H., 118, 130
Ewalt, P., 99, 111, 118, 124, 130

Fairbank, J. A., 200, 216
Fairweather, G., 286, 294
Falke, R. L., 153, 170
Farkas, M., 272, 274–275, 279–280
Fawcett, S. B., 203, 216, 286, 294
Ferdinande, R. J., 81, 86
Ferris, P. A., 167, 170
Field, G., 235, 271, 273, 279
Fiorentine, R., 137, 149
Fischer, J., 68, 78, 86, 119, 130, 176, 193,
    196–197, 200, 215
Fitz-Gibbon, C., 174, 193, 197
Fleishman, J. A., 272, 274, 279
Fleiss, J., 193, 197
Fleming, M. L., 118, 124, 131, 174, 197, 237,
    250, 256, 279
Flexner, A., 39–40, 54
Flores, R., 105, 110
Fodor, I. G., 106, 112
Frankfather, D. L., 4, 21
Franklin, J., 275–276, 279
Freddolino, P. P., 272–274, 279
Freud, A., 4, 22
Freundlich, A., 107, 111
Frost, A., 275–276, 279
Frumkin, M., 138, 149

Gallagher, D. E., 155, 170
Gallagher, J., 221, 249
Gallagher, R. M., 175, 197
Gambrill, E. D., 103, 108, 111, 191, 197
Gardner, J. R., 5, 7–8, 10–12, 14–15, 21
Garrison, V., 87
Garvin, C. D., 122, 130
General Accounting Office, 18, 22, 92

Gerhart, U. C., 8, 22, 87, 99–101, 111, 158, 170, 174, 185, 197
Germain, C. B., 14, 41–42, 45, 49–50, 53–54, 87, 97, 111, 162, 170
Gilchrist, L. D., 125, 132
Gilson, B., 193, 196
Giordano, J., 53–54
Gitterman, A., 5–7, 13, 15, 22, 53–54, 87, 97, 111, 180, 197
Glaser, B. G., 51, 55
Goering, P. N., 272, 274–275, 279–280
Golan, N., 120–121, 130
Goldberg, G., 209, 216
Goldfinger, S. M., 4, 22
Goldman, H. H., 16, 22, 114, 132, 225, 251
Goldstein, E. G., 119, 130
Goldstein, J., 4, 22
Goldstrom, I., 28, 36
Gonwa, T., 37–38
Goodwin, S. E., 106, 111
Gordon, E., 155–156, 159, 169
Gordon, W. E., 41, 54
Gottlieb, B. H., 153–154, 170
Graham, K., 271, 279
Gray, B., 221, 250
Green, J. W., 248
Greenberg, J., 114, 130
Greene, V., 36, 153, 170
Greenson, R. R., 123, 130
Grisham, M., 138, 149
Grosskopf, B., 272, 276, 279
Gruber, M. L., 189, 197
Grusky, O., 137, 149, 153, 160, 170
Gundlach, J. H., 193, 197
Gutwirth, L., 154, 169
Gwyther, L. P., 87

Hackett, T. P., 175, 197
Hagen, J. L., 204, 216
Hamilton, G., 41, 54
Hamilton, M. A., 221, 250
Hammaker, R., 272, 274, 279
Hanig, D., 272, 276, 279
Hanks, J. W., 53–54
Harbin, G., 221, 249
Harrison, L., 221, 249–250
Harshberger, D., 272, 275, 278
Hartup, W. W., 106, 111
Hasenfeld, Y., 221–223, 249
Haskins, B., 238, 249
Hawkins, R. O., 53, 55
Hearn, G., 41, 54
Heiman, J. R., 274, 276, 281
Hemphill, D. P., 107, 111
Hennessy, C. H., 178, 197
Hereford, R. W., 256, 279
Hersen, M., 78, 87, 107, 111
Highlights, Champaign, Illinois Region v. Child Welfare Training Center, 185

Hilsberg, B. L., 153, 170
Hogarty, G. E., 12, 22, 51, 53–54, 115, 117, 130–131
Hollingshead, A. B., 235, 250
Hollis, F., 116, 119, 131, 153, 170, 175, 198
Holloway, S., 53–54
Holloway, W. B., 221, 250
Holyrod, K. A., 107, 111
Honeyfield, R., 99, 111, 118, 124, 130
Honnard, R., 192, 197
Horejsi, C. R., 70, 86, 139, 149
Horowitz, A., 115, 130
Horton, C., 107, 112
Horwitch, M., 221, 250
Howard, D. S., 41, 54
Hudson, W. W., 78, 87

Intagliata, J., 8, 12, 22, 82, 86–87, 115, 130, 137, 149, 174–175, 187, 196, 255, 257, 271, 279
Iodice, J. D., 160, 168, 170
Isles, P., 221, 250
Iverson, L. H., 238, 250

Jacobi, J. E., 220, 249
Jacobs, C., 53–54
Jamison, P. W., 81, 86
Jarrett, R. B., 200, 216
Jeffers, S., 221, 250
Johnson, C. A., 274, 279
Johnson, P., 9, 22, 256–257, 279
Johnson, P. J., 201, 216
Johnson, S. D., 221, 250
Jurkiewicz, V., 153, 170
Jurmain, R., 153, 170

Kagan, S. L., 221, 250
Kahn, A. J., 235, 238, 250
Kailes, J. I., 87
Kane, R. A., 97, 102, 111, 180, 190, 193, 197, 234, 237, 239, 250, 257, 272, 279
Kane, R. L., 193, 197, 234, 237, 250, 272, 279
Kanter, J. S., 71, 78, 85, 87
Kaplan, S. J., 105, 110
Karls, J. M., 5, 14, 22, 70, 80, 86, 88, 205, 216, 225, 234
Kay, T. L., 247, 251
Kaye, L. W., 153–155, 170
Kazdin, A. E., 120, 131
Keating, D., 159, 170
Kelley, E. J., 247, 250
Kemper, P., 238, 250
Kentera, A., 12, 22
Kessler, R., 12, 21
Kinard, E., 118, 124, 131
King, J., 273, 280
Kinross-Wright, J., 274, 278
Kirshstein, R., 137, 149
Kirwin, P. M., 220, 250
Kisthardt, W., 115, 127, 132

Klett, C., 115, 131
Knickman, J., 276, 278
Kolisetty, N., 118, 124, 131
Kotler, P., 247–248, 250
Krumboltz, J. D., 105, 111
Kulys, R., 160, 170
Kurtz, L. F., 69, 87, 114–115, 131

Lamb, H. R., 10, 22, 116–117, 122, 127–128, 131, 201, 216
Lancee, W. J., 272, 274–275, 279–280
Land, D., 272, 274, 279
Lannon, P. B., 272, 274, 279
Lanoil, J., 200, 216
Lantz, E., 274, 281
Lauffer, A., 225, 250
Launier, R., 49, 54
Lawton, L. P., 79, 87
Lazarus, A. A., 64, 121, 131
Lazarus, R. S., 44, 49, 54
Lazer, W., 247, 250
Learner, R. M., 272, 274, 276, 278
Leavitt, S. S., 126, 129, 131, 136, 149
Lee, P., 41, 54
Levendusky, P., 107, 111
Levin, E. I., 12, 21
Levin, H., 152, 169
Levine, I. S., 118, 124, 131, 174, 197, 237, 250
Levine, S., 223–224, 250
Levinson, R. W., 91, 111, 135, 149
Libby, M., 174–175, 187, 196
Liberman, R. P., 126, 131
Lindsay, V., 221, 249
Linn, M., 115, 131
Litwak, E., 224, 250
Loomis, A., 136–137, 149
Loomis, F. J., 138, 149
Los Angeles County Department of Mental Health, 87, 134, 149, 201, 216
Lowy, L., 87
Lum, D., 53–54
Lycan, C., 276, 278

Madiasos, M. G., 272, 280
Maguire, L., 162, 170
Mahaffey, M., 53–54
Mahoney, M. J., 106, 111
Mandersheid, R., 36, 38
Marion, T. R., 154, 170
Marshall, C. A., 167, 170
Martin, D. P., 193, 196
Mason, M., 275–276, 279
Mathews, R. M., 203, 216
Maxmen, J. S., 175, 197
Mayer, J. B., 153, 159, 170
Mazel, R. M., 153, 170
McCann, J. E., 221, 250
McCarthy, E. J., 247, 250
McCoin, J. M., 271, 279–280

McDermott, C. J., 205, 216
McFall, R. M., 105, 112
McGoldrick, M., 53–54
McGowan, B. G., 202, 204, 208, 216
McKechnie, R. J., 107, 111
McRea, J., 276, 278
Means, R., 221, 250
Meenaghan, T. M., 193, 197
Melnick, G., 12, 22
Messinger, K., 5, 7–8, 10–12, 14–15, 21
Meyer, C. H., 87, 118, 124, 131
Meyer, R. G., 107, 111
Middleman, R., 209, 216
Miller, G., 275–276, 279
Miller, I., 180, 197
Miller, L., 138, 149
Miller, L. S., 272, 280
Miller, P., 138, 149
Minahan, A., 138, 140, 149
Mink, G., 8, 21, 62, 64, 82–86, 122–124, 127–128, 130, 143, 147, 149, 181, 185, 212, 215
Mitchell, K. R., 107, 111
Modrcin, M., 84, 87, 122, 124, 131, 145–146, 148–149, 272, 280
Monahan, D., 36, 38, 153, 170
Morningstar, G. C., 247, 251
Morris, L., 174, 193, 197
Morrissey, J. P., 272, 274, 279
Morrow, H., 272, 280
Moses, A. E., 53, 55
Moxley, D. P., 70–71, 87, 114, 127–128, 131, 183, 197, 204, 208, 272, 274, 279
Mueser, K. T., 126, 131
Muller, J., 271–272, 279–280
Muraco, W., 273, 280
Murphy, P., 87

National Association of Social Workers, 63
    Ad Hoc Committee on Advocacy, 200, 215
National Conference on Social Welfare, 256, 280
Nelson, H., 153, 170
Nock, S. L., 153, 170
Northern, H., 68, 80, 87
Novaco, R. W., 106, 111
Nurcombe, B., 175, 197

Obershall, A., 204, 216
Oden, S., 106, 111
Olvera, G., 274, 276, 281

Paine, S. C., 286, 294
Pallard, W. E., 193, 196
Pankratz, L., 107, 111
Parad, H. J., 121, 129, 131
Parker, F. L., 221, 250
Patterson, S. L., 162, 170
Patti, R., 121, 131, 201, 216
Peak, T., 154, 171

Pearce, J. K., 53–54
Pearson, R. E., 152, 154, 157–158, 170
Peele, R., 10, 22
Perlman, B., 12, 22
Perlman, H. H., 124, 131
Perlmutter, F., 138, 149
Peterson, C., 174, 198
Pinderhughes, E., 117, 131
Place, P., 221, 249
Platman, S. R., 87, 225, 250
Podell, J., 87
Poertner, J., 240–241, 250, 272, 280
Pollane, L., 114–115, 131
Powell, T. J., 157, 170
Powers, G. T., 193, 197
Prahalad, C. K., 221, 250

Quam, J. K., 188, 197
Quinlan, J., 129, 131

Raines, J. C., 122–123, 131
Random House Dictionary of the English Language, 134, 149
Rapp, C. A., 5, 8, 10–11, 15–16, 22, 84, 87, 115, 122, 124, 127, 131–132, 145–146, 149, 208, 215, 240–241, 271–275, 279–280
Red Horse, J. G., 53, 55
Redlich, F. C., 235, 250
Rees, 200
Reich, C., 202, 216
Reid, P., 193, 197
Reid, W. J., 13, 22, 70, 87, 116–117, 121, 132
Rein, M., 91, 111
Reisch, M., 214, 216
Reiss, D. J., 51, 53–54
Rhea, B., 153, 170
Richards, M., 87
Richmond, Mary, 40–41, 55
Rist, R. C., 221, 250
Ritvo, R., 136, 149
Rivera, A. M., 221, 250
Roberts-DeGannaro, M., 16, 22, 116–117, 124, 132
Rogowski, A., 174, 198
Rose, S., 276, 280
Rosenberg, M., 47, 55
Rossiter, C. M., 154, 171
Rothman, J., 23–24, 26, 36, 38–40, 42, 51, 224, 247, 250–251, 256, 271, 280, 286, 294–295
Rubin, A., 5, 9, 11–13, 22, 201, 216, 266, 280
Ryndes, T., 220, 251

Sanborn, C. J., 117, 122, 124, 128, 132
Sancier, B., 203, 216
Savage, A., 61, 88, 118, 169, 171, 208–210, 216
Schamess, G., 118, 132
Schinke, S. P., 125, 132
Schlesinger, E. G., 53–54
Schneider, B., 97, 100–102, 112

Schneider, L. D., 77–78, 87
Schwab, J. J., 242, 251
Schwartz, S. R., 4, 16, 22, 114, 132, 225, 251
Scott, R. A., 176, 197, 235–236, 251
Seabury, B., 122, 130
Seekins, T., 203, 216
Segal, S. P., 10, 18, 21–22, 157, 170
Selby, L., 129, 131
Seltzer, M. M., 153, 159, 170
Sharratt, S., 274, 278
Shelton, J. L., 107, 111
Shenassa, E., 286, 295
Shinkfield, A., 193, 197
Shore, B. K., 155–156, 159, 169
Shupe, J., 274, 276, 281
Sievert, A. L., 203, 216
Silber, B., 272, 274, 280
Silverstone, B., 62, 64, 66, 83, 87
Simon, B. L., 180, 196
Siporin, M., 124, 132
Skinner, B. F., 119
Smith, C. A., 272, 274, 280
Smith, C. J., 272, 274, 280
Smith, G. C., 154, 171
Smith, M. J., 4, 21
Smith, R., 221, 250
Solnit, A., 4, 22
Solomon, P., 275, 280
Solovitz, B., 275–276, 279
Sommers, R., 274, 281
Sosin, M., 201–202, 208, 216
Sovronsky, H., 272, 278
Spanos, N. P., 107, 112
Speigler, M. D., 120, 126, 132
Spitzer, R., 193, 197
Srouf, L. A., 47, 55
Stedman, D. J., 220, 251
Stefanik-Campisi, C., 154, 170
Steffan, P. A., 153, 170
Stein, L., 115, 132, 174, 197, 272, 280
Stein, T. J., 191, 197
Steinberg, R., 36, 38, 138, 148, 150
Stone, C., 88
Strauss, A. L., 51, 53–55
Struening, E. L., 77–78, 87
Struening, E., 154, 169
Stufflebeam, D., 193, 197
Sullivan, H. S., 47, 55
Sullivan, W. P., 115, 127, 132

Tarail, M., 138, 150
Tasto, D. L., 107, 112
Taylor, S. E., 153, 170
Ten Broek, E., 191, 197
TenHoor, W. J., 11, 22, 234, 251
Teresa, J. G., 247, 251
Test, M., 10, 22, 115, 132, 174, 197, 272, 280
Tharp, R., 120, 132
Thomas, E. J., 286, 295

Thompson, A., 160, 171
Tierney, K., 153, 160, 170
Toomey, B. G., 193, 197
Toseland, R. W., 154, 171
Towle, C., 41, 55
Tracy, E. M., 175, 198
Tripodi, T., 193, 197
Tumblin, A., 286, 295
Turner, 220
Turner, F. J., 175, 198
Turner, J. C., 11, 22, 234, 251
Twentyman, C. T., 105, 112

U.S. Department of Health and Human Services, 138–139, 150
U.S. General Accounting Office, 18, 22, 92

Van den Bergh, N., 53, 55
Van Doornick, W. J., 106, 110

Wallace, C. J., 126, 131
Walsh, E. J., 204, 215
Wan, T. T., 276, 280
Wandrei, K., 14, 22
Warheit, G. J., 242, 251
Warland, R. H., 204, 215
Wasmer, D., 272, 274, 278
Wasylenki, D. A., 272, 274–275, 279–280
Watson, D., 120, 132
Webster's Ninth New Collegiate Dictionary, 198
Weick, A., 115, 127, 132
Weil, M., 5, 22, 70, 80, 86, 88, 90, 99, 112, 148, 150, 189, 192, 198, 205, 216, 220, 225, 234, 251, 265, 280
Weiss, C. H., 193, 198
Weiss, R., 12, 21, 115, 123, 127, 130
Weissert, W. B., 276, 280
Weissman, H., 61, 88, 118, 169, 171, 208–210, 216

Wells, J., 273, 280
Wells, S. J., 64, 88, 179, 190–191, 198
Werner, H. D., 120, 132
Westbrook, T., 107, 111
White, M., 5, 9, 11, 20, 22, 138, 149
White, P. E., 223–224, 250
White, R. G., 107, 111
White, R. W., 46–47, 55
Whitehead, A. N., 23, 33
Whittaker, J. K., 175, 198
Wiegerink, R., 220, 251
Wilcox, B., 286, 294
Wiltberger, H. E., 221, 250
Wiltse, K. T., 191, 197
Wimberly, E. T., 207, 215
Wintersteen, R., 8, 22, 272, 274–275, 280
Wiseman, L. D., 220, 249
Witheridge, T. F., 272, 274, 278
Wodarski, J. S., 160, 168, 170
Wolf, E., 122–123, 132
Wolfe, J. L., 106, 112
Wolkon, G. H., 63, 88, 174, 192, 197–198
Wolowitz, D., 207, 216
Wolpe, J., 119, 132
Woodberry, L. G., 135, 150
Woods, M. E., 153, 170, 175, 198
Wright, R. G., 274, 276, 281

Yegge, L., 235, 271, 273, 279
Yordi, C., 272, 281
York, J. L., 256, 279
Young, D., 272–274, 278

Zald, M. N., 265, 281
Zaltman, G., 247–248, 250
Zimet, S. G., 106, 110
Zolik, E., 274, 281